Moral Philosophy

Theories and Issues

Moral Philosophy

Theories and Issues

FOURTH EDITION

EMMETT BARCALOW
Western New England College

Australia • Brazil • Canada • Mexico • Singapore • Spain
United Kingdom • United States

Publisher: Holly J. Allen
Philosophy Editor: Steve Wainwright
Assistant Editors: Lee McCracken, Barbara Hillaker
Editorial Assistant: Gina Kessler
Technology Project Manager: Julie Aguilar
Marketing Manager: Worth Hawes
Marketing Assistant: Alexandra Tran
Marketing Communications Manager: Stacey Purviance
Creative Director: Rob Hugel

Executive Art Director: Maria Epes
Print Buyer: Nora Massuda
Permissions Editor: Joohee Lee
Production Service: Matrix Productions Inc.
Copy Editor: Ann Whetstone
Cover Designer: Yvo Riezebos Design/Adrienne Aquino
Cover Image: S. Calatrava/Superstock
Compositor: Integra
Text and Cover Printer: Courier-Stoughton

Library of Congress Control Number: 2005938194

ISBN-13: 978-0-495-00715-9
ISBN-10: 0-495-00715-3

Thomson Higher Education
10 Davis Drive
Belmont, CA 94002-3098
USA

For more information about our products, contact us at:
Thomson Learning Academic Resource Center
1-800-423-0563

For permission to use material from this text or product, submit a request online at
http://www.thomsonrights.com.
Any additional questions about permissions can be submitted by e-mail to
thomsonrights@thomson.com.

Contents

Preface

I wrote the first edition of this book because of problems I was having in my ethics class. I began my teaching career by using primary sources, generally from anthologies. Unfortunately, I found that most of my students had great difficulty understanding what they read. That led many of them to stop reading. Most of those who continued to read the assignments felt frustrated by their inability to understand and to follow an author's arguments. The other objection was that the works were too abstract and theoretical. If I focused solely on ethical theories, my students grumbled that they wanted to discuss real issues. I finally abandoned my efforts to have them read primary sources except in small doses.

I first turned to anthologies of articles on moral issues, but they didn't pay enough attention to moral theories. I next turned to single author texts because, unlike primary sources, they were written for today's college students, not for professional philosophers or the educated public of centuries gone by. However, none of them seemed to work for me and my students. Some focused too much on theories, while others focused too much on ethical issues. Some were written for students with better preparation than most of the students I encountered, while others seemed to be written for students with less preparation. Finally, I decided to write my own book.

A ROAD MAP

The book begins with the structure of moral arguments and the basic presupposition that moral judgments require reasons. It then discusses the standard model of moral reasons: both nonevaluative claims about the way the world is, as well as moral principles. That chapter also introduces students to such considerations as impartiality and universality, and it ends with a discussion of basic moral principles and intuitionism. From there the book moves to natural law and theory and what is for most people the starting point of moral justification and reflection, religion. Although this chapter recognizes the importance of religion for moral reflection, it ultimately concludes that there are good reasons for investing in secular forms of moral justification.

If we do not or cannot rely on nature or God's law to serve as the foundation of morality, various forms of ethical skepticism often result. Chapter 3 covers realism, nihilism, subjectivism, and relativism. The next step is to examine some realist theories. Chapter 5 examines utilitarianism, Chapter 6 examines Kantian moral theory, and Chapter 7 focuses on virtue theories. Chapter 8 covers an approach to moral and political issues that is central in much contemporary discourse—human rights. The focus centers on the United Nations Universal Declaration of Human Rights. The final chapter devoted to moral theories deals with feminism and sexual equality.

Chapter 10 includes discussions of sex outside marriage, the role sex plays or should play in achieving happiness, pornography, adultery, prostitution, homosexuality, and same-sex marriage. Chapter 11 deals with three issues of life and death: abortion, suicide, and euthanasia. Chapter 12 begins a series of chapters on social and political issues. It deals with economic equality, poverty, and equal opportunity. Chapter 13 deals with the thorny issues of racism and affirmative action. Chapter 14 covers capital punishment, Chapter 15 war and peace, and Chapter 16 issues about the environmental threats. After Chapter 16, there are guidelines for moral decision making, guidelines for thinking about case studies, and a set of case studies for discussion.

Many students think that having an opinion on a moral issue is the end of the story, even if people have different opinions. It's as though they are saying, "That's what I think about that. You can think what you want and I'll think what I want." The book tries to get them to see that having an opinion on a question or issue is the beginning of the story rather than the end of it. The important question is not so much "What do you think?" but "What justification is there for thinking that? Is what you think reasonable or unreasonable, justified or unjustified?" The major tasks of philosophy, whether moral philosophy or some other branch, include both the creative enterprise and the critical enterprise. The creative enterprise formulates answers to philosophical questions or solutions to philosophical problems; the critical enterprise evaluates the truth and reasonability of alternative answers or solutions by carefully investigating the justifying reasons for and against each answer or solution. I encourage students to take both enterprises seriously.

Each chapter begins with a moral issue and ends with exercises designed to encourage students to apply what they have learned in the chapter to lifelike situations and with a list of suggested readings for further research. Most of the exercises are appropriate for motivating class discussions as well. Most of the chapters on moral theories also have information about resources available on the World Wide Web.

WHAT'S NEW IN THIS FOURTH EDITION

Objectives have been added to each chapter. Also, most chapters now begin with a real life case study of a moral issue relevant to the content of the chapter. For example, Chapter 7 now begins with the story of Robert Courtney, the toxic pharmacist.

Chapter 1 has been completely rewritten to simplify the material on the justification of basic moral principles and to strengthen the discussion of all-things-considered singular moral judgments and their justification. In this edition, only Intuitionism is covered in the first chapter's discussion of justifying basic moral principles. In justifying singular moral judgments, new emphasis is placed on Donald Davidson's analysis of the logical structure of moral principles, whereby a principle such as "Stealing is wrong" is analyzed as "The fact that this act is an act of stealing is *a* reason to think it's wrong." This helps motivate the idea that reasoning with respect to singular moral judgments is a process like comparing the weights of different objects. It requires comparing the weight of reasons on the side of the rightness of an act with the weight of reasons on the wrong side of the act, where reasons take the form of moral arguments.

Chapter 2 has been substantially rewritten to include an extended discussion of natural law theories, in both their religious and secular forms. The content of Chapter 3 remains the same, but the text has been revised to improve its clarity and logical structure.

Chapter 7 on virtue and vice now includes a discussion of the Socratic view on the unity of the virtues and brings attention to the views of John McDowell that character affects how we perceive situations that present moral issues. In his view, people with different character traits see the world differently.

The subject of Chapter 14 has been changed from crime and punishment to capital punishment. The discussion of whether murderers have forfeited their right to life or whether they *deserve* the penalty of death has been expanded. A discussion of torture and cruel, inhuman, and degrading treatment in the context of interrogation has been added to Chapter 15.

The number of case studies has been reduced, and several new, extended case studies have been added, including one on the McWane company and one on the allegations of the torture of detainees in U.S. custody in Guantanamo Bay, Afghanistan, and Iraq.

ACKNOWLEDGMENTS

I want to thank the reviewers whose comments were so helpful during revision of the manuscript: Pat Aspell, St. Phillips' College; Clint Dunagan, Northwest Vista College; Scott Erbe, Western Michigan University; and H. Scott Hestevold, University of Alabama. I also want to thank the reviewers of the manuscript for the previous editions: Susan J. Armstrong, Humboldt State University;

Jean Badgley, Brookdale Community College; Julia J. Bartkowiak, Clarion University of Pennsylvania; Ronald R. Cox, San Antonio College; Erick R. Egertson, Midland Lutheran College; Susanne E. Foster, Marquette University; Roger W. Gilman, Northeastern Illinois University; Brenda S. Hines, Highland Community College; Peter Horn, Capital University; Robert Kane, University of Texas, Austin; John Modschiedler, College of DuPage; Wayne P. Pomerleau, Gonzaga University; Bambi Robinson, Southeast Missouri State University; Bruce B. Suttle, Parkland College; Rosaleen Trainor, Seattle University; and Brian Wallace, Capital University. Of course, I remain responsible for (and blameworthy for) any errors or inadequacies that remain in the text.

1

Morality and Moral Reasoning

OBJECTIVES

- To understand the distinction between singular moral judgments and moral principles
- To understand the difference between basic and nonbasic moral principles
- To understand the structure of moral argument and the two kinds of premises: descriptions of what is the case and moral principles
- To understand the logical structure of moral principles
- To understand the nature of all-things-considered singular moral judgments
- To understand the place of impartiality in the moral point of view
- To understand the difference between impartiality and universality
- To understand Intuitionism in moral theory.

INTRODUCTION

In September 1998, 18-year-old David Cash Jr. and his friend Jeremy Strohmeyer were in a gambling casino in Nevada. Both had been drinking. Around 3:00 a.m. they encountered a seven-year-old girl, Sherrice Iverson, in a video arcade playing video games while her father gambled. They began playing games with her, such as throwing wet paper towels at each other. Then, security cameras show her running into the men's room with Cash and Strohmeyer close behind. The cameras showed Cash leaving the men's room a few minutes after entering and hanging around outside. They showed Strohmeyer emerging 24 minutes later. They never showed Sherrice come out alive.

According to Cash, Strohmeyer grabbed Sherrice in the men's room, clamping his hand over her mouth, and pulled her inside one of the stalls. Cash went into the next stall and peered over the wall. Strohmeyer was undressing the struggling little girl. Cash said he told Strohmeyer to stop. When Strohmeyer paid no attention to him, Cash simply left the men's room and waited outside. When Strohmeyer emerged from the men's room 24 minutes later and told Cash he had just molested and murdered Sherrice, Cash's only question was, "Was she aroused?"

When Sherrice's body was found, the security cameras led to Strohmeyer and Cash. Strohmeyer was charged and later said he felt remorse, acknowledged that what he did was wrong, and blamed alcohol and drugs. Cash, however, wasn't charged because in Nevada, as in most of the country, there's no law requiring people to act to stop a crime in progress. Unlike Strohmeyer, Cash showed no remorse or sense of guilt. After all, he pointed out, he hadn't molested or murdered Sherrice. He simply did nothing to prevent it. Afterwards, a reporter for the *Los Angeles Times* asked Cash if he felt sympathy for Sherrice. He replied that he worried about himself first and said he wouldn't lose sleep over someone else's problems. In that interview he also said that his new fame or notoriety would help him meet women at the university he attended. When public outrage reached a crescendo, Cash continued to insist that he had done nothing wrong.[1]

MORAL JUDGMENTS

As humans, we make moral judgments or evaluations. We cannot help ourselves. It's part of human nature. It's difficult to imagine anyone *not* having an opinion about whether Strohmeyer and Cash did anything morally wrong. Our opinions about whether either of them did anything morally wrong are examples of moral judgments.

We judge things all the time. For example, you may have to decide whether to take one job or another, whether or not to marry someone you're dating, whether to live in one location or another, and whether to buy a house or rent. In deciding what to do, we make judgments about what it would be better or best to do.

Many of the judgments mentioned above are what we call prudential judgments, judgments made from the point of view of self-interest or prudence. When we judge things from a prudential point of view, we're trying to ascertain which of the alternatives is best for us. We make all sorts of judgments from all sorts of points of view. You may judge a book bad because it's boring, a movie good because it's exciting, a law unjust because it unfairly applies only to one category of people, an action or omission wrong, a teacher mediocre because he mumbles, and so on. Here we're interested in moral judgments—judgments made from a moral point of view.

Philosophical Questions about Moral Judgments

If we judge that David Cash did wrong in not saving Sherrice Iverson, several philosophical questions inevitably arise in the minds of thoughtful people. One question is whether our judgment is true or false. We may wonder, "Could we be mistaken? Might Cash not have done anything wrong even though we believe he did wrong in not saving Sherrice?" This question presupposes that the judgment or claim that Cash did wrong is either true or false and that people who make moral judgments can be either correct or incorrect. If we think of moral judgments as moral beliefs, we are assuming that a person's moral beliefs may be true and thus correct, or false and thus mistaken.

But this leads to another question that people have. Are moral judgments either true or false? Instead, might they be neither true nor false? Perhaps moral judgments simply aren't the sort of things that can be true or false. For example, the order "Do not smoke" is neither true nor false. Perhaps there are no moral truths. Then our judgment that Cash did something wrong is not true, but neither is Cash's judgment that he didn't do anything wrong true.

To resolve these problems, we need to examine the reasons for thinking that moral judgments are true or false, and the reasons for thinking that moral judgments are neither true nor false. We must ascertain where the weight of reasons lie or which view has better arguments in its favor.

If moral judgments are neither true nor false, the next natural question is, What is their status? Are all moral judgments equally arbitrary, or are some more reasonable than others, even if they are neither true nor false? If some are more reasonable than others, how can we figure out which are more reasonable? For example, we can ask whether it's more reasonable to judge that Cash did wrong or more reasonable to judge that Cash didn't do wrong in not saving Sherrice.

But suppose we conclude that moral judgments are true or false. A natural question then is, How do we distinguish between moral truths and moral falsehoods? Put another way, how do we distinguish between moral right and wrong? Are there tests for moral rightness and wrongness? If yes, what are they, and how reliable are they? And can we say that people have moral knowledge, that sometimes they can actually know what's right and wrong?

These are some of the basic questions we will be trying to answer. But as we explore these issues, we will see that careful distinctions need to be made, and that sometimes in order to answer a question, there are several prior questions we need to resolve first.

Kinds of Moral Judgment

Singular Moral Judgments, Mediate Moral Principles, Basic Moral Principles.   The first complication that confronts us is that there are several kinds of moral judgment. What may be true of one kind of moral judgment is not necessarily true of another kind of moral judgment. The first distinction is between singular moral judgments and moral principles. If you judge that it was wrong of Cash not to save Sherrice Iverson, you are making a singular moral judgment. A singular moral judgment is a judgment of a specific, concrete item, such as a particular act or omission of a particular person. Singular moral judgments are judgments of something with a specific location in space and time. On the other hand, you may make a judgment of a *kind* of act or omission, a generalization such as, It's wrong not to save innocent children when we can. Such generalizations are moral principles.

Both singular moral judgments and moral principles may be expressed in a variety of ways. For example, instead of using the concepts of right and wrong, I could have said, "Cash should have saved Sherrice" or "Cash had a duty to save Sherrice." As we will see, there are an ample number of concepts we can employ in making moral judgments.

Moral judgments can differ also in the object that is judged. We can judge acts and omissions, as we did with Strohmeyer and Cash, but we can also judge people. Such judgments usually focus on what we call a person's character. You might say that Cash was a bad or evil person overall, or focus on parts of his character by judging him to be cruel, cowardly, unfeeling, etc. Such judgments of people can take the form of singular moral judgments of a particular person, but they can also take the form of generalizations or principles that apply to a kind of person or a kind of character trait. Thus, I might say that cowardly people are despicable or that unfeeling people are bad.

Finally, as we will see below, a natural line of reasoning seems to lead to the conclusion that there are differences between what I shall call *mediate* moral principles and basic moral principles. To simplify, when I speak of moral principles, I will have in mind mediate principles. If I am speaking about basic principles, I will identify them as basic.

Moral Judgments and Moral Reasons

We will make a fundamental assumption. If someone makes a moral judgment, he or she presupposes or is committed to the view that there are good reasons for the judgment. Should we accept this assumption?

Imagine that someone said that a particular action was morally wrong (a singular moral judgment). Now suppose he went on to say, "But there is absolutely no reason to think it was wrong." Surely this is at the very least highly paradoxical. How can something be morally wrong if there is absolutely no reason to think it's wrong?

If someone sincerely said, "This is morally wrong, although there is no reason to think it's wrong," I would doubt that we mean the same thing when we think about, utter, or write this sentence. Perhaps we mean different things when we use such concepts as "morally wrong" and a "reason," or we mean something different when we use the terms "there is" and "no." As I use the concept of something's being morally wrong, there must be a reason to think it's wrong. The idea that something can be morally wrong although there is no reason to think it's wrong doesn't seem to make any sense.

However, in saying that someone who makes a moral judgment is committed to or presupposes that there are reasons for the judgment, I do not mean that the individual consciously made the judgment on the basis of those reasons. I also do not mean that the individual is aware of what those reasons are at the time of making the judgment. Rather, the point is that the individual is committed to the view that if he reflects carefully on it, he will be able to identify reasons that support the judgment. If, after reflecting on it, he is unable to come up with reasons and concludes from that that there are no reasons supporting it, he will withdraw the judgment.

If there must be reasons for moral judgments, what do we have in mind? The kind of reasons at issue here are justifying reasons, not explanatory reasons. A justifying reason confers reasonability or justification on a judgment or action. In one kind of paradigm case, it provides a reason to think a claim is true. For example, the fact that there are thick black clouds overhead is a reason to think it will rain (a reason to think that the claim "It will rain" is true). Another paradigm case of a reason involves reasons for action that make the action reasonable. For example, the fact that a building is on fire is a reason to leave the building (unless, perhaps, one is a firefighter).

An explanatory reason does not confer reasonability. For example, if I say that you believe something because you were brainwashed to believe it, I am explaining your belief but not providing a justifying reason for thinking your belief is true. Similarly, if I say that you unconsciously doodled on an employment application because you were nervous, I am explaining why you did it, but not giving a reason that make your actions reasonable. The moral reasons we focus on are justifying reasons, not explanatory reasons.

MORAL ARGUMENTS

A common and seemingly natural way to think of justifying reasons is as being embodied in arguments as premises. For example, consider how you might argue for the singular moral judgment that it was wrong of Cash not to save Sherrice Iverson.

1. Sherrice was an innocent child whose life was in danger.
2. Cash could have saved her at no cost or risk to himself, but didn't.
3. It's wrong not to save innocent children whose lives are in danger when we can *at no cost or risk to ourselves.*
4. Therefore, it was wrong of Cash not to save Sherrice.

The conclusion, a singular moral judgment, seems to follow from these premises. The premises constitute the justifying reasons for thinking it was wrong of Cash not to save Sherrice.

The premises in a moral argument take two different forms. The first two are claims about what is the case. They are what we might call descriptions of the universe. The third premise or reason is a moral principle. We will say, then, that there are two kinds of reason or premise in a moral argument (an argument with a moral judgment as conclusion): descriptions of the way the world is and moral principles.

The form of a moral argument can also be seen in a possible argument Cash might give for thinking he didn't do anything wrong.

1. There is no law requiring people to save others when their lives are in danger.
2. If there is no law requiring us to do something, then it is not illegal to refrain from doing it.
3. Therefore, it was not illegal to not save Sherrice.

4. *If something is not illegal, it is not morally wrong.*

5. Therefore, it was not morally wrong to not save Sherrice.

In this argument, the first two reasons or premises are descriptions of the way the world is. (Or perhaps the second is a description of how we define the term "illegal.") The third reason is a moral principle. Moral principles are another form of moral judgment.

Below we will take up the plausibility of the moral principle that Cash appeals to in our imaginary discussion with him, the principle that if something isn't illegal, it's not morally wrong, either. For now, I want to focus on the basic fact that in justifying a singular moral judgment, we appeal to moral principles. (We could also speak of moral rules.)

Although it may not seem so, it is important to understand the logical form of a moral principle. Take the moral principle that lying is wrong. On the surface, it seems to say that all acts of lying are wrong. But most of us, on reflection, don't think that all lies are wrong. What if I lie because that's the only way to save an innocent person's life? But if not all acts of lying are wrong, does it follow that the moral principle that lying is wrong is simply false?

According to the twentieth-century American philosopher Donald Davidson, if I say that lying is wrong, what I mean is: The fact that something is a lie is *a* reason to think it's wrong. That is, the fact that it's an act of lying counts on the side of its being wrong rather than on the side of its being right. And the fact that something you said is a lie is not morally neutral, as might be the fact that something you said was said quickly. Thus, if I say that it's wrong not to save innocent people from death, what I'm saying is that the fact that an act will save an innocent person from death is *a* reason to think that it would be wrong not to do it.

But this makes singular moral judgments complicated. In concrete situations, more than one moral principle may apply. For example, suppose you can save an innocent life, your own child's, but only by breaking into a closed pharmacy and stealing medicine. Let's suppose that you believe that breaking and entering, as well as stealing, are wrong, but you also believe that it's wrong not to save innocent lives when you can, especially if it's your own child's life that's at stake. It may appear that whatever you do is wrong, because whichever you do, you are violating a moral principle you believe. But would it really be equally wrong to steal the medicine as it would be to let your child die?

All-Things-Considered Singular Moral Judgments

The conflict seems more tractable if we view moral principles as Davidson does, that is, as stating that something is *a* reason to think it's wrong or right. In our imaginary situation, we have a reason to think it would be wrong to break into the pharmacy to steal medicine and a reason to think it would be wrong not to (it will lead to the death of our child). What we are called on to do, then, is to reach an "all-things-considered" singular moral judgment. That is, we are called on to weigh the reasons to think that an act is wrong and the reasons to think the act is right, and to decide which reasons are better or "weightier." If the moral reasons for stealing the medicine outweigh the moral reasons against stealing it, then our all-things-considered judgment should be that the act is right. On the other hand, if our moral reasons against are weightier than our moral reasons for, our all-things-considered moral judgment should be that it would be wrong to break into the pharmacy and steal the medicine. To repeat, when we are called on to make a singular moral judgment, it must be an all-things-considered judgment. Then, too, the moral principles we appeal to in judging pick out a feature or features of the act or situation—such as being a lie, being an act of stealing, or leading to the death of an innocent child—as a reason or reasons for or against its rightness or wrongness. We must balance the reasons for and against to determine which reasons are weightier.

Absolute Moral Principles

There is a controversy about whether there are any moral absolutes, that is, kinds of action that are wrong no matter what the circumstances. For example, if lying is wrong no matter what the reasons or circumstances, then the moral principle that lying is wrong is *absolute*. On the other hand, if there are situations in which lying is not wrong, then the principle against lying is not absolute. For example, if the principle is absolute, then it is always wrong for a doctor to lie to her patient, regardless of the consequences.

Given the logical structure of moral principles as described by Davidson, it seems highly unlikely that there are any absolute moral principles. In concrete situations, moral principles may conflict, and it is not easy to think of one that may never ever be outweighed by other principles. Take a truly terrifying example that involves application of the moral principle that murder is wrong. Imagine a prisoner given the choice of killing a fellow prisoner, in which case he himself and ten other prisoners will be spared, or having his captors kill him, the prisoner he has been ordered to kill, and the ten other prisoners. It is not immediately obvious (to me) that it would be wrong to kill the fellow prisoner if that is the only way to save the others. (In a case like this, I don't pretend to know what the right thing is.)

Less perplexing may be a different case involving a general principle against killing human beings. Suppose that an escaped prisoner is about to murder your children and the only way to prevent it is to kill him. Would it be wrong to kill him, even though we believe that, in general, it's wrong to kill other human beings? The point is that moral principles provide reasons to think actions are wrong or right, but they are like weights that are added to and subtracted from a scale to get a total weight.

Universality

Although there may be few, if any, absolute moral principles, moral principles are universal. That is, if they apply, they apply to everyone. If the fact that an act is an act of killing a human being is a reason to think it's wrong, then it's a reason to think it's wrong whether you are the killer and I am the victim or you are the victim and I am the killer. This fact always goes on the "against" side, never the "for" side.

Returning to David Cash, the universality of moral principles suggests that to be consistent, Cash must say that if he were in Sherrice's position and someone did nothing to save him, the potential savior would have done nothing wrong. If it's not wrong to fail to save someone whose life is in danger, then that's true (or applicable) whether Cash is the potential savior or the victim.

EVALUATING MORAL ARGUMENTS

Are all moral arguments equally good (or bad)? No. Here are some ways to evaluate moral arguments.

Nonmoral Claims Must Be True or Reasonable

First, the nonmoral claims about what is the case, the claims frequently called descriptive, need to be evaluated as to their truth or falsity (or their reasonability). For example, suppose that in defending himself Cash claims that he tried to contact security to save Sherrice, but his pleas for help were ignored. This claim is false. So if he presents this as a reason to think he didn't do anything wrong, it's not a good reason. Similarly, suppose that Cash claims that his life would have been in danger if he tried to contact casino security to save Sherrice. This, too, is false. Justifying reasons must be true; if they're false, they cannot really justify what they are supposed to justify.

Sometimes, we don't know for certain whether a claim is true or false. In such cases, we have to use our judgment to decide whether the claim is probable, plausible, or reasonable. If a claim is implausible or unreasonable, it is not a good justifying reason. For example, suppose that Cash says he did nothing to save Sherrice because he knows that if she lived, she would grow up to be a mass murderer who would rival Hitler, *and* that he was doing the world a favor. We are not in a position to say with certainty that Cash's claim is false, but I assume you agree with me that it is highly implausible because we have no evidence for it or for the claim that Cash has a reliable way to foretell the future. Therefore, his claim is not a good justifying reason.

Deductive Validity and Inductive Strength

A second requirement is that there be the right relation between the premises and conclusion of the argument. The strongest relation is deductive validity. If an argument is deductively valid, then its conclusion cannot possibly be false if all its premises are true. Here is an example that has nothing to do with ethics.

1. All dogs have fleas.
2. *Rex is a dog.*
3. Therefore, Rex has fleas.

If all the premises are true (they may not be), the conclusion has to be true. Therefore, this argument is valid.

Here's another example.

1. If something is not illegal, it is not morally wrong.
2. *Failing to save someone is not illegal.*
3. Therefore, failing to save someone is not morally wrong.

Not all good arguments are deductively valid. For example, suppose that a detective has ten pieces of evidence that point to Jones as the killer and no evidence that points in another direction. It doesn't guarantee that Jones is the killer, but it may make it more or less probable, perhaps highly probable. If the conclusion is probably true if all the premises are true, then it is an inductively strong argument. Inductive strength is a matter of degree. Some arguments are stronger than others.

Perhaps this is most obvious when we consider statistical arguments. Compare the following two arguments.

1. 98 percent of English majors like to read.
2. *Jill is an English major.*
3. Therefore, (probably) Jill likes to read.

1. 75 percent of college freshmen are under age 25.
2. *Jill is a college freshman.*
3. Therefore, (probably) Jill is under age 25.

Both arguments are inductively strong because their premises make their conclusions probable, but the first is stronger than the second.

If the conclusion of a moral argument is an all-things-considered singular moral judgment, then the argument will be more like that of a detective weighing the pieces of evidence, for and against a hypothesis, than like a standard deductively valid argument. That is, the argument, if it is a good argument, will be more like an inductively strong than a deductively valid argument.

Soundness and Cogency

As we will be using the term, a sound argument is a deductively valid or inductively strong argument with all true premises. If one of the premises is false, it cannot be a sound argument. Finally, a cogent argument is an argument that is sound and takes into account all the available relevant information.

THE CONCEPT OF MORAL JUDGMENT

We speak of moral judgment and moral arguments. We can also speak of moral beliefs, moral principles, moral rules, moral laws, moral codes, moral duties, moral rights, etc. We are tacitly dividing discourse and thought into what pertains to morals and what doesn't. We are contrasting what is in the domain of morals with what isn't. For example, when I speak of a good book, I am probably applying aesthetic criteria, whereas if I speak of a good person, I am surely applying moral criteria. The former is in the aesthetic domain whereas the latter is in the moral domain. If I distinguish legal duties and rights from moral duties and rights, the former is in the domain of legislation and law, whereas the latter is in the domain of morals.

But how do we distinguish between the domain of morals and other domains? Several logical and conceptual requirements have been suggested. One is that the moral domain is a domain of impartiality.

Impartiality and the Moral Point of View

David Cash made it clear that he did not care about Sherrice's needs when he chose to do nothing to save her. He was operating from a purely selfish or self-interested point of view. Many philosophers claim that by definition the concept of *moral* judgment and action is judgment that is *not* based purely on self-interest. In order to qualify as a *moral* judgment, the person must judge from an *impartial* point of view. Thus, if Cash claims that he did nothing wrong *from a moral point of view* (as opposed to, say, a purely self-interested point of view), then he is committed to the claim that he did nothing wrong *from an impartial point of view*. (Of course, Cash may refuse to make a *moral* judgment.)

Although we might be tempted to think that whether Cash did the morally right or wrong thing depends on whether he had the proper moral motivation and tempted to think that the proper moral motivation is a motive that is not purely self-interested but instead impartial, we should resist the temptation. Cash's motive is not relevant to the issue of whether his acts or omissions were morally right or wrong. If he had saved Sherrice, it would have been the right thing to do regardless of what his motives might have been. Even if he saved her purely out of self-interest rather than care and concern for her interests, it would have been the right thing to do. Motives are relevant to judging the person (as good or bad, praiseworthy or blameworthy), but not the person's behavior.

If you're judging from an impartial point of view, then you are counting the interests of everyone likely to be affected, and giving each person's interests equal weight. The paradigm would be a referee in a game or a judge in a court of law, who is neutral, neither favoring nor disfavoring anyone. If I'm the coach of a team playing against another team, I'm not impartial. I'm biased, and my bias will affect my judgment, whether consciously or unconsciously. The opposite would be David Cash, who apparently cared only about himself. But impartiality is not contrasted only with pure selfishness. We might be very altruistic, but only to members of our family or to some group with which we identify.

Bias or partiality was responsible for some of the horrible atrocities in history. The best known example is probably the Nazi extermination of Jews. Individual Nazis may not have been purely self-interested, like David Cash. Instead many were wholly biased in favor of their nation or "race" and considered only the interests of fellow Germans or fellow members of the "Aryan" race. The interests of non-Germans or non-Aryans merited no concern or consideration. Other examples include the Turkish massacre of Armenians before and during World War I, "ethnic cleansing" in Bosnia in the late 1980s and early 1990s, the genocide in Rwanda in the early 1990s, black slavery in the United States, and the treatment of Native Americans by European settlers (killing them and stealing their land). If the people responsible for these atrocities had judged from an impartial point of view, they could not possibly have judged their actions to be morally right.

Many philosophers point out that morality does not require us to be absolutely 100 percent impartial as between our interests, or our friends' and family members' interests, on the one hand and the interests of casual acquaintances or strangers on the other hand. This is connected to the point that the rightness or wrongness of action is not dependent on the person's motives. If I pay for my child's braces but not for the braces of a stranger's child, I am not blameworthy from a moral point of view, even though I did not decide what to do from a purely impartial perspective. I favored my child over the stranger's child. But my action, when judged from an impartial perspective, can (I think) be shown to be morally acceptable. From an impartial point of view, it is defensible for parents to favor their children's' interests when deciding what to do and how to spend their money. (Of course, there are limits. If I kill a stranger's child in order to get a heart suitable for transplantation into my child, I am sacrificing too much of the stranger's child's interests in furthering my own child's interests.) The task is to distinguish acceptable partiality from unacceptable partiality. Thus, as Marilyn Friedman suggests,[2] the easiest way to do this is to identify specific forms of partiality that we agree are unacceptable except in special circumstances, such as those based on gender, race, ethnicity, sexual orientation, caste, economic class, religion, and age. Following Friedman, we might say that the requirement of impartiality in moral deliberation and action is that we *minimize* such named and nameable biases.

The requirement of impartiality can play an important role in moral argument. We can rationally criticize our own or another's moral views by showing that we would not have the view in question if we were judging from the kind of impartial perspective required by morality. If a moral belief or claim would not be accepted if we were judging from the impartial perspective, then it is not justified or reasonable from a moral point of view.

The impartiality requirement is supposed to help provide guidance in moral judgment and action. In deciding what to do, I can ask myself whether it would be acceptable from an impartial point of view. If not, it's morally wrong. That is, if an impartial person would think it wrong, then it's wrong. Similarly, I can use it to judge the behavior of others, for example, David Cash. I can ask whether what he did can be considered morally acceptable from an impartial point of view. If an impartial person would think that it was wrong of Cash not to save Sherrice, then it was wrong. Of course, because the idea of an impartial person is an ideal (few if any of us are completely impartial), this leaves us with the problem of determining what an impartial person would think.

Harm, Benefit, and Morality

Another feature of the concept of the *moral* domain may be that the context must be one in which issues of harm and benefit arise. That is, a moral judgment is a judgment about a moral issue. But that naturally leads us to ask what makes an issue a moral issue.

Suppose I'm a painter wondering whether to use a certain shade of red in the picture I'm painting. Is that a moral issue? Or suppose I'm wondering whether to wear a coat and tie to class today. Is that a moral issue? Surely not. But if not, why not? Isn't it because whatever I do, it won't have much of an impact, if any, on important interests of people? Regardless of what shade of red I use or whether I wear a coat and tie, there doesn't seem to be anyone who will be harmed or benefited.

However, we could transform the issue of how I dress into a moral issue. Suppose that an insane terrorist has warned that he will kill someone if I don't wear a coat and tie to class today. Now it is a moral issue.

There is one other feature related to this. The fact that something will harm someone is not neutral from a moral point of view. But it can count as a reason for thinking an act is *wrong* or for thinking an act is *right* when we're weighing reasons to reach an all-things-considered judgment. Which is it? Surely according to our concept of morality, it counts as a reason for thinking an action is wrong. Similarly, the fact that something will benefit someone is not neutral from a moral point of view. But does it count on the side of right or the side of wrong when weighing moral reasons? Surely it counts as a reason to think something is right rather than wrong. In fact, on reflection, many people probably would agree with the following two important claims.

> Necessarily, the fact that an act causes harm is a reason to think it is morally wrong rather than morally right.

> Necessarily, the fact that an act is beneficial is a reason to think it is morally right rather than morally wrong.

Imagine arguing with someone about whether it's wrong to torture young children. Suppose you point out that torture is very harmful and the other person agrees but says that's why he thinks it's not wrong to torture young children. How could we make sense of this reply? And given impartiality, it doesn't matter who is benefited or harmed; it carries the same valence in reaching an all-things-considered singular moral judgment.

Harm reduces well-being; benefit increases well-being. The well-being involved can be physical or psychological. Forms of physical harm include death, injury, disease, disability, and physical pain. Behavior can also cause psychological harm by: (1) creating or intensifying such painful psychological states as loneliness, fear, depression, hopelessness, despair, unhappiness, anxiety, and sadness; and (2) by eroding such positive psychological states as self-confidence, self-esteem, self-respect, happiness, and feelings of self-worth.

Admittedly, we don't always think that something harmful is morally wrong, but that's generally because we think that there will be benefits that will outweigh the harms. Being stuck with a needle is harmful, but if it's the only way to provide the medicine you need, it's not morally wrong for a doctor to stick you with a needle. The anticipated benefit outweighs the brief and mild pain (harm) of the needle. Similarly, to kill someone causes harm, but people who favor the death penalty think it's not wrong to kill someone who has been convicted of a serious crime because they think that the benefits outweigh the harms. That is, in an all-things-considered judgment, the fact that someone is harmed is only one factor. Its weight on the side of the action's being wrong may be outweighed by factors on the side of its being right.

Finally, this provides a means of answering the question of who or what "counts" from a moral point of view. Whose interests must be factored in and weighed when we make impartial moral judgments? The answer seems to be anything that can be harmed or benefited. For example, if people of a different race, ethnicity, or religion can be harmed or benefited by our behavior, their interests cannot be ignored or discounted. But that also leaves open the very real possibility that it is not only humans whose interests count from a moral point of view. For example, it seems that one could plausibly argue that all living things can be harmed or benefited. If so, then in order to be impartial, we would need to factor their interests into our calculations when judging from a moral point of view.

Morality and Freedom

A third much discussed requirement is that of freedom. The issue centers on what precisely is the object of evaluation when making moral judgments. Paradigmatically, it is free actions. Ordinarily, if we see a cat "playing" with a mouse before killing it, we do not make moral judgments about the cat or its behavior. Why? Because the cat is not a free agent and it did not "freely choose" to play with the mouse. Instead, we say that its behavior is instinctual, hard-wired into its brain. The same may be said of other animals that are not capable of free action. It is inappropriate to judge them or their actions from a moral point of view.

Now consider another life form. In Milton's *Paradise Lost*, Satan, a spiritual being like other angels, rebels against God and is thrust from heaven. Later, he corrupts the innocent Adam and Eve, leading to their expulsion from the Garden of Eden. Reading the poem, we naturally judge Satan and his actions from a moral point of view. (We also judge Adam and Eve from a moral point of view.) What is the difference between Satan and a cat? Satan has what we call free will. His behavior is the result of conscious choice. He has the capacity to reflect on and resist the onslaught of desires and impulses that a cat cannot reflect on or resist. If Satan feels a strong desire to torture Adam and Eve, he has the capacity to choose not to. Finally, we can point again to David Cash. We judge him and his actions from a moral point of view only because we assume that he is a free agent.

We will call a being that can freely choose how to act a moral agent. Moral judgment presupposes the existence of moral agents who are both the judger and the judged.

Whether people have free will is a lively and controversial issue in an area of philosophy called *metaphysics*. Some people have argued that human free will is an illusion. Historically, there have been two lines of argument, one theological and the other scientific. Some theologians have claimed that God has designed the universe down to the smallest detail and that nothing occurs that was not willed by God. Consequently, once God, who is timeless, has willed a sequence of events, those events will necessarily occur in that sequence. But that seems to encompass all human actions, as well. So whatever we do, we do necessarily.

A second line of argument, one that is based on science, starts with the assumption that every event has a cause and that causes "physically necessitate" their effects. For example, it is a law of nature that pure water at a certain pressure will freeze when its temperature goes below 32 degrees Fahrenheit. So if the temperature of pure water in a glass at that pressure slips below 32 degrees, it must freeze. The *effect* is the water freezing. The *cause* is the drop in its temperature. According to this line of argument, all human actions are events that have causes. For example, suppose you raise your hand in class. Why? You want to answer the teacher's question and you know that you won't be called on unless you raise your hand. The cause is your desire to answer a question and your belief that in order to do so, you must raise your hand.

Admittedly, the cause of many human actions are far more complicated, with multiple factors cooperating to bring about the behavior. Consider the explanation for your choice of a major. The balance of reasons for and against tipped in favor of the field you chose. Given all those reasons and their relative weights, surely the only way you could have made a different decision is if some of the factors influencing your decision were different. Or so opponents of free will argue.

Whether we have free will depends on what exactly we mean by "free" when we speak of free choices, as well as on the theological and scientific "facts." But what seems difficult to deny is that morals presuppose freedom. If human freedom is an illusion, then perhaps it is no more legitimate to make moral judgments about humans than about cats.

MORAL DISAGREEMENT

Appealing to What "We" Agree On

On more than one occasion, I have appealed to what "we" believe or what "we" agree on. For example, I spoke of what forms of partiality (based on race, etc.) that "we" agree are unacceptable from a moral point of view. Who are "we"? I wish I could say that it is all human beings, or even better, all rational agents or moral agents, but you and I know that there is a lot of disagreement about moral issues. In effect, when I speak of "we," I am referring to people who agree with me.

Many, if not most, of my basic moral views are common in "my" culture, so when I say that "we" agree, perhaps all I can legitimately mean is that most people in "my culture" agree. Is that twenty-first-century U.S. culture? Twenty-first-century Western culture? Perhaps it's more restricted—twenty-first-century U.S. white college-educated middle class culture. If that is the case, then appeals to what "we" believe probably carry little weight from the point of view of justification.

Perhaps, though, I should not appeal at all to what "we" agree on, but rather to what we would agree on if we were judging impartially and had adequate knowledge of the facts. But then, aren't I claiming to know what judgment an impartial person with adequate knowledge of the facts would make? Can I know that?

To defuse this objection, let's think in the following way. If I claim that "we" agree on something and try to use this to justify anything, take it as a question addressed to *you,* the reader. Take it that I am asking whether on reflection, *you* agree. I need not worry about anyone else's agreement or disagreement except yours.

Why Do People Disagree?

How can we explain moral disagreement? What is its extent and scope?

We seem to have a tendency to attend to and remember disagreement more than agreement. There may be more agreement in moral judgments than we realize. For example, how many people do you think believe that it wasn't wrong of Strohmeyer to molest and murder Sherrice Iverson? Note that even Strohmeyer and Cash, once they were no longer under the influence of alcohol and drugs, agreed that it was wrong. I haven't done empirical research, but I'll bet that if you described the case to people, regardless of their sex, race, ethnic background, religion, or class, virtually no one would believe that Strohmeyer did nothing wrong. Similarly, how many people do you think believe that it wasn't wrong of Cash to do nothing to save Sherrice? Cash believes it, but it doesn't appear that there are many people who agree with him. Again, although I haven't done empirical research, I bet that the vast majority of people agree in judging that it was wrong for Cash to do nothing.

In explaining moral disagreement, we need to distinguish between agreeing about singular moral judgments and moral principles. In many cases, examples of moral disagreement ultimately may presuppose a wide area of agreement.

Sometimes disagreement isn't over moral principles at all. Suppose that members of a tribe kill their parents after they reach age sixty. We think it's wrong, they think it isn't wrong. Why? Don't they believe in honoring and respecting their parents? They very well may agree with us on this, but suppose they believe that people spend eternity in the same physical condition they were in at death. After age sixty, the likelihood of a variety of disabilities and injuries dramatically increases with each passing year. One may become crippled, blind, deaf, filled with pain from arthritis, and so on. What loving child would want his or her parents to spend an eternity like that? They could argue that it is more loving to kill their parents when they are still healthy and have not yet been debilitated by old age. What we disagree on are the facts of the matter, not the moral principles.

Similarly, suppose that we disagree on whether government should provide support to those who cannot work. Why? I may think it's wrong because it promotes unhealthy dependence and leads to many people voluntarily with-drawing from the labor force. You may believe that it's right because you believe it doesn't lead to the bad consequences I envision and because you believe that if such people are not helped by the government, many of them will die. The point is that the basis of the disagreement may not be "moral" at all.

Another reason people disagree is that their self-interest is affected, often dramatically affected, by the outcome of the judgments and the decisions based on those judgments. Suppose that our material well-being would be strongly affected by whether Earth is a sphere. You would gain but I would lose if it is. The probability of our disagreeing about whether Earth is spherical would be much higher. On a more realistic level, one could argue that some of the disagreement about global warming is explained by the fact that some people stand to lose a lot if the hypothesis that Earth is warming dangerously and that the warming is caused primarily by human activity is true.

Sometimes disagreement may be explained by people giving different weights to different moral principles. That is, they may agree in accepting the moral principles, but not in their priority when there is a conflict. For example, we may agree that autonomy or freedom is an important moral value, but when it comes to people choosing to end their lives, we may weigh the value differently, with one of us thinking people should not be permitted to end their lives and one thinking they should be.

MORALITY AND LAW

In our imaginary conversation with David Cash, he defended his inaction by claiming that if something is not illegal, then it's not morally wrong either. Is that true? Are moral right and wrong identical to what the human laws forbid or require? If we focus on some cases, it can seem plausible. It's against the law to murder, torture, rape, kidnap, and steal. These things are also morally wrong, so they're both illegal and immoral. So doesn't that show that something is immoral if, and only if, it's illegal? Most people say no because they can think of counter-examples.

First, laws vary from jurisdiction to jurisdiction. The laws of California are not identical to those of Massachusetts; the laws of the United States are not identical to those of China. Laws also change over time. The laws of the United States today are different from those that existed before the Civil War; the laws of Germany today are different from those that existed during the Nazi era (1933–1945). Most people claim that moral right and wrong do not vary according to one's position in space or time. Second, laws are created by human beings in the context of politics, where the power of different groups determines what the laws will be. Laws are passed by the politically powerful or are the product of negotiation and compromise among influential groups. Even in a democracy such as the United States, wealthy corporations and individuals may be able to use their power to get laws passed that benefit them. Isn't it implausible to say that wealthy individuals and corporations not only have the power to make things legal but also the power to make things morally right or morally wrong?

But concrete cases are the most persuasive consideration. It was not illegal to enslave African Americans in the Southern states before the Civil War, yet almost everyone today agrees that slavery is and was morally wrong. It was not against the law in Nazi Germany to exterminate Jews, yet today almost everyone agrees that it is and was immoral. We feel so certain that slavery and genocide are immoral that we cannot accept any principle that is in conflict with these judgments. Yet if Cash's principle is correct, then neither enslaving African Americans nor exterminating Jews were morally wrong. Given all these considerations, Cash's principle seems deeply implausible. Law and morality are not identical.

BASIC MORAL PRINCIPLES

In the logic of moral arguments, we justify singular moral judgments by appealing to moral principles. We said earlier that we can request a reason for any moral claim, including the claim that a specific moral principle is true or binding on us, so we can be asked to justify moral principles. We can justify most moral principles the same way we justify singular moral judgments—by constructing an argument that has nonmoral claims about the way the world is and moral principles as premises. Here's an example.

1. Lying harms people.
2. *It's morally wrong to harm people.*
3. Therefore, it's morally wrong to lie.

(Recall that when we claim that lying is wrong, we are saying that the fact that an act is an act of lying is a reason to think it's wrong.) The first premise is a claim about what is the case, a description of the world. The second premise is a moral principle, a principle more general than the principle that says lying is wrong. The principle that harming people is wrong may be applied to justify not just a principle against lying, but principles against kidnapping, murder, rape, assault, stealing, and so on.

But presumably, justification must stop somewhere. Many philosophers claim that it stops at basic moral principles. A basic moral principle can justify other, nonbasic, moral principles, but it cannot be justified in the same way, that is, by appeal to other, more general moral principles.

If there are basic moral principles, several questions arise. Is there just one, or are there more than one? What is the content of the basic moral principle or principles? That is, what exactly does it or do they say? Can the basic moral principle or principles be justified? If so, how?

Several of the moral theories that we will examine in later chapters, Utilitarianism and Kantianism being the major ones, are based on the idea that there is only one basic moral principle. Here we will focus on the idea that there are several basic moral principles. To further narrow the focus, we will examine a view called *Intuitionism*.

INTUITIONISM

According to Intuitionism, basic moral principles are self-evident. (According to some versions of Intuitionism, not only are basic moral principles self-evident, but nonbasic moral principles, as well as all-things-considered singular moral judgments are self-evident. We will focus on a form of Intuitionism that holds that only basic moral principles are self-evident.) We see an appeal to self-evidence in the famous words of Jefferson in the Declaration of Independence: "We hold these truths to be self-evident, that all men are created equal, that they are endowed by their Creator with certain inalienable rights, that among these are life, liberty, and the pursuit of happiness. . . ." But what does it mean if we say that a basic moral principle is self-evident?

Jefferson speaks of "truths" being self-evident, so we might say that it is the truth of a basic moral principle that is self-evident. We are saying that a basic moral principle is self-evidently true.

Before tackling the question of the self-evident, we should begin with what is merely evident. What do we mean if we say, e.g., that it is evident that it will rain soon? Surely we mean that there is evidence that it will rain. (The evidence might be roiling dark clouds, flashes of lightning, driving winds, and the rumble of thunder.) If something is evident, there is evidence for it. But we seem to mean something a little stronger than that. We seem to mean that there is the kind or quantity of evidence that makes it obvious, sufficient evidence to guarantee that we're justified in believing what is evident.

Imagine two detectives investigating a crime scene. One says, "It is evident that the killer came in through the window." Surely she means that there is easily visible evidence that makes it obvious that the killer came in through the window, and that it would not be reasonable to doubt that the killer came in through the window.

What is evident has supporting evidence. If challenged, the detective could point, for example, to the open window, the broken glass on the floor, and a muddy print of a shoe to explain why she thinks it's evident that the killer came in through the window. However, if something is self-evident, it has no supporting evidence beyond or in addition to itself and, and this is crucial, one needs no evidence beyond the self-evident itself to be justified in believing it.

Contrast the following two claims: (1) It will rain here tomorrow at noon. (2) Either it will rain or it won't rain here tomorrow at noon. Are either of them true? I won't know until tomorrow at noon whether the first is true. Why? I have to see what the weather is like here tomorrow at noon to know whether or not it's raining. I have to see raindrops or wet streets, feel drops on my head, hear the sound of raindrops drumming on the roof, and so on. I cannot just look at the claim or sentence itself and know whether it's true or false. I need evidence beyond or in addition to the claim itself.

However, I do know that the second is true. I don't have to wait until tomorrow or to look at evidence to know whether it's true or false, or to be justified in believing it. We can say that the second claim is self-evident. If a claim is self-evident, its truth can be determined without having to look at evidence and one is justified in believing it even if one has no evidence for it beyond the claim itself.

If someone asks me for evidence to prove it's true that either it will rain here tomorrow or it won't, I can explain why it's true, but I can't really provide evidence. Given the meaning of "either...or," it's true if it rains and true if it doesn't rain. There are only those two possibilities, and the claim is true whichever of the two possibilities is actualized. So no matter what happens tomorrow, it is true that either it will rain or it won't rain.

A claim such as "It will rain tomorrow or it won't" is not just true, it's necessarily true. It could not possibly be false no matter what happens. Philosophers say it's true in all possible worlds, not just the actual world. Claims that are necessarily true are said to be self-evident. Once we understand them, we can just "see" immediately that they are true.

Here's another example. Contrast (3) All bachelors are unmarried with (4) All bachelors are lonely. I can't know whether (4) is true until I've checked out some bachelors to see if they're lonely. If I find even one who isn't, then (4) is false. However, I can know that (3) is true without ever seeing a single bachelor, at least provided that I know the meaning of the term *bachelor*. I know I'll never find a married bachelor no matter how long I look because if someone is married, he cannot be a bachelor. Being unmarried is part of the meaning of "bachelor." We can say that "All bachelors are unmarried" is true by definition. It is necessarily true and therefore self-evident. For a more philosophical example, we can turn to Aquinas. He said that given the meaning of "angel," it is self-evident that angels are immaterial or nonphysical.

According to Intuitionists, there are basic moral principles that are self-evident. We can know that they are true without having to have evidence. More specifically, we can know they are true without having to have moral arguments that prove they are true, moral arguments that derive them from other moral principles and claims about the facts. These principles are necessarily true.

In order to make this less abstract, let's look at examples of principles that Intuitionists claim are self-evident. British philosopher W. D. Ross (1877–1971) claimed that there are (at least?) seven basic moral principles that are necessarily true, hence self-evident. He claimed that it is self-evident that we have the following moral duties:

1. Duties to others we have because of our previous acts
    a. Duty of fidelity (duty to keep promises, agreements, and so on)
    b. Duty of reparation (duty to compensate others for harms we caused)
    c. Duty of gratitude (duty to show gratefulness for benefits conferred on us)
2. Duties to others independent of our previous acts
    a. Duty of beneficence (duty to help others in need)
    b. Duty of nonmaleficence (duty to not harm others)
    c. Duty of justice (duty to be just to others)
3. Duties to ourselves (duty to improve ourselves physically, intellectually, and morally so that we reach our full potential)

Ross called these *prima facie* duties. That is, they're duties we have, but in a concrete situation, our duties may conflict, in which case one or more must be overridden. For example, suppose that I am a doctor with a patient and I'm trying to decide whether to tell her the truth—that her illness is terminal and that it is highly probable that she will die in less than six months and close to certain that she will die within a year. However, this patient is prone to depression, and if I tell her the whole truth, she will give up all hope. If patients have hope, they live longer and have a higher quality of life than patients who feel hopeless. Finally, this patient has told me that she would rather not know the truth if it is that she's going to die soon.

Suppose I agree that I have a duty to tell the truth. Does that mean that in this situation I should tell the truth? Not necessarily. I have other duties as well, and some of those duties push in the opposite direction. I have a duty to help others, and in this case, keeping her hopes alive will help. I also have a duty not to harm. The truth probably will shorten her life and reduce its quality, surely harms. Finally, I have made no promise to or agreement with my patient to tell the truth, so I would not seem to be violating the duty of fidelity.

But is it necessarily true and thus self-evident that I have a prima facie duty of fidelity to keep promises I've made? That is, is it necessarily true that if I have promised to do something, I have a moral duty to do it (even though in concrete situations that duty may be overridden)? Surely that depends on what it means to say that someone has a moral duty to do something. For our purposes, we will say that having a moral duty to do something means that it's morally wrong not to do it. In turn, that means that in trying to reach an all-things-considered singular moral judgment, the fact that you promised to do something always weighs in on the side of doing it. Alternatively, if you did not do that thing, the fact that you promised to do it weighs in on the side of the moral wrongness of the omission.

But if a basic moral principle is necessarily true and self-evident, shouldn't everyone agree that it's necessarily true? If there are people who deny that a basic moral principle is necessarily true, doesn't that prove that it isn't? No. I may not believe a claim that is necessarily true because I don't understand it. The necessarily true and self-evident is what we might call "irresistible" in the way of belief only if we understand it. To see that "Either it's raining or it's not raining" is necessarily true, I must understand the meaning of "not" and "either...or." Also, our intellect in a sense can be short circuited by our emotions. If it's in my self-interest that a claim not be necessarily true, that may interfere with my capacity to see that it's necessarily true. When we speak of "moral blindness," that may be part of what we have in mind.

Intuitionism is the claim that there are several basic moral principles that are self-evidently true because they are necessarily true. As I am using the term, Intuitionism makes no commitment on the question of how we know these basic moral principles. More specifically, Intuitionists are not claiming that we have something like a "sixth sense" or moral sense that enables us to know or "see" basic moral principles. More modestly, and in line with tradition, we can take it that according to Intuitionism, reason is the source of our knowledge of necessary truths, including basic moral principles.

According to intuitionists, if someone says that there is absolutely nothing morally wrong about breaking a promise, he shows that he does not completely understand the concepts of promising, breaking a promise, moral wrongness, moral duty, and other related concepts. Similarly, if someone says that there is absolutely nothing morally wrong about harming people, failing to help them when they are in need, failing to compensate people for harm we caused them, failing to show gratitude for benefits conferred, and being unjust, Intuitionists would say he doesn't understand the network of concepts employed and presupposed in these claims. The person does not mean what we mean when we employ these moral concepts, even if he uses the same words.

One or Many?

Ross lists seven principles he identifies as basic and self-evident. We'll call such Intuitionists "pluralists." On the other hand, some people think that there is only one basic principle that is necessarily true and self-evident, although they may disagree on what that principle is. It is not that they disagree that we have the duties Ross says we have or think that the principles he lists are false rather than true. Rather, they think these duties or principles are true, but can be derived from some more basic principle. We examine some of these theories in later chapters.

Basic Moral Principles Are Neither True Nor Justified?

One alternative to Intuitionism says that the basic moral principles that end our chains of justification in moral argument are not necessarily true, or even true, and we are not justified in believing them. Rather, they are arbitrary assumptions that may have a psychological explanation but no justification. Perhaps we believe them because that's what we were taught. They think Intuitionists are right that they cannot be justified by appeal to other moral principles, but in their view, that means that they cannot be justified at all. We believe them and think they are true, but we have no justifying reasons for thinking they are true. We just believe them and treat them as basic in the sense that we derive other principles from them. We will examine these theories, nonobjectivist or non-cognitivist theories, in Chapter 3.

Agreement on Basic Moral Principles

I shall assume that you, the reader, agree with Ross that we have at least the six moral duties to others that he identifies. (We will discuss the Ross's seventh duty later.) That is, I shall assume that we agree that

> the fact that an act is one of failing to live up to an agreement is a reason to think that the act is morally wrong.

> the fact that an act is one of failing to compensate someone for a harm one caused is a reason to think that the act is morally wrong.

the fact that an act is one of failing to show gratitude for a benefit conferred is a reason to think that the act is morally wrong.

the fact that an act is one of failing to help others is a reason to think that the act is morally wrong.

the fact that an act is one of harming others is a reason to think that the act is morally wrong.

the fact that an act is unjust is a reason to think that the act is morally wrong.

That is, I shall assume that we agree on which side of the moral rightness/wrongness scale used in reaching all-things-considered moral judgments each factor belongs. We can then employ them in moral argument and reasoning whether or not we think them necessarily true and self-evident.

However, even if we agree on this, note how many questions are left unanswered. For example, no standards for the sufficiency or adequacy of compensation are set. An eye for an eye is one concrete instance of a rule of compensation. Or take the idea of showing gratitude. Is a "thank you" sufficient? As for helping others, am I doing something wrong if I don't help everyone who needs it, if I help only some of them? And are there limits to how much help I have a duty to provide, or the risks or sacrifices I must accept? And how do I determine whether an act is just?

One important lesson from this is that we cannot employ these principles as if they are ingredients in a recipe. Considerable judgment is required in applying them and answering some of these thorny questions. And the answers to these questions may not be self-evident.

Duties to Ourselves?

Ross claims that it is necessarily true and self-evident that we not only have moral duties to others, but also moral duties to ourselves. Specifically, we have a moral duty to improve ourselves. Take David Cash as an example. Suppose we take him to be morally deficient in that he fails to do his duty, lacks compassion, and is indifferent to the interests of others. Ross would say that Cash has a moral duty to improve his character if he recognizes his deficiencies, and a moral duty to be sufficiently reflective so that he achieves self-knowledge about his moral deficiencies. There is something wrong if someone acknowledges their moral deficiencies but is not motivated to do anything about it.

But there is more to it than this. Ross also thinks that we have a moral duty not to waste our talents and potential. I think Ross would agree that most people have a wide variety of potential capabilities. You may have the potential to be a good physician, a good musician, a good manager, and a good actor. You probably cannot actualize all of these disparate talents. Therefore, you do not have a moral duty to actualize all of them, but you do, according to Ross, have a moral duty to actualize at least one of them, and to actualize our potential generally takes work. What this duty forbids is wasting all our talents and abilities where we have the opportunity to actualize them. If you intentionally spend all your time gambling or watching television, you are wasting your talents, and Ross thinks this is wrong, a violation of our moral duty to ourselves.

Of the duties Ross identifies, this is probably the most controversial. Many philosophers do not think it makes sense to say that we have any moral duties to ourselves. But Ross's view can perhaps be made more plausible if we accept the duty he identifies but deny that it is really a duty to ourselves. We could say that it is a duty to others, because what we are and do affects others in so many ways. If I am and remain morally deficient, if I waste all my talents and fail to actualize any of my potential, it doesn't only affect me. Obviously, David Cash's moral deficiencies affected others. And if you could have been a good physician, musician, manager, or actor but become none of these, you fail to make a contribution to others that you could have made.

Even if we agree with Ross that we have a moral duty to improve ourselves and actualize our potential, many would strongly disagree that it is necessarily true and self-evident that we have this duty. If we do disagree with Ross on this, Ross can only ask us to reflect more carefully on the question of whether we have such duties. He could ask us to reflect on whether we really can deny that the fact that someone fails to correct moral deficiencies or wastes all his potential is a reason to think the person has acted wrongly. Unfortunately, that is one of the well-known limitations of Intuitionism. At some point, we may face a situation where one person says a principle is necessarily true and self-evident whereas another denies this. Is there a reliable test to determine whether a principle is or isn't necessarily true, a test that is more formal than the directive, "Reflect on it some more"? It seems that there isn't.

Reflective Equilibrium

According to twentieth-century American philosopher John Rawls, as moral agents our goal should be to create and sustain a "reflective equilibrium" between our singular moral judgments and our moral principles. We should aim for consistency. (It's possible that consistency should include feelings and emotions, and nonmoral beliefs, as well as moral judgments.)

For example, suppose I have learned that my wife is a spy for an enemy country, with whom we are at war. I love my country, and I love my wife. I believe that we should be loyal to those we love and loyal to our country. We should not harm our loved ones or harm our country. I face a choice. I can keep her secret, which will significantly harm my country, or I can reveal her secret to the authorities, which will significantly harm her. If I denounce her to the authorities, I can warn her so that she can escape or not warn her so that she will be arrested, tried, and punished. I believe many people will be seriously harmed if my wife continues to spy for the enemy. If she is caught, there is a very high probability that she will be executed. What's the right thing to do?

Suppose I believe that loyalty to country comes before loyalty to loved ones. I think spies should be executed, both as punishment for wrongdoing and deterrence for further spying. I believe it's wrong to help criminals escape. But

I believe that I should warn my wife before denouncing her so that she can escape punishment. To be consistent, I must either give up some of the principles or give up the judgment that I should warn my wife so that she can escape.

EXERCISES

In constructing moral arguments for exercises 1 through 4, be sure to appeal both to nonevaluative beliefs about what the facts are and to moral principles. Wherever necessary, clarify the concepts that you employ in the argument.

1. Did David Cash do anything morally wrong when he failed to save Sherrice Iverson?

2. In June 2001, the governor of Texas vetoed a bill passed by the Texas legislature that would have made it illegal to impose capital punishment on anyone who is mentally retarded, generally defined as having an IQ below 70. First, construct an argument defending the governor's veto; then, construct an argument opposing it. Which argument do you consider stronger? Why? Do you agree with the governor's veto? Why or why not?

3. Several male high school students talk an 18-year-old girl they know to be mildly retarded into having sexual relations with them. (We'll call her Joan.) Because they are not using force or coercion and because they consider her to have freely consented, they believe that they are doing nothing wrong. They argue as follows:

   Joan is 18 and freely consented to have sex with us.

   There's nothing wrong with having sex with an 18-year-old girl who has freely consented to it.

   Therefore, there's nothing wrong with our having sex with Joan.

   Do you agree? Why or why not? Construct an argument to defend your view. What criticisms, if any, do you have of the boys' argument?

4. Is it morally wrong for tobacco companies to market cigarettes to children and adolescents?

5. Timothy maintains that abortion is immoral unless it is necessary to save the life of the mother. When he learns that Frieda, a girl he despises, has had an abortion although her life was not threatened, he strongly condemns her action as immoral. However, when he learns that Gloria, a girl he likes very much, has had an abortion in similar circumstances, he maintains that she has not done anything immoral. Are there any defects in Timothy's moral judgments? If yes, explain them.

6. If Cash judged that he did nothing morally wrong in not saving Sherrice, would it make sense to say that he reached that conclusion while judging his own behavior from an impartial point of view? Do moral judgments presuppose or require an impartial point of view?

7. Of the six moral duties to others that Ross identifies, which, if any, do you think we do not have? (Which duties, if any, did Cash violate?)

8. Do you think that any moral principles are necessarily true and self-evident?

9. If we have a duty to keep our promises, is it always wrong to break a promise?

10. Do we have a moral duty to help everyone who needs help? If not, then why couldn't David Cash use this to excuse his behavior?

11. "An eye for an eye" is a principle of compensation. Many people think it is an appropriate principle. Others do not. Gandhi said that if we follow it, soon the whole world will be blind. Jesus repudiated it in the Sermon on the Mount and told us to "turn the other cheek." Is it an appropriate principle of compensation?

12. In the case where I must decide whether to turn in my wife, who is a spy, and decide whether to warn her so that she can escape if I do turn her in, what would be the right thing to do? Construct an argument to defend your judgment.

ENDNOTES

1. *Time.com,* Law section (7 September 1998).

2. Marilyn Friedman, *What Are Friends For? Feminist Perspectives on Personal Relationships and Moral Theory* (Ithaca, NY: Cornell University Press, 1993), p. 31.

2

Natural Law and Divine Commands

OBJECTIVES

- To understand the natural law theories of the Stoics, Aquinas, Hobbes, and Philippa Foot
- To understand what is meant by natural and unnatural and their connection to moral right and wrong in natural law theories
- To understand the difference between theological and secular natural law theories
- To understand the Divine Command Theory of Morality

INTRODUCTION

Cloning and Genetic Engineering

In 1997, the world was startled to learn of the existence of the world's first clone—a sheep named Dolly. Dolly developed from the unfertilized egg of another sheep, so her genetic structure was identical to that of its mother/father, unlike other sheep brought into existence via sexual intercourse between a male and a female sheep, which leads to a blending of their genes. In effect, Dolly is an almost exact copy of its mother/father. Dolly also started life in a petrie dish rather than a sheep's womb. Not everyone approved of the manner of Dolly's conception.

Recently, the birth of the first cloned dog was announced. This raises an interesting possibility. People attached to their pets don't have to lose them through death. They can create clones of them, exact copies, before they die.

Because dogs and cats are influenced by their experiences, a cloned dog that starts out as an exact physical copy of its mother/father will not necessarily remain an exact copy. But if its experiences are nearly identical to those of its parent, it probably will remain a very close copy. But should people clone their pets? Many people think we shouldn't.

A major worry is the possibility of cloning human beings. Suppose you have a child who dies young due to an accident. If it were possible to create a clone of your child before he or she died, creating an exact genetic copy, would you? Should you?

Here's a bit of science fiction. A billionaire is near death. His doctor tells him that he can be cloned. The clone will not have any of the billionaire's memories, and his character and personality will not remain the same because they are influenced by experience, but his entire set of genes will be passed on to a baby that might live many years after he is dead. He can leave his entire fortune to the baby and appoint guardians to bring the baby up in a way most likely to duplicate his own character and personality. Would it be morally right for him to do this?

Here's a final example. Suppose a company can genetically enhance a fetus in the womb. The company can increase intelligence, athletic ability, creativity, and so on. It can also provide immunity from a variety of deadly diseases. If there are genetic abnormalities in the fetus, such as abnormalities that would lead to blindness or mental retardation, the company can correct them. Is that a good or a bad thing? Would it be morally right to genetically enhance fetuses in the womb?

Many people who condemn such actions say that they are unnatural, and morally wrong *because* they are unnatural. Some condemn such acts by saying that those who do them are playing God, and humans should not play God.

Cosmetic Surgery

It's natural for humans to age, and aging brings on certain characteristic effects. Many men lose their hair; everyone's skin wrinkles to some extent; everyone loses muscle mass and bone density. Strength, endurance, and vigor decline. But suppose we could create a drug that would stop all the natural effects of aging. Suppose it enabled people to maintain all the physical characteristics of youth for hundreds or thousands of years. Critics might say that it would be unnatural and therefore wrong to create and use such a drug.

This drug is in the realm of science fiction, but face lifts, collagen injections, silicon or saline breast implants, and drugs to grow hair and enhance sexual potency aren't. Then, too, many athletes take performing enhancing drugs. Is it unnatural to have breast implants or take drugs to enhance sexual potency or athletic performance? If it is unnatural, does that alone make these things morally wrong?

According to one important philosophical tradition, basic moral principles are laws of nature. What's natural is morally right and good, whereas what's unnatural is morally wrong and bad.

Same-Sex Marriage

Some states have legalized same-sex marriage. Other states forbid it and have sought to define marriage as a relation between a man and a woman. Some opponents claim that same-sex marriage is unnatural while a conventional marriage between a man and a woman is natural. Because they believe that what's unnatural is wrong and what's natural is right, they oppose same-sex marriage.

A related underlying issue is homosexuality. Presumably, only gay men and lesbian women would take advantage of same-sex marriage. But many Americans believe that homosexuality is unnatural, and immoral because it's unnatural. Are same-sex marriage and homosexuality unnatural and therefore immoral?

STOICISM

The ancient Stoics, whose intellectual roots go back to classical Greece of the fourth and third centuries BCE, claimed that nature should be our guide. They thought that certain moral values and rules of conduct are built into nature. Putting it metaphorically, nature issues commands to us.

But how are we to understand what nature is, let alone what nature requires and forbids? On one level, as we know now, it's obvious that nature is made up of physical matter, from the very small (atoms and subatomic particles) to the very large (solar systems and galaxies). But nature also is exemplified in processes. Over time, the properties and relations of the physical things making up the universe change. For example, a person is born, changes from being a baby to a teenager, from a teenager to a mature adult, from a mature adult to an old person, and then dies. Similarly, in the spring a tree grows leaves, which change color in the fall and finally drop to the ground, leaving the tree branches bare again.

Process and change are essential to nature, but how are we to understand these natural processes and changes? Are they entirely random and chaotic, or do they follow patterns? The Stoics considered matter to be inert, incapable of changing unless some active principle (what we might call force or energy) caused it to change. For example, if a leaf grows on a tree or changes its color, they thought that there must be an immaterial power causing it. The same thing applies if we think of the movement of the sun, the outside air changing from hot to cold or wet to dry, and the movement of a wolf's legs as it chases a deer. One change is triggered by another, which in turn was triggered by a previous change, and so on into the far distant past, and each change is the result of the activity of some immaterial force or power acting on or through inert matter. Thus, they believed that there are no uncaused changes. An uncaused change is like creation of something from nothing, which they said was impossible. Furthermore, causes necessitate. That is, if the cause is present, the effect must occur. For example, if you reduce the temperature of a glass of pure water below 32 degrees Fahrenheit, it must freeze.

Changes and processes follow patterns; they are orderly rather than chaotic. Winter is followed by spring, which is followed by summer, which is followed by fall, which is followed by winter. Summer is never immediately followed by spring. Water freezes when its temperature falls below 32 degrees. It does not freeze if the temperature is higher, and it always freezes when it is below 32 degrees. People go from being young to being old, never from being old to being young. Released stones fall, they never rise.

Nature exemplifies regularities. It is orderly rather than disordered. Undoubtedly, the most important aspect of this natural order is that it is hospitable to life. It creates and maintains systems where there are a profusion of living things—insects, birds, snakes, fish, mammals. It looks, in fact, as if it were designed to support the myriad forms of life we encounter. But design requires a designer.

The Stoics believed that everything that exists and everything that occurs is the product of intelligence. God designed and directs everything. In fact, the Stoics believed that God pervades everything. God is the active principle that exists everywhere in the universe and causes everything that occurs in the passive, inert matter of which the universe is composed. Some Stoics apparently thought that "the world and the heavens are the substance of God."[1] Everything that happens, then, happens because of God's activity and occurs as part of God's intentions for the universe.

Events unfold according to natural laws that were established by God. Because the natural order of things is established and maintained by God, the Stoics believed that it must be good and must conform to God's intentions and plans. If wolves live in packs ruled by the strongest male, then that's part of the natural order and God wanted it that way; it must be for the best. Not only is it the way wolves live, it's the way wolves should live. If a wolf lives an isolated existence like a bear, it is living contrary to nature, which is not good. Everything both does and should conform to the natural order of things.

Some laws of nature are irresistible. It's impossible to violate them. For example, it's not possible for water to flow up hill or remain a liquid when its temperature drops below 32 degrees Fahrenheit. It's impossible for a fish to breathe in the air or for a cat to breathe underwater. With respect to laws of nature that are irresistible, it doesn't make sense to urge us to act in accordance with them, because we cannot help but do that. When it comes to standards for evaluating human behavior, then, the Stoics cannot have in mind only natural laws that are irresistible, that we *must* live by. The laws they have in mind must be laws that we are capable of breaking or violating.

Often we say that a certain pattern or regularity is natural because that's the way things are most of the time, not necessarily all of the time. It's natural for it to snow in winter in New England, but there may be an occasional winter when it doesn't snow. We would probably call such a winter unnatural.

But the natural/unnatural dichotomy is not based merely on statistics. In the Stoics' view, the universe was created by God for a purpose. Because they share reason with the divine, humans are the most special and important parts of the universe. Everything else in the universe is designed to further the well-being of humans. Thus, animals were created to serve humans. For example, according to the Stoic Chrysippus, dogs were created to help us hunt, and leopards, bears, and lions were created to give us practice in being courageous.[2] Similarly, they probably would say that trees were created to provide shade, fuel for cooking and heating, and material to build ships, houses, and furniture.

What serves the interests of those things that directly benefit humans indirectly benefits us. For example, birds provide food, sport, decorations, and entertainment to humans. The worms that birds eat, then, indirectly benefit humans by benefiting the birds that directly benefit us.

Each thing, then, must be designed to have features that will enable it to fulfill its function. In order to provide us with practice in being courageous, bears and leopards need to have characteristics that make them dangerous and fearsome, such as sharp teeth and claws. Something is acting in accordance with nature, then, when it is doing what it was designed to do, and it is able to do what it was designed to do only if it has the right characteristics. So it's natural for leopards and bears to threaten people, and natural for them to have sharp claws and teeth.

In order for something to serve human interests, it must exist. Therefore, when it comes to living creatures, the Stoics claimed that each has an innate drive for self-preservation to keep itself in existence. The Stoics saw that there are different kinds of living things, what we today would call species. What enables a member of one species to survive will not necessarily enable a member of another species to survive. For example, put a polar bear in the tropics and it will die; put an alligator at the North Pole and it will die. Try to feed seals on grass and they will die; try to feed cows on fish and they will die.

Given the kind of creature something is, it will have a specific way of life or "nature" characteristic of things of its kind, a way of life it must pursue if it is to continue to exist and do what it was designed to do. For example, part of a fish's way of life or nature is to live and swim in water. Now it seems unproblematic that a living creature must or should live and act in the ways necessary for it to survive, but less obvious that it must or should act and live in ways that enable it to do what it's designed to do. The Stoics' idea that every living thing was designed and intended to benefit humans in various ways is deeply controversial.

The Stoics believed that everything, because it was created by God, has a "proper function." When it comes to parts of living beings, it makes sense to speak of their proper functions. These are the contribution each part makes to the life and functioning of the whole living thing. Thus, the heart has the proper function in mammals of circulating blood. Blood has the proper function of oxygenating tissues. But the idea that each living organism has a proper function designed to benefit humans or benefit the whole universe is less plausible. For example, the idea that a leopard has the proper function of providing us with practice in being courageous seems far-fetched. What is the proper function of a porcupine or a dandelion?

But with respect to ethics, the Stoics, of course, had to focus on human beings. They claimed that what is natural in human ways of living and behaving is right; what is unnatural is wrong. In turn, then, what is natural for humans is what enables us to fulfill our proper function. But are we designed to fulfill a function?

Under the description "human being," it may not be obvious that we have a function, but if we are described as someone's son, brother, or parent, for example, then the Stoics claim that we have a function may seem more obvious. For example, in order to function well as a parent, one must act to further the well-being of one's children. If a father neglects the interests of his children, he is not fulfilling his proper function as a father. Thus, Epictetus said that for each role we can play, such as citizen, friend, or farmer, there are certain actions appropriate to the role. Our reason enables us to distinguish between what is appropriate for someone in that role and what is inappropriate. Thus, reason tells me that it is inappropriate to reveal the confidences of a friend because that is incompatible with being a friend.

However, what if we think about humans only under the description "human being"? Chrysippus apparently thought that one vital function is reproduction. If we don't reproduce, we'll become extinct. Therefore, he said that it is natural for us to have children. Also, because we are social beings, it is natural for us to create families and communities that enable us to survive, live well, and reproduce. Because certain forms of behavior will enable us to remain part of a community whereas other forms of behavior will probably lead to our being expelled or killed, it is natural and right to behave in ways that will secure our membership in the community. For example, if we steal from others in the community, we may be punished.

Some Stoics also maintained that because we alone have reason, we have the proper function of contemplating the universe and God. In essence, we were designed to think and know, so that's our proper function. What's natural for us, then, is to exercise the faculties that enable us to think and know, and live in a way that will sustain and develop these capacities. Thus, it would be unnatural to be drunk all the time, because it prevents us from exercising these capacities and threatens to physically destroy them.

Finally, the Stoics sum up their doctrine by claiming that what is natural and right for us is to obey reason. Reason issues commands. Some acts and omissions are contrary to reason. Reason forbids them. It is natural and right for us to follow reason's dictates and unnatural and wrong to go against reason's dictates. However, there is great controversy over what, if anything, reason forbids or commands, just as there is over whether, simply as humans, we have a proper function.

THOMAS AQUINAS

Stoic thought influenced St. Thomas Aquinas (1225–1274). According to Aquinas, God created each thing with its own proper ends and an inclination to perform its own proper acts, that is, acts that are aimed at enabling it to achieve its proper ends. This applies both to whole things and parts of things.

Consider human creations. We create things with proper ends, and those ends are the functions or purposes of our artifacts. The proper ends of a hammer include punching nails into and pulling nails out of wood. The proper end of a screwdriver is to turn screws to make them spiral in or spiral out of some material. The parts are designed to enable these artifacts to achieve their proper ends. A screwdriver has one end for grasping and another end to fit into the grooves of the head of a screw. A hammer has at one end both a claw for pulling and a hard round surface to hit the head of a nail. It is difficult if not impossible to use a screwdriver to drive in a nail or a hammer to screw in a screw.

Aquinas thought that God would not create anything that had no purpose or function. Therefore, everything in creation has a purpose or function—a proper end—even if we don't know what it is. But we can often take an educated guess by understanding what something can do. What something can do it was probably designed by God to do. Grass can feed certain animals, so it probably was designed to feed those animals. That is its function or purpose, its proper end. Similarly, because dogs can guard a house or a field of sheep, that is probably at least one of their proper ends. Because horses can pull plows and wagons, and carry people, that is probably one of their proper ends. In order that dogs may guard sheep, dogs must be fierce and sheep must be meek. In order for horses to pull and carry for humans, they must be big, strong, and docile.

According to Aquinas, it is always natural and right for something to act in a way that will enable it to reach its proper end or fulfill its function. It is natural for horses to pull plows, so there is nothing wrong with harnessing a horse to a plow. (But what if a horse is born that is incapable of pulling a plow? That is a defect in the horse.) What is less clear is whether it's always wrong if something does not act in furtherance of its natural ends. For example, what if someone buys a horse and lets it simply graze in the field, so that it never pulls or carries anything for its human owner? It is not at all obvious that this would be wrong. Perhaps Aquinas thinks that something is always permitted but not necessarily required to do what enables it to reach its proper end.

According to Aquinas, the proper end of humans is happiness. We were created to be happy. However, because we are a combination of mortal material body and immortal immaterial soul, our proper end is not limited to achieving happiness in this life. Our proper end is eternal happiness. Therefore, doing what will enable us to achieve eternal happiness is natural and right, whereas doing what will prevent us from achieving eternal happiness is unnatural and wrong.

What will enable us to achieve eternal happiness is perfect union with God. But that requires that we know and love God. Knowing and loving God, we will naturally conform to the moral laws that God has established, moral laws that "exist in God's mind." Failing to conform to God's laws prevents us from achieving union with God, so failing to conform to God's laws is unnatural in that it prevents us from achieving our proper end. According to Aquinas, God has established several self-evident basic or primary moral laws "written on the human heart," the most fundamental of which is that we should do what's good and avoid doing what's evil. Other primary laws are that we should love God, love our neighbor, and avoid doing harm to others. From these primary laws, secondary laws can be derived, such as the laws forbidding us to kill, steal, and lie, and laws requiring us to honor our parents and do acts of charity.

Most of the moral laws (laws of nature) deal with our relations with other people. Their aim is to enable us to live together in peace and harmony. Because we are naturally social beings, we live together in groups. It is important that we act in ways that will not lead to the destruction of the groups of which we are a part. Aquinas thought that we can acquire knowledge of these laws either by revelation from God or by the exercise of human reason, which is itself a reflection of God's reason. And because we are rational as well as social beings, it is natural for us to follow the dictates of reason.

However, some moral laws do not regulate our relations with others. One set of laws regulates our relations with God. That includes the prohibition against worshipping false gods or graven images. This is a moral law we can know only if God reveals it to us. Another set of laws regulates our conduct that affects only ourselves. That includes a prohibition against self-destruction. Because we have a natural inclination to preserve ourselves, implanted by God, it is unnatural and wrong to go against this natural inclination and act in self-destructive ways. Aquinas thinks this can be known by human reason as well as by divine revelation.

If the primary moral laws are written on the human heart and the secondary moral laws are obvious implications of these primary laws in light of their function of enabling people to live together in conformity with their nature as social beings, why do people disagree on moral issues? Aquinas claimed that such things as bad customs we have inherited, bad habits we have acquired, and sin can interfere with our capacity to recognize, let alone conform to, the moral laws.

The fact that we are naturally social beings can be used to justify a variety of moral laws that are necessary for social harmony. For example, it enables us to make sense of prohibitions on murder, theft, and deception, and requirements that we sometimes be charitable and help others when the need is great and the cost or risk is low. But when it comes to more controversial issues, applying Aquinas's natural law theory presents a variety of difficulties.

For example, he claims that we have a natural inclination to reproduce. Therefore, reproducing is one of our proper ends. But does that entail that each of us has a duty to reproduce, or only that it is morally permissible for us to reproduce? Clearly, if no one reproduced, the human race would become extinct, and presumably God does not want us to become extinct. It would be wrong and unnatural if humanity failed to reproduce itself. But that doesn't require that each of us reproduces, only that some of us do. Is it plausible to claim that childlessness is unnatural and morally wrong because we have a natural inclination to reproduce?

How do we know whether the fact that something is our proper end entails that we are *obligated* to act in conformity with it or merely that we are permitted? After all, "proper" (the English translation of a Latin word) might seem to imply something like acceptable—not improper. What reason is there to think that we are required? If Aquinas claims that God commands us to act in conformity with our proper ends, a skeptic can ask, How do you know that?

Aquinas seems to have inferred that reproduction is one of our proper ends from the claim that we have a natural inclination to reproduce. But is every natural inclination a proper end? For example, humans can be incredibly cruel. Many people think that we have a natural inclination to cruelty that can be extinguished only through learning. If it is a natural inclination, is it one of our proper ends? Would it then be right to be cruel and wrong not to be cruel? And if our having a natural inclination to act in certain ways doesn't guarantee that these ways of acting are among our proper ends, how do we know what acts are and what acts aren't?

According to Aquinas, not only does whole organism have proper ends, but so, too, do their parts. The proper end of an eye is to see and of an ear is to hear. What about human genitalia? Their proper end has been said to be reproduction. That's what they're for. Many natural law theorists maintain that it is wrong to use our genitalia in ways that are contrary to their proper end of reproduction. That seems to mean using our genitalia in a way intended to prevent reproduction (pregnancy) from occurring. This has been used to justify the claim that the use of artificial methods of birth control, such as the pill or condoms, and forms of sex that cannot lead to pregnancy, such as anal or oral sex, are morally wrong. But if being a proper end entails no more than that we are permitted to act in certain ways, then a prohibition on employing a part of us in a way contrary to its proper end seems groundless, unless, again, one claims that God commands us not to use parts of ourselves in ways contrary to their proper ends. But if that's the justification, how do we know that is true?

Let's return to some of the issues with which we began this chapter. Can we apply Aquinas's natural law theory to the issues of genetic engineering, such as cloning? One possibility is to say that genetically reengineering something, such as a mouse, is making it act contrary to its proper end, which is to reproduce itself. In genetically reengineering it, it does not reproduce an exact copy of itself. The problem with this strategy is that even without genetic reengineering, a pair of mice won't produce exact copies of either mouse. So the proper end of a mouse cannot very well be to reproduce exact copies of itself. If being genetically reengineered does not make a mouse act contrary to its proper end of reproduction, does a mouse have other proper ends that reengineering would violate?

It may be, though, that the fear is that genetic engineering will create an entirely new species of organism. What will be its proper end if it was created by humans, not by God? Will it even have a proper end if it is created by humans? And will its creation lead to the extinction of the original species? If so, the proper end of that species will not be achieved, unless by a substitute species that can play the same role in God's plans.

These worries seem overblown. If we create a form of bacteria that eats oil in order to clean up oil spills in the ocean, can't we say that its proper end is to eat oil and clean up oil spills? Then, too, if we create a new species, it doesn't guarantee that the original species will become extinct.

But perhaps it's not that we're acting contrary to the mouse's proper end, but rather that we are interfering with the natural operation of the physical laws of nature, or the "natural order." But what does that really mean? We're certainly not altering the laws of nature. We can't. No one can change the laws of gravity, for example. We're acting in conformity to these laws because we couldn't do genetic engineering if it were against the physical laws of nature. But we can distinguish between events unfolding with humans playing no causal role and events unfolding with humans playing a causal role. If the route of a river changes because of human intervention, we played a causal role in its reconfiguration. On the other hand, if a river changes course without our having done something to change it, we didn't play a causal role; it's part of the "natural" order. We can say that we interfered in the former case, but not the latter.

But is it wrong for humans to play a causal role in the world? How could it be wrong when it's unavoidable? We interfere in the operation of the laws of nature if we build a dam, clear a forest, plant crops, take an antibiotic to cure a bacterial infection, take an anesthetic to have a painless operation, take an antidepressant to reduce depression, and so on. What reason is there to think it's wrong? In addition, we should recognize that we are part of nature, part of the natural world. In one important sense, what we do is as natural as anything else. There must be more to the objection to genetic engineering than that it is going against the "natural order" of things.

An entirely different line of argument would be that genetic engineering has a high probability of having harmful effects. But then we abandon natural law theory. That isn't basing condemnation of genetic engineering on a prohibition on interfering with the operation of the laws of nature.

For many philosophers, the ultimate problem for Aquinas's theory is that it is based on theology. It depends on the idea that God gives things and their parts "proper ends" and then forbids us to use things or act in ways contrary to their and our proper ends. It also presupposes that God forbids us to change the "natural order" of things. But there are purely secular versions of natural law theory. One is that of the British philosopher Thomas Hobbes (1588–1679).

HOBBES

According to Hobbes, laws of nature are "convenient articles of peace, upon which men may be drawn to agreement."[3] Like the Stoics and Aquinas, Hobbes recognized that humans are social animals. We are far more likely to survive and flourish if we are part of a community rather than living as isolated beings. However, sociability has its dangers, because there is nothing as threatening as other human beings. We can do terrible things to each other. In order to preserve the communities we need, there must be certain rules that everyone is required to follow. According to Hobbes, these rules are the Laws of Nature. As Hobbes put it,

> A Law of Nature . . . is a precept or general rule, found out by reason, by which a man is forbidden to do that which is destructive of his life or taketh away the means of preserving the same, and to omit that by which he thinketh it may best be preserved.[4]

He identifies the following Laws of Nature.

1. Seek peace with others.
2. Give up your right to do as you please provided that others are willing to give up their right to do as they please.
3. Do what you promised or agreed to do.

4. Show gratitude for benefits conferred.

5. Strive to accommodate yourself to the other members of your community. (This seems to imply the necessity of compromise.)

6. Pardon those who have offended you if they genuinely repent and ask forgiveness.

7. Pursue vengeance only to secure a future good, not to punish past transgressions.

8. Do not show contempt or hatred for another person.

9. Do not be arrogant or overly full of pride.

10. Do not reserve to yourself a right you are not willing that others have.

11. When judging between people, be impartial and treat them equally.

12. Things that cannot be divided should be held in common.

13. Let questions of property and right be decided by an impartial procedure.

14. Let the procedure be either first possession or a procedure that all agree to. . . .

15. Provide safe conduct for mediators or ambassadors of peace.

16. In controversies, let a judge or arbitrator decide; do not rely on force.

17. Do not try to be the judge in your own case.

18. Let only those who are unbiased and impartial be judges and arbitrators.

19. Judges should decide questions of fact by examining the testimony of witnesses.

He says that all the Laws of Nature can be derived from what has been called *the silver rule*—Do not do to others what you would not want them to do to you. According to Hobbes, violating any of these Laws of Nature will undermine a community. It is because of our human nature that the violation of any of these laws will undermine or destroy a community of human beings. If we were not offended by another's pride or arrogance, for example, or by their contempt, and if we were not motivated by feeling offended to harm those who offended us, these would pose little threat to the community.

If we don't seek peace with others, the first law, it is an invitation to perpetual war, and everyone's life, including our own, will be in Hobbes's memorable phrase "solitary, poor, nasty, brutish, and short." One who doesn't seek peace with others becomes an outlaw or an outcast. Similarly, if we simply do as we please, the subject of the second law, we are bound to clash with others, and it will lead to the perpetual war that we all have reason to avoid. However, we have a reason to give up the right to do as we please only if others are also willing to give up that right. If you restrain yourself while others don't, you're just leaving yourself open to being taken advantage of and harmed. Therefore, you have reason to restrain yourself only if there is an agreement between you and others, who agree to restrain themselves. Once you agree with others, you are part of a social contract. The third Law of Nature says that you should do what you promised or agreed to do. The fact that you agreed obligates you to do what you agreed to do.

The nineteen Laws of Nature listed above deal with our behavior toward others. Hobbes also says that there are purely self-regarding Laws of Nature that forbid any self-destructive behavior, such as drunkenness and intemperance. That is because for Hobbes, the Laws of Nature are principles of enlightened self-interest or rules of prudence. Nature implanted in us a drive for self-preservation, and it is rational to act to preserve ourselves but irrational to act in ways likely to lead to our own destruction. The Laws of Nature that are other-regarding, not only self-regarding, are rules to follow if you want to live a reasonably satisfactory life in a community. If you violate these rules, not only will it jeopardize the existence of your community, but it is like playing Russian roulette because you risk getting caught and punished. Those who violate these rules are counting on their ability to fool the rest of their community and on the community's inability to detect their transgressions. Hobbes thinks this is a foolish and irrational risk. People tend to overestimate their own intelligence and cleverness while under-estimating everyone else's intelligence and cleverness.

Hobbes's natural law theory provides a way to discover the true or reason-able rules of morality and to justify adopting them. We employ our reason to ascertain what laws are necessary to create and maintain enough social harmony to preserve our society or community. Those rules are the right rules. Hobbes recognizes, though, that different communities may require different systems of rules, so what system is right for one society may not be right for another. He also recognizes that a community may be able to maintain social harmony while being at war with other communities. However, the first law of nature—seek peace—applies to relations among groups as well as relations among individuals within groups.

How might Hobbes's theory be applied to some of the concrete moral issues with which we began this chapter, such as genetic engineering or same-sex marriage? We must ask whether they are incompatible with the survival and harmony of the community to which we belong. Would our community dis-integrate and life be solitary, poor, nasty, brutish, and short if scientists engaged in genetic engineering or same-sex couples married?

Like Aquinas, Hobbes views the moral rules or Laws of Nature as having the function of enabling human beings to be happy. But whereas Aquinas emphasized eternal happiness because he viewed humans as a combination of immaterial soul and material body and because he believed that God would some day resurrect us, Hobbes emphasized happiness in this life. He was a materialist who believed that we are composed entirely of physical matter. Consequently, he thought that the only happiness we could have is the temporary happiness of this life.

PHILIPPA FOOT

Contemporary British philosopher Philippa Foot takes the concept of goodness as basic for moral evaluation, and the questions for her are, What is a good action? and What is a good human being? She wants to focus, though, on what she calls natural goodness. The key to the answers for her questions will depend on identifying features of human nature in the sense of essential characteristics of our species, where the identification of a thing's species determines "what it is for members of [that] particular species to be as they should be, and to do that which they should do."[5] (Unlike Aquinas, who thinks that each species has a proper end such that it makes sense to ask such things as, What is the purpose of bees?, Foot does not say that each species has a function or purpose. She only says that each species has a characteristic form of life.)

Foot suggests that when we make judgments about the life or behavior of a living organism, evaluation is based on the form of life of the species to which the organism belongs. According to Foot, "The way an individual *should be* is determined by what is needed for development, self-maintenance, and reproduction."[6] Each species has a characteristic way of life that determines how members of that species engage in the basic life processes of self-maintenance and reproduction. For example, self-maintenance for deer relies on swiftness to outrun predators. A deer that is slow has what Foot calls a natural defect, a defect that lowers its chances to survive and reproduce. Similarly, owls hunt at night, so they must have eyes that enable them to see in the dark. An owl that cannot see in the dark has a natural defect. Therefore, it is good for a deer to be swift and good for an owl to be able to see in the dark. These are instances of natural goodness. They ground judgments that a deer should be fleet of foot and an owl should be able to see in the dark. (It would not be a big stretch to say that it's a law of nature that deer should be swift and owls should be able to see in the dark.)

Foot points out that some organisms live cooperatively, for example, wolves, which hunt in packs. A wolf that refuses to participate in the hunt probably will not survive. Perhaps more to the point, if many or most wolves behaved in that way, the entire species probably would become extinct.

What about the form of life of human beings? Foot says that the form of life of human beings is more rich and complex than the form of other organisms, so that the form of human "ultimate good" goes far beyond the basic life processes of survival and reproduction. But given our nature as rational beings who need to live as part of a society, and who need such social bonds as love and friendship, we can focus on possible defects that would reduce our ability to get what we need. For example, what if we could not learn a language or recognize faces? What if we could not understand other people, or see or hear, for that matter? Foot uses the word *deprivation* rather than defect. We are deprived if we cannot see, hear, speak, understand a language, understand other people, have a sense of humor, distinguish between different faces, or remember factual information or past experiences. Therefore, it is naturally good that we have the capacities to do these things, and we should have these capacities.

The evaluations in terms of what is naturally good or a natural defect or deprivation are based on what Foot referred to as the "ultimate" human good. Something is a natural deprivation for a human being if it interferes with a human's chances of getting or experiencing the "ultimate" human good. But what is that ultimate human good that serves as the standard of what we should do or be able to do? She firmly rejects the idea that the ultimate human good is happiness, at least as conventionally understood. Rather, the ultimate human good is to live a good life, which is not the same as a happy life. She recalls that on his death bed, the deeply unhappy philosopher Ludwig Wittgenstein said that he had had a wonderful life, and the anecdote of a psychiatrist who had a lobotomized patient who, according to the psychiatrist, was happy spending every day just picking leaves. But she admits that she has no single concept to replace that of happiness, so she qualifies it and calls it *deep happiness* (of a grown up human being), which distinguishes it from the happiness of a pig or a child. A child might be happy reading comic books and watching television all day long, but that is not the deep happiness Foot has in mind. A grown up human being (the form of life of the species directs us here) is capable of experiencing and doing so much more, and would not be happy with what would make a child happy. In terms of psychological states, it includes such states as satisfaction, joy, and contentment, but deep happiness is not determined solely by our psychological states; it is not merely "in the mind."

According to Foot, if deep happiness is identified with the ultimate human good, it must include what we do, how we live, not just what mental states we have or had. She gives an example of someone on his death bed who regrets having spent all his life in activities he now considers trivial and regrets that such activities made him happy at the time. He now feels that he wasted his life and did not have a good life. Thus she says that, "possible objects of deep happiness seem to be things that are basic in human life, such as home, and family, and work, and friendship."[7] She also mentions raising children, artistic creation, and exploration, in short, virtually anything that we would tend to consider "important." Deep happiness comes from love and friendship, satisfying work one considers significant, exercises of creativity. Foot also thinks that deep happiness is connected to such sentiments as pride and honor, and although this is not an attitude she mentions, she also probably would include self-respect. We should, then, have the capacities that will enable us to live such lives, do such things, and have such sentiments and attitudes that will bring us deep happiness. She also is convinced that traditional vices such as cruelty, dishonesty, and cowardice prevent us from achieving deep happiness. (Foot certainly does not think that she has presented a full and adequate explanation of deep happiness.)

But how is this scheme connected to laws of behavior exemplified in evaluations of moral right and wrong? The point is that the fact that something would help us achieve the deep human happiness we are capable of achieving gives us reasons for action. It's right to behave in ways that will enable us to achieve deep happiness and wrong to act in ways likely to prevent us from achieving deep happiness.

THE DIVINE COMMAND THEORY

Aquinas's natural law theory is based on theology ultimately, on what God commands. It is right to obey God's command and wrong to disobey. This is connected to the Divine Command theory of morality, perhaps one of the oldest and widely accepted moral theories. For example, we see it in Sophocles's *Antigone,* written and performed in Greece almost 2,500 years ago. The hero, Antigone, deliberately disobeys the commands of the king, Creon, who ordered her not to bury her brother after he was killed in a failed attempt to seize power. When she disobeys his command, Creon is enraged. He believes that it is morally wrong to disobey the commands of a king. But Antigone thinks she did the right thing in burying her brother because she is doing what the gods command. According to the religious beliefs of her society, if a body is not properly buried with the right religious rituals, its soul is not released into the underworld. Zeus, the king of the gods, commands us to bury our close relatives—such as father, mother, brothers, or sisters—with the proper rituals. This is a way of honoring and respecting our family. Thus, as Antigone sees it, the commands of the king are in conflict with the commands of the gods. To her, it is obvious that the commands of the gods—the moral rules they establish—take priority. When Creon asks, "You dared to break this law?" Antigone replies:

> Yes, because I did not believe
> that Zeus was the one who had proclaimed it. . . .
> The laws they have made for men are well marked out. . . .
> These laws are not for now or for yesterday, they are alive forever;
> and no one knows when they were shown to us first.[8]

Many of the world's major religions are based on so-called sacred writings said to be the word of God (or Allah). According to these traditions, God has issued commands to us that constitute the moral law we should follow. The moral laws are God's commands. Both Judaism and Christianity share the Ten Commandments. In addition to The Ten Commandments, Christians turn for guidance to the pronouncements and stories of Jesus in the New Testament. Muslims turn to the Koran and the traditions of Islam for moral guidance. Hindus turn to the Vedas, sacred scriptures of Hinduism believed to have been revealed by the Hindu gods.

There are two versions of the Divine Command theory. According to one version. God's commands *make* things morally right and wrong. On this view, if stealing is wrong, it is only because God forbids it. If God did not forbid it, it would not be wrong. Consequently, we cannot say that God forbids stealing *because* it is wrong. According to this version, the existence of moral right and wrong depends entirely on God. In fact, it might entail that *morally wrong* means nothing more than "forbidden by God." On this view, if God did not exist, *nothing* would be morally right or wrong. As for moral knowledge, on this version, the only way for human beings to acquire moral knowledge is to have it revealed to them by God. There can be no source of moral knowledge independent of God's revelation.

According to the second version, God's commands don't make things right or wrong. Rather, God commands us to do some things *because* they're morally right and forbids us to do other things *because* they're morally wrong. We should obey God's commands because we can be certain that what God commands is morally right, not because God created or made morality, but because God is all-knowing and infallible—God has perfect knowledge of right and wrong. Therefore, God cannot make a mistake.

To put the point provocatively, even if God did not exist, the same things would be morally right and wrong. God knows what's morally right and wrong rather than makes things morally right and wrong.

On this version, human beings can come to know moral truths either through divine revelation or through the use of reason. Thus, we can learn that murder and stealing are wrong by having God reveal their wrongness to us, or we can figure it out for ourselves that stealing and murder are wrong. And even if God didn't exist to prohibit murder and stealing, they would still be morally wrong.

Problems for the Divine Command Theory

A number of problems face the Divine Command theory.

Of course, we can accept that the moral laws are God's commands only if we believe that God exists. Not everyone believes that. There are both atheists (those who believe that God doesn't exist) and agnostics (those who neither believe God exists nor believe that God doesn't exist but rather suspend judgment). In moral argument, appeals to what God commands fail unless those we are arguing with believe that God exists.

Even among theists, appeal to God's commands can present problems. Theists may disagree on what God commands. The problem is, How do we know what God commands? We can appeal to what our religion considers the revealed word of God; for example, a Christian can consult the Bible or a Muslim can consult the Koran. However, such sacred writings do not provide explicit guidance on every moral issue that a person may face. For example, no sacred scriptures mention genetic engineering. Then, too, sacred writings require interpretation, and people's interpretations may differ. How do we know which interpretation is correct? For example, in the Sermon on the Mount, Jesus says, "You have heard that it was said, 'An eye for an eye, and a tooth for a tooth': But I say to you, Do not resist an evil doer. But if anyone strikes you on the right cheek, turn the other also" (Matthew 5:38–39). Should we interpret this passage as condemning capital punishment? Similarly, Jesus encountered a man who asked what he should do to ensure that he went to heaven. "Jesus said to him, 'If you wish to be perfect, go, sell your possessions, and give the money to the poor, and you will have treasure in heaven.'" The man, who was rich, wasn't pleased to hear this, but "Jesus said to his disciples, 'Truly I tell you, it will be hard for a rich man to enter the kingdom of Heaven'"[9] (Matthew 19:21–24). Should we interpret this passage as requiring people to give away their wealth to the poor in order to ensure that they don't die rich? But can we guarantee that our interpretation of sacred writings is correct? If so, how?

Different religions disagree, moreover, about which writings are truly sacred scriptures—the word of God or the gods. Christians and Jews do not accept the Hindu Vedas. Hindus and Buddhists do not accept the Bible. Of course, atheists deny that any writings are the word of God. The question is, How do we know what writings really are sacred—the word of God? If a certain book contains statements claiming that it is the word of God, does that prove it really is the word of God? What evidence could there be to show that writings really are God's words?

But even if someone accepts a religion's sacred scripture as the authentic word of God, she may not believe that every word in it is God's. Many liberal Protestants believe that the Bible was divinely inspired, but that human voices are mingled with God's voice among its pages. The problem, then, is to determine what is the genuine voice of God and what are merely the voices of human beings. Passages in sacred writings may truly reveal God's law, but there is at least the possibility that instead they embody the moral convictions of the human beings who wrote them down. For example, if a passage in the Bible directs us to stone adulterers to death, how confident can we be that these are God's words rather than the words of the human author?

If we do not rely on sacred writings that are considered revelations of God's law, we may consult our conscience, hoping that God will speak to us in an audible and intelligible voice. What we hear may be God's voice, but it also may be our own voice, reflecting our moral traditions and upbringing. How can we determine whether it is God's voice? And even if it is God's voice, what we hear may require interpretation, just as sacred writings do. How can we determine whether our interpretation is correct? For example, apparently the consciences of many white Southerners prior to the Civil War told them that enslaving blacks was not morally wrong. Probably many of them sincerely believed that it was God's voice. Few of us today find that believable. Similarly, many white Southerners prior to and during the era of civil rights struggles in the 1950s and 1960s sincerely believed that it is not morally wrong to discriminate against blacks. Presumably their consciences told them that segregation laws and denial to blacks of the right to vote were not morally wrong. Was that the voice of God? Few of us today find that at all believable.

Religion and a Meaningful Life

Philippa Foot spoke of deep human happiness as a basis for judgments of natural goodness. That deep happiness included a conception of one's life and projects as being meaningful and significant. But sometimes life can seem pretty meaningless and insignificant. We may reflect that human life is confined to the planet Earth, and Earth is merely one tiny planet in a huge universe that's composed of billions and billions of stars, a tiny point that's no more significant from a point of view that encompasses the whole than one atom of water in all the world's oceans on Earth. We're not in some privileged place in the universe, because there is no privileged place in the universe. We're located on an average planet circling an average star in an average galaxy that probably contains hundreds of millions of stars, a galaxy that's just one of billions of galaxies. So from the point of view of the universe, the home of human life seems pretty tiny and unimpressive.

As for the human species itself, according to science, human life has existed on Earth only for a tiny fraction of its existence, a few tens or hundreds of thousands of its four or five billion year history. We're a very recent addition to a universe that seems to have gotten along quite well for billions of years without us. Will our species still be here a million or ten million years from now? The dinosaurs ruled the Earth for hundreds of millions of years, but eventually they died out. The same may happen to human beings. In fact, well over 95 percent of the species that have existed are now extinct. Or our species may evolve into something unimaginable—if we do not become extinct first. But unless we can colonize space, we're definitely fated to die out in a few billion years when the sun dies out in our solar system, because the sun is the engine of life. In a sense, the human species is like a soap bubble floating in a bath tub that thinks it has always existed and always will exist.

If Earth and human life in general look trivial and insignificant from this point of view, consider the life of a single individual alive today. Even if you're the president of the United States, you're only one individual among six or seven billion now existing. Hundreds of millions of people came before you. Tens and hundreds of billions of people will come after you as the centuries and millennia roll on. Your existence probably will span fewer than a hundred years of the billions of years that rolled by before you were born and will roll by after you die. No matter who you are or what you do, some day you'll be forgotten; there won't be anyone alive who will even suspect that you existed. It may take ten years or ten thousand years after you die, but you'll be forgotten.

Given these reflections, one might think that nothing about human life matters, whether on the level of individuals or the species, at least from a cosmic point of view. But for many people, religion can provide significance and meaning that's otherwise lacking. (Of course, other nonreligious considerations may also provide an antidote, such as the reflection that trying to judge human life in general and our own lives in particular from such a cosmic perspective is not appropriate.) First, even if the human species is limited to a tiny speck in the universe, religion can teach that it's a place important to God. Similarly, even if human beings are a relative newcomer to the universe and Earth, religion can teach that it came into existence as part of God's plan and for God's purposes. It is a species loved and valued by God, with a role to play that God considers important. (Think of Aquinas's view that humans have a proper end.) As for individual humans, religion can teach that God loves and values each one, and loves and values them equally. Each has a role to play in God's plans. Even if their earthly status is modest, they may have a very important part to play in God's purposes. Regarding death, most religions teach that we have (or are) immortal souls that will continue to exist long after our bodies die.

We should question, though, whether religion is necessary if we are to consider the life of our species or of individual people meaningful and significant. Can life be meaningful and significant without religious belief?

EXERCISES

1. Presumably, a Stoic would say that abusing one's own children or parents is unnatural and therefore morally wrong. In what way might it be unnatural? Why would that make it morally wrong?

2. Do humans have proper ends, as Aquinas claims? If yes, what are our proper ends? What are the implications with respect to what actions are right or wrong?

3. Do all our parts have proper ends? If yes, is it morally wrong to use our parts in ways contrary to their proper ends? What makes an act "contrary" to a thing's proper end?

4. Hobbes viewed Laws of Nature as rules that must be followed if a group and its members are to survive and thrive. He thought that there are good reasons for each of us to adopt and live by the Laws of Nature because that enables us to survive in a group or society. What rules would you include in this system of Laws of Nature?

5. If God doesn't exist, is nothing morally forbidden or required?

6. If God exists, how does God want us to treat nonhuman animals? How do you know?

7. Does anyone know what God's laws are? If yes, how do we acquire knowledge of God's laws?

8. What responses do you have to the following words of the Dalai Lama?

> I believe there is an important distinction to be made between religion and spirituality. Religion I take to be concerned with faith in the claims to salvation of one faith tradition or another, an aspect of which is acceptance of some form of metaphysical or supernatural reality. . . . Connected with this are religious teachings or dogma, ritual, prayer, and so on.
>
> Spirituality I take to be concerned with those qualities of the human spirit—such as love and compassion, patience, tolerance, forgiveness, contentment, a sense of responsibility, a sense of harmony—which bring happiness to both self and others. . . . There is no reason why the individual should not develop them, even to a high degree, without recourse to any religious or metaphysical belief system. This is why I sometimes say that religion is something we can do without. What we cannot do without are these basic spiritual qualities.
>
> . . . [E]ach of the qualities noted is defined by an implicit concern for others' well-being. . . . Thus spiritual practice according to this description involves, on the one hand, acting out of concern for others' well-being. On the other, it entails transforming ourselves so that we become more readily disposed to do so.[10]

SUGGESTED READINGS

Robert M. Adams. *The Virtue of Faith*. New York: Oxford University Press, 1987.

Saint Augustine. *Confessions*. Translated by Henry Chadwick. New York: Oxford University Press, 1991.

J. B. Schneewind, ed. *Moral Philosophy from Montaigne to Kant*, Vols. 1 and 2. Cambridge: Cambridge University Press, 1990.

INTERNET RESOURCES

Christian Classics Ethereal Library (www.ccel.org/). A huge collection of important texts in the Christian tradition, all online.

David Hume, *The Natural History of Religion* (www.utm.edu/research/hume/wri/nhr/nhr.htm). The complete 1757 text online.

His Holiness the Dalai Lama of Tibet (www.earthlight.co.nz/hhdl/). A website containing a biography of the Dalai Lama, information about Tibet, and transcripts of several speeches.

ENDNOTES

1. Diogenes Laertius in *The Hellenistic Philosophers*. Edited by A. A. Long and D. N. Sedley (Cambridge, England: Cambridge University Press, 1987), p. 266.

2. Ibid., p. 329.

3. Thomas Hobbes. *Leviathan*. Edited by Edwin Curley (Indianapolis, IN: Hackett, 1994), p. 78 (Part I, Chapter XIII, Paragraph 14).

4. Ibid., p. 79 (I, XIV, 3).

5. Philippa Foot. *Natural Goodness* (New York: Oxford University Press, 2001).

6. Ibid., p. 33.

7. Ibid., p. 88.

8. Sophocles. *Antigone*. Translated by Richard Emil Braun (New York: Oxford University Press, 1973), Lines 550–562.

9. All translations are from *Holy Bible: The New Revised Standard Version* (New York: Oxford University Press, 1989).

10. His Holiness the Dalai Lama, *Ethics for the New Millenium* (New York: Riverhead Books, 1999), pp. 22–23.

3

Realism, Nihilism, Subjectivism, and Relativism

OBJECTIVES

- To understand moral realism
- To critically examine the concepts of moral truth and moral facts
- To understand moral nihilism
- To understand noncognitivism and logical positivism
- To understand moral subjectivism
- To understand moral relativism
- To distinguish among nihilism, subjectivism, and relativism
- To understand the reasons that count in favor of and count against realism, nihilism, subjectivism, and relativism

INTRODUCTION

On June 7, 1998, James Byrd Jr. of Jasper, Texas, a 49-year-old disabled African American, was walking home late at night from a friend's anniversary party when three white men offered him a ride. Byrd may have known one of the men. Unknown to Byrd, the three men were white supremacists. They drove Byrd to a deserted spot and beat him for no other reason than that he was black. Then they chained him by the ankles to the back of the pickup truck and dragged him for a few miles on a bumpy road. According to a pathologist's testimony at the trial, Byrd "turned over and over to relieve the pain as his flesh was torn away and his [bones] ground up on the blacktop."[1] He was dragged for almost two miles, alive until "his head, shoulder, and right arm were torn off by a concrete drain pipe at the foot of a driveway."[2]

MORAL REALISM

If one of the murderers were to say that he did nothing wrong in dragging Byrd to his death, a fellow white supremacist who agrees might say, "That's true." On the other hand, if someone disagrees, he might reply, "That's false." But are sentences that express moral judgments true or false? Moral realists, also called moral objectivists, think that they can be true or false, but, many people in our culture deny this.

The question of whether there are any moral truths is sometimes connected to another question, namely, whether some moral judgments are better justified or more reasonable than others. Can some be better justified or more reasonable if moral judgments are neither true nor false? The answer appears to be yes. A command, for example, is neither true nor false, but we can evaluate it as justified or reasonable, and compare the justifiability or reasonability of one with another. Similarly, we can evaluate the reasonability of an emotion, such as fear or anger, although neither fear nor anger is true or false (although the claim that someone is feeling fear or anger is true or false). In the first chapter, we saw that moral judgments seem to require justification. If there is no justification for a moral judgment, it isn't reasonable. We also saw how moral judgments can be justified by moral arguments, and that not all moral arguments are equally strong.

Even if the justifiability or reasonability of moral judgments is not dependent on whether they are true or false, other issues are. People often change their minds about moral issues, but it's hard to understand why someone would change her mind unless she thought that her original moral judgment was mistaken. For example, consider a white supremacist who experiences a conversion. He once believed that it is not wrong to harm people of color and Jews, but he now believes that it is wrong. What other attitude can he have toward his former moral judgment other than that he had been mistaken and his current moral judgment other than that it is not mistaken? That is, it certainly seems natural to describe him as thinking that his former moral belief is false and his current moral belief true. But that presupposes that moral judgments (beliefs or sentences) can be true or false.

Similarly, suppose that you are discussing a moral issue with someone, say abortion. Let's assume that you think that abortion is sometimes wrong but not always wrong, whereas the other person believes that abortion is always wrong. If you disagree, that seems to entail that you think you have a true moral belief and the other person has a false moral belief.

So, can moral judgments be true or false? Is moral realism true? It's difficult to evaluate moral realism without answering the question, What is truth? That is, what are we claiming when we say that a sentence, any sentence, is true? We may be tempted to say something like, "A true sentence corresponds to the facts whereas a false sentence doesn't," but is the nature of facts and the relation of "correspondence" between facts and sentences any clearer than the nature of truth?

If the cup on my desk is blue, isn't it a fact? And if it's a fact, then that's the way the world (the universe) is. There is a cup on my desk and it has the property of being blue. This fact, we may feel tempted to think, is composed of the cup, my desk, and the property of being blue. Those are (at least some of) its constituents or parts.

If the truth of a sentence depends on there being a fact with which it agrees or corresponds, then moral sentences can be true only if there are moral facts, such as the fact that dragging James Byrd to his death was wrong. The moral fact, then, would be composed of the dragging (an event) and its property of being wrong. What seems problematic to many people, though, is the property of being wrong. It certainly is different from the property of being blue. Is the property of being wrong as "real" as the property of being blue?

I can detect the property of being blue simply by looking. So can you. But can I detect the property of being wrong simply by looking? Note that I can determine whether the cup has the property of being blue only if I see or saw the cup. Can I determine whether the dragging has the property of being wrong only if I see or saw the dragging? If I never actually saw the dragging, does that mean I am forever barred from being able to determine by myself whether it had the property of being wrong? Are only actual witnesses able to tell us whether it had the property of being wrong? What if I just think about the idea of the dragging? Will that enable me to determine whether it has the property of being wrong?

One problem may be that we are thinking of facts as something we can visualize or picture. We can determine whether there is a picturable fact, such as the fact that there is a blue cup on my desk, merely by looking because it's picturable. We cannot determine just by looking whether it is a fact that the dragging had the property of being wrong because it isn't picturable. (The fact that Byrd was dragged to his death may be picturable, but the fact of the dragging's wrongness isn't.) But must something be picturable to be a fact?

Surely not. It is a fact that the number 5 is odd and the number 6 is even, but that fact is not picturable so that you could detect it just by looking. Similarly, how would the picture of a bachelor differ from the picture of that same person if he weren't a bachelor? The fact that someone is a bachelor isn't picturable. I cannot tell just by looking whether someone has the property of being a bachelor. Does that mean that it cannot be a fact that someone is a bachelor (and therefore that claims about someone being a bachelor are neither true nor false)?

Then too, how would the picture of someone who fears death differ from the picture of that same person if she didn't fear death? I cannot tell just by looking at someone whether she fears death. Does that mean that it cannot be a fact that someone fears death and that a claim that someone fears death is neither true nor false? If that doesn't follow, then being picturable is not necessary for facts. Therefore, even if the presence or absence of moral properties is not picturable and thus ascertainable by just looking, it does not follow that there are no moral facts or true moral sentences.

One possible strategy is suggested by the example of the property of being a bachelor. We define being a bachelor in terms of other properties, most of which can be detected empirically. Part of the definition of being a bachelor is that one is unmarried. Because it is very difficult, if not impossible, to prove a negative claim, we focus on the property of being married. How do we define being married? We define marriage at least in part in terms of various legal rights and duties. For example, if two people are married to each other, they have a legal right to part of each other's economic resources. How do we ascertain whether two people are married to each other? In order to determine that, we have to ascertain whether they correctly performed certain ceremonies or rituals, these to be determined by the local laws or conventions. For example, they must both sign a valid marriage license within a certain period of time before the ceremony. The ceremony must be performed by someone licensed to perform marriages. If any of the legal requirements are not met, the two people aren't "really" married. But if two people are married, it is a fact that they are married, and the claim that they are married is true or false.

Perhaps being wrong is a property like being married and can be defined in empirical terms. For example, we might define being wrong as violating certain standards whose purpose or function is to promote social harmony or minimize harm to people. Whether moral terms can be plausibly defined in a way that makes the idea of moral facts less problematic is a controversial and difficult issue that cannot be pursued here in any detail. The point I wish to emphasize is that thinking of moral properties more along the lines of the property of being married rather than the property of being blue may make the idea of moral properties and facts less problematic.

Why Think That Moral Judgments Can Be True or False?

One reason is that otherwise, a fundamental logical law seems to be violated, the so-called law of excluded middle. According to this law, two contradictory sentences cannot both be true. One must be true and the other false. Thus, consider the two sentences, "Dogs are mammals" and "Dogs are not mammals." They contradict each other. They are inconsistent. Therefore, they cannot possibly both be true. One must be true and the other false. If someone says that they're both true, we must assume that either he is irrational or that he doesn't mean what we mean by "not."

Similarly, consider two moral sentences: "Slavery is always wrong" and "Slavery is not always wrong." They certainly appear to contradict each other. If they contradict each other, they cannot both be true. But then, one must be true and the other false (even if we don't know with absolute certainty which is true).

Another consideration is that if moral sentences and beliefs are neither true nor false, then it can seem puzzling to talk of someone making a mistake about a moral issue. And if we cannot make a mistake about a moral issue, it's difficult to explain why someone would ever change his mind. Yet most of us probably have at least at some time changed our minds about a moral issue. If we have changed our minds, that seems to show at least that we *think* we can make moral mistakes. If we think we can make moral mistakes, doesn't that commit us to the view that moral sentences and beliefs are either true or false?

However, many people reject moral realism. What theories do they put in its place? We shall examine three: moral nihilism, moral subjectivism, and moral relativism.

MORAL NIHILISM

According to moral nihilists, nothing is morally right or wrong because moral judgments are neither true nor false. (The word *nihilism* comes from the Latin word *nihil*, which means "nothing.") It follows that it was neither right nor wrong to drag James Byrd Jr. to his death. Similarly, suppose that a sadist is torturing someone a moral nihilist loves. The nihilist cannot say or think that what the sadist is doing is morally wrong. If nothing is really morally right or wrong, then it's not really wrong for the sadist to slowly torture to death the nihilist's loved one.

Why do nihilists think that moral judgments are neither true nor false? Some, called *noncognitivists*, say that moral sentences aren't true or false because they are not used to describe, to state a fact; rather, they're used to do something else that cannot be evaluated as true or false. We can use language (sentences) to do many things. For example, rather than use a sentence to state a fact (for example, that it's noon), we can use it to ask a question: What time is it? A sentence used to ask a question is neither true nor false. Imagine someone replying to "What time is it?" with "That's true." We can also use language to make recommendations, or issue commands, for example, "Look before you leap." That sentence is neither true nor false because it's an imperative. Noncognitivists claim that sentences used to express moral judgments, such as "This is morally right/wrong" or "This is morally good/bad" are neither true nor false because they are not used to make claims about what the universe is like or state facts, but instead are used merely to express feelings or attitudes, such as moral approval or disapproval. Thus, "White supremacists dragged James Byrd to his death" is either true or false because it states a supposed fact about the universe. It's true if it is a fact. On the other hand, sentences such as "It was morally wrong for the white supremacists to drag James Byrd to his death" don't state a supposed fact or make a claim about what the universe is like. Instead, it expresses the speaker's or writer's negative attitude or feelings toward the action. "It was wrong for the white supremacists to drag Byrd to his death," on this view, is rather like saying that they dragged him to his death and following it with "Boo!" or a downward gesture with one's thumb or the holding of one's nose to express a negative attitude. But neither "Boo" nor the gestures are true or false.

Are moral sentences used for nothing more than to express someone's feelings or attitudes? Critics of noncognitivism point out that sentences can be used for many purposes simultaneously. For example, "The bridge is weak" can be used to describe a bridge and to warn an unwary motorist. "You're obese" can be used to describe, but also to insult or to warn. They're not mutually exclusive. If these sentences can be used to express feelings or attitudes, among other things, does it follow that they are neither true nor false? Given agreement on the meaning of weak and obese, and the criteria or standards for weakness in bridges and obesity in people, the sentences can also describe or state facts and thus be true or false. That is, given criteria for what makes a bridge weak, for example, having a high probability of collapsing when it is bearing weights there is a high probability it will have to bear, then saying it's weak says that it fails to meet the criteria of strength in bridges and therefore is weak. There may be some question about the exact line between strong and weak, and what the probability of its collapsing is under different weights, so that we're not sure whether a given bridge is weak, but closer to the edges there won't be. In many cases, it will be straightforwardly true or false whether a bridge is weak, even though the sentence "The bridge is weak" can be used to warn as well as describe.

Might moral sentences such as "Slavery is wrong" be like such sentences as "The bridge is weak"? That is, might they be true or false because although they express attitudes, they also describe or state facts? The point is that the mere fact that a sentence is used to express an attitude or feeling does not prove it's neither true nor false, because it may be that it's used to do other things as well that do make it true or false.

Interestingly, when we express moral judgments in some ways rather than others, noncognitivism is obviously true. When we speak of moral rules, such as "Do not commit murder" or "Do not steal," we clearly are employing imperatives that are neither true nor false. But when we express moral judgments using such so-called "thick" concepts as cruel, we clearly are describing as well as evaluating. "He's cruel" can be straightforwardly true or false, even if used to express a negative attitude. (We also should point out that noncognitivists can say that some moral judgments are more justified, rational, or reasonable than others even if they are neither true nor false, just as we can say of some orders or recommendations. Those who do are not really nihilists, because nihilists say not only that no moral judgment is true or false but also that no moral judgment is more justified, reasonable, or rational than any other.)

Some noncognitivists, sympathetic to a movement known as *logical positivism*, claim that if a sentence is not verifiable or confirmable by observation and perception (or empirical tests), then it is meaningless. If it's meaningless (or *cognitively meaningless*), it's neither true nor false. "The ball is red" is verifiable or confirmable because we can tell whether the ball is red just by looking at the ball. Therefore, it's meaningful. On the other hand, the sentence (or string of words) "The baby belief had its loud hair cut" is not verifiable or confirmable by using our senses; therefore, it is meaningless. (We can't tell whether or not the baby belief had its loud hair cut by looking. Are some beliefs baby beliefs? Do some beliefs have hair? Is some hair loud?) Because it's meaningless, it's neither true nor false.

According to these philosophers, we cannot verify or confirm a moral sentence such as "Slavery is always wrong" by using our senses. Therefore, such sentences are meaningless. Therefore, they're neither true nor false.

But the example of "The baby belief had its loud hair cut" seems to have gotten things backwards. It's not meaningless *because* it cannot be verified by the senses; it cannot be verified by the senses because it's meaningless. The question to ask is what reason there could possibly be to think that a sentence is meaningless just because it can't be verified or confirmed by appeal to our senses. Almost all philosophers today reject this. In fact, it's self-undermining. Take the sentence "A sentence that cannot be empirically confirmed or verified is meaningless." Is this sentence itself empirically confirmable or verifiable? No. Therefore, if the sentence is true, it's meaningless! Therefore, it's not true.

Some philosophers also object that some noncognitivists seem to overlook the role of perception and observation in moral reasoning, even if it is not exactly the same as verification or confirmation in the natural sciences. Reasons for moral judgments almost always include confirmable and disconfirmable empirical claims. For example, claims about harm are generally crucial in moral reasoning, and we must appeal to observation and perception to determine whether something is harmful and how harmful it is. (Consider the role of claims about harm in all-things-considered singular moral judgments, as well as mediate moral principles.) Probably most philosophers think that moral nihilists haven't proved their case.

According to Plato in his Socratic dialogue *Theaetetus*, the Greek philosopher Protagoras claimed that "Man is the measure of all things: of the things which are, that they are, and of the things which are not, that they are not."[3] Socrates in the dialogue goes on to explain what he thinks Protagoras meant: "...as each thing appears to me, so it is for me, and as it appears to you, so it is for you."[4] Thus, the day may feel hot to you and cool to me. In that case, it is hot for you and cool for me. If we ask which it really is, whether it's really hot or really cool, Protagoras would say that the question betrays a mistaken assumption: there is no one way that the day *really* is. It's neither really hot nor really cool. It's relative. It's hot for (or to) you and cool for (or to) me. If it feels warm to a third person and cold to a fourth, then it's also warm for (or to) the third person and cold for (or to) the fourth. But the day itself is neither objectively hot, warm, cool, or cold.

Similarly, suppose we ask each other what we think of the novel *Moby Dick*. You may find it fascinating, and I may find it boring. In that case, it's boring for me but not for you. But suppose we ask whether it's *really* boring or *really* not boring. Protagoras would say we've made a mistake. It's not objectively one thing or the other. Being boring is entirely relative. It's boring to some people and not boring to others.

But according to Socrates, Protagoras's relativism applies to more than questions of whether the day is hot or *Moby Dick* is boring. As Socrates interprets him, Protagoras claims that whatever appears to someone to be true is true for that person; the person cannot make mistakes or have false beliefs. As he summarizes Protagoras, "whatever the individual judges by means of perception is true for him;...no man can assess another's experience better than he, or can claim authority to examine another man's judgment and see if it be right or wrong;...only the individual himself can judge of his own world, and what he judges is always true and correct...."[5] But suppose you dream that you're flying and you come to believe from that experience that you really were flying. According to Socrates, Protagoras claims that I can't correctly say to you, "Oh, you're mistaken, you weren't really flying, you only dreamed that you were flying." It's true to you that you were flying and false to me, but there's no objectively true or false answer to the question "Were you really flying?" All truths are relative to a perceiver. We should not say that something is true (or false), period. Instead, we should express it in a relative way and say that it's true *to or for* certain people, and false *to or for* others.

But we're more interested in moral claims, not claims about whether someone was really flying or only dreamed that he was flying. Socrates says that Protagoras' relativism includes claims about the moral concepts of justice and right. According to Protagoras, "whatever any community decides to be just and right, and establishes as such, actually is what is just and right for that community and for as long as it remains so established."[6] There are two different doctrines in tension here. One is that the individual person is the measure of all things, including moral things, while the other is that the community is the measure of all things. We'll call the first doctrine—that the individual person is the measure of what is right and wrong—*moral subjectivism*, while we'll call the second doctrine—that a community is the measure of right and wrong—*moral relativism*.

Saying that moral right and wrong are relative either to individuals or groups should be distinguished from another version of relativism that claims that moral right and wrong are relative to circumstances.

According to this view, things aren't right or wrong, period. Rather, they're right in some circumstances and wrong in others. For example, killing may be wrong if one kills an innocent person to steal her money but not if one kills a terrorist to save the lives of innocent hostages. Similarly, stealing may be wrong when it's to buy drugs but not wrong when it's to feed your starving children. This kind of relativism is not what we have in mind when we talk of moral subjectivism and moral relativism.

MORAL SUBJECTIVISM

Moral subjectivists claim that whatever an individual believes to be right or wrong is right or wrong for that individual. What if we ask whether what an individual believes to be right is "really" right? Subjectivists say that nothing is "really" right or wrong. Put another way, if we ask whether an individual's moral beliefs are "really" true, the subjectivist says there is no such thing as "real" truth applicable to moral beliefs and moral sentences. That is, every moral belief of every individual is true; none are false. But the truth that subjectivists have in mind is what we might call *subjective* truth rather than *objective* truth.

A belief or sentence is said to be *objectively* true if it is true independent of what anyone believes, perceives, or feels. It is true because that's the way the real world is, independent of all observers. For example, "Earth has one moon" is objectively true. It would still be true even if there were no observers with minds around to see that it's true. Similarly, if there really are no witches (with supernatural powers), an individual who believes that witches don't exist has an *objectively* true belief and an individual who believes that witches do exist has an *objectively* false belief.

If moral subjectivism is true, no one can have an *objectively* true or false moral belief. Rather, each has a *subjectively* true belief. But that seems to entail that contradictory moral sentences can both be *subjectively* true and that if they contradict, it is not the case that one of them must be false. That is, if I believe that it was wrong to drag James Byrd to his death and a white supremacist believes that it was not wrong, we're both correct and both have *subjectively* true beliefs. Neither of us has an *objectively* true belief, but then again, neither of us has an *objectively* false belief, either.

According to moral subjectivism, the highest and only court of appeals on moral matters is an individual's own moral code. There are no moral facts; there are no valid moral standards that apply to an individual except the standards he accepts.

Reasons Supporting Moral Subjectivism

Moral Beliefs Are Based on Feelings.   One common argument for moral subjectivism is as follows:

1. Moral beliefs are based only on feelings.
2. Feelings are subjective and are neither true nor false.
3. Therefore, moral beliefs are subjective and are neither true nor false.

This argument has several problems. First, if being "based on" means being caused by, it is not obvious that the first premise is true. Many moral beliefs are learned from the moral teachings of family, friends, religious groups, and teachers; they may not be caused by or associated with any feelings. If you were taught at an early age that stealing is wrong, how is that belief based on feelings?

Although feelings often do play a role in moral evaluation, they are not alone. Often experience, reason, and imagination also play a crucial role in the generation of moral beliefs. Consider this example. A visitor from the United States sees Nazi thugs drag an old Jewish man from his home and beat him to death in the street. The Nazis believe that they are not doing anything wrong. The visitor from the United States believes that they are. It may be that the Nazis believe and act as they do in part because they hate Jews and lack sympathy and compassion for the old man they are beating to death. But we should ask why they hate Jews and why they lack sympathy and compassion. Feelings do not stand alone. They have causes rooted in perception, imagination, belief, reasoning, and so on. These Nazis may hate Jews because they have been brainwashed into believing that Jews are destroying their society. They may have no compassion or sympathy for their victim because they lack the imagination necessary to imagine his suffering as well as because of their beliefs about Jews. Similarly, the visitor from the United States may believe as he does because he does not hate Jews and because he does have sympathy and compassion for the man being beaten to death. But his feelings also do not stand alone. They have causes.

The second premise is also problematic. Feelings are neither true nor false, but it does not follow that they cannot be assessed or evaluated as reasonable or unreasonable. Consider fear. If someone feels intense fear at the sight of a mouse, the fear is unreasonable given that mice pose no threat. Similarly, we often maintain that hatred of people because of their religion or race is irrational. Hating Jews, Arabs, African Americans, or Asians is almost universally regarded as irrational. If a moral belief is based on a feeling such as hatred, it does not follow that it is then immune from questions about whether it is justified or rational, because we can ask whether the feeling is justified or rational.

Finally, the cause of a belief has little to do with whether it is true. Suppose that a doting mother believes that her son did not commit a heinous crime only because she loves him. She bases her belief in his innocence solely on her feelings. Would it follow that her belief is neither true nor false? Of course not. Whether her belief is true depends on whether he committed the crime. The same logic applies if the belief based on feelings is a moral belief.

People Disagree about Moral Issues.   According to this argument, if individuals disagree about an issue, then they're both equally right. And since on all moral issues we can find individuals who disagree, it follows that whatever an individual believes about a moral issue, he or she has a true belief.

The mere fact that people disagree about an issue proves nothing. People disagree about virtually everything. For example, people disagree about whether Lee Harvey Oswald killed JFK. It simply does not follow from this that the claim that he did is neither true nor false. Suppose that there is someone who believes that you don't exist. This need not be as outlandish as it may sound. For example, imagine you're speaking to someone who is psychotic and thinks that you're a figment of his imagination. He believes you don't exist. You believe you do. Because there is disagreement, does it follow that the claim that you exist is neither true nor false? But how could it possibly be the case that you neither exist nor don't exist? If two people disagreed about whether you exist, that simply would not show that there is no truth to the matter. Therefore, the fact that people disagree about moral issues does not show that no moral claim is true or false.

We should keep in mind that not all moral disagreement involves disagreement at the level of moral principles. Disagreement over a particular moral issue could arise even when the societies accept the same moral principles, if they have different beliefs about the nonmoral facts. If society A believes that human sacrifice is morally right and we believe it's morally wrong, does that prove we have different basic moral principles, for example, that they place a lower moral value on human life than we do? No. It may be that they believe that the entire universe will be destroyed if they do not periodically sacrifice humans to the gods whereas we believe no such thing. If they didn't believe this, they wouldn't believe that human sacrifice is morally right. On the other hand, if we did believe this, we probably would believe that human sacrifice is morally right. (And would the fact that we disagree show that the claim that the gods will destroy the universe if we don't sacrifice to them neither true nor false?)

Moral disagreement may also be due to applying the same moral principle in different circumstances. Recall that a different version of moral relativism, one that we are not disputing, claims that what is morally right in one set of circumstances may be morally wrong in other circumstances. (According to this version of relativism, moral right and wrong are relative to circumstances, not relative to the beliefs of societies or individuals.) Suppose that there are two societies, A and B. A is an affluent, technologically advanced society with extensive, accurate information about reproduction and reliable methods of birth control. Population growth has been controlled, and overpopulation is not a problem. B, on the other hand, is technologically backward and poised on the edge of subsistence, barely able to support its current population. People in B lack accurate information about reproduction and have no reliable methods of birth control. If unchecked, population growth will outstrip available resources, leading to widespread starvation, malnutrition, and disease. Now suppose we ask whether infanticide is morally wrong. It may be easy to agree that infanticide is morally wrong in society A, but less easy to agree that it's morally wrong in society B because of the difference in circumstances. That two societies disagree about a moral issue does not show that they accept different moral principles, but even if they do, it doesn't guarantee that each has an equally true or reasonable moral belief.

No One Can Prove Who Is Correct in a Moral Dispute.   Moral subjectivists might argue as follows: no one can prove who is correct in a moral dispute. If no one can prove who is correct, then either both are equally correct or neither of them is correct.

Can no one prove who is correct in a moral dispute? It depends on what we require for *proof*. If we prove something only if we show that it is certain (or certainly true)—that we couldn't possibly be mistaken—then most people probably would agree that we cannot prove who's correct in moral disputes. But then, we probably cannot prove who is correct in most nonmoral disputes, either. In most cases—nonmoral as well as moral—we are more interested in whether we have *adequate justification* for what we believe; we look for high probability, not certainty.

If two societies disagree about a moral issue, that doesn't automatically mean that they both are equally justified in what they believe. In order to determine whether they are, we have to look at their justifications. And while it's possible for both to be equally justified, it also could be that one society has far better and weightier reasons for its moral belief than does the other society. For example, one society's moral belief may be based on false and unreasonable nonmoral beliefs. In that case, its justification is defective. Or it may have made mistakes in reasoning, thinking that one claim implies another when it doesn't. In those cases, perhaps the society that has justification of its moral beliefs that don't have these defects has "proved" its case.

But even if in a relaxed sense we cannot "prove" who is correct, it simply does not follow that either both are equally correct or neither is correct. There are lots of disputes where we probably will never be able to prove who is correct, such as whether God created the universe or whether there is intelligent life in another galaxy. But that should not lead us to think that there is no fact of the matter, that both views are equally correct or neither is.

The Virtue of Tolerance.   Many people think that it is good to be tolerant of other people's views and that everyone has a right to believe what they believe, and they think that moral subjectivism provides a strong ground for toleration. From that, they may go on to think that moral subjectivism is true. But even if acceptance of a theory will have good consequences, that does not show that the theory is true. Furthermore, it is not even clear that acceptance of moral subjectivism will have such good consequences as increased tolerance for different views.

Does moral subjectivism provide fertile ground for the virtue of tolerance? On the one hand, it would seem so, because a subjectivist cannot be dogmatic and say that someone they disagree with is wrong. But if subjectivism is fertile ground for the virtue of tolerance, we need to keep in mind that's it not the only possible ground; there are also grounds that are not subjectivist. Perhaps more to the point, though, because a subjectivist cannot say that anything is "really" wrong, subjectivism provides rather slippery grounds for the virtue of tolerance, because a subjectivist cannot say that intolerance is really wrong. According to a subjectivist, the claim that we should be tolerant is no more objectively true than the claim that we should not be tolerant.

Problems for Moral Subjectivism

Can a Subjectivist Have Any Moral Beliefs?   Moral subjectivism is committed to a view that seems to make the idea of having moral beliefs or making moral judgments unintelligible. Suppose that you're a moral subjectivist. You believe that when two people disagree on a moral issue, neither is mistaken. Both have (subjectively) true beliefs. Suppose that you and I disagree about whether it was wrong to drag James Byrd to his death. You say it was wrong; I say it wasn't wrong. Now if you *say* that it was wrong, that seems to express your belief that it was wrong. Add to that your commitment to moral subjectivism, and you're saying that you believe it was wrong to drag James Byrd to his death but it's equally true that it was not wrong to drag him to his death. But then I must wonder how it can make sense to believe that it was wrong to drag him to his death but equally true that it wasn't wrong. If you believe that it was and wasn't wrong, then you don't believe that it was wrong. But then we're not really disagreeing because disagreement means that one person believes one thing and another believes the opposite.

Moral Inquiry.   Suppose that you have not yet made up your mind on a moral issue, for example, whether it is wrong for a teacher to have sexual relations with one of his or her students. How would you go about trying to answer the question? If moral subjectivism is correct, it doesn't matter what you believe or why. Whatever you believe will be (subjectively) true, and you are guaranteed that you cannot possibly make a mistake. Therefore, it doesn't matter whether you flip a coin, ask your mother, consult a public opinion poll, or carefully weigh pros and cons in order to decide what to believe. But many people think that makes a mockery of the serious business of moral inquiry. According to them, moral inquiry should be a matter of weighing reasons.

Types of Moral Judgment. Recall that we have distinguished between all-things-considered singular moral judgments, mediate moral principles, and basic moral principles. According to Donald Davidson, the logical structure of mediate moral principles, for example, that lying is wrong, is something like this: The fact that an act is a lie is a moral reason for thinking that it's wrong. Now according to subjectivists, someone who says "The fact that it's a lie is a moral reason to think it's right" is no less correct than someone who says it's a moral reason to think it's wrong. But how can that be? How can we be equally correct whether we put the fact that something is a lie on the side of its wrongness or the side of its rightness? According to Davidson, if someone says that the fact that something is a lie is a reason to think it's right, we should have serious doubts that we mean the same thing when we talk about a "lie" or a "moral reason" for or against. If we don't mean the same thing by "lie" or "moral reason," then we are not really disagreeing; rather, we are arguing past each other.

Philippa Foot has pointed out that if subjectivism is true and people mean the same thing by "moral reason," we could have some truly outlandish consequences. For example, a subjectivist cannot object if someone says that the fact that you put on your left sock before your right sock this morning is a moral reason for thinking that everything else you do today is wrong. But surely whether someone puts on his left sock before his right is irrelevant from a moral point of view. It cannot be a reason for thinking something is right or wrong. Someone who thinks it is relevant surely doesn't mean what we mean by a moral reason.

Summary. If moral subjectivism is true, it is not self-evident or obvious. Many people think that the reasons that count against subjectivism are stronger and weightier than the reasons that count in favor of moral subjectivism. What do you think?

MORAL RELATIVISM

According to cultural relativism, different cultures accept different moral principles and make different moral judgments. Thus on many (but not necessarily all) moral issues, different cultures have different views. This seems obviously true given the wealth of data from history, anthropology, and other social sciences. For example, some cultures think polygamy is morally wrong, while others don't; some cultures think slavery is morally wrong, while others don't.

If cultural relativism is true, what are the implications? According to some people, cultural relativism entails moral relativism. Recall the claims of Protagoras in Plato's *Theaetetus*. In one version of his relativism, "Man is the measure of all things," but in another version, he said that the community is the measure of all things. Socrates took that to mean that whatever a particular community believes about a moral issue is true for it, and there is no other kind of objective or nonrelative truth or falsity. That means that a community cannot make a mistake in its moral judgments and have an objectively false moral belief. Whatever it thinks is morally wrong *is* morally wrong (for it). According to moral relativism, there are no universal moral principles that every society should accept. What about individuals? Protagoras seems to say that the morality of one's society is binding on its individual members and is the standard of moral truth for them. But the moral principles of one society, although they legitimately govern the behavior and moral judgments of the members of that society, do not apply to other societies. According to this view, we are never justified in applying moral standards or principles to an individual or society that are not part of the moral code that the society accepts. Thus, we are never justified in making an unrelativistic moral claim, such as "Slavery is wrong, period," nor can such a claim be objectively true. All we can say is something like, "In this society, slavery is morally wrong," Similarly, we cannot legitimately say that a society that believes that slavery is morally right has a false or unreasonable moral belief. If we did, we would be judging that society by appealing to our moral code rather than its moral code.

But according to relativists, we shouldn't judge another society's moral code using the standards of our own moral code because our moral code is no more true, reasonable, or justified than their moral code. All we can say is that slavery is wrong in our society. According to relativists, if my society considers slavery, subordination of women, suicide bombing, racial discrimination, and religious persecution morally right whereas yours considers them morally wrong, neither society is mistaken or has a false belief. There is no objective truth, but each society's moral beliefs are "relatively" true.

Some moral relativists also claim that an individual's moral beliefs are true if and only if they are consistent with the moral beliefs of his or her society. Suppose that according to society A's moral code it's morally right for men to dominate women, while according to society B's it's morally wrong. According to moral relativism, men dominating women is morally right in society A and morally wrong in society B. Suppose that Brad and Brenda are members of society A. Brad believes that it's morally right for men to dominate women while Brenda believes it's morally wrong. According to this version of moral relativism, Brad has a true moral belief and Brenda has a false moral belief.

What reasons are there to think that the relativist's claims are true?

Does Moral Disagreement Entail Moral Relativism?

Some people seem to think that moral relativism follows directly from the fact that societies disagree on a lot of moral issues. But as we saw with respect to subjectivism, the fact that people disagree does not show that they're both equally correct. The same is true if societies disagree. If one society believes that microbes but not demons cause illness while another believes demons cause illness, both societies cannot possibly have true beliefs. Mere disagreement doesn't show that both societies must be right.

We also should keep in mind that not all moral disagreement involves disagreement at the level of moral principles. Disagreement over a particular moral issue could arise even when the societies accept the same moral principles, if they have different beliefs about the nonmoral facts. If society A believes that human sacrifice is morally right and we believe it's morally wrong, does that prove we have different basic moral principles, for example, that they place a lower moral value on human life than we do? No. It may be that they believe that the entire universe will be destroyed if they do not periodically sacrifice humans to the gods whereas we believe no such thing. If they didn't believe this, they wouldn't believe that human sacrifice is morally right. On the other hand, if we did believe this, we probably would believe that human sacrifice is morally right.

No One Can Prove Who's Correct in a Moral Dispute.   Moral relativists might argue that because no one can prove which society is correct in a moral dispute, then we cannot say that one of them is correct and the other incorrect; instead, we should consider them both equally correct. What we said about this argument when used by subjectivists also applies when used by relativists.

Tolerance Is a Virtue

Some people accept moral relativism because they think that people should not judge or try to change other societies and they think that moral relativism requires that kind of toleration. Many of us are familiar with the dismal history of efforts to change cultures. For example, Christian missionaries set out to convert the Native Americans. In doing so they devalued Native American culture, considering it inferior. In some cases, they destroyed that native culture in trying to refashion it in the image of their own. Similarly, the British in India generally had contempt for Indian culture. Applying British standards, the British masters were contemptuous of what they considered typical Indian personality and character traits, the religions, customs, and institutions of India, and so on. The British thought they had a duty to take on the "white man's burden" of civilizing the uncivilized peoples of the world by ruling them for their own good and changing their cultures to be more like Western European cultures.

What we said above about the virtue of tolerance as a ground for subjectivism also applies as a ground for relativism. For example, if another society rejects tolerance and thinks it should change other cultures, a relativist cannot say it's wrong. It may be wrong relative to his culture's moral code, but as a relativist, he must say that his society's moral code is no more true or correct than the other society's moral code.

Shouldn't People Conform to the Moral Code of Their Society?

Some people accept moral relativism because they think that people should conform to the moral code of their society and because they believe that moral relativism entails that people have that duty. However, moral relativism does not entail that people have that duty. A moral relativist cannot say that people should conform to the rules of their society, period. That's not a "relative" claim. And while there may be good reasons for people to conform to most of the rules of their society, what reasons are there for thinking that people should obey every rule? Some of the world's greatest moral leaders, such as Martin Luther King Jr. and Gandhi, claimed that people should obey the just rules but disobey the unjust ones. The Fugitive Slave Laws in the United States prior to the Civil War made it a crime to harbor an escaped slave and required people to cooperate with the authorities in returning escaped slaves to slavery. Was it morally wrong to defy those laws?

Furthermore, we should look critically at the idea of a "society's" moral code. It seems to imply that it's the code that everyone in the society accepts, but is there such a code? Not likely. No society is completely homogenous. Many are composed of a variety of subgroups. For example, in the United States there are significant differences in moral beliefs among those living in the Northeast, the Southeast, and the far West. There are also significant differences among those living within the Northeast. The moral beliefs of rural people are often different from the moral beliefs of urban people. Those of liberal Protestants are different from those of Catholics and conservative Protestants. The moral beliefs of orthodox Jews are different from those of other Jews. What, then, is "our society's" moral code if we mean the moral code of the United States? It can only be the moral beliefs of the majority or of a powerful minority. Even if we know what the majority of people in our society believes about a particular moral issue, do we have a moral duty to conform to its moral beliefs simply because it is the majority? Is the majority always right? No. What counts is not the number of people who believe that something is right or wrong, but rather the weight of the arguments.

Relativism and Moral Inquiry

Suppose that you have not yet made up your mind on a moral issue. For example, suppose you wonder whether it is morally wrong for a 15-year-old girl to have an abortion because she's been raped. How would you go about trying to answer the question? If moral relativism is correct, you should consult a public opinion poll to find out what a majority of people in your society believe about it. If a majority believes it is wrong, then it is wrong; if a majority believes it isn't wrong, then it isn't. But is consulting a public opinion poll really the best way to answer moral questions? Wouldn't it be better to carefully examine the reasons for and against the claim that it's wrong for the 15-year-old rape victim to have an abortion? Weighing reasons in moral inquiry, however, seems to be incompatible with moral relativism.

CONCLUSION

We seem forced to choose between moral realism and some form of anti-realism, such as nihilism, subjectivism, or relativism. None of these moral theories is entirely unproblematic. Each has its defenders and opponents, its strengths and weaknesses. Ideally, philosophers try to decide what to believe by carefully weighing the arguments and reasons for and against various claims or theories to determine what, all things considered, is most reasonable. It is up to you now to take on the role of a philosopher and decide which of these moral theories it's most reasonable to believe.

EXERCISES

1. Which is more reasonable, moral realism or moral anti-realism? If moral anti-realism is more plausible, which version is most plausible—nihilism, subjectivism, or relativism?

2. Are moral claims true only if there are moral facts? Are there moral properties and facts? If yes, how are we to understand moral properties? How can we detect their presence or absence?

3. Is tolerance a virtue? If it is, is that a good reason to think that either moral subjectivism or moral relativism is true?

4. Can a moral nihilist or subjectivist have moral beliefs?

    For the following exercises, try to reflect on them from the perspectives of moral realism, moral nihilism, moral relativism, and moral subjectivism. Which perspective makes the most sense to you? Why?

5. According to "tribal law" among some Arabs, not only is it morally right that relatives of a rape victim kill the rapist but it is also morally right that her relatives kill the rape victim as well for bringing shame to the family. In 1996, a 3-year-old girl in a town on the West Bank was raped by a 25-year-old man seeking revenge against her father because of a quarrel over money. According to tribal law, it would have been morally right for the child's relatives to kill her. Her relatives intended to do just that until Palestinian leader Yasir Arafat intervened to forestall the killing.[7] Is it morally wrong to kill a rape victim? Does it matter whether she is 3, 23, or 83?

6. Imagine that you take a trip in a time machine back to Germany in 1939. You witness a group of Nazis drag an old man out of a house where he had been hiding and beat him to death. Was it morally wrong for them to beat him to death?

7. If you could go back in time and assassinate Adolf Hitler before he began the Holocaust and World War II, would it be right?

8. In 1864, a U.S. Army officer, Colonel John Chivington, ordered his troops to attack a peaceful Cheyenne village, despite the fact that the Native Americans, under the chieftainship of Black Kettle, had been guaranteed safety by the local military commanders in what is now Colorado.

According to Dee Brown:

> Captain Silas Soule, Lieutenant Joseph Cramer, and Lieutenant James Connor protested that an attack on Black Kettle's peaceful camp would violate the pledge of safety given the Indians . . ., "that it would be murder

in every sense of the word," and any officer participating would dishonor the uniform of the Army. Chivington became violently angry at them and brought his fist close to Lieutenant Cramer's face. "Damn any man who sympathizes with Indians!" he cried. "I have come to kill Indians, and believe it is right and honorable to use any means under God's heaven to kill Indians." The camp held 600 Cheyenne Indians, two-thirds of them women and children. Without warning, the soldiers under Chivington's command attacked the sleeping, unguarded village at dawn. The Indians were massacred. Robert Brent, a soldier who reluctantly participated in the attack, offered the following eyewitness account.

I saw five squaws [female Indians] under a bank for shelter. When the troops came up to them they ran out and showed their persons to let the soldiers know they were squaws and begged for mercy, but the soldiers shot them all. . . . There seemed to be indiscriminate slaughter of men, women, and children. There were some thirty or forty squaws collected in a hole for protection; they sent out a little girl about six years old with a white flag on a stick; she had not proceeded but a few steps when she was shot and killed. All the squaws in the hole were afterwards killed. . . . The squaws offered no resistance. Every one I saw dead was scalped. I saw one squaw cut open with an unborn child, as I thought, lying by her side. . . . I saw the body of White Antelope with his privates cut off, and I heard one soldier say he was going to make a tobacco pouch out of them. I saw one squaw whose privates had been cut out. . . . I saw a little girl about five years of age who had been hid in the sand; two soldiers discovered her, drew their pistols and shot her. . . . I saw quite a number of infants in arms killed with their mothers.
A total of 28 men and 105 women and children were killed.[8]

Clearly, some of Colonel Chivington's soldiers believed that massacring Indians was wrong. However, Chivington himself and many of his soldiers believed that it was not wrong. It is quite likely that at the time, most whites in the West, who were a majority, believed that it was not wrong to kill Indians. Was it wrong for the soldiers to massacre Black Kettle and his people?

SUGGESTED READINGS

David Copp and David Zimmerman, eds. *Morality, Reason, and Truth*. Totowa, NJ: Rowman and Allanheld, 1984.

Stephen Darwall. *Philosophical Ethics*. Boulder, CO: Westview Press, 1998.

William Frankena *Ethics*, 2d ed. Englewood Cliffs, NJ: Prentice-Hall, 1973. (See especially Chapter 6.)

Gilbert Harman. *The Nature of Morality*. New York: Oxford University Press, 1977. (See especially Chapters 1–4, 8, and 9.)

John Ladd ed. *Ethical Relativism*. Belmont, CA: Wadsworth, 1973.

Ellen E. Paul, Fred Miller, and Jeffrey Paul. *Cultural Pluralism and Moral Knowledge*. Cambridge, England: Cambridge University Press, 1994.

Louis Pojman. *Ethics: Discovering Right and Wrong*. Belmont, CA Wadsworth, 1990. (See especially Chapter 2.)

Walter Sinnott-Armstrong and Mark Timmons. *Moral Knowledge? New Readings in Moral Epistemology*. Oxford: Oxford University Press, 1996.

David Wong. *Ethical Relativity*. Berkeley: University of California Press, 1984.

INTERNET RESOURCES

Ethics Update (http://ethics.acusd.edu). A Web page dedicated to both ethical theory and applied ethics. See the resources under ethical relativism.

Plato, *Protagoras* (http://classics.mit.edu/Plato/protagoras.html). The complete dialogue online.

ENDNOTES

1. "Jasper, Tex., and the Ghosts of Lynchings Past," *New York Times* (25 February 1999), Editorial.

2. "Pathologist Testifies Byrd Was Alive When Decapitated," *New York Times* (23 February 1999).

3. Plato, *Theaetetus*, in *Plato: Complete Works*, John M. Cooper, trans. M. J. Levett, revised by Myles Burnyeat (Indianapolis, IN: Hackett, 1997), section 152a.

4. Ibid., 152a.

5. Ibid., section 161d.

6. Ibid., section 177d.

7. "Palestinian Court Dispenses Justice," *Boston Sunday Globe* (20 October 1996), p. A6.

8. Dee Brown, *Bury My Heart at Wounded Knee* (New York: Washington Square Press, 1981), pp. 85–88. (Originally published in 1970.)

4

Psychological Egoism and Moral Egoism

OBJECTIVES

- To understand the concept of commonsense morality
- To understand and critically evaluate the plausibility of psychological egoism
- To understand and critically evaluate the plausibility of moral egoism
- To understand the relation between psychological egoism and moral egoism
- To understand and appreciate the difference between a psychological theory and a moral theory

COMMONSENSE MORALITY

According to what we might call *commonsense* or traditional morality, harming others to benefit ourselves—or some group with whom we identify—is generally wrong, and helping others when the need is great and the cost of help small is generally right. Examples of harmful behavior that commonsense morality considers wrong are murder, torture, treason, terrorism, genocide, enslavement, rape, stealing, and lying. According to commonsense morality, not all wrongs are equal. Torture is worse than stealing. The fact that you or a group to which you belong would benefit from such behaviors makes no difference; they would still be wrong according to commonsense morality. Similarly, commonsense morality says that we should help others when the need is great and the cost to us is small, even if we would not benefit from it and even if we would suffer a net loss. If someone is drowning and you could save her by throwing her a rope, commonsense morality says that you should throw her the rope, even if you gain nothing you value by saving her, and even if you would be a net loser by it (perhaps you get your clothes muddy and wind up with a dry-cleaning bill). Commonsense morality does not demand that you jump into the water to save the drowning person if you're not a good swimmer, or if there would be significant danger to you. But according to commonsense morality, it would be wrong for you to do nothing—to merely walk away and let the person drown. (Once again, let's remind ourselves that a principle that requires us to help someone in need places that help on the side of the rightness of the action when weighing aspects of the action and the situation for an all-things-considered singular moral judgment, and the weight increases with the urgency of the need.)

Sometimes commonsense morality dictates that we should do things, even if we will not benefit from doing them or even if doing them would impose a net cost on us. Similarly, commonsense morality says that we should refrain from doing some things even if we would benefit from doing them. Commonsense morality says that sometimes we should sacrifice our own self-interest in order to further or protect the interests of others.

Is commonsense morality correct? Some people claim that commonsense morality is wrong. They claim that we do not have a moral duty to sacrifice our own self-interest in order to benefit or protect others. We have no duty to refrain from harming others if it would be in our self-interest to harm them, and we have no duty to help others if it would not be in our self-interest to help them. On this view, it's not wrong to harm people to benefit ourselves and it's not wrong to fail to help others when we don't benefit from helping them. As we will understand this theory, it claims that from a moral point of view, the smallest gain or loss in terms of self-interest always outweighs even the most urgent needs of others in all-things-considered singular moral judgments. This claim, called Moral Egoism, conflicts with commonsense morality. Is Moral Egoism correct, or is commonsense morality correct?

What reasons are there for thinking that Moral Egoism is correct and commonsense morality incorrect? One reason appeals to the principle that *ought* implies *can*. According to this principle, it makes sense to say that morally you *ought* to (or should) do something (have a moral duty to do it) only if you *can* do it. For example, suppose someone says that morally we ought to (we have a moral duty to) breathe underwater for at least ten minutes a day. That claim would be absurd because it is physically impossible for us to breathe underwater. It is absurd to claim that we have a moral duty to do something that is physically impossible for us. On the other hand, if you *can* eat without putting your elbows on the table, then it would not be absurd to claim that you have a moral duty to refrain from eating with your elbows on the table (although it surely is false or unreasonable, it's not absurd). Similarly, if we could not possibly refrain from scratching when we itch, it would be absurd to claim that we have a moral duty not to scratch when we itch.

The principle that *ought* implies *can* has interesting implications for commonsense morality. If people *cannot* sacrifice their own self-interest in order to refrain from harming others or to help others (because of our psychological makeup), then "*ought* implies *can*" entails that commonsense morality is mistaken. If we *cannot* help others if we don't benefit by it, then it makes no sense to say that we ought to help others or that it's morally wrong not to help others. If we *cannot* refrain from harming others when we would benefit by it, then it makes no sense to say that we ought to refrain from harming others or that it is morally wrong to harm them. But why should we think that people *cannot* sometimes sacrifice their own self-interest in order to benefit others or to refrain from harming them?

A theory called Psychological Egoism, if true, may entail that people *cannot* ever sacrifice their own self-interest in order to benefit others or to refrain from harming them. If Psychological Egoism is true and entails that people *cannot* sacrifice self-interest, then commonsense morality is mistaken and Moral Egoism is correct. Before we examine Moral Egoism, then, let's investigate Psychological Egoism.

PSYCHOLOGICAL EGOISM

Psychological Egoism is a descriptive theory about human nature and behavior, whereas Moral Egoism is a theory about moral right and wrong. Sometimes Psychological Egoism is expressed as the theory that:

> Everyone always behaves selfishly.

The term *selfishly* is used purely descriptively rather than evaluatively, because Psychological Egoism is a theory about human psychology, not a theory about moral right and wrong. It's a theory about how people do behave, not about how they should behave. According to this theory, we always behave selfishly because that's human nature; it's how we're "built." But what does it mean to call an action *selfish*?

According to *Webster's Dictionary*, *selfish* means

> 1: concerned excessively or exclusively with oneself; seeking or concentrating on one's own advantage, pleasure, or wellbeing without regard for others
> 2: arising from concern with one's own welfare or advantage in disregard of others.[1]

The dictionary definition of *selfish* emphasizes *disregarding* the interests of others in order to advance or protect our own interests. If everyone were selfish according to this definition, would commonsense morality violate the principle that *ought* implies *can*? Not necessarily. When we speak of disregarding and sacrificing the interests of others, do we mean *some* others, *most* others, or *all* others? And do we mean *some* of the time, *most* of the time, or *all* the time? The rule that "ought" implies "can" is violated only if you disregard *everyone's* interests *all* the time. If you consider the interests of some other people some of the time, then obviously, you *can*. Are humans built in such a way that we "must" be selfish in the sense of disregarding the interests of everyone else all the time? Surely, that would be the case only if we as a species are incapable of caring about anyone but ourselves, but there seems to be ample evidence that we are capable. Although there are people such as David Cash (who did nothing to save Sherrice Iverson)—people who care for no one but themselves—they seem to be a small minority of human beings. (If we were all like David Cash, our species might have become extinct long ago.) Most of us do care about other people—at least, we care about *some* other people. Consider the love of parents for their children or the romantic love that one adult has for another. Reflect on your own case. Is there no one you care about other than yourself?

Note that acting in your own self-interest is not always "selfish." You're acting to further your own self-interest if you go to the doctor for a physical examination or work overtime for a promotion or extra money, but there's nothing selfish about these unless you're disregarding and sacrificing important interests of others.

Perhaps a better formulation of Psychological Egoism would be:

Everyone's actions are always ultimately based on self-interest.

Suppose that you volunteer to work in the local hospital every other Saturday. According to this formulation of Psychological Egoism, your action is ultimately based on self-interest. What does that mean?

Ordinarily, when people act they act for a reason. Reasons may vary widely. Consider three people who do unpaid volunteer work at the local hospital every other Saturday. Green volunteers because he is a politician looking for votes; he believes that by volunteering his time at the hospital he will impress voters with his altruism. Brown is a businesswoman who wants to get more business; she hopes to impress potential clients with her good character by volunteering at the hospital. Finally, Black feels compassion and sympathy for the sick; she wants to help reduce suffering and make a constructive contribution to her community. She knows that the local hospital is financially strapped and understaffed and that patient care will suffer unless unpaid volunteers fill in some of the gaps. She wants to help, and she believes that she can help by volunteering her time every other Saturday.

An individual's action is based on self-interest if the reason or motive for the action is to increase his or her own well-being or to prevent a reduction in well-being (to prevent harm to himself). On the surface, doing unpaid volunteer work at a hospital looks like it's *not* based on self-interest because it seems to benefit others rather than the agent. But if we look below the surface at the agent's actual reasons or motivation, we can see that Green's and Brown's actions are ultimately based on self-interest. They are volunteering their time because they believe that they will benefit. Their intention is to benefit themselves through benefiting others. If they didn't benefit from volunteering, they would not volunteer. We might diagram the structure of their motivation or reasons as follows:

I want to benefit myself → I will benefit by volunteering → I volunteer → I benefit and others benefit.

The main goal of the action is to benefit the agent himself, not to benefit others. It may be that as a result others will benefit, but that benefit is not part of the motivation. Benefiting others is a means to an end (benefiting the agent himself), rather than an end in itself. In both cases, the action only appears to be altruistic; ultimately it benefits, and it is intended to benefit, the agent. These seemingly altruistic actions are ultimately based on self-interest.

However, what of Black? Is her action also ultimately based on self-interest? Even if we say that it is, surely it's obvious that the structure of her motivation or reasons is quite different from that of Green and Brown. We might diagram the structure of her motivation or reasons as follows:

I want to benefit others → I will benefit them by volunteering
→ I volunteer → Others benefit and I benefit.

Black's main concern is to benefit others rather than to benefit herself. Of course, she may benefit from her action because she gets satisfaction or happiness from helping other people. But her intention is to benefit others rather than herself, even though as a result of her action she also benefits. Her action may *not* be based on self-interest in the sense of being undertaken in order to benefit herself.

The claim that everyone's actions are always ultimately based on self-interest entails that every time we look below the surface of someone's action, we will discover that it was motivated by the desire to further that person's own self-interest, as in the cases of Green and Brown. What reason is there to think that this rather sweeping generalization about *every* action of *every* person is true? Do Psychological Egoists have proof of this claim? What would such proof look like? It is by no means obvious that there is or even could be proof of this theory. And if it is possible for people to have the structure of motivation I have attributed to Black, then Psychological Egoism is probably false.

But even if Psychological Egoism in this form is true, would it follow that commonsense morality violates the principle that *ought* implies *can*? If Psychological Egoism is true, given human nature is it physically impossible for people to benefit others or to refrain from harming others? No. If it's in your self-interest to benefit others—for example, because you benefit financially or get happiness from it—then you can. For example, if giving your sibling a birthday gift makes you happy, then you'll give the gift. Then, too, if you love someone and would be made unhappy if she died in a fire, that may lead you to risk your life in an attempt to save her. Similarly, if it's not in your self-interest to harm others, then you can refrain from harming them. It seems obvious that human nature does not prevent people from ever helping others or from avoiding harming others. However, what about cases where self-interest and commonsense morality diverge? Commonsense morality says that people should refrain from harming others even when it is in their self-interest and help others even when it's not.. Psychological Egoism then poses the following questions: if it's not in your self-interest to benefit others, then given human nature (our psychological makeup), is it physically possible for you to benefit them anyway? Similarly, if it's in your self-interest to harm others, then given human nature, is it physically possible for you to refrain from harming them anyway?

Our beliefs are a part of the cause of our actions. Many people think that we have *moral* beliefs. Suppose someone believes that he has a moral duty to minimize the harm he causes others and to help people when the need is great, even if it requires him to sacrifice some amount of self-interest. This belief may lead him sometimes to sacrifice his self-interest. Perhaps David Cash acted as he did because he does not have this belief. The point is that many, if not most of us, do have such moral beliefs.

Psychological egoists seem to think of human nature (our human psychology) as both universal and fixed or unalterable. However, opponents of Psychological Egoism might object that human nature, especially our psychological nature, is both remarkably variable and alterable. Consider the psychological makeup of an Adolf Hitler and a Mother Teresa; surely there are vast and fundamental differences. Moreover, a person's psychological nature (and moral beliefs!) can change. At the extreme, it may be possible to alter the genetic makeup of the whole human species through genetic engineering. On a less dramatic and sweeping level, an individual's psychological makeup (and moral beliefs) can be altered by conditioning, social circumstances, learning, and experiences. Human beings in one society or set of social circumstances may, on average, have one kind of psychological makeup and system of beliefs, while human beings in another society or set of social circumstances have a very different kind of psychological makeup and system of beliefs.

Thus, there seems to be no good reason to think that commonsense morality violates the requirement of *ought* implies *can*. The theory of Psychological Egoism cannot be used to defend the claim that commonsense morality is mistaken because it requires human beings to do things that, given human nature, they physically cannot do. Human beings can do what commonsense morality requires of them. The question, then, is whether the claims of commonsense morality are correct. Moral Egoists maintain that they are not.

MORAL EGOISM

Psychological Egoism is a theory about human nature; Moral Egoism is a theory about morality. According to Moral Egoism—in contrast to commonsense morality—it's always morally acceptable to do what we believe to be in our own self-interest. People have no moral duties to one another. Moral egoists claim that morality never requires people to sacrifice their own self-interest to help others or to avoid harming others; rather, morality permits people to do whatever is in their own self-interest. In weighing reasons for all-things-considered singular moral judgments, the interests of others carry no weight; only reasons of self-interest have weight. We can imagine someone like David Cash defending his attitudes and judgments in the following way.

> It's a jungle out there, a dog-eat-dog world. Nice guys finish last. The strong prey on the weak, and the weak go under. You can't afford to reach out a helping hand to the other guy, because he'll either bite it off or drag you under with him. The world doesn't owe you anything, and you don't owe the world anything. The only rule is, look out for number one!

For example, take a used-car salesperson who cheats his customers, disguising serious defects in the cars he sells. If he's a moral egoist, he'll claim that anything that helps him sell cars is in his self-interest and is therefore morally acceptable, because it's never wrong for him to do what's in his own self-interest.

In many situations, it is not wrong to pursue our self-interest. Eating properly and exercising regularly are in our self-interest, yet it's certainly not wrong to eat properly and exercise regularly. However, the case is less clear when our self-interest is in conflict with the interests of others. For example, although it may be in the self-interest of the owner of an apartment building to torch it and collect the insurance, it is not in the interests of the tenants, the fire department, or the insurance company that the building be torched. When people's interests collide, is it always morally acceptable for people to do what's in their self-interest, regardless of any effect on the interests and well-being of others? Do reasons that focus on the interests of others have no moral weight? Moral Egoism entails that theft, rape, torture, assault, and murder are morally acceptable if the agent believes that they are in his or her self-interest, that the only moral reasons that have weight are reasons of self-interest.. Surely that is a startling claim. What reason is there for thinking that morality permits us to simply look out for number one? One is that ultimately everyone benefits if people pursue their own self-interest.

Moral Egoism and the Common Good

Adam Smith (1723–1790), the intellectual godfather of capitalism, maintained that the common good is best promoted when people focus on their own private good. When people pursue their own self-interest, he claimed, an unintended consequence is that everyone is better off.

For example, if Joe concentrates on making Sam rather than himself happy, the result may be that neither will be happy. In neglecting his own happiness, Joe may fail to be happy. And despite his best efforts to make Sam happy, he may not succeed. He may be mistaken about what will make Sam happy, or if his goals are correct, his means may be ineffective. According to Smith, each individual is most likely to achieve happiness for himself if he concentrates on making himself rather than other people happy. Therefore, the best way of maximizing happiness is for each person to concentrate on making himself happy and to leave his neighbor's happiness to his neighbor, who after all can be expected to know best what will make him happy and how to achieve it. (We will ignore Smith's economic reasons.)

This defense of Moral Egoism has several problems. First, its justification appeals to principles that at least appear to be in conflict with Moral Egoism; that is, the justification proceeds in terms of what is good for *others* rather than only what is good for ourselves. But if Moral Egoism is correct, the good of others should not count when we are considering what we morally should or should not do. When you're considering what to do, you should think about what's good for you, not what's good for others.

Second, the argument seems to be based on a false dichotomy; either you focus exclusively on your own self-interest when deciding what to do or you focus exclusively on the interests of others. It suggests that you can do either what's in your self-interest or what's in the interest of others, but not both. But surely we can often do both. We can do things that make both us and others happy, things that benefit us and benefit others.

Third, the argument misleadingly suggests that we must choose between always pursuing our own self-interest and never pursuing our self-interest. Both are extremes. In fact, we could choose to pursue self-interest 80 to 90 percent of the time and promote or protect the interests of others 10 to 20 percent of the time. We can do sometimes one, sometimes the other, and sometimes both simultaneously.

Finally, the argument ignores the very different ways in which people can make themselves happy. Some ways of making ourselves happy are harmless. If I go out bird-watching or go to a movie, I'm not harming anyone. But other ways of making ourselves happy are toxic to others. Suppose that a man derives happiness from raping children. Should he do what makes him happy and ignore its effect on the children he rapes? According to commonsense morality, we should not make ourselves happy in ways that impose serious harm, or the risk of serious harm, on others. Pursuing our own self-interest while ignoring its effects on others is not likely to maximize happiness and make everyone better off.

The Meaning of a "Moral" Reason

As we have seen, the American philosopher Donald Davidson thinks that we should question whether we mean the same thing by the words we use if there is too fundamental a disagreement. A moral egoist in effect claims that reasons that refer to the interests of others carry no moral weight. That means that they're not moral reasons at all. A moral egoist denies that the fact that we will harm another person is a moral reason counting in favor of an action's wrongness, and denies that the fact that we will help another person is a moral reason counting in favor of an action's rightness. The only moral reasons are reasons that refer to our own self-interest.

Davidson's point is that we should conclude that the moral egoist doesn't mean the same thing we do when he speaks of a "moral reason." As most of us understand the concept of a moral reason, the fact that we will harm someone definitely is a reason weighing in on the side of its moral wrongness and the fact that we will help someone definitely is a reason weighing in on the side of its moral rightness. We might call these *conceptual* truths.

Moral Egoism and Universality

As we saw in the first chapter, moral principles are often said to be universal. They apply to everyone. Given universality, if it is morally acceptable for you to do what is in your self-interest regardless of its effect on others, then it is morally acceptable for others to do what is in their self-interest regardless of its effect on you. If Moral Egoism is correct, then a person who tortures and kills you or someone you love has done nothing wrong so long as it was in that person's self-interest. A moral egoist is committed to the view that the fact that someone's action will seriously harm her is no reason to think that the other person is doing anything morally wrong. Someone who cannot accept that implication of Moral Egoism cannot consistently accept Moral Egoism.

Moral Egoism and Social Harmony

Many people maintain that a purely self-interested point of view is inconsistent with a moral point of view because morality has a specific function - to resolve conflicts between people so that they can live together in harmony. If everyone does whatever is in his or her self-interest regardless of how it affects the interests and well-being of others, people cannot live together peacefully. In order to fulfill its function, morality sometimes requires people to sacrifice their own self-interest in order to benefit and protect others. For example, if everyone always stole, lied, broke promises, and assaulted and killed people when it was in their self-interest, no group could survive. Thus, many people claim that morality requires that people sometimes follow the common good rather than their own private good.

Samuel Pufendorf (1632–1688) wrote, "In the natural [moral] law it is asserted that something must be done because the same is gathered by right reason as necessary for sociability between men."[2] The natural law "is so adapted to the rational and social nature of man, that an honorable and peaceful society cannot exist for mankind without it."[3] Pufendorf pointed out:

> Man is indeed an animal most bent upon self-preservation, helpless in himself, unable to save himself without the aid of his fellows, highly adapted to promote mutual interests; but on the other hand no less malicious, insolent, and easily provoked, also as able as he is prone to inflict injury upon another. Whence it follows that, in order to be safe, he must be sociable, that is, must be united with men like himself, and so conduct himself toward them that they may have no good cause to injure him, but rather may be ready to maintain and promote his interests. The laws, then, of this sociability, or those which teach how a man should conduct himself, to become a good member of human society, are called natural laws.[4]

Thus, Pufendorf claimed:

> Among the absolute duties, i.e., of anybody to anybody, the first place belongs to this one: let no man injure another. For this is the broadest of all duties.... Again, it is likewise the most necessary duty, because without it the social life could in no way exist. For with the man who confers no benefit upon me.... I can still live in peace provided he injure me in no way.... But with the man who injures me, I cannot by any means live peaceably....[5]

> Further, the next most basic duty is that every man promote the advantage of another, so far as he conveniently can. For since nature has established a kind of kinship among men, it could not have been enough to have refrained from injuring ... others; but we must also bestow such attentions upon others ... that thus mutual benevolence may be fostered among men.[6]

Many philosophers have insisted that morality requires people to do what is for the common good rather than what is in their own self-interest when the common good and their own private good are in conflict.

Moral Egoism directly contradicts this view. If Moral Egoism is true, it's morally acceptable for people to completely ignore the interests and well-being of others. Critics of Moral Egoism maintain that life in a society of moral egoists would be, in the memorable words of the philosopher Thomas Hobbes (1588–1679), "solitary, poor, nasty, brutish, and short."[7]

Modified Moral Egoism

Some moral egoists, such as Ayn Rand and her followers, take what appears to be a more moderate position. We might call them modified moral egoists. As Ayn Rand puts it, "Man—every man—is an end in himself, not the means to the ends of others. He must exist for his own sake, neither sacrificing himself to others nor sacrificing others to himself. The pursuit of his own rational self-interest and of his own happiness is the highest moral purpose of his life."[8]

Given other things she says elsewhere, when she talks of "sacrificing" ourselves to others it seems that in her view, any time we do something for others that is not in our immediate self-interest, we're *sacrificing* ourselves to them. Thus, not only are we sacrificing ourselves to others if we become slaves and devote our every waking hour to serving someone else's interests, but we're sacrificing ourselves if we help someone to get up who has fallen down and we get no material or psychological reward for it. She often speaks as though there is no difference between always, sometimes, and never sacrificing our interests to protect or promote the interests of others. She speaks as though if we ever sacrifice ourselves to others, we are giving up any chance of achieving any happiness for ourselves.

Most people probably agree that we should not always sacrifice ourselves to others. After all, everyone wants some happiness in their lives, and if we live totally for others and not at all for ourselves, we probably won't achieve much if any happiness (unless we're someone like Mother Teresa). But that doesn't mean that the only alternative is to never sacrifice ourselves to or for others. Even if you sometimes sacrifice yourself to others, you still may be able to achieve a great deal of happiness over the course of your life. (Many people claim that we're unlikely to achieve much happiness over the course of our lives if we don't sometimes sacrifice ourselves for others.) And not all sacrifices are equal. Suppose I sacrifice my suit in the process of saving someone's life because it gets dirty and torn. That's a lot different from sacrificing my life or health.

Perhaps Ayn Rand's position is that we are not put on earth *merely* to serve others. But Rand's position seems to be more extreme than that. In her view, we are not put on Earth *ever* to serve others. Someone making a counterargument would point out that we live with and are perpetually dependent on others to provide us with most of what we need and want. For the first quarter of our lives we're dependent on adults for everything, including the food we eat, the clothing we wear, and the shelter that keeps the rain and snow off our heads. As we develop, we learn and employ a language that we didn't create; others created it. As we accumulate knowledge, we learn mostly what others discovered or created. We learn from books written by others and teachers who are other human beings; we don't teach ourselves. Our very identity—who we are, determined by such things as our beliefs about ourselves and the universe, our personality and character traits, and our attitudes and feelings—is influenced, if not created by, interactions with others.

When we reach adulthood, we still are dependent on others. If we're sick, we don't cure ourselves; we depend on doctors, nurses, hospitals, and medicines. Generally, we don't grow our own food, make our own clothing, or build our own houses. We drive cars we didn't build on roads we didn't build. We could go on and on. Now one might say that generally we pay for what we receive, but we can't pay the people from the past, now dead, who bequeathed us almost everything we depend on today. How do you pay the people who invented metallurgy or the internal combustion engine? You might say that when they were alive they got paid by others for what they produced, but even if that's true, you didn't pay them, although you reap the benefits of what they produced. Even if we buy what we get from people who are currently alive and producing today, that doesn't change our dependence on them. That is, others do serve us in so many ways that it's difficult to enumerate them all, and we couldn't survive unless they did serve us. Even if we pay them for serving us, the fact remains that they are serving us. (And in turn, if we're doing productive work, paid or unpaid, we're serving others.)

The Ayn Rand position would be more plausible if we didn't have to depend on each other in these ways, if instead we fit the profile of the self-made rugged individualist who depends on no one but himself or herself. But such a person is a myth. No one is self-made; everyone is dependent on others, from the richest individual in the world to the poorest. We depend on and benefit from the social, political, and economic system as a whole. Perhaps that generates duties to do what will keep that system healthy. It is an empirical question (a question whose answer can be determined only by appeal to perception and observation) whether leaving each other alone is sufficient to keep the system healthy, but people opposed to Ayn Rand's position doubt it. Those who doubt it think that the benefits we get (and accept) from the system obligate us to do our part to keep the system going, which requires giving to others as well as receiving from them.

For many people, both the position that Ayn Rand attacks, and Ayn Rand's position itself, are extreme and difficult to justify. The former advocates virtual enslavement to others, while the latter implies that we only have duties to leave each other alone. Rather, the truth lies somewhere in the middle for many. We shouldn't spend our whole lives doing nothing but serving others, but we shouldn't spend no part of our lives serving others, either. We shouldn't sacrifice all of our interests to protect or further the interests of others, but we shouldn't sacrifice none of our interests to protect and further the interests of others. But reasonable people can and do disagree about where in the middle range the truth lies about our positive obligations to others.

Yet from a theological point of view, many people repeat the slogan that God helps those who help themselves. I recently saw an interesting variation on this: God helps those who help others. Perhaps, if God exists, both are true.

Short-Term Versus Long-Term Self-Interest

Moral egoists may distinguish between a person's short-term self-interest and a person's long-term self-interest. What may be in a person's immediate or short-term self-interest may not be in his or her long-term self-interest. For example, it may be in a person's short-term self-interest to steal from her roommate because she will get money she wants and not be caught. However, if success at this theft encourages her to further thefts, she may eventually be caught and punished, which would not be in her self-interest. The short-term benefit of stealing has to be weighed against its potential long-term effects. Similarly, it may be in our short-term self-interest to smoke a cigarette because it makes us feel good; however, the long-term effects of continuing to smoke may include various serious health problems that would not be in our self-interest.

Moral egoists may insist that it is morally acceptable for people to do whatever they believe is in their long-term self-interest, but not necessarily what they believe is in their short-term self-interest; that is, long-term self-interest takes priority over short-term self-interest. They may then claim that if we do what we believe is in our long-term self-interest, rather than what we believe is in our short-term self-interest, we will not behave as critics assume that moral egoists will behave, like a David Cash. Moral egoists who pursue their long-term self-interest will not ignore the interests and well-being of others, because they will recognize that it is not in their long-term self-interest to do so. Such moral egoists will often sacrifice their short-term self-interest in order to benefit and protect others, because they believe that doing so is in their long-term self-interest. Thus, they might claim that life in a society of moral egoists who pursue their long-term rather than their short-term self-interest would not be "solitary, poor, nasty, brutish, and short."

British philosopher and theologian Joseph Butler (1692–1752) made this point in the following way:

> Neither does there appear any reason to wish that self-love were
> weaker in the generality of the world, than it is. . . . Men daily, hourly
> sacrifice the greatest known interest, to fancy, inquisitiveness, love or
> hatred, any vagrant inclination. The thing to be lamented is, not that
> men have so great regard to their own good or interest in the present
> world, for they have not enough; but that they have so little to the
> good of others. . . . Upon the whole, if the generality of mankind were
> to cultivate within themselves the principle of self-love; . . . and if
> self-love were so strong and prevalent, as that they would uniformly
> pursue this as their supposed chief temporal good, without being
> diverted from it by any particular passion; it would manifestly prevent
> numberless follies and vices.[9]

Butler maintained that long-term self-interest is rarely if ever in conflict with the common good. People are happier in the long run if they care about others, refrain from harming others, and benefit others.

Critics might point to two problems with this view. First, why must long-term self-interest take priority over short-term self-interest? That assumption is crucial for maintaining that, although it is not morally acceptable to pursue our short-term self-interest regardless of its effect on the interests and well-being of others, it is morally acceptable to pursue our long-term self-interest. Second, what if a person believes that it is in his or her long-term self-interest to ignore the interests and well-being of others? Might that person be mistaken? And even if mistaken, Moral Egoism entails that it would be morally acceptable for him or her to ignore everyone else's interests and well-being in pursuing his own long-term self-interest. Critics of Moral Egoism find that position unacceptable.

EXERCISES

1. During World War II, the Nazis ordered Jews in Nazi-occupied countries to wear a yellow Star of David on their clothing so that they could be instantly identified as Jews. The purpose was to make it easier to persecute and ultimately exterminate the Jews. In Denmark, after the Nazi order was broadcast, the king and queen appeared in public with yellow Stars of David sewn to their clothing, although they were not Jewish. Almost overnight, virtually all Danes were wearing yellow Stars of David on their clothing, although only a minute percentage of the population was Jewish. As a result, Denmark—alone of Nazi-occupied countries—saved almost all of its Jewish population from the Holocaust. Why do you think that a non-Jewish Dane would sew a yellow Star of David to his or her clothing? When a non-Jewish Dane wore the emblem, was it a selfish act? Was it a purely self-interested act?

2. Have you ever stopped to give directions to a stranger when asked or paused to let a stranger's car into traffic on a congested highway? If you have, why did you do it? Was it a selfish act? Was it a purely self-interested act?

3. According to the Dalai Lama, "When we act to fulfill our immediate desires without taking into account others' interests, we undermine the possibility of lasting happiness."[10] In his view, "altruism is an essential component of those actions which lead to genuine happiness."[11] Thus, he continues,

   Spiritual acts we can describe in terms of...love, compassion, patience, forgiveness, humility, tolerance, and so on which presume some level of concern for others' well-being. We find that such spiritual actions we undertake which are motivated not by narrow self-interest but out of concern for others actually benefit ourselves. And not only that, but they make our lives meaningful.[12]

   Do you agree?

4. Imagine that you are walking down the street when you see an apparently frail old woman fall in her driveway. She attempts to get up, but is unable to. You do not see anyone else in the immediate vicinity who would be in a

position to help her. She is a stranger and this is not the neighborhood where you live. What would you do? Why would you do it? Do you think you would be doing anything morally wrong if you didn't help her, but instead simply kept on walking? What might someone such as Ayn Rand say about this? Is what you think about this case the same as what Ayn Rand would probably say about it?

5.   Imagine that you are walking through a park in winter and you see a young child fall though the ice. You can see no one else who could help. You have a cell phone with you so you could dial 911 to summon aid. You also have a rope in the car that you could throw to the child to try to keep her head above water until professional help arrives. Perhaps with the rope you could even pull the child to safety. The child is a stranger to you. You are late for a business meeting that is important to you. Would you be doing anything wrong if you did nothing but instead continued driving to your business meeting without even calling 911?

6.   Recall David Cash from Chapter 1 who did nothing while his friend raped and murdered Sherrice Iverson. What would a moral egoist say about his behavior? What would Ayn Rand say about his behavior? What do you think of his behavior?

7.   White owns a chemical company. To increase his profits, he's decreasing his costs by disposing of toxic chemical wastes in a residential area. The toxic waste is contaminating the water supply of about 30 percent of the local residents. White's country has no laws forbidding his action.

   a.   Develop an argument to persuade people that White isn't doing anything wrong because he's simply doing what's in his self-interest.

   b.   Develop an argument to persuade people that White is doing something wrong, even if it is in his self-interest.

   c.   Do you think that White's action is morally wrong?

8.   The fictional character Superman is not protrayed as a psychological egoist. He is constantly risking his life to save humanity, and although he could harm other people with complete impunity, he doesn't. Why? Do you think that if Superman existed, he would be exclusively self-interested? Do you think he would be a moral egoist?

SUGGESTED READINGS

Joseph Butler. "Fifteen Sermons." In *British Moralists, 1650–1800*, vol. 1. Edited by D. D. Raphael. Indianapolis, IN: Hackett, 1991.

His Holiness the Dalai Lama. *Ethics for the New Millennium*. New York: Riverhead Books, 1999.

Joel Feinberg. "Psychological Egoism." In *Reason and Responsibility*, 5th ed. Edited by Joel Feinberg. Belmont, CA: Wadsworth, 1981.

INTERNET RESOURCES

Thomas Hobbes, *Leviathan* (www.knuten.liu.se/~bjoch509/works/hobbes/leviathan.txt).

Friedrich Nietzsche, excerpts from *Beyond Good and Evil* (www.cwu.edu/~millerj/nietzsche/bge.html).

Friedrich Nietzsche, abridged version of *Human, All Too Human* (http://inquiria.com/nz/hah_title.html).

ENDNOTES

1. *Merriam-Webster's Collegiate Dictionary*, 10th ed. (Springfield, MA: Merriam-Webster, 1994).

2. Samuel Pufendorf, "On the Duty of Man and Citizen," in *Moral Philosophy from Montaigne to Kant,* vol. 1., ed. J. B. Schneewind (Cambridge, England: Cambridge University Press, 1990), p. 158.

3. Ibid., p. 161.

4. Ibid., p. 163.

5. Ibid., p. 165.

6. Ibid., p. 167.

7. Thomas Hobbes, *Leviathan* (New York: Collier, 1962), chap. 13, p. 100. (Originally published in 1651.)

8. Ayn Rand, "Introducing Objectivism," http://aynrand.org/objectivism/io.html.

9. Joseph Butler, "Fifteen Sermons," in *British Moralists: 1650–1800,* vol. 1, ed. D. D. Raphael (Indianapolis, IN: Hackett, 1991), pp. 335–336. (Originally published in 1726.)

10. His Holiness the Dalai Lama, *Ethics for the New Millennium* (New York: Riverhead Books, 1999), p. 53.

11. Ibid., p. 61.

12. Ibid.

5

Utilitarianism

OBJECTIVES

- To understand the concept of a consequentialist moral theory
- To understand the concept of utility and its relation to other concepts, such as pleasure, happiness, and well-being
- To understand Act Utilitarianism
- To understand Rule Utilitarianism and its relation to Act Utilitarianism
- To apply act and Rule Utilitarianism
- To critically evaluate both act and Rule Utilitarianism

INTRODUCTION

Suppose that you're trying to make up your mind about whether capital punishment is morally wrong. As we saw in the first chapter, moral judgments require reasons, so in making up your mind you should weigh the reasons for and against capital punishment. For example, you might think that with capital punishment, there's a high probability that at least some innocent people will be executed because of mistakes. Without capital punishment, no innocent person can possibly be executed by mistake. That counts as a reason for thinking that capital punishment is morally wrong (at least if it's wrong to execute innocent people). On the other hand, we may also think that capital punishment is a better deterrent than other punishments, even life in prison without parole, so that with capital punishment for murder, there will be fewer murders. That counts as a reason for thinking that capital punishment is morally right (at least if it's right to save people from being murdered).

Similarly, suppose that you're trying to decide whether it would be morally wrong to torture suspected terrorists during interrogation in order to get important information that might save lives. The fact that torture harms the victim and causes great suffering—sometimes permanent injuries or death—is a reason to think it's wrong, but the fact that it might provide information that will save the lives of innocent people is a reason to think it's right.

In thinking in these ways, we're focusing on the *consequences* of actions and policies. One important strand of commonsense moral thinking is the view that moral right and wrong depend solely on the consequences of actions. To put it loosely, according to *consequentialist* moral theories, if the good consequences outweigh the bad, it's morally right; if the bad consequences outweigh the good, it's morally wrong. Consequentialists consider this to be a basic moral principle.

Consequentialist thinking is pretty common. In many ways, it just seems like common sense. For example, if you're trying to decide whether to go to college, you probably weigh the costs and benefits. Some costs are monetary. You pay tuition and fees, perhaps room and board, buy books, and forego some earnings while you're in college. Other costs are not monetary. You spend a lot of time in class and studying. As to benefits, some of those are monetary. If you have a college degree, you'll probably earn a lot more over the course of your life than you will if you don't have a college degree. Other benefits are less tangible. With a college degree, you may be able to have a job or career that is more satisfying than the job you would have without the degree. The work may be more interesting and challenging; you may have more autonomy; the work conditions may be safer, healthier, and more comfortable. In addition, you will learn things that make life more interesting, including things about yourself. You may discover skills, talents, and abilities you didn't know you had. You will have opportunities for acquiring self-knowledge and engaging in self-development. Thus, if in your view the benefits outweigh the costs, you will probably go to college, but if you think the costs will outweigh the benefits, you probably won't.

Cost-benefit analyses for making business decisions are another example of consequentialist thinking. A company will do something only if it thinks the benefits will outweigh the costs, which are expressed in monetary terms. If Atlas Casket Company believes that it will earn an extra $25,000 annually if it invests $200,000 in remodeling, it will probably spend the money to remodel.

This basic principle leaves us with several problems. First, with respect to moral arguments and moral thinking, what counts as a good consequence and what counts as a bad consequence? According to many consequentialists, relevant consequences are any increases or decreases in pleasure, happiness, or well-being. (Some also talk of the satisfaction of desires or preferences.) Here we will take it that the relevant consequences are changes in well-being. But then, we must consider what constitutes a state of well-being and what increases or decreases it. There are subjectivist and objectivist views of well-being. According to subjectivist views, a person's well-being is determined entirely by her mental states. Whatever mental states a person considers positive are positive, and whatever mental states she considers negative are negative for her. For example, if you consider sadness and depression negative, then they decrease your well-being, but if I consider them positive, they increase my well-being. Alternatively, we could say that someone is in a state of well-being if she is satisfied with her life, and that her well-being increases if she feels more satisfied and decreases if she feels less satisfied. But different people are satisfied by different things.

On the other hand, according to objectivist views of well-being, well-being cannot be determined solely from the person's own point of view. A slave may feel satisfied and think she's happy with her life because she has been brainwashed into thinking that she deserves to be a slave and has lost all hope of anything better. She may think the acme of well-being is being beaten only once a week and fed two meals a day. But that leaves objectivists with the problem of specifying the objective conditions that promote well-being. Some of the things that have been suggested include having our basic needs for food, clothing, and shelter met; having adequate physical and mental health; being relatively free of discomfort or pain, whether physical or psychological; having our needs for the love, friendship, affection, and respect of others met; having self-respect; having an adequate amount of liberty or freedom; having an adequate number of our desires met; and having adequate opportunities for self-development and the actualization of our potential. Then, given our social circumstances, whatever is necessary for or conducive to these things is also part of our well-being. Decreases in any of these things decrease our well-being; increases in these things increase our well-being.

We will focus on objective measures of well-being. Once we have decided that an increase in well-being is a good consequence and a decrease in well-being a bad consequence, the next question is, whose well-being counts from a moral point of view? For example, in the cost-benefit analyses, only the interests of the person or company making the decision counted. There are a variety of possibilities. It is easy to assume first that at most, only the well-being of human beings counts. But as we will see in a later chapter, many people now question that assumption and broaden the scope of moral concern. Some include all sentient beings, such as deer, bears, dogs, dolphins, and rabbits. Others widen the area of concern to include all living beings, such as plants. Still others include even ecosystems with their living inhabitants.

Sentient beings are conscious. If there is intelligent life on other planets, they would be sentient beings. But sentience seems to be a matter of degree. The sentience or consciousness of humans includes the capacity to be aware of the physical world via perception; to feel painful and pleasurable sensations; to be aware of themselves as separate independent beings with a past, present, and future; to form complex beliefs and belief systems, including beliefs about themselves; to form complex desires and intentions; to have feelings such as depression and elation; to have emotions such as love and hate; and so on. Other nonhuman animals may have some of these capacities, but not others. For example, a dog probably doesn't have the same capacity for self-awareness that a human being has.

If sentience is the criterion of counting from a moral point of view, that leaves open the question of whether all sentient beings count equally from a moral point of view. If there are degrees of sentience, then perhaps it would make sense to speak of different moral weights. For example, in that case, we might say that the well-being of a dog counts, but counts less than the well-being of a human. Suppose that A will lead to the death of a dog while B will lead to the death of a human. We could say that from a moral point of view, the death of a human is worse than that of a dog.

For the sake of simplicity, we will limit moral consideration to humans in this chapter. That is, we will ignore the well-being of nonhuman creatures or things as if it doesn't count from a moral point of view. However, we should keep in mind that this is only for the sake of simplicity. It may be very difficult to justify counting only human well-being from a moral point of view.

If we count only human well-being from a moral point of view, another question naturally arises. Which humans? One possibility is that only one human's well-being counts in moral deliberation—the deliberator's. Thus, suppose you're the deliberator trying to decide what it would be morally right to do. In weighing consequences, you could limit yourself to consequences that affect you. If the good consequences to you outweigh the bad consequences, then it's morally right. If the bad consequences to you outweigh the good consequences, then it's morally wrong. In essence, this is Moral Egoism.

We need not repeat the objections to Moral Egoism we already have examined. Here we will only ask the question, What reason is there to think that only the agent's well-being counts from a moral point of view?

Well, if it's not only your well-being counts from a moral point of view when you're trying to distinguish right from wrong, then perhaps the well-being of your family and friends also counts, but no one else's. The same problems arise, however. Maybe from your, your friends', and your family's point of view, only your well-being counts, but from other people's perspective, there's no reason to think that. They will insist that their well-being also counts. No matter how you try to draw the boundaries—limiting moral concern to your friends and family, or to people like you in such fundamental respects as race, ethnicity, religion, class, and sexual orientation, the boundary looks arbitrary. (Consider the Nazi's limitation of moral concern to "Aryans," a wholly irrational and arbitrary line.) There doesn't seem any way to adequately *justify* limiting moral concern in such a way. In addition, if *impartiality* is constitutive of the moral point of view, as most philosophers claim, it's difficult to see how drawing lines based on such features as race and religion is consistent with that. We seem driven to the view, then, that the only nonarbitrary moral boundary is one that includes all of humanity. In that case, from a moral point of view, all humans count, and count equally. That means that my interests are no more or less important than your interests.

The consequentialist moral theory we will examine is called *Utilitarianism*. According to Utilitarianism, moral right and wrong are determined solely by the balance between increases and decreases in the well-being of everyone affected, that is, the total well-being. There are two versions of Utilitarianism. Act Utilitarianism is applied to individual concrete actions. Rule Utilitarianism is applied to kinds of actions. For example, we could apply Act Utilitarianism to the question of whether it was morally wrong of John Wilkes Booth to assassinate Abraham Lincoln. That was an individual concrete act. We could apply Rule Utilitarianism to the question of whether it is always morally wrong to assassinate political leaders, a kind of act.

ACT UTILITARIANISM

According to the standard account, Act Utilitarianism says that we should always act in ways that will maximize the total well-being of everyone affected. Alternatively, only the act that will, under the circumstances, produce the greatest increase in total well-being (or the smallest decrease in total well-being) is morally right.

Consider the case of David Cash from Chapter 1. How would an act utilitarian judge it? Sherrice's well-being drastically decreased because she was raped and murdered. So did the well-being of her family and friends. Even the well-being of her murderer drastically decreased; he will spend the rest of his life in prison. As for Cash, he may be shunned by people, not hired for jobs, fired, and so on, if people learn of his past. If Cash had stopped the rape and murder, everyone's well-being would have increased. According to Act Utilitarianism then, stopping the rape and murder was the morally right thing to do and not stopping it was morally wrong.

Let us imagine that we can quantify increases and decreases in well-being. Suppose that Jones owns a truck-cleaning firm and discovers that nontoxic solvents for cleaning trucks are roughly three times as expensive as toxic solvents. The runoff from Jones's operation ultimately finds its way into the wells of nearly 100 families to the south of him. Scientific studies suggest that long-term exposure to the toxic solvents will probably damage an individual's immune system and may cause neurological problems. Because he will have more profits if he uses the toxic solvents and because he does not live in the area of water contamination, Jones will be happier, and hence have more well-being, if he uses the toxic solvents. However, if Jones uses the toxic solvents, the well-being of the people whose wells will be contaminated by the runoff will be reduced because they will be injured by long-term exposure.

Let's assume that Jones would gain 100 units of well-being by using the toxic solvents and would lose 200 units of well-being by using the more expensive nontoxic solvents. On the other hand, using the toxic solvents would decrease the well-being of each of the 100 neighboring families by 20 units, for a total of 2,000 units, whereas using the nontoxic solvents would increase their well-being by 5 units, for a total of 500 units. These assumptions result in the following table:

	Use Cheaper Toxic Solvents	Use More Expensive Nontoxic Solvents
Jones	+100	-200
Neighbors	-2,000	+500
Total	-1,900	+300

According to Act Utilitarianism, the right thing to do is to use the more expensive nontoxic solvents because that will increase total well-being 300 units, whereas using the toxic solvents will reduce total well-being 1,300 units.

Let's look at one final example. Again, let's assume that we can quantify increases and decreases in well-being. Two people, Alpha and Omega, need a heart transplant, but there's only one heart available. Who should get it? Let's approach the question as an act utilitarian would. An act utilitarian will ask how much total well-being will be produced of Alpha gets it and how much if Omega gets it. Suppose we uncover the following facts. Alpha has a spouse and three young children whose well-being will decrease if Alpha dies. Omega has neither a spouse nor children. Alpha's parents are alive, and Alpha has two siblings as well as aunts and uncles; each of them will have a decrease in well-being if Alpha dies. Omega has no living relatives. Alpha is a teacher beloved by many students whose well-being will decrease if Alpha dies. Omega works alone at home and has no coworkers. Suppose we then find that the increases and decreases in well-being are summarized in the following table.

	Alpha Gets Heart	Omega Gets Heart
Alpha	+5,000	-5,000
Omega	-5,000	+5,000
A's spouse and children	+2,000	-2,000
A's parents and siblings	+1,500	-1,500
A's aunts/uncles	+500	-500
A's students	+250	-250
Total	+4,250	-4,250

An act utilitarian would say that it would be morally right to give the heart to Alpha and morally wrong to give it to Omega, because giving it to Alpha will produce more total well-being.

One feature of Act Utilitarianism must be emphasized. We can't apply Act Utilitarianism to determine the moral rightness and wrongness of *kinds* of actions. For example, if we ask an act utilitarian whether it is morally right to torture suspected terrorists during interrogation, she won't say yes and she won't say no. Rather, she will say that it depends. Sometimes it will be; sometimes it will not be. We must judge things on a case-by-case basis. We can determine whether it would be morally right to torture a specific individual, but each case will be different. If torturing a suspect will produce more total well-being because it provides information that saves many innocent lives, information that could be gotten in no other way, then it's morally right. But if there will be more total well-being if this individual is not tortured because no information that saves lives will be extracted, then it is morally wrong. We must examine the situation with care.

This raises an important point. We can employ a test of moral right and wrong to determine after the fact whether an act was right, or use it before the fact to provide guidance in what we should do. One use is backward-looking into the past, the other is forward-looking into the future.

Suppose I'm trying to apply Act Utilitarianism to determine whether it would be right to torture this specific suspected terrorist. If total well-being increases, it will be right, but if it decreases, it will be wrong. It will increase if I extract information that saves lives, but it will decrease if I don't. Thus, I will be doing the right thing if I extract information, but the wrong thing if I don't.

My problem is that my ability to see into the future is limited. I do not know with certainty that torturing this suspect will provide information that will save lives. She may have no useful information. (She may not even be a terrorist; she's a "suspected" terrorist. Even if she is a terrorist, she may not have the kind of information that will lead to innocent lives being saved.) If she has information, torture may not work. If she's tortured, in order to end the torture she may provide misinformation (falsity rather than truth) that leads to more rather than fewer innocent lives being lost. How do I use Act Utilitarianism to figure out what's the right thing to do, then?

I have no choice but to count on what consequences I think are most probable. If I think it's probable that she has information she will reveal under torture that will save innocent lives and that therefore total well-being probably will be increased if I torture her, then surely I should torture her. But how probable must it be? Is a 60 percent probability enough? 75 percent? 90 percent? Or must it be higher, say 99 percent? And what kind of torture would I be justified in using? How much agony would I be justified in imposing on the terrorist? It may not be wrong to shout at her, push her, or slap her, but may I thrust needles under her fingernails? How about beating her, burning her with cigarettes, shocking her with electric current, breaking her arm, or cutting off a finger? Of course, people throughout the ages have used much ingenuity to invent refined torture techniques and machines that are ghastly and terrifying. Are there limits beyond which we may not go?

To this is connected the issue of how long torture may go on. No matter what information a suspect provides, there is always a possibility that she knows more. Therefore, in theory, torture should continue until the death of the victim, no matter how long that takes, unless it reaches a point where I am almost certain that she has no more information that might save innocent lives.

Applying Act Utilitarianism in this forward-looking way may sometimes be easy, but in many cases it will be deeply problematical, as in the case of torturing suspected terrorists. And we must admit that there is a tension between forward-looking and backward-looking applications. If I torture to death a suspected terrorist and get no information that saves innocent lives, I have reduced total well-being without any compensating gain. There would have been more total well-being if I had not tortured the suspect. I gambled that torturing her would turn out to be the right thing according to Act Utilitarianism, but I lost the gamble. It wasn't. It just *seemed* to be the right thing to do.

There is one final complication with Act Utilitarianism that has not been emphasized. There have been only two alternatives in most of our examples, but in real life, we usually have far more than two. Act Utilitarianism requires us to select the *best* alternative. For example, suppose that I want to donate $100 to a charity. Let's assume that total well-being will increase if I donate the $100 to any of a thousand charities, but the amount of increase varies among them. I must donate the $100 to the one charity that will produce the greatest increase in total well-being. (If, say, ten charities tie for first place, then I may give to any of the ten.) If I donate to a different charity, one that will produce a lesser increase in total well-being, then I'm doing the wrong thing.

Act Utilitarianism has a number of strengths. It provides us with a clear test of right and wrong that is purely empirical. We must use perception and observation of the world in order to determine what's morally right and wrong. And on this view, moral judgments are objectively true or false. Whether choice A will produce more total well-being than choice B is a matter of fact. And moral rightness depends wholly on whether one choice will produce more total well-being than another choice. If choice A will produce more total well-being than any alternative choice, then it's *true* that A is morally right and the other alternatives morally wrong. Act Utilitarianism also makes it clear that the point or purpose of morality is closely linked to human interests. The facts that are relevant are about human well-being or happiness. Morality then will contribute to increasing human well-being or minimizing decreases in human well-being. Furthermore, Act Utilitarianism doesn't rely on disputed theological assumptions as the divine command theory does. Moral right and wrong are independent of God's existence and will. Even if God doesn't exist, some things are really morally right and other things really morally wrong.

But many people reject Act Utilitarianism. Why?

Objections to Act Utilitarianism

Act Utilitarianism Requires Too Much.   Critics believe that Act Utilitarianism requires too much of people. According to Act Utilitarianism, it is wrong for people not to do whatever will produce the *most* total well-being. Suppose that you are considering going to a movie with your friends. The problem is that there are a lot of other things you could do instead. For example, you could tutor illiterate adults or work as a volunteer in a hospital, each of which would probably produce more total well-being than would be produced by your going to the movies. Therefore, according to act utilitarians, it would be wrong for you to go to the movies.

Of course, what was said of going to the movies applies to almost anything we do. If we watch television, listen to music, or walk in the park, there are alternative courses of action that would have produced more total well-being; therefore, it would be wrong to do these things. Critics of Act Utilitarianism find this consequence of the theory highly implausible; the requirement to *maximize* total well-being would probably ensure that no matter what we do, it's always the wrong thing because we could have done something else that would have produced more total well-being.

Act Utilitarianism Requires Too Much Impartiality.   A second related objection is that Act Utilitarianism requires us to be too impartial. Suppose that both my child and a stranger's child need an operation for the same life-threatening illness. The doctors and hospital won't operate unless they are paid.

I can pay for only one. The other child's parents cannot pay for either. No one else will pay for the children's operations. Whose operation should I pay for? Act Utilitarianism tells me that I should pay for the operation that will produce the most total well-being. If there would be more total well-being if the stranger's child got the operation, it would be morally wrong for me to pay for my child's operation instead of the stranger's child's operation. But many people would say that I have a special obligation to my child that I don't have to the stranger's child. They think it would be wrong of me to let my child die to save a stranger.

But perhaps there are alternative versions of Act Utilitarianism that can overcome these objections. The basic problem seems to be the requirement that we *maximize* total well-being. Why think that from a moral point of view, we must be well-being maximizers? One alternative is to forbid us to do what will reduce total-well-being, at least if there is an alternative action that will not reduce it. Thus, if I could do five things, one of which would reduce total well-being and four of which would not, I am forbidden to do that which will reduce well-being, but I'm permitted to do any of the remaining four alternatives. Similarly, if I could do action A or not do A, and doing A will reduce total well-being whereas not doing A won't, then it would be wrong to do A. I will leave you to think of other possible variations that do not require maximization of well-being.

Act Utilitarianism Ignores the Distribution of Happiness

Another problem is that both versions of Act Utilitarianism focus exclusively on total well-being and ignore its distribution. Suppose that you can do either act A or act B. Let's assume that acts A and B will increase your well-being the same amount. However, if you do A, you will reduce the well-being of five people by 10 units each for a total reduction of 50 units of total well-being. On the other hand, if you do B, you will reduce one person's well-being by 50 units. The decrease in total well-being is the same. According to Act Utilitarianism, alternatives A and B are equally right because all that counts is total well-being. Similarly, suppose that you face a choice between acts C and D. Again, they will produce the same amount of well-being for you. If you do C, you'll increase the well-being of five people by 10 units each; if you do D, you'll increase the well-being of one person by 50 units. As before, the total increase in well-being is the same. According to Act Utilitarianism, they are equally right.

However, many critics deny this. They claim that it's worse to impose great losses on one person than to impose slight losses on several people, and it's better to produce a moderate increase in well-being for several people than to produce a large increase in well-being for only one person.

Act utilitarians claim that their critics are mistaken. First, they claim that their critics' assumption that it's better to harm or benefit several people a little rather than one person a lot is simply mistaken. How can critics justify this claim? If they claim that it's self-evident, act utilitarians can simply deny it. Second, they insist that their critics oversimplify reality. Act utilitarians claim that it is very difficult to come up with realistic examples of situations in which one action would produce a moderate loss (or increase) of well-being for several people, the alternative would produce a large loss (or increase) in well-being for one person, and the total change in well-being would be the same. If it's a real rather than a made-up case, they say, if we are thorough in examining the facts, we will almost always find that the total change in well-being is not the same. And they think it's highly likely that we would find that benefiting (or harming) many in small increments will produce more total well-being than would benefiting (or harming) one person a lot.

Act Utilitarianism Ignores Duties

Some critics object to its fundamental assumption that the rightness or wrongness of an individual action is determined solely by its future consequences. They think that it unjustifiably ignores past behavior that might create obligations and duties. For example, if John promised to take you to the doctor this afternoon, then according to common sense morality he has a (prima facie) moral duty or obligation to take you. Suppose, though, that he's an act utilitarian. On reflection he realizes that he would produce more total well-being if he works at a soup kitchen for the homeless instead of taking you to the doctor. He concludes that the right thing to do is work at the soup kitchen. The fact that he promised to take you to the doctor is irrelevant. Commonsense morality disagrees.

Act utilitarians might reply that in many cases, violating what we take to be a duty will reduce total well-being in the long run.

RULE UTILITARIANISM

Suppose that Sabrina is considering killing her uncle. He is the most hated man in town because he's a miser who often sues people for trivial things. Although he wants to go on living, he is old and sickly, suffering from painful maladies and depression. She's convinced that he'd be better off dead. She has a drug that will make it appear that he died of a heart attack, so there's no chance of her being caught. His fortune will be left to her, and she will use the money for various charitable purposes that will increase total well-being. Everyone in the town will be happy when they learn of her uncle's death; no one will mourn him. Therefore, Sabrina reasons that killing him will produce more total well-being than not killing him. According to Act Utilitarianism, it would be morally right for Sabrina to kill her uncle. Critics say that even if more total well-being would result from killing him than from letting him live, it would nonetheless be morally wrong to kill him because it would violate an obviously correct moral principle or rule that says it is morally wrong to commit murder. Regardless of the effect on total well-being, if Sabrina killed her uncle it would be murder.

Commonsense morality generally has us apply a variety of moral principles or rules in judging and deciding, such as, "We should not lie, steal, or commit murder." (Alternatively, the principles might be expressed as, "It is morally wrong to lie, steal, or commit murder.") Act Utilitarianism has us apply only one moral principle or rule: maximize total well-being, and as we have seen, critics find that problematic. Yet there is something plausible about basing moral right and wrong on the effects on people's well-being. Is there any way to combine moral principles or rules with a utilitarian test of moral right and wrong that looks to the effects on people's well-being?

Rule Utilitarianism says that we should obey correct moral principles or rules. If "it's morally wrong to commit murder" is a correct moral principle or rule, then Sabrina should obey it. And if she murders her uncle, she will have done something morally wrong, regardless of the consequences of her act. Similarly, if "We should not lie" is a correct moral principle, then Sabrina shouldn't lie; if she does, she will do what's morally wrong.

The problem is to distinguish between the correct and incorrect (or true and false) moral principles or rules. How do we know whether a principle forbidding us to murder is correct? What about a principle forbidding us to wish for people's death? Similarly, we could follow a moral principle that says it's wrong to lie, or we could follow a moral principle that says it's not wrong to lie. Which of the two conflicting principles is correct?

Rule utilitarians provide us with a test for moral principles or rules based on the effect on total well-being. We must ask what would be the effect on total well-being if people followed a rule permitting us to lie, or instead followed a rule forbidding us to lie. If there would be more total well-being if people lie, then the principle permitting lying would be correct. On the other hand, if there would be more total well-being if people do not lie, then the principle forbidding lying would be correct.

Rule utilitarians, then, say that the right thing to do is to follow the correct moral rules that apply in a given situation. In turn, the correct moral rules are those that would produce more total well-being if followed than if they're not followed. A rule is incorrect if there would be more total well-being if people did not follow it.

But one advantage of Act Utilitarianism is that moral principles cannot come into conflict because there is only one. If there is more than one principle, they can conflict in a given situation. For example, a principle forbidding lying can come into conflict with a principle requiring us to save innocent lives. Which takes priority? Because Rule Utilitarianism recognizes many different moral rules, there can be conflicts. For example, it may turn out in a given situation that a rule requiring us to be loyal to friends comes into conflict with a rule requiring us to inform the police if we know that a crime is going to be committed. Which rule has priority?

Fortunately, Rule Utilitarianism has a way to resolve such conflicts. If conflicting rules apply in a given situation, we should appeal to Act Utilitarianism. The right thing to do is what will produce most total well-being. If we apply negative Act Utilitarianism, it would be wrong to do what will reduce total well-being if there are any alternatives that do not reduce it. If every alternative will reduce total well-being, then the right thing to do is what will reduce it the least amount. Thus, suppose I know that my brother is planning to blow up a building but I have promised to keep quiet. Suppose that by the rule utilitarian test, the following rules are all correct and apply in this situation:

Be loyal to close family.

Keep promises.

Prevent harm to innocent people.

If I tell the police, I will be disloyal to my brother and will break a promise. If I don't tell the police, many innocent people will die or be seriously injured. Which rules should I follow? Since there will be a huge decrease in total well-being if the building is blown up, much greater than if I inform on my brother, I should follow the rule that requires us to prevent harm to innocent people, rather than the rules that require us to be loyal to close family and to keep promises.

Advantages of Rule Utilitarianism

Rule Utilitarianism does not seem to be as open as Act Utilitarianism to the objection that it requires too much. Rule utilitarians could very plausibly maintain that there would be more total well-being if everyone followed the rule "Get some rest and relaxation" than if everyone followed its opposite, "Don't ever rest or relax." Unlike the well-being-maximizing version of Act Utilitarianism, Rule Utilitarianism probably won't forbid going to the movies, listening to music, and so on, because it does not require people to always do what will produce the most total well-being. Similarly, problems with the distribution of happiness are less likely to arise with Rule Utilitarianism; even if in some concrete circumstance two alternative actions would produce the same total amount of happiness but a vastly different distribution of it, the question is what rule is correct in this circumstance. And we may find that a rule that tells us to impose small harms on many people, rather than a large harm on one; or to give small benefits to many people, rather than a large benefit to one, will produce more total well-being.

Then, too, whereas critics say that Act Utilitarianism focuses exclusively on the future consequences of an action—ignoring past behavior that may have created duties and obligations—Rule Utilitarianism does not. For example, a rule utilitarian must look at the future effects on total happiness of the practice of keeping or breaking promises. If the practice of keeping promises would produce more total happiness than the practice of breaking them, then a rule requiring you to keep promises is correct. And in that case, you should keep this particular promise because you should follow correct moral rules. Therefore, the fact that you made a promise is relevant under Rule Utilitarianism in a way that it may not be under Act Utilitarianism.

An Objection to Rule Utilitarianism

Critics of Rule Utilitarianism find that in at least some cases, applying it yields conclusions that are inconsistent with their own moral convictions. For example, suppose that in a society 1 out of 100,000 babies is born with green skin. Because everyone without green skin detests green-skinned infants, everyone, including the parents of green-skinned infants, would feel happier if the babies are killed at birth than if they are not killed. If green-skinned infants were allowed to live, they would be shunned and could never live a normal life in that society. Let us suppose that, because of people's intense revulsion to green-skinned people, total well-being in the society would be greater if they followed a rule permitting the killing of green infants than there would be if they don't. (The well-being of 100,000 people, we will suppose, outweighs the well-being of one infant.) According to Rule Utilitarianism, "Kill green-skinned infants" is a correct moral rule. Critics disagree. According to their moral convictions, it is wrong to kill green-skinned infants.

Rule utilitarians might respond by maintaining either that such examples are highly unrealistic and implausible or that the moral convictions of their critics are wrong and without foundation. They might insist that an example such as the society's killing of green-skinned infants is farfetched and based on a very super-ficial sketch that leaves out too much detail. If such a society really existed, closer inspection would almost surely show that total happiness really isn't maximized by killing green-skinned infants. And if on closer inspection the very improbable turned out to be true and the total increase in well-being would be greatest if all green-skinned babies were killed, then those who think it would be wrong to kill green skinned-babies in these circumstances are simply mistaken. The fact that they assert that it would be morally wrong doesn't make it so.

PROBLEMS FOR ALL VERSIONS
OF UTILITARIANISM

To apply either Act or Rule Utilitarianism with any precision, we must be able to measure and compare increases and decreases in people's well-being. However, many critics of Utilitarianism point out that we have no reliable way of making such measurements and comparisons. In our examples, I assigned numbers to increases and decreases in well-being, but the numbers assigned were arbitrary. Perhaps we can justifiably say that someone's well-being increased and someone else's decreased, but we cannot measure the amount of increase or decrease. Yet we must do so to apply Act and Rule Utilitarianism.

A utilitarian could concede that changes in well-being cannot be measured with any precision, yet insist that precise measurements are often unnecessary; comparative judgments can be made with some reliability in a large percentage of cases. Take the case of a truck cleaning company that can choose to use either cheaper toxic cleaning substances that will get into the wells of neighboring families, or more expensive, nontoxic products. An act utilitarian could say that even if we can't make precise measurements, the nonquantitative judgment that there would be more total well-being if Jones used nontoxic cleaning solvents is very well-founded. Similarly, a rule utilitarian could say that the judgment that there would be more total well-being if people followed a rule forbidding stealing than there would be if they followed a rule permitting stealing is well-founded, even if we can't say by precisely how much.

EXERCISES

1. In the summer of 2001, a controversy erupted in the United States over stem cell research. Many scientists believe that using stem cells to treat certain serious conditions, such as Parkinson's disease, might very well lead to great improvements for patients or even cures. But the stem cells used in these medical procedures and the research performed to develop those procedures come from human embryos. In most cases, the embryos were conceived for different purposes—generally for treating fertility problems in couples who want to have a baby but are having trouble. Many embryos are created by joining the woman's egg with a man's sperm outside the womb, and then some are implanted in the woman's womb. Most embryos, though, are not used and eventually are discarded. It is these about-to-be-discarded embryos that are harvested for stem cells for scientific research. The controversy was mainly about whether the federal government should provide funds for medical research using stem cells. The antiabortion movement claims that harvesting stem cells from a human embryo kills it. They oppose both the research and the federal funding of it, maintaining that it is morally wrong to use stem cells from human embryos for any purposes. They further claim that killing a human embryo is murder. Others claim that it's not morally wrong because the human embryo is going to be discarded anyway and will certainly die. Using harvested stem cells from it will actually give its life and death some meaning. They focus on the potential benefits from the research. And they say that an embryo isn't a person; therefore, it can't feel pleasure or pain, be happy or unhappy. Try to reason about this case applying both Act and Rule Utilitarianism.

2. According to a story in the *New York Times* (18 March 1992), two executives of a food company were charged with knowingly selling eggs tainted with salmonella, which causes food poisoning, and with falsifying lab reports to hide the fact that the eggs were tainted. (For our purposes, assume that the charges were true.) Obviously, their motive was to benefit themselves and their company. Let's imagine that when confronted, they claim that they thought that no one would really get sick from eating the tainted eggs and that, therefore, they didn't think they were doing anything morally wrong. Try to reason about this case applying both Act and Rule Utilitarianism.

3. Brad has a date with Sara. He hopes to encourage her to drink enough to get drunk so that he can either seduce her or have her pass out so that he can have sex with her while she's unconscious. He knows that he'll get pleasure from having sex with Sara, and he thinks that there won't be any harm to Sara because if she's conscious and consents while drunk she will experience pleasure and won't feel bad about it later and if she is unconscious from

having passed out she won't even know it happened. What do you think of Brad's reasoning? Try to reason about this case applying both Act and Rule Utilitarianism.

4. Phil has gone to Boston to view the St. Patrick's Day parade. For the first time, a gay-pride group of homosexual and lesbian Irish Americans has been permitted to march. As they pass him on the parade route, Phil shouts out insults, makes threatening gestures and remarks, and finally throws a rock at the group. Try to reason about this case applying both Act and Rule Utilitarianism.

5. Dave has been drinking heavily at a party and is drunk. His friends have urged him to stay the night so he won't drive home drunk, but Dave has refused and has become aggressive. One of his friends wants to hide his car keys and disable his car so that he can't drive home drunk. Another friend says they should just let Dave do what he wants. Would it be morally wrong of Dave to drive home while drunk? What would be the morally right thing for his friends to do? Try to reason about this case applying both Act and Rule Utilitarianism.

6. Sandra works at an amusement park for the summer at the admission counter. Her best friend has asked her to let her in for free. Sandra has been told by her supervisor that no one is allowed into the park unless they have purchased a ticket. Sandra feels loyalty toward her best friend and fears that her friend will be angry with her if she doesn't let her into the park for free. But she also worries that if she gets caught, she will be fired. She likes and needs the job. Was it morally wrong of Sandra's friend to ask her to let her into the park for free? Would it be morally wrong of Sandra to do what her friend asks? Try to reason about this case applying both Act and Rule Utilitarianism.

7. Sherman is producing and marketing a pill that he claims cures cancer. He knows that it has no effect on cancer, but he also knows that desperate cancer patients will buy the pill. He reasons that they will probably die anyway and taking the pills will give them some hope, which is a benefit. And taking the pills won't hurt them because the pills are harmless. He also thinks that he won't get caught and be punished for it, and he will make millions of dollars in a fairly short time selling the pills. Try to reason about this case applying both Act and Rule Utilitarianism.

8. Apply Act and Rule Utilitarianism to the question of whether it would be wrong to torture a suspected terrorist to get information that might save innocent lives.

SUGGESTED READINGS

Jeremy Bentham. "An Introduction to the Principles of Morals and Legislation." In *The Utilitarians*. New York: Doubleday, 1961.

Fred Feldman. *Introductory Ethics*. Englewood Cliffs, NJ: Prentice-Hall, 1978. (See especially Chapters 2–5.)

John Stuart Mill. "Utilitarianism." In *The Utilitarians*. New York: Doubleday, 1961.

Anthony Quinton. *Utilitarian Ethics*. New York: St. Martin's Press, 1973.

INTERNET RESOURCES

The Bentham Project (www.ucl.ac.uk/Bentham-Project/). Includes many online texts of Bentham's works, including *Principles of Moral and Legislation*.

John Stuart Mill, *Utilitarianism*. (http://utilitarianism.com/mill1.htm). The complete text online.

6

Kantian Moral Theory

OBJECTIVES

- To understand the difference between consequentialist and nonconsequentialist moral theories
- To understand Kant's concept of the good will and its relation to the concept of duty
- To understand the Universal Law formulation of Kant's Categorical Imperative
- To understand what maxims are and how they differ from universal laws
- To understand the concept of inconsistency in willing that a maxim becomes a universal law
- To understand the Respect for People Formulation of Kant's Categorical Imperative
- To understand the concept of a person

> Do not impose on others what you yourself do not desire.
> CONFUCIUS (551–479 c.e.), *THE ANALECTS*

> Always treat others as you would like them to treat you.
> JESUS, THE SERMON ON THE MOUNT (MATTHEW 7:12)

INTRODUCTION

At one time, wars were fought with swords and spears in hand-to-hand combat. Eventually, human ingenuity developed new technologies that allowed for mass killing, some at a distance, such as artillery and bombs, some at relatively close range, such as machine guns. But until the twentieth century, soldiers primarily killed enemy soldiers rather than civilians in battle. (Of course, there are many instances throughout history of the massacre of civilians after battles.) The technology of mass killing at a distance improved during the twentieth century, and at the same time, it became more and more common to target civilians, not just enemy soldiers.

According to Jonathan Glover, the British naval blockade of Germany during World War I was among the first instances of mass killing of civilians at a distance during war time. The British government deliberately prevented supplies of such essentials as food from reaching Germany, knowing that it would mean mass starvation of civilians, including women, children, and the elderly. A goal was to break civilian morale, which in turn might lead people to pressure their government to end the war. But the British continued the blockade after the armistice of November 11, 1918 ended the fighting in order to increase the pressure on Germany to comply with all Allied demands during the peace negotiations. Between 425,000 and 800,000 civilians died as a direct result of the blockade.[1] Psychologically, it was easier to justify civilian deaths caused by a blockade than it might have been to justify directly killing civilians with weapons, and the fact that the policy makers didn't have to see the starving and starved people helped maintain emotional distance from the consequences of their decisions.

According to Glover, the naval blockade of World War I made it easier for decision makers to order the bombing of enemy cities during World War II. By 1944, the Allies had total command of the air over Europe and had developed the capacity for precision bombing that would have allowed them to destroy military targets instead of bombing cities. It is now clear that targeting Germany's oil installations would have practically crippled the German army. Nevertheless, the Allies continued to bomb cities, knowing that most of those killed would be civilians, arguing that it would disrupt industrial production and reduce morale.

From July 24, 1943 to August 3, 1943, the city of Hamburg was systematically bombed. Incendiary bombs caused firestorms. About 40,000 people died, almost all civilians. Annalies Schmidt later described seeing some women and children who had died: "...their brains tumbled from their burst temples and their insides from the soft parts under their ribs. How terribly these people must have died. The smallest children lay like fried eels on the pavement."[2] A raid on Darmstadt on September 11, 1944 killed almost 12,000 people.

Again according to Glover, the bombing of cities with conventional bombs, killing tens of thousands of civilians in each city, made it easier for the U.S. government to decide to drop atomic bombs on the Japanese cities of Hiroshima and Nagasaki in August 1945. With the complications of radiation sickness, about 140,000 Japanese died within a year and 200,000 within five years in Hiroshima. (The atomic bomb kept on killing long after it exploded.) The bomb dropped on Nagasaki a few days later killed 70,000 within a year and 140,000 within five years.

According to consequentialists, even the mass killing of civilians during war is not inherently wrong. They could justify any instance of it by claiming that the good consequences outweigh the bad. Of course, it would be objectively right only if the good consequences really outweigh the bad. That is, if the premise in their moral argument that the good consequences outweigh the bad is false or unreasonable, their argument is defective and justification fails.

On the other hand, nonconsequentialists claim that some actions are inherently wrong regardless of the consequences. Thus, a nonconsequentialist could say that even if the good consequences of slaughtering civilians during war outweigh the bad, it is inherently wrong. But how do we determine what actions are inherently wrong and what actions aren't? Is there a test?

The most influential nonconsequentialist moral theory is that of the German philosopher Immanuel Kant (1724–1804). The test he devises to determine whether an action is inherently wrong is based on the intellectual requirement of logical consistency. If we contradict ourselves, we are inconsistent. According to Kant, when an action is inherently wrong, we would contradict ourselves if we think it is not wrong.

KANT AND THE GOOD WILL

Kant began his *Foundations of the Metaphysics of Morals* with the words "Nothing in the world—indeed nothing even beyond the world—can possibly be conceived which could be called good without qualification except a GOOD WILL."[3] Goods such as wealth, power, and fame; talents such as strength, agility, intelligence, skill, and endurance; character traits such as courage, industriousness, and perseverance are all good, but they are not good without qualification because they can be put to evil purposes. Wealth can be used to destroy people; strength and intelligence can be used for murder; courage can be used for robbery. All such goods can be used for evil ends unless a person has a good will. Therefore, only a good will can be good without qualification.

To understand the concept of will, we begin by asking how we can explain human actions. Suppose that Pablo carries an umbrella to work. How can we explain why he brought the umbrella rather than leaving it home? Part of the explanation might be that Pablo believed that there was a high probability of rain that day. If it rained, he would get wet, and if he used an umbrella, he could stay dry even in the rain. But these beliefs are not enough to explain why he brought the umbrella. After all, if he desired to get wet rather than stay dry, he would still have no reason to bring an umbrella. A crucial part of the explanation has been omitted: his desires. We can complete our explanation of Pablo's action by adding that he desired to stay dry rather than get wet. Now we have a plausible explanation of his action.

But there's still one ingredient missing, according to Kant. We have to decide whether to act on a desire. After all, sometimes we decide to resist a desire rather than satisfy it. Consider an alcoholic who has a desire for a drink, someone trying to quit smoking who has a desire for a cigarette, or a dieter who has a desire for a piece of chocolate cake. In each case, the individual must decide whether to satisfy the desire or resist it. In cases like these, we usually think (and so does the person involved) that one ought to resist the desire and not act to satisfy it.

In such cases we often talk of "willpower." We say that the individual who successfully resists the temptation of desire has willpower, whereas the person who succumbs and acts to satisfy the desire lacks willpower. This concept suggests the following model of human action: The agent starts with a cluster of beliefs and desires that are motives to action; they are like forces that get the body into action. The agent, however, must (or at least should) evaluate the desires to determine whether they should or shouldn't be satisfied. The role of evaluator is played by the agent's reason. When reason functions as evaluator, it is also governor, because it is the last thing that determines the will, which in turn determines action. In any event, before a desire can be acted on, there must be an act of willing to attempt to satisfy the desire. The agent must choose or decide to either act or not act on the desire. Only then does the body act. Thus, we might imagine human action schematically in the following way:

Beliefs + desires → Evaluation by reason → Act of will to satisfy desire (decision) → Action to satisfy desire.

When reason is not functioning as evaluator, the model becomes:

Beliefs + desires → Act of will to satisfy desire → Action to satisfy desire.

Kant recognized that desires often conflict. Sometimes acting to satisfy one desire will guarantee that we cannot satisfy another desire. In such cases, we must decide which desire to satisfy. If we are rational, we will let our reason decide between conflicting desires. No action will be undertaken until our will has been activated. So our will is master of our actions. According to Kant, if we are rational, our will won't be the slave of our desires, merely doing their bidding. Our will instead can cooperate with our reason and master our desires.

If the one thing that is good without qualification is a good will, what makes a will good and what makes it bad?

Kant was a supporter of what we have called commonsense morality. He thought that the moral views common to most people are pretty much correct. Therefore, he would think that a person with a good will would not commit major moral offenses such as murder or robbery, would not commit minor moral offenses such as maliciously gossiping about people, and would help people in need.

Kant took these things for granted. But he recognized that a person might have a good will and not be able to actually do any of the things a good person would do, or refrain from doing the things a good person would not do. Similarly, someone might do all the things that a good person would do and refrain from doing all the things that a good person would not do, and yet not have a good will. For example, someone may contribute to charity only because it's in his self-interest, perhaps a politician who believes that he will gain votes by (publicly) contributing to charity. Kant does not think that his contributing money to charity shows that he has a good will.

What about performing actions that normally would be considered an indication that someone lacks a good will? Suppose someone acts in a way that is deeply offensive or insulting to someone else. Would that necessarily show that he or she lacks a good will? No—not if he or she did not intend to be offensive or insulting.

Thus, Kant points out that we cannot tell whether someone has a good will by looking only at what that person does or does not do, or only at the effects or consequences of his actions. One's intentions are the key to whether one has a good will. It is what one wants or tries to accomplish—what one wills—that counts. A person has a good will if he or she tries to do what is right and tries to avoid doing what is wrong. But the trying must be a genuine trying, a summoning of all of one's capacities to work hard toward doing what's right and to refrain from doing what's wrong.

Kant says that the concept of duty contains the concept of a good will, but it probably would be more accurate to say that the concept of a good will entails the concept of duty. One has a good will if one tries to do one's duty. But Kant emphasized that for a will to be truly good, it must try to do its duty from a purely moral motive, rather than from a self-interested motive. That purely moral motive is the desire to do one's duty out of respect for the moral law. A person with a good will respects the moral law and tries to act dutifully because he or she desires to act in ways that conform to what his duties are.

"In summary, the first proposition of morality is that to have genuine moral worth, an action must be done from duty. The second proposition is that an action done from duty does not have its moral worth in the purpose which is to be achieved through it, but in the maxim whereby it is determined."[4]

ACTIONS AND MAXIMS

Kant believed that people act as they do for a reason (whether or not they are immediately conscious of the reason or engage in deliberation before acting). For example, suppose that Brown and Gray each contribute $1,000 to charity. According to Kant, each has a reason for his or her action. Let's assume that we know their reasons. Brown approves of the goals of the charity and wants to help it accomplish its goals. Gray knows that the names of large contributors will be publicized; he wants to impress his business associates and customers, which he thinks will improve his business.

Kant believed that when people act for a reason, they're following a maxim—a kind of personal rule of action. Of course, people do not always consciously formulate maxims and then deliberately follow them. Rather, people often act *as though* they formulate and follow maxims. However, Kant seemed to assume that we can discover what maxim we follow, even if we did not consciously formulate and follow it. Given Brown and Gray's reasons for contributing to charity, we might express the maxims they were following as M1 (Brown's maxim) and M2 (Gray's maxim).

M1. I will contribute to charity when I approve of the charity's goals and I want to help it achieve its purposes.

M2. I will contribute to charity when I think that doing so will help improve my business and I want to improve my business.

A maxim takes the form "I will do action X in circumstance C for purpose P." It is a personal principle of action, a kind of prescription of how a person will act in certain circumstances to achieve what he or she wants. Thus, a maxim must specify: (1) what I will do, (2) the concrete circumstances in which I will do it, and (3) why I will do it.

For example, suppose that a social worker faces the following situation. The agency where she works is funded by the state. In order to save money, the state has instituted a screening system. All children who are referred to the agency for counseling must be given a questionnaire designed to quantify the severity of their problems or symptoms. Children who score 80 or above will receive treatment; children who score below 80 will not receive treatment. The social worker and her colleagues believe, first, that the questionnaire's results are not entirely reliable; and second, that almost all children who score in the 70s on the questionnaire need services. Consequently, they consider falsifying the results of the questionnaire so that children who actually score only in the 70s will have a score of 80 entered in their records. Their intention is to deceive the state authorities so that treatment for these children will be authorized.

What maxim would the social worker and her colleagues be following? We must be careful not to identify a maxim that is overly general, such as:

I will deceive people.

It must be qualified to include the circumstances and the motivation. Will the social worker deceive everyone under all circumstances? No. A more accurate statement of the maxim would be:

I will deceive state authorities by falsifying the scores of children on a questionnaire designed to quantify the severity of their psychological symptoms/problems when I believe that the test is probably unreliable and when falsification is necessary in order to get children the help that, in my best professional judgment, they need.

The action contemplated is an act of deception, but we must expand the description of the act to include: (1) the circumstances (the deception is limited to deception of state authorities about the results of a questionnaire that may not be reliable and may deprive children of services that they need), and (2) the motive (the deception is intended not to benefit the social worker but to benefit others). So a maxim must be properly qualified.

Of course, self-deception is possible. Ascertaining the maxim one actually follows (or would follow) requires a great deal of self-reflection. Some people may not be able to engage in such deep reflection because they are not fully aware of their own motives. Others may rationalize and convince themselves that they are following one maxim when in fact they are following a different maxim. However, people who are conscientious will try to be honest with themselves about the maxims they follow (or would follow).

According to Kant, an action done from duty has moral worth based only on the maxim that the agent follows, which specifies the action, the circumstances, and the motive. But surely an action cannot have moral worth if the agent is following a bad maxim, such as "I will kill people whenever it is advantageous to me." Presumably an action has moral worth if and only if the maxim being followed is a morally acceptable maxim. But what makes a maxim morally acceptable or morally unacceptable?

Before turning to this question, however, let us reflect a bit more on the maxims and behavior of Brown and Gray. Did Brown or Gray do anything wrong in contributing to charity? If they were following morally unacceptable maxims, then they were doing something wrong, but if they were following morally acceptable maxims, they were not doing anything wrong. Whether they did anything wrong, then, depends on whether their maxims are morally acceptable. Surely neither did anything wrong. However, Kant would say that Gray's actions lacked *moral worth* because the maxim he followed was purely self-interested. (Lacking moral worth, their actions do not merit praise; but it does not follow that because they lack moral worth, they merit condemnation instead.) So once again, we face the task of distinguishing between morally acceptable and morally unacceptable maxims.

Thus, whether we are talking about the moral worth of actions or the rightness and wrongness of actions, we need to distinguish between morally acceptable and morally unacceptable maxims. We require a test of maxims that will enable us to distinguish between those that are and those that are not morally acceptable to act on.

Kant did not think that we need to invent a totally new test to determine the rightness and wrongness of maxims. He believed that there is a test that most ordinary people apply and that has been endorsed by most of the world's major religions, including Christianity. This test is the so-called Golden Rule: Treat people the way you think you should be treated. However, he did think that the Golden Rule needed to be made more precise in order to be applied correctly. He called his reformulation of the Golden Rule *the Categorical Imperative*. It's an imperative because it takes the form of a rule. It's categorical because it applies in all circumstances, regardless of an agent's desires, and because it binds all rational agents.

THE CATEGORICAL IMPERATIVE

Universal Law Formulation

Kant's first formulation of the Categorical Imperative was "I ought never to act in such a way that I could not also will that my maxim should be a universal law."[5] Because the Categorical Imperative is commanded by a person's own reason, it applies not just to that person but to all creatures with reason, that is, to all rational creatures. Because an essential feature of the moral law is universality, it is the essence of the Categorical Imperative. Therefore, it cannot be expressed merely in terms of "I." Thus, more formally, Kant presented the following universal law formulation of the Categorical Imperative:

Act only according to that maxim by which you can at the same time will that it should become a universal law.[6]

According to Kant, all people—in all times in all places—are morally forbidden to act on maxims that they can't consistently will to be universal laws. But what does this formulation mean?

Maxims and Universal Laws

According to Kant, an action is morally acceptable if and only if the maxim the individual follows is morally acceptable. Kant maintained that a maxim is morally acceptable if and only if one could consistently will it to be a universal law. According to Kant, people are morally forbidden to act on maxims that they cannot consistently will to be universal laws. To determine whether we can consistently will a maxim to be a universal law, we must transform the maxim from a personal policy expressed in terms of "I" into a universal policy that applies to everyone.

Recall Brown's maxim (M1) and Gray's maxim (M2):

M1. I will contribute to charity when I approve of the charity's goals and I want to help it achieve its purposes.

M2. I will contribute to charity when I think that doing so will help improve my business and I want to improve my business.

To determine whether their maxims are morally acceptable, we must transform M1 and M2 into universal laws and determine whether Brown and Gray can consistently will that the maxims they're acting on become universal laws. A maxim only applies to the individual whose maxim it is; a universal law applies to everyone. Thus, M1 becomes UL1, and M2 becomes UL2:

UL1. Everyone will contribute to charity when they approve of the charity's goals and they want to help it achieve its purposes.

UL2. Everyone will contribute to charity when they think that doing so will help improve their business and they want to improve their business.

If Brown can't consistently will that the maxim she's following, M1, becomes the universal law UL1, then M1 is an immoral maxim, and the action she performs in following that maxim is immoral. The same applies to Gray and his maxim (M2). What might prevent Brown (or Gray) from consistently willing that M1 (M2) become the universal law UL1 (UL2)?

Inconsistencies in Willing That a Maxim Becomes a Universal Law

Kant's test of maxims involves looking for contradiction. Contradiction or inconsistency is always a relationship between two things. "I am sleepy" contradicts "I am not sleepy." "2 + 2 = 4" is inconsistent with "2 + 2 = 5." According to Kant, a maxim is unacceptable if willing it to be a universal law generates contradiction. In order to generate contradiction, just as "I am sleepy" must be juxtaposed with "I am not sleepy," the universal law must be juxtaposed with something else. What might that something else be?

To answer this question, let's analyze one of Kant's own examples. Kant asks us to imagine a prosperous man who "sees others (whom he could help)... struggle with great hardships." He asks himself whether it is morally acceptable for him to *not* help them. His maxim might be expressed as:

M3. When I am prosperous, I will refrain from helping others if I won't benefit from helping.

The question for Kant would then be whether he can will that maxim to be a universal law of nature without contradicting himself. The universal law would be:

UL3. When people are prosperous, they will refrain from helping others if they won't benefit from helping.

Kant claims that the man cannot possibly will UL3 without contradicting himself.

It is . . . impossible to will that such a principle should hold everywhere as a law of nature. For a will which resolved this would conflict with itself, since instances can often arise in which he would need the love and sympathy of others, and in which he would have robbed himself, by such a law of nature springing from his own will, of all hope of the aid he desires.[7]

The key to this passage is that willing the universal law conflicts with desires the man has. According to Kant, the man desires or will desire help, but by willing UL3 he virtually guarantees that this desire will be frustrated. He will not get help if or when he needs it. Thus, one potential source of contradiction is for a universal law to conflict with our desires in the sense of making it virtually certain that the desires will be frustrated. Thus, one test of whether our willing a universal law generates contradiction is to juxtapose the law with our desires. If the law would virtually guarantee that our desires would be frustrated, then there is a contradiction in our willing. We are willing that our desires be satisfied at the same time that we are willing something that will virtually guarantee that our desires will *not* be satisfied.

But how does Kant know that the man in his example desires help? First, Kant emphasizes that human beings are both rational and "dependent." Rational beings who are dependent inevitably need help. (Kant would give angels as an example of *independent* rational beings.) Humans, because they are dependent as well as rational, are vulnerable to a variety of harms; therefore, they need others to refrain from harming them. Additionally, they always need the help of others at various stages and points in their lives. Kant implies that rational beings desire or want what they need. (It would be irrational not to want what we need.) Therefore, since the man in his example is a dependent rational being, he will inevitably need help even if he does not need help at this moment; he knows he will need help; and he desires what he needs. Kant would probably maintain that the man necessarily desires the help he will inevitably need because he is rational. (If he does not desire the help he will inevitably need, he is not rational.) Therefore, it is necessarily the case that the man desires help, even if he does not desire *specific* help at this precise moment.

Let's return for a moment to Brown and Gray who contributed money to charity for a variety of reasons, some of them purely self-interested. If they have no desires that would almost certainly be frustrated if their maxims became the universal laws UL1 and UL2, then they are not contradicting themselves. Their maxims pass the test. They would be doing nothing wrong by acting on their maxims (even if their actions would lack moral worth and not be praiseworthy because they are purely self-interested). There is no reason to think that Brown and Gray must have some desires that would be frustrated if UL1 and UL2 become universal laws of nature. Therefore, it seems reasonable to assume that their maxims pass the test.

However, one problem with this test is that it appears to be subjective. It depends on one's desires, and different people have different desires. Kant certainly did not intend his test to be subjective.

Is there a solution? Perhaps. Kant claims that all rational beings necessarily pursue or desire happiness:

> There is one end, however, which we may presuppose as actual in all rational beings . . ., so far as they are dependent beings. There is one purpose which they not only can have but which we can presuppose that they all do have by a necessity of nature. This purpose is happiness. It belongs to [a rational being's] essence.[8]

Someone whose goal in life is to be as unhappy, rather than happy, as possible would not be rational.

If there are no limits or requirements regarding what can constitute happiness for rational dependent beings, then Kant's claim, even if true, cannot provide a solution to our problem. However, if there are limits or requirements, it may be able to provide a solution. Kant would probably agree that happiness for rational dependent beings, all other things being equal, requires continued existence, health, some degree of liberty, and enough resources to meet one's basic needs. Imagine someone's claiming that death, illness, or poverty would make him or her happy as an end in itself (rather than as a means to some other valued end), while admitting that he or she has no good reason for wanting to be dead, ill, unfree, or poor. Such a claim would be irrational. Similarly, if dependent rational beings care about other people (and probably almost all care about some other people), then their happiness will require that those they care about be happy. Kant would probably agree that the happiness of rational beings also requires that the lives, health, liberty, and access to basic resources of those they care about be preserved.

If there are some desires that all rational dependent beings necessarily have and others that necessarily no rational dependent being has, then the test of the Categorical Imperative is not wholly subjective. For example, consider the prosperous man in Kant's example who considers not helping others in need. We suggested that he necessarily has a desire that he receive help when he needs it. Such a desire is inherent in all human beings, all of whom are dependent rational beings. Kant could say that no human being lacks the desire to be helped. Therefore, no rational dependent being could will UL3 without contradiction.

But suppose that both Arnold and Brad are thinking of cheating on their spouses. If Arnold wouldn't want his spouse to cheat on him, he couldn't will that his maxim become a universal law without contradicting himself. However, if Brad doesn't care whether his spouse cheats on him, he could. Must all dependent rational beings desire that their spouses not cheat on them?

Unfortunately for Kant's claim of objectivity, it is not obvious that, as a rational dependent being, Brad must desire that his wife be faithful to him. Therefore, in applying the Categorical Imperative we may find that it is wrong for Arnold but not for Brad. If this reasoning is correct, then there is an element of subjectivity in applying the Categorical Imperative. Given agents with different desires, some actions may be wrong for some people but not for others. However, if Kant is correct—that there are some desires that all rational dependent beings necessarily have and others that they necessarily do not have—then *some* actions are wrong for every human being; namely, those actions whose maxims, if transformed into a universal law, would conflict with desires that all rational dependent beings necessarily have.

Kant considered one more possible source of inconsistency: We could will something to be a universal law that couldn't possibly be a universal law. To take Kant's own example, suppose that A borrows money by making a promise to repay that he does not intend to keep. The maxim he's following is:

> M5. I will make a promise to repay a loan that I don't intend to keep when I need money.

M5 is morally acceptable only if A can consistently will that it become the universal law.

> UL5. Everyone will make promises to repay loans that they don't intend to keep when they need money.

According to Kant, UL5 could not possibly be a universal law because if everyone followed it, soon no one would be able to follow it because the practice of lending money on the basis of a promise to repay would soon be extinguished. UL5 is self-destroying. It would not take long for people who lend money to realize that people were following UL5, and when they did, they simply would stop lending money on the basis of a promise to repay. Once promises were no longer accepted, the practice of lending money would cease. Therefore, it would be impossible for everyone to make false promises to repay a loan with no intention to repay.

There are, then, two primary ways that inconsistency can arise in willing that a maxim become a universal law. First, in some cases, if a maxim became a universal law, it would jeopardize our own survival and happiness. Because as dependent rational creatures we will that our survival and happiness *not* be jeopardized, we would be willing contradictory things. Second, we may will something to be a universal law that couldn't possibly be a universal law.

We can use the Categorical Imperative to rationally criticize our own or others' behavior. Consider the acts of genocide committed by Serbs in Bosnia, primarily against Muslims, and by Hutus in Central Africa, primarily against Tutsis. Imagine that Sara is having a discussion with a Serb or Hutu who has participated in these acts of genocide. Challenging him, Sara asks what maxim he was following. He replies that he was following:

> M6. I will participate in killing members of groups that my people despise or fear in order to exterminate them.

Sara, applying the Categorical Imperative, asks him whether he can consistently will that M6 become a universal law.

> UL6. Everyone will participate in killing members of groups that their people despise or fear in order to exterminate them.

Sara points out that UL6 will probably lead to acts of genocide against his own people in order to exterminate them. Surely he wills that acts of genocide against his own people, which could lead to his own murder or the murder of many people he cares about, *not* occur. Thus, he contradicts himself. He wills a universal law that will probably ensure that acts of genocide against his people will occur, at the same time that he wills that acts of genocide against his people will *not* occur.

Duties Derived from the Categorical Imperative

Kant derived a variety of duties from the Categorical Imperative. For example, he argued that everyone has a duty to help those in need, using the following reasoning:

> A ... man, for whom things are going well, sees that others (whom he could help) have to struggle with great hardships, and he asks, "What concern of mine is it? Let each one be as happy as heaven wills, or as he can make himself; I will not take anything from him or even envy him; but to his welfare or his assistance in time of need I have no desire to contribute." If such a way of thinking were a universal law of nature, certainly the human race could exist. . . . It is nevertheless impossible to will that such a principle should hold everywhere as a law of nature. For a will which resolved this would conflict with itself, since instances can often arise in which he would need the love and sympathy of others, and in which he would have robbed himself, by such a law of nature springing from his own will, of all hope of the aid he desires.[9]

In a later work, Kant again maintained that:

> to be beneficent, that is, to promote according to one's means . . . the happiness of others in need, without hoping for something in return, is every man's duty.

For every man who finds himself in need wishes to be helped by other men. But if he lets his maxim of being unwilling to assist others in turn when they are in need become public, that is, makes this a universal permissive law, then everyone would likewise deny him assistance when he himself is in need.... Hence the maxim of self-interest would conflict with itself if it were made a universal law, that is, it is contrary to duty.[10]

Kant also claimed that gratitude or "honoring a person because of a benefit he has rendered us"[11] is a duty, and it is a duty generally to respect other rational agents.

THE CATEGORICAL IMPERATIVE: "RESPECT FOR PEOPLE" FORMULATION

Kant provided a second formulation of the Categorical Imperative that he claimed is equivalent to the first. Whereas the first formulation is expressed in terms of universal law, the second formulation requires that we treat all people with respect:

Act so that you treat humanity, whether in your own person or in that of another, always as an end and never as a means only.[12]

In *The Metaphysics of Morals,* Kant elaborated:

Man regarded as a *person* ... *is* exalted above any price; for as a person ... he is not to be valued merely as a means to the ends of others ..., but as an end in himself, that is, he possesses a *dignity* (an absolute inner worth) by which he exacts *respect* for himself from all other rational beings in the world. He can measure himself with any other being of his kind and value himself on a footing of equality with them.[13]

Trees, insects, snakes, and squirrels are living beings, but they're not persons (or people). Human beings, although only one species among many, are thought to be special. What makes them special? What makes them people? To Kant it is rationality; in his view, it is reason that makes persons especially valuable. However, contemporary thinkers generally focus on at least three major features that define what we might call "personhood":

1. People are conscious; they're aware of their environment and can perceive the world around them.

2. People are self-aware; they're aware of themselves as separate beings persisting through time with a past, present, and future.

3. People have a developed capacity or ability to reason; they can think, solve problems, communicate, and so on.[14]

Because trees, insects, snakes, and squirrels don't have all of these characteristics, they're not people. However, that doesn't mean that only human beings are people. If there is intelligent life elsewhere in the universe, alien beings who satisfy these criteria, they would be people even though they're not human beings. Consider the creature E.T. from the movie of the same name. Although viewers knew that E.T. was not human, they certainly thought of E.T. as a person. Similarly, it may be possible for nonbiological organisms to have these characteristics; if so, they would also be people. Consider the robot R2D2 from the *Star Wars* movies or the android Data from the television series *Star Trek: The Next Generation*. If such nonbiological organisms existed, they would be people and not mere things.

Kant insisted that people are supremely valuable and that they should not be treated as we might treat things that are not people, such as television sets or cows. Kant also seems to presuppose that all people have equal moral worth or value. In his view, it's morally permissible to use mere things purely as means to our ends. For example, it's morally permissible for you to use your television set as you please (as long as you don't use it to harm people). If you would derive satisfaction from smashing it to pieces, it's morally acceptable for you to do so. Similarly, many people believe that it's morally acceptable to raise cows in order to eat them. But it is not morally acceptable to use people purely for our own purposes, because people have inherent and equal moral worth.

Let us say that if we use another person purely for our own purposes, we are *merely* using the person. We do and must use people all the time for our own purposes, but it does not follow that we *merely* use them. For example, suppose you hire a tutor in calculus. You're using the tutor for you own ends, but you are not merely using that person. Here, it would be helpful to distinguish between hiring a tutor in calculus and enslaving or raping people. In the second and third cases you are merely using people, but not in the first case.

How does the tutor–tutee relationship differ from the slave–master or the rapist–victim relationship? First, the tutor–tutee relationship, unlike the slave–master and the rapist–victim relationship, is purely voluntary. We merely use another person when we enter into the relationship against the person's will. Second, there's mutual and roughly equal benefit in the tutor–tutee relationship, but not in the slave–master or rapist–victim relationship. You benefit by receiving instruction, and the tutor benefits by receiving payment. The same cannot be said of the slave–master and rapist–victim relationship. Finally, we may presume that in the tutor–tutee relationship there is mutual respect and consideration of one another's interests and well-being, manifested in such behaviors as politeness, honesty, and openness. Each refrains from insulting, manipulating, exploiting, degrading, humiliating, or otherwise harming the other. Again, the same cannot be said of the slave–master or rapist–victim relationship. Rape and enslavement can serve as paradigm examples of *merely* using people.

According to Kant, because people are special, because they have great (and equal) value or worth, they should be treated with respect, which means that they should never be treated merely as a means. We treat others with respect when: (1) we ensure that our interactions with them are purely voluntary, (2) we ensure that our interactions with them are mutually beneficial or are just and fair, and (3) we ensure that we take account of their needs, desires, and interests.

Kant emphasized that we must treat other people with respect simply because they're people, but he also emphasized that we should treat ourselves with respect because we, too, are people. He thought that we have duties to others, but also duties to ourselves. For example, he maintained that every person has a duty of self-perfection:

> This duty can . . . consist only in *cultivating one's capacities* . . . *the* highest of which *is understanding*. . . . Man has a duty to raise himself from the crude state of his nature, from his animality . . ., more and more toward humanity . . .; he has a duty to diminish his ignorance by instruction and to correct his errors.[15]

As for our duties to others, Kant insisted that when we are acting toward others from the duty of beneficence, we must never undermine their self-respect or humiliate them, for that would violate the requirement that we treat people with respect.

> We shall acknowledge that we are under obligation to help a poor man; but since the favor we do implies that his well-being depends on our generosity, and this humbles him, it is our duty to behave as if our help is either merely what is due him or but a slight service of love, and to spare him humiliation and maintain his respect for himself.[16]

Finally, let us return to the issue of the mass killing of civilians during war time. Suppose that it is certain (of course, it never is) that killing 10,000 civilians in a bombing raid on a city will end a war quickly and save the lives of 100,000 soldiers. A consequentialist might argue as follows:

1. Bombing this city, which will kill 10,000 civilians, will save the lives of 100,000 soldiers.

2. It is better to kill 10,000 people to save 100,000 people than not to kill 10,000 people and have 100,000 people die.

3. The right thing to do is what will save more lives.

4. Therefore, it is right to bomb the city, killing 10,000 civilians.

According to this reasoning, only the number of lives counts; the fact that those killed are innocent civilians and those saved are soldiers doesn't matter.

A Kantian, however, might conclude that killing civilians in war, no matter how many lives might be saved, is inherently wrong. My maxim might be "I will bomb a city, killing civilians, when more lives will be saved than lost." Given that I and people I love may some day be among the civilians killed in a bombing raid on a city, and that I will those I love to continue to live, I would be willing contradictory things.

Many people aren't comfortable with either the consequentialist or the Kantian position. The consequentialist position seems to imply that if even one more person would be saved than is killed, it would be right to bomb cities and kill civilians. It would be right to kill 99,999 civilians to save 100,000 soldiers who would otherwise die. Many people find this view implausible. On the other hand, the Kantian position seems to imply that it would be wrong to kill one person even if it would save a billion people from death. Many people find this implausible, too. They think that numbers aren't wholly irrelevant. Thus, some people think that the consequentialist position permits too much while the Kantian position permits too little.

EXERCISES

1. In the summer of 2001, a controversy erupted in the United States over stem cell research. Many scientists believe that using stem cells to treat certain serious conditions, such as Parkinson's disease, might very well lead to great improvements for patients, or even cures. But the stem cells used in these medical procedures and the research that must be done to develop them come from human embryos. In most cases, the embryos were conceived for different purposes—generally for treating fertility problems in couples who want to have a baby but are having trouble. Many embryos are created by joining the woman's egg with a man's sperm outside the womb, and then some are implanted in the woman's womb. Most embryos, though, are not used and eventually are discarded. It is these about-to-be-discarded embryos that are harvested for stem cells for scientific research. The controversy was mainly about whether the federal government should provide funds for medical research using stem cells. The antiabortion movement claims that harvesting stem cells from a human embryo kills it. They oppose both the research and federal funding of it, maintaining that it is morally wrong to use stem cells from human embryos for any purposes. They further claim that killing a human embryo is murder. Others claim that it's not morally wrong because the human embryo is going to be discarded anyway and will certainly die. Using harvested stem cells from it will actually give its life and death some meaning. They focus on the potential benefits from the research. And they say that an embryo isn't a person; therefore, it can't feel pleasure or pain, be happy or unhappy. Try to reason about this case applying Kant's Categorical Imperative.

2. Brad has a date with Sara. He hopes to encourage her to drink enough to get drunk so that he can either seduce her or have her pass out so that he can have sex with her while she's unconscious. He knows that he'll get pleasure from having sex with Sara, and he thinks that there won't be any harm to Sara, because if she's conscious and consents while drunk, she will experience pleasure and won't feel bad about it later, and if she is unconscious from having passed out she won't even know it happened. What do you think of Brad's reasoning? Apply Kant's Categorical Imperative to determine whether it would be morally wrong for Brad to do what he intends.

3. Phil has gone to Boston to view the St. Patrick's Day Parade. As a gay-pride group of homosexual and lesbian Irish-Americans march past him on the parade route, Phil shouts out insults, makes threatening gestures and remarks, and finally throws a rock at the group. Apply Kant's Categorical Imperative to determine whether Phil's actions are morally wrong.

4. Apply Kant's Categorical Imperative to try to determine whether capital punishment is morally wrong. Focus on the following questions. If someone you loved were murdered, would you think that the murderer should be executed? If someone you loved were convicted of murder, would you think that he should be executed? Do we show respect for murder victims if we do

not execute their murderers? Do we show respect for murderers if we execute them? If people commit murder, does the moral requirement to treat them with respect no longer apply?

5. Dave has been drinking heavily at a party. His friends have urged him to stay the night so he won't drive home drunk, but Dave has refused and has become aggressive. One of his friends wants to hide his car keys and disable his car so that he can't drive home drunk. Another friend says they should just let Dave do what he wants. Would it be morally wrong of Dave to drive home while drunk? What would be the morally right thing for his friends to do? Apply Kant's Categorical Imperative to answer these questions.

6. Sherman is producing and marketing a pill that he claims cures cancer. He knows that it has no effect on cancer, but he also knows that desperate cancer patients will buy the pill. He reasons that they will probably die anyway and taking the pills will give them some hope, which is a benefit. Additionally, taking the pills won't hurt them because the pills are harmless. He also thinks that he won't get caught and be punished for it, and he will make millions of dollars in a fairly short time selling the pills. Apply Kant's Categorical Imperative to determine whether Sherman is doing anything wrong.

7. Explain the difference between Rule Utilitarianism and the universal law formulation of the Categorical Imperative.

8. Pedro claims that the principle "treat others as you want them to treat you" is dangerous. He says that a masochist who enjoys having pain inflicted on him would then inflict pain on others in following this principle. He claims that a masochist could consistently will as a universal law a principle permitting people to inflict pain on others. Consuela disagrees. She says that a masochist could not consistently will that such a principle be a universal law and that "Treat others as you want them to treat you" does not have that consequence. With whom do you agree, and why?

9. The Categorical Imperative's requirement to treat people with respect applies to ourselves because we are people, too. What would be some ways of treating yourself with disrespect? What are some ways of treating yourself with respect? Do you agree that we should treat ourselves with respect?

10. Could committing suicide ever be a way of treating yourself with respect?

SUGGESTED READINGS

Fred Feldman. *Introductory Ethics*. Englewood Cliffs, NJ: Prentice-Hall, 1978. (See especially Chapters 7 and 8.)

Immanuel Kant. *Foundations of the Metaphysics of Morals*, 2nd ed. Translated by Lewis White Beck. New York: Library of Liberal Arts, 1990. (Originally published in 1785.)

Immanuel Kant. *The Metaphysics of Morals*. Translated by Mary Gregor. New York: Cambridge University Press, 1991. (Originally published in 1797.)

Onora Nell. *Acting on Principle.* New York: Columbia University Press, 1975.

Roger J. Sullivan. *Immanuel Kant's Moral Theory.* New York: Cambridge University Press, 1989.

Roger J. Sullivan. *An Introduction to Kant's Ethics.* Cambridge, England: Cambridge University Press, 1994.

Robert Paul Wolff. *The Autonomy of Reason. A Commentary on Kant's Groundwork of the Metaphysics of Morals.* New York: Harper Torch, 1973.

INTERNET RESOURCE

Immanuel Kant. *Fundamental Principles of the Metaphysics of Morals.* Translated by T. K. Abbott. (http://ethics.acusd.edu/theory/Kant/Groundwork/Groundwork.html).

ENDNOTES

1. Jonathan Glover, *Humanity: A Moral History of the Twentieth Century* (New Haven: Yale University Press, 1999), pp. 64–66.
2. Ibid., p. 78.
3. Immanuel Kant, *Foundations of the Metaphysics of Morals,* 2nd ed., trans. Lewis White Beck (New York: Library of Liberal Arts, 1990), p. 9. (Originally published in 1785.)
4. Ibid., pp. 15–16.
5. Ibid., p. 18.
6. Ibid., p. 38.
7. Ibid., p. 40.
8. Ibid., p. 32.
9. Ibid., p. 40.
10. Immanuel Kant, "The Doctrine of Virtue," in *The Metaphysics of Morals,* trans. Mary Gregor (New York: Cambridge University Press, 1991), p. 247. (Originally published in 1797.)
11. Ibid., p. 248.
12. Kant, *Foundations of the Metaphysics of Morals,* p. 46.
13. Ibid., p. 230.
14. Compare this definition with those discussed in Chapter 11 on abortion.
15. Kant, *Foundations of the Metaphysics of Morals,* p. 191.
16. Ibid., p. 243.

7

Virtue and Vice

OBJECTIVES

- To understand Aristotle's theory of virtue, including the role of the concepts of flourishing and the golden mean
- To understand the view of the unity of the virtues
- To understand the role of perception in the virtues
- To understand the nature of individual virtues as character traits involving behavior, feelings and emotions, attitudes, and ways of perceiving
- To understand epicurean views of virtue and vice
- To understand Stoic views of virtue and vice
- To understand Hobbes and Hume's views of virtue and vice
- To understand Hindu and Buddhist views of virtue and vice
- To understand the traditional seven deadly sins

INTRODUCTION

In 2003, 51-year-old Missouri pharmacist Robert Courtney pleaded guilty in federal court to intentionally diluting the medications of thousands of patients who filled their prescriptions at his pharmacy over a nine-year period. The prescriptions he diluted included antibiotics, fertility drugs, blood clotting medications, and chemotherapy treatments for cancer patients. The first time tests were done on the medications he dispensed, it was found that he had diluted them anywhere from 40 percent of the proper dosage to nearly zero.

No one could believe that someone would be so ghoulish as to deliberately dilute medications, especially medications of the seriously ill and dying. Robert

Courtney seemed an unlikely ghoul. He sang in his church choir and donated hundreds of thousands of dollars to his church. He was often described as very gentlemanly. He was a picture of solid respectability, seemingly a pillar of his community.

But what made Robert Courtney stand out in his community was his money. Without it, he would not have been a big man in his church, donating hundreds of thousands of dollars. Without his money, he would not have lived in a huge mansion in the most exclusive neighborhood of Kansas City, nor driven about in an expensive Mercedes. Without his money, he would have been just plain, obscure, ordinary Robert Courtney.

Courtney didn't jump from being a law-abiding pharmacist to what many people would consider a moral monster in one giant leap. Rather, he did it in stages. He began by purchasing discount pharmaceuticals from the black or gray market. Then one day, he diluted, but only slightly diluted, the medication of a dying patient, a patient who would die regardless of the strength of the chemo-therapy drugs. He probably convinced himself that he wasn't really doing any harm. But gradually, he made the concentrations of medication lower and lower, and diluted more and more medications of more and more patients. It didn't matter whether the patient would have lived or been helped if the medication had been at its proper dosage.

By the time he was caught, Courtney had amassed a fortune of nearly 20 million dollars. It is impossible to know how many people he killed in order to accumulate that fortune. Even now, it is hard to accept that once, Robert Courtney was a college student who looked pretty much like every other college student.

At his trial, Courtney was asked why he had done such terrible things. He said he didn't know. Many observers think they can at least partly explain his behavior. He was greedy, greedy for money and what it could buy—expensive houses, expensive cars, but perhaps most of all, respect and notice. Greed goes far beyond the more acceptable trait of ambition.

But in explaining Courtney's behavior, surely we should include what he seemed to lack, not just what he had in super abundance. Obviously, he lacked compassion and sympathy for his victims. He also lacked honesty, justice, kindness, and a sense of responsibility.

We are explaining Courtney's behavior in terms of character traits, some of which are traditionally called *virtues* (the good or praiseworthy traits) and others called *vices* (the bad or blameworthy traits).[1] We are at the same time, though, describing Courtney and evaluating him. We could apply general terms such as right/wrong and good/bad, and say that Courtney was a bad man and that he did what is morally wrong. However, we could also apply what have been called *thick* moral concepts as virtue and vice terms and say that Courtney was greedy, cruel, lacking compassion, and dishonest and that he did things that were cruel, dishonest, and so on. Thus, we can apply virtue and vice terms both to people and to actions. We can speak of cruel people and cruel acts (or acts of cruelty).

THE DALAI LAMA

Both utilitarianism and Kant's Categorical Imperative rely on rules for making moral decisions and judgments. But according to the Dalai Lama, spiritual leader of Tibetan Buddhism, "no one should suppose it could ever be possible to devise a set of rules or laws to provide us with the answer to every ethical dilemma. . . . Such a formulaic approach could never hope to capture the richness and diversity of human experience."[2] (This is a point also made by Aristotle.)

The Dalai Lama suggests an approach to moral judgment and action that instead of applying moral laws and rules focuses on virtues and vices. The point is that in any situation we should act as people who are virtuous (who have the virtues and lack the vices) would act. According to the Dalai Lama, the virtues or positive traits include compassion, empathy, love, concern for others and sensitivity to their suffering, patience, kindness, humility, gentleness, affection, tolerance, forgiveness, generosity, warm-heartedness, self-discipline and self-restraint, and altruism. Vices or negative traits include hatred, anger, pride, lust, greed, envy, indifference to the suffering of others, bias, cruelty, violence, selfishness, and inconsiderateness.

If we apply a virtue or vice term to a person, we are attributing a specific *character trait* to that person. A character trait is a disposition to act, think, and feel certain things under certain specified conditions. For example, a person who is cruel has the tendency or disposition to intentionally cause people to suffer, to want people to suffer, and to feel pleasure from causing suffering. The cruel person almost surely lacks such feelings or emotions as compassion, sympathy, guilt, and remorse. Similarly, an honest person has the tendency always or almost always to tell the truth, even in circumstances where he or she would benefit from lying, desires to tell the truth, and has such feelings as guilt or remorse if she lies. Finally, as we will see below, according to contemporary philosopher John McDowell, virtues and vices affect the way we perceive and constitute a kind of "sensitivity" to features of the world.

Acts that exemplify a virtue are, insofar as they exemplify that trait, morally right, whereas acts that exemplify vices, insofar as they exemplify that trait, are morally wrong. Alternatively, we might say that the fact that an action exemplifies a virtuous trait is a reason for thinking it's morally right, whereas the fact that an action exemplifies a vicious trait is a reason for thinking it's morally wrong.

One important question in morality is, "What kind of person should I be (or strive to be)?" The kind of person you are depends on what character traits you have or lack. (The question "What kind of person should I be?" naturally raises the companion question, "What kind of person am I?" Answering that question accurately requires a great deal of self-knowledge, and it's not always easy to achieve self-knowledge. We can engage in self-deception.)

One philosophical problem we face in employing concepts of virtue and vice is that of identifying which traits are virtues and which are vices. Another problem is to specify what makes a trait a virtue or vice. If cruelty is a vice, why is it a vice? If kindness is a virtue, what makes it a virtue?

Which Are the Virtues, Which Are the Vices?

The following table lists traits that almost everyone today considers virtues and traits that almost everyone considers vices. We can call it the commonsense view of virtue and vice.

Moral Virtues

Compassion	Integrity	Patriotism	Sincerity
Courage	Justice	Politeness	Strength
Faithfulness	Kindness	Prudence	Tactfulness
Generosity	Loyalty	Reliability	Tolerance
Gratitude	Mercifulness	Responsibility	Trustworthiness
Honesty	Modesty	Self-control	Unselfishness
Humility	Open-mindedness	Self-reliance	Being loving
Independence	Patience	Self-respect	Sensitivity

Moral Vices

Arrogance	Greed	Jealousy	Shamelessness
Callousness	Ignorance	Laziness	Tactlessness
Cowardice	Impatience	Manipulativeness	Unreliability
Cruelty	Imprudence	Mercilessness	Unscrupulousness
Dishonesty	Ingratitude	Prejudice	Untrustworthiness
Disloyalty	Insincerity	Promiscuity	Weakness
Envy	Intolerance	Rudeness	Self-absorption
Faithlessness	Irascibility	Selfishness	Insensitivity
Fanaticism	Irresponsibility	Servility	

ARISTOTLE ON VIRTUE

What makes one trait a moral virtue and another a moral vice? One view is that virtues and vices are identified in terms of benefit and harm. There are at least three possibilities. One is that a virtue benefits its possessor and a vice harms her. Thus, according to this view, if courage is a virtue, it is because it is in one's self-interest to be courageous, and if cowardice is a vice, it is because it is contrary to one's self-interest to be cowardly. A second possibility is that a virtue benefits others whereas a vice harms others. According to this view, if kindness is a virtue, it is because it leads its possessor to benefit others, and if cruelty is a vice, it is because it leads its possessor to harm others. Finally, a third view is that virtues benefit both their possessors and others, whereas vices harm both their possessors and others.

One of the earliest and most influential theories of virtue is that of the Greek philosopher Aristotle (384–322 B.C.E.). Aristotle said that virtues are character traits it's good for a human being to have, good in the sense of contributing to their possessors' well-being or happiness. In his view, a virtue (many translators prefer the term *excellence*) is a character trait that helps its possessor achieve happiness or a state of well-being; it helps its possessor "flourish." On the other hand, a vice makes it more difficult for its possessor to achieve happiness or a satisfactory state of well-being.

For Aristotle and other ancient Greeks, the point of ethical reflection is to achieve happiness, advance our own interests, or attain what is good or best for us. There are, then, two major issues to confront. First, what is most likely to make us happy? Second, how can we get what is most likely to make us happy?

Happiness/Eudaimonia

According to Aristotle, what we do and should seek is our own happiness. But *happiness* doesn't quite capture the concept Aristotle employs, *eudaimonia*. When we speak of happiness, we could be referring to fleeting temporary states. For example, we could say that eating ice cream or watching a football game makes us happy. Eudaimonia, however, is a state that doesn't apply to a person merely at a specific moment in his or her life. Rather, it applies to the entire course of one's life. We cannot say that you have achieved eudaimonia during the three hours you are watching a football game, even though we might say that you were happy while you were watching it. Instead, whether you achieved the state of eudaimonia depends on the overall course of your entire life.

It is easiest to see what Aristotle has in mind if we imagine someone near death reflecting on the life she has lived. She might ask herself whether she had a good life. She wouldn't necessarily mean a morally good life. It is more plausible to think of her asking herself whether her life worth living, whether it was meaningful and satisfying, whether it had in it enough of the things she values, such as love, achievement, joy, contentment, excitement, or pleasure. She might ask herself what she would do differently if she had her life to live over again. If she would not make many changes in her life, she might say that she had achieved a life that exemplified eudaimonia.

According to Aristotle, most people try to achieve eudaimonia by focusing their lives on getting either pleasure, wealth, or honor (fame). (I will revert to using the concept of happiness, with the warning that it does not refer to a psychological state that one can be in during relatively short spans of time.) He thinks they are mistaken about what constitutes the good life for a human being, mistaken about what brings what we might call genuine, long-lasting happiness. As one of the earliest systematic biologists, Aristotle thought in terms of the concept of *flourishing*. Biologists ask under what conditions members of a certain species or subspecies flourish. Obviously, it's good for a living organism to flourish, but what constitutes flourishing depends on its species. Aristotle asked under what conditions a human being will flourish, just as he might ask under what conditions a deer or lion will flourish.

Flourishing

Compare a flourishing rose bush with a flourishing cactus. A rose bush is flourishing if it has a lot of bright colored flowers and vibrant green stems. A flourishing cactus (at least of certain varieties) doesn't flower. Something is flourishing if it is as "normal members of its kind are." We also can say that it is actualizing its full potential, determined by the kind of thing it is. (We saw this above in Philippa Foot's contribution to natural law theory.) The conditions that enable a rose bush to flourish differ markedly from the conditions that enable a cactus to flourish. Give a cactus as much water as a rose bush needs and it will die from too much water. Give a rose bush as much water as a cactus needs and it will die from too little water.

According to Aristotle, we also can talk meaningfully of a human being flourishing or not flourishing. Humans are members of the same species. Therefore, a human who is in a state or condition normal or natural for her species, or who can do the kinds of things members of her species can do, flourishes. Human flourishing isn't like rose bush flourishing. We don't grow a profusion of flowers on our bodies if we're flourishing. Perhaps we can understand what human flourishing is by focusing on what is contrary to flourishing.

If a child is malnourished, its growth will be stunted. He will be shorter and weigh less than he has the potential for. His intellectual capacities will be affected, so that here, too, he will not reach his full potential. He will have less energy than he could have and be lethargic. His immune system will be suppressed, so that he will be more susceptible to disease. He may go blind. He probably will have a shorter life span than he could have. He is not flourishing in that many aspects of his full potential are blocked or compromised.

If a child is abused or neglected by her caretakers, she may be unable to form close attachments to people. She may be unable to trust people, may feel little pity, kindness, or compassion, and may feel insecure or hostile.

A flourishing human, then, is and can do what a "normal" human can be and do. First is physical survival. She can live at least to an average age. She can also reach her full physical potential. If one is genetically programmed to be far shorter or taller than average, that doesn't necessarily mean one isn't flourishing if it does not shorten one's life or make one feel negative emotions on account of it. But if one's sensory capacities are less acute than the average, it generally detracts from flourishing. People who are blind or deaf are generally thought to be missing something valuable. They cannot see a sunset or hear a piece of music. People who cannot smell lose many pleasures and enjoyments, from the sweet smell of a rose to the taste of their dinner. If someone's tactile senses are affected, he may fail to feel pain that warns of damage and wind up losing parts of himself, and get no pleasure from sex.

"Normal" humans can walk and run; can see, hear, taste, smell, and feel; can understand a language and speak, read, and write; can understand a joke and see humor in a situation; can remember facts and experiences; can recognize different people; can count, and add, multiply, and divide, and solve basic mathematical problems; can feel such emotions as sorrow and joy, love and hate, pride, self-respect, and fear; and can form attachments to other people. These are aspects of human flourishing. They are valuable. Anything that interferes with or diminishes one's capacities for or enjoyment of these things, such as undue restrictions on liberty or constant pain or discomfort, interferes with human flourishing.

Aristotle claimed that we have not achieved genuine happiness if it depends on anything that can be taken away from us. In part, that's because we will always be subject to fear and insecurity over the possible loss of what's necessary or important for our happiness. And he thought that we take things to be necessary for happiness that aren't, such as wealth, power, fame, and physical pleasure. Then too, pursuing pleasure, wealth, fame, and power can have unhappy consequences. We can become jaded with these things and discover that they do not bring the happiness and contentment that we expect from them. How many people have attained their heart's desire of wealth, fame, or power only to feel it turn to dust and ashes in their hands? Pursuit or attainment of these things can also bring unpleasant side effects. The pleasure of drink can lead to a hangover; the pleasure of sex can lead to diseases such as AIDS; wealth and power can bring a host of false friends and real enemies.

According to Aristotle, we are rational animals; therefore, reason—the only thing that separates us from other animals, such as cows, pigs, and horses—is most central to our flourishing. He said that the maximally happy life for a human is a life devoted to what he called *contemplation*. What does contemplation include? First, Aristotle says that humans have an innate desire to know and learn. Contemplation involves acquiring knowledge; we are a curious species. We want to know how things work, why things happen as they do, what the truth is about a variety of things. Finding the answers to our questions—satisfying our curiosity—brings us happiness. Ignorance is frustrating. But ignorance and misinformation are dangerous as well. For example, if I don't know that rivers flood during intense rain storms, I may build my house in a place prone to flooding and lose everything, including my life. Then there are the joys of reading and thinking. As an intellectual, Aristotle was especially sensitive to these as sources of pleasure and happiness.

When Aristotle said that a life of contemplation is the best life for a human being, he probably did not mean that contemplation alone is sufficient for human happiness. Rather, his point perhaps was that a human being cannot live a fully human life without the activities of contemplation and that these activities should play a central role in a human being's life. Whatever other goods human beings pursue should be consistent with and not opposed to reason. Finally, other goods, such as wealth, power, attractiveness, friends, and prestige or fame, should be put into perspective. Although they are goods, they are not the highest good. They should not come to dominate a person's life, nor should they be pursued in a way that interferes with the highest activities of the rational soul. In order for us to flourish, then, all parts of our human nature must come into play and all the needs based on our human nature must be met. These include biological, social, and mental. But for Aristotle, the needs of reason are most central.

Virtue, Vice, and Flourishing

According to Aristotle, certain character traits make it more likely that we will flourish, while other traits makes it less likely that we will flourish. Traits that contribute to our flourishing are virtues; traits that detract from our flourishing are vices. Knowledge of the character traits that are most and least likely to promote flourishing can provide us with at least the outline of a blueprint or recipe for achieving a happy life. We are most likely to achieve happiness over the course of our whole lives if we have as many of the virtues and as few of the vices as possible. Alternatively, we are most likely to achieve happiness over the course of our entire lives if as many of acts of ours as possible exemplify virtues and as few as possible exemplify vices. Thus, if the trait of kindness will enable us to flourish and the trait of cruelty will not, then kindness is a virtue and cruelty a vice. Alternatively, if kind acts enable us to flourish and cruel acts don't, then kind acts are virtuous acts and cruel acts are vicious acts.

Aristotle thought that flourishing requires that we reach a "golden mean" of neither too much nor too little of the things that are of value to us. For example, we need food, but too much or too little will harm us. Similarly, pleasure may be valuable, but too much can harm us and too little can needlessly deny us something that makes life enjoyable and worth living. Although it may seem odd at first to say it, fear is of value to us because it motivates us to escape from dangerous situations. But we can have too much fear or too little fear. The trick is to determine where on the continuum between too much and too little is the appropriate place to be. According to Aristotle, then, each individual virtue lies in an appropriate mean between too much and too little of something. This is a reason for connecting virtue to knowledge. Virtue involves the knowledge of where the appropriate mean is.

According to Aristotle, the following traits are virtues: courage, temperance, liberality (generosity), proper pride, good temper, ready wit, modesty, and justice. Aristotle does not claim that these are the only virtues, only that they are some of the virtues. They enable us to flourish and achieve happy lives. *Courage* lies in a mean between having too much fear and too little fear. The courageous person knows what should and should not be feared, and how much fear is appropriate. The courageous person acts on that knowledge in the sense that she feels only the appropriate amount of fear for the appropriate things, and she behaves in ways appropriate to the situation. She doesn't lose her head and act foolishly, increasing her danger, nor does she act in a foolhardy way by ignoring the danger.

Briefly, *temperance* is having moderate desires for physical pleasures and acting in moderate ways with respect to pleasure. For example, a temperate person eats, drinks, and engages in sex neither too much nor too little; desires for these things are neither too strong nor too weak. As for *liberality,* a liberal person gives and wants to give neither too much nor too little to others. Someone with *proper pride* thinks neither too much nor too little of herself and avoids the extremes of arrogance and obsequiousness. A person with *good temper* is neither too quick nor too slow to anger. This person is not quarrelsome, but also will not let people walk all over her. Someone with *ready wit* is not a clown always ready with a joke to make people laugh, but rather is a good conversationalist. He or she has interesting things to say and says them well. *Modesty* is related to proper pride. A modest person does not exaggerate deeds or abilities, does not brag, and is not arrogant. But neither does this person deflate his or her deeds or abilities either. As for *justice*, a just person gives people what they are due or owed. We might also say that a just person does not violate others' rights.

We tend to think that virtues and vices come in pairs. For example, courage is paired with cowardice, temperance with self-indulgence, honesty with dishonesty, and so on. However, Aristotle maintained that when thinking of traits as virtues and vices, we must think of triples. Every virtue is a mean between two vices, which are extremes, too much or too little of something (the *golden mean*). For example, as we saw, courage is a mean between feeling too much and too little fear. Aristotle warns us that the mean is not the exact middle. The mean is what is appropriate according to reason. The standard of appropriateness is human flourishing, and it is reason that discovers where between two extremes we are most likely to flourish. Think of honesty, a virtue according to common-sense morality. (Even though Aristotle doesn't list it among his virtues, he probably would agree that it is a virtue.) Too little honesty—either lying or concealing our thoughts—will alienate people, making it more difficult to satisfy our social needs. But too much honesty—absolute truthfulness and openness (revealing all our thoughts)—will also alienate people. If I reveal it to people every time I don't like the clothes they're wearing or their hair style, I will alienate them. Many people also approve of "little white lies" intended to protect people's feelings. Suppose the person you love asks you if you think he or she is overweight. If you think your partner is overweight, but you also know that he is very sensitive about it, admitting that you think he's overweight will hurt him. It's obvious that he's looking for reassurance. Many people would think that you should lie. If virtue is a mean between two extremes, then we should be honest and open only to the extent or degree that it will enable us to flourish. How much truth and openness will maximize our chances of flourishing must be found out by reason.

Temperance is also a mean between two extremes, according to Aristotle. We can want too much physical pleasure, but we can also want too little physical pleasure. The person who wants too much physical pleasure eats and drinks too much, becomes promiscuous or engages in unsafe sex, or becomes addicted to alcohol, cigarettes, or drugs. Such behavior will adversely affect his or her health, and will probably shorten his or her life. On the other hand, a person who denies himself all physical pleasures will deny himself often harmless experiences and activities that would make his life more pleasant and rich. Imagine never allowing ourselves to have good-tasting food, a hot bath, or other harmless physical pleasures. Aristotle finds nothing admirable in such behavior because there is no good reason to deny oneself all physical pleasures. The virtue of temperance involves a mean between overindulgence and underindulgence in physical pleasures. When physical pleasures become unhealthy or addictive, they should not be pursued. But if they are not unhealthy, addictive, or otherwise harmful, they may be pursued. Again, it takes the judgment of reason to know where the mean between overindulgence and underindulgence lies.

Aristotle includes justice among the virtues. How does justice help its possessor flourish and how is it a mean between two extremes? If you are just, doesn't that primarily benefit others? According to Aristotle, a just person treats people who are equal in relevant respects in the same way, and people unequal in relevant respects differently. We also might think of the just person as giving people what they deserve and respecting others' rights. For example, if you discriminate against people on the basis of irrelevant characteristics—say, by refusing to hire a black applicant simply because she is black—you are behaving unjustly. Blacks and whites are equal in what is relevant to consideration for jobs, yet you are treating them differently. Obviously, if someone has the character trait of being just, it benefits others because the just person will not oppress or exploit others or otherwise unjustifiably harm them.

Aristotle concedes that justice benefits others. Does it also benefit its possessor, or does it harm its possessor? We are all familiar with the cynical slogans "Nice guys finish last," and "No good deed goes unpunished." Sometimes it seems that injustice pays better than justice, that vice pays better than virtue. Those who rise to the top in business and politics often seem to be ruthless and unscrupulous. But Aristotle thought differently. He thought that being just to others benefits the just person in the long run, and that being unjust to others harms the unjust person in the long run.

Injustice alienates those who are treated unjustly. They will try to retaliate. At the very least they will avoid the unjust person. And even people who are not themselves treated unjustly will, if they know of the injustice, avoid the unjust person and strongly disapprove of his or her behavior. They will know that they cannot trust him or feel confident that he will not treat them unjustly. (Would you want to do business with someone you believe to be unjust?) Therefore, an unjust person will have few if any people who are genuine friends or who like or love him, and can never feel secure that he or she is invulnerable to retaliation. Of course, an unjust person may think that unjust acts will go undetected and unpunished, but that cannot be guaranteed. Also, because human beings are social animals, we depend on others; we cannot flourish outside a society or community. Injustice injures the community, whereas justice strengthens it. If most people behaved unjustly to each other, they could not live together in peace and harmony, and they could not maintain a community. Those who injure their community ultimately injure themselves.

On the other hand, the just person has nothing to fear. Being just will make that person many genuine friends and few enemies. He or she will be loved and respected, rather than feared and hated. Business dealings and political aspirations will prosper. Although it is possible that a just person could appear to others to be unjust or that an unjust person could appear to be just, it is highly unlikely in the long run. Aristotle concerns himself with the happiness of our lives as a whole over the long run.

However, even if it is true that wealth, power, and fame come more readily to the unjust than to the just (which is debatable), Aristotle did not think that wealth, power, and fame are important ingredients of flourishing or well-being.

In fact, they sometimes seem to interfere with flourishing. If we have these things, we often fear losing them and feel insecure. We lack peace of mind. If we don't have them, we may strive so hard to acquire them that we sacrifice all other ingredients of flourishing, such as love and friendship, or we may feel deeply dissatisfied with our lives because we have not acquired them.

One possible difficulty for Aristotle's account is that the traits he focuses on may be most conducive to flourishing *as a free citizen in 4th century* B.C.E. *Athens*. But Aristotle clearly intended his account to be more universally applicable than that. One question, then, is whether the traits he identifies as virtues will help us flourish whether we are living in the fourth century B.C.E. or the twenty-first century C.E., whether we are living in Athens or in the United States.

Virtues and Vices as Guides to Action

For Aristotle, knowledge of which traits are virtues and which are vices (or which acts are virtuous and which are vicious) provides guidance. First, it provides us with guidance on what kind of person to be. We should try to acquire and keep the virtuous traits and extinguish the vicious traits. It also provides us with guidance on how to act. In any situation, we should try to act as a virtuous person would act. Knowing about the virtues, we will know what virtue is called for in any given situation. If we know what virtue is called for, we should try to behave the way someone with that virtue would behave. For example, if I'm in a burning building, I will know that courage is called for and I should try to behave the way a courageous person would behave. On the other hand, I know that loyalty is called for in friendship. Therefore, I should try to behave toward friends the way a loyal person would behave. Knowing about loyalty, I know that a loyal person would not betray the confidences of a friend behind his back.

THE UNITY OF VIRTUE

Can someone have just one virtue in an otherwise vicious character? Socrates, the teacher of Plato, who in turn was the teacher of Aristotle, thought that the virtues come in a package—we either have all of them or none. If we have one, we have them all. This has seemed highly implausible to many philosophers, but if we take a modest view and say that if we have any virtues, then we have all or most of the rest at least to some degree, it may seem more plausible. We asked above whether courage could lead to wrong action, where, for example, we might speak of the courage of a train robber. Aristotle thought that a virtue could not lead to wrong action, so whatever it is that the train robber has should not be called courage. There may be a connection between this thought and the idea of the unity of the virtues (we have all or none). A vicious person who does vicious things cannot be said to have the single virtue of courage. Similarly, suppose a person is disloyal. If she acts disloyally, is she likely nevertheless to be honest? Disloyalty often requires deception—efforts to seem loyal when one is not.

The virtues do seem to be connected in some way. It's difficult to imagine that someone could be kind yet dishonest, or trustworthy yet irresponsible, or sensitive yet self-absorbed. Character traits may not be entirely independent of each other. For example, consider once more the toxic pharmacist, Robert Courtney. What specific virtues might it be plausible to attribute to him?

Before moving on, let's look more carefully at the nature of some of the traditional virtues.

Compassion

According to most religious tradition, as well as commonsense morality, compassion is one of the most important virtues. For example, the Dalai Lama emphasizes compassion as a fundamental virtue. Similarly, Jesus both exemplifies compassion and urges us to be compassionate. The gospels frequently describe him as feeling compassion, especially for the weak, helpless, and despised, as well as for those not considered "respectable" by the world's standards. Jesus tried to teach his followers to be compassionate or act compassionately. Surely the story of the good Samaritan is meant to teach us to be compassionate. Those without compassion passed by the man who had been beaten and robbed and lay unconscious on the ground. The Samaritan who helped him had compassion for his plight.

We can see what the absence of compassion leads to. Obviously, Robert Courtney lacked compassion for his victims, which made it easier for him to dilute their medications. The Nazis had no compassion for Jews, which made it easier for them to try to annihilate them. But what is compassion?

If we have the character trait of compassion, we have the tendency to have unpleasant feelings when we are aware of other people's suffering. We are not indifferent to or unaffected by their suffering, and we are not made happy, glad, or satisfied by it. In a sense we share in their suffering; we ourselves suffer if we are aware of others' suffering.

What the compassionate person does in light of the unpleasant feelings is crucial. In order to escape or avoid unpleasant feelings, we could close our eyes and ears, and turn away. But that's not compassion. If we are compassionate, we don't simply want to stop feeling bad; we want to stop or reduce the other person's suffering. It is that which will make us feel better, not turning away and forgetting about it. So compassionate people have a desire to relieve others' suffering and generally act to relieve suffering.

Compassionate people seem to perceive the world differently from people who lack compassion, as McDowell points out. Take Robert Courtney. Because he lacked compassion, he probably did not see the harm and suffering he caused. When he looked at his customers, perhaps he saw money, not people. It's hard to imagine that he would have diluted the medications of his customers had he perceived them the way a compassionate person would have perceived them.[3] A compassionate person is, as McDowell would say, sensitive to the suffering in the world. The compassionate person is attentive to it, is not blind to it. And the compassionate person views the fact that someone is suffering as a reason to act to relieve that suffering.

Similarly, take a Nazi concentration camp guard. If he were compassionate, how would he perceive the helpless tormented Jews in his custody? Again, it's hard to imagine that the guard could see the Jews the same way a compassionate person would see them. Perhaps the guard lacking compassion perceived the Jews as little more than lice or vermin, and simply did not see their suffering.

Courage

A courageous person has the tendency to neither exaggerate nor minimize the magnitude of the danger she faces in any given situation. For example, a courageous person recognizes that she is in great danger if she has fallen into a ravine with hungry lions but not much danger if she has fallen into a ravine with poison ivy. (As with compassion, courage seems to affect how we perceive situations.) Courage also has to do with our feelings of fear in a situation of perceived danger. With a courageous person, the magnitude of the fear she feels is appropriate to the magnitude of the danger she faces. It would be a mistake to think that a courageous person never feels fear. Of course she does. But she doesn't feel great fear in situations of little danger, or little fear in situations of great danger.

Another aspect of courage involves our response to the fear we're feeling. Even if the magnitude of our fear is appropriate to the magnitude of the danger we face, how our fear affects our actions matters. Suppose that a firefighter is trapped in a burning building and feels intense fear. If the fear makes him lose his head and do foolish things likely to reduce his chances of survival, he lacks courage. If instead of panicking, he thinks carefully, examines his situation, and acts in ways that offer him some hope of saving himself, that's courageous. A courageous person does not feel more fear than the circumstances warrant, and does not act inappropriately because of his fear.

Did Robert Courtney have courage, or was he a coward? Did it take courage to dilute the medications knowing that there was a danger of getting caught and punished? The fact that he did it in secret surely would suggest that he was not courageous, but there is also an issue brought up by Socrates, who thought that if a character trait is a genuine virtue, it can never lead its possessor to act wrongly. Thus, even if there was danger and Courtney felt an appropriate amount of fear, but acted despite the fear, Socrates would say that isn't courage. It is courage only when we act rightly, as we should.

Self-Control/Self-Discipline

Self-control or self-discipline can seem quite paradoxical. The person doing the controlling and the person being controlled, or the person doing the disciplining and the person being disciplined, are the same person. What sense can we make of that?

Let's consider situations where we feel tempted to bring up issues of self-control. Suppose that someone is always going on diets and is always violating them. She wants to lose weight, and she doesn't want to succumb to the temptations she feels to overeat. However, she almost always succumbs to those temptations. For example, when she sees a piece of chocolate cake, she is ambivalent and feels conflict. She wants to eat it, yet at the same time, she doesn't want to eat it. Unfortunately, when she sees chocolate cake, the desire to eat it is generally stronger than the desire not to. But after she eats the cake, she feels angry and disappointed with herself. Because we think that it is more reasonable to refrain from eating cake when we have a weight problem, we say that she lacks self-control. If she had self-control, she would not act on the desire to eat cake.

Similarly, suppose that someone has a bad temper. He gets angry easily and when he gets angry, he becomes violent, damaging property and hurting people. Because we think that it is not reasonable to damage property and hurt people when we're angry, we say that he lacks self-control.

Probably the most common way of explaining the trait of self-control is to speak of different parts of a person. If we say that one part of a person controls another, it's not exactly the same thing that is both controlling and controlled. In the case of the dieter, one part of her desires to lose weight, go on a diet, and stick to it. But in situations of temptation, another part of her wants to gorge herself on foods that violate her diet. In the case of the man with the bad temper, we could say that part of him could and should control the part of him that gets angry too easily and too intensely.

According to the ancient Greeks, there's a part of a person that reasons or thinks and a part that feels. According to this view in its most general form, reason is the part that thinks, while another part enables us to have such feelings and emotions as the pleasurable sensations we get from having sex, eating, and drinking; desires for pleasurable sensations (such as lust); anger or rage; and love or hate. Either our reason rules our behavior or our feelings and emotions rule our behavior. The Greek ideal was to have reason always rule (controlling behavior) and feelings and emotions to be ruled. In part this was because in their view, reason takes into consideration our long-term interests, whereas feelings and emotions demand instant gratification regardless of the long-term consequences. Reason recognizes that our goal should be happiness over the course of our entire lives, not just for the moment.

According to this view, someone's desire to lose weight by dieting comes from her reason. Her reason understands that in the long run she will be healthier and happier if she loses weight and keeps it off. But her feelings and emotions disregard this. Because of that part of her, she has a strong urge or desire immediately to eat chocolate cake when she sees it, regardless of the long-term consequences. As for the man with a short fuse, his anger and rage come from his feelings and emotions. His reason should (and probably does) understand that when his behavior is ruled by his anger or rage, he often does things contrary to his long-term interests, things that either are self-destructive or destructive to others. He may break a window or television; then he has to pay for it. He may hit a wall with his fist, injuring his hand. He may injure other people, leading to trouble with the law. For example, in a moment of "road rage," a man reached into the car of a driver who had provoked him, grabbed her little dog from the seat beside her, and threw it into oncoming traffic on the highway. The dog was killed. The man went to jail for it.

Similarly, consider people in the grip of addictions, for example, an alcoholic or a drug addict. The individual may wish to refrain from drinking or using drugs but in moments of temptation, simultaneously wish to drink or use drugs. We might say that reason, which looks to the long term, produces the desire to refrain from drinking or using drugs. This desire is long lasting. It is not a desire of the moment that may disappear as suddenly as it arose. It may extend over the person's whole life. The desire to drink or use drugs, on the other hand, is produced by feelings and emotions. It is transitory. It comes and goes. Sometimes it lasts for an hour, other times for a day or a week. Sometimes there are years between episodes of having the desire to drink or use drugs; at other times, it's only a matter of days or hours. We might say that if the addict has self-control, reason will rule, leading to resistance to drink or use drugs. If reason is not in control, his feelings and emotions will rule and he will succumb to the temptation. (We might also speak of "higher" and "lower" selves. Our higher self puts our long-term happiness before short-term happiness, but our higher self also tries to live up to the requirements of morality.)

So far, we have described self-control as a matter of reason, rather than feeling and emotion ruling our behavior. But we often talk of people controlling their own thoughts, feelings, and desires, not just their actions. For example, we might talk of a dieter having so much self-control that she has extinguished her desire for chocolate cake so that she isn't even tempted when she sees it. Similarly, we could talk of someone having so much self-control that he no longer even feels anger in circumstances where once he would have felt intense rage. Again, it is one part of the mind controlling another: reason controlling the very nature and existence of our desires, feelings, and emotions, not just supplanting them as ruler of our behavior.

We also sometimes talk of someone controlling his own thoughts. Suppose that you have a fear of flying. If you are in an airplane, you have intense visual images of a crash. Surely you don't *want* to feel this fear, and you don't *want* to have these disturbing images. But sometimes we say that we can't help it. We have the fear and the frightening images even though we don't want to have them. But suppose that by an act of will, you are able to stop having the frightening images. We might say that you have self-control if you can keep the frightening images out of your mind and that you lack self-control if you can't. And once more, we might explain it by saying that your reason controls your thoughts when you can keep the images out of your mind.

Reason generally controls behavior, thoughts, and feelings with a self-controlled person; reason does not with a person who lacks self-control. But self-control is a matter of degree. (Do you think that Robert Courtney had self-control?)

Arrogance

An arrogant person has a very high opinion of himself and feels superior to most people. We should say that an arrogant person is arrogant *about* something. A person can be arrogant about looks, intelligence, wealth, fame, talent, birth, and so on, thinking that with respect to that characteristic, he or she is superior to others. Of course, one is generally arrogant about only things that are highly valued in one's society (and when one shares those values). In our society, for example, it's unlikely that someone would be arrogant about being unemployed, as though that is a form of superiority. For example, aristocrats in eighteenth- and nineteenth-century Britain were arrogant about their "noble" birth or blood, and the superior intellect and taste they thought came with it, so that they felt vastly superior to "commoners," no matter how wealthy.

Arrogance about one valued characteristic often spreads in a person's psyche. Consider a great conductor who believes (correctly) that he is superior to most others in his conducting ability. He may then come to believe that he is superior to others in almost every way that counts. He may believe he is superior in culture, wisdom, judgment, manners, looks, importance, social value, and so on. He may come to believe that he is perfect. (Arrogance frequently is linked with self-deception. It is often the case that people aren't really superior in the ways they think they are. They often fail to see their flaws, imperfections, and limitations.)

Arrogance affects behavior. An arrogant person behaves arrogantly. For example, most aristocrats in eighteenth- and nineteenth-century Britain refused to socialize or intermarry with commoners. Sometimes arrogance comes out in both verbal and nonverbal behavior. It may manifest itself in tones of voice that are patronizing or peremptory, or in disdainful sneers. It may manifest itself in words, as with an abusive husband who tells his wife that she's worthless.

A person who is not arrogant does not consider herself superior to others even if in important ways that person really *is* superior. Or, if she recognizes superiority in one area, she minimizes its importance and does not allow it to spread within the psyche.

Arrogance, then, is first a matter of belief and feeling. It then may lead to (but doesn't have to lead to) behavior that reveals the belief in one's superiority and others' inferiority. But then, here is another example where virtues and vices affect how we perceive ourselves and the world. An arrogant person surely does not see himself or others the way a more humble person sees herself.

Selfishness/Self-Absorption

A selfish person focuses on and is primarily or exclusively interested in himself or herself, rarely about other people except as ways to the achievement of his or her ends. If we're selfish, we tend to ignore the interests and desires of others. Almost all of a selfish person's desires are for good things for that individual, rarely good things for others (unless it also provides good things for him). It may be that selfishness involves valuing our own good more than the average person and valuing the good of others less than the average person. Alternatively, it may involve valuing our own good more than we *should* and valuing the good of others less than we *should*.

What ways of behaving are characteristic of selfishness? A selfish person spends almost all his or her time trying to satisfy desires for good things and trying to promote and protect selfish interests instead of other peoples' interests. A selfish person often acts in ways that harm others. For example, a selfish person may think only about his or her own sexual pleasure and ignores the partner's need for pleasure.

Responsibility

We call some people responsible and others irresponsible. For example, suppose that a babysitter spends all his time on the telephone and doesn't pay any attention to the small child he's paid to watch. While he's on the telephone, the child begins to draw with his crayons on the dining room wall. When the parents come home, they find the dining room wall covered in crayon drawings. They probably would call the babysitter irresponsible. On the other hand, suppose that in writing her first letter applying for a job, a young woman stresses that she is a very responsible person. What does she mean?

The babysitter is irresponsible because he had duties as a babysitter that he neglected. He had a duty to monitor the child's activities and pay attention to what the child was doing, as well as to pay attention to the child's health and safety. By talking on the telephone the whole time, he showed that he didn't take his responsibilities seriously; he didn't make the slightest effort to do what he had a duty to do and probably didn't think for even a moment of what his duties were.

On the other hand, the young lady who wrote in her letter of application that she is a very responsible person is telling the prospective employer that she would take her duties as an employee, whatever they may be, very seriously. She will think about her duties so that she knows what they are, and she will try hard to make sure that she does whatever is her duty. That seems to entail that as a responsible person, she has a desire to do her duty. Her being a responsible person goes far beyond her job, of course. If she is a very responsible person, we might imagine that she fulfills her duties as a student: she turns school assignments in on time, prepares for her classes, and doesn't cheat. Similarly, we might imagine that she fulfills her duties as a member of a family—as a daughter or sister. For example, she might do her assigned chores around the house without having to be constantly reminded. If she's going to be home much later than she said she would be, she will call to let her parents know so that they won't worry. She won't lie to her parents or intentionally break the rules they have set for her.

So far, we've said that a responsible person thinks about what his or her duties are, has a desire to do his or her duty, and strives to do what he or she has a duty to do. We can also say that a responsible person *takes* responsibility for his or her actions. One part of taking responsibility involves causal responsibility. Suppose that Tim causes an accident by suddenly swerving into the lane on his right while driving at high speed on the highway. Tim hadn't been paying attention because he was talking on his cell phone, almost missed his exit, and swerved to get off the highway before passing his exit. Suppose that after the accident he's questioned by police and insists it wasn't his fault, although he knows it was. He is not taking responsibility; he is not acknowledging the causal role his actions played. Suppose that doesn't work. Next, he might invent false excuses, such as "The sun blinded me." Or he might invent mitigating circumstances that lessen his blameworthiness, such as "I was racing to the hospital because my son was in an accident and is in critical condition."

A person who takes responsibility would do none of these things; he or she would acknowledge that it was his or her fault.

EPICUREANS

Aristotle denied that pleasure is the highest good for a human being. Hedonists disagree. According to hedonism, what makes life worth living—the secret of happiness—is pleasure. Hedonists claim that only pleasure is intrinsically good and only pain is intrinsically bad. All other good things are good only because they increase pleasure (or decrease pain), and all other bad things are bad only because they increase pain (or decrease pleasure). Hedonists claim that we achieve happiness and the good life by maximizing pleasures and minimizing pains. The Greek philosopher Epicurus (341–270 B.C.E.), founder of Epicureanism, is perhaps one of the most famous hedonists. Epicurus was a materialist who believed that everything that exists is composed of physical matter, the smallest bit of matter being the atom. Thus, according to Epicurus, the soul, like the body, is physical and composed of atoms, albeit a much finer variety of atoms. At death, when the soul detaches from the body, we cease to exist; all consciousness permanently ceases. Therefore, according to Epicurus, happiness must be achieved while we are alive.

In Epicurus's view, if we are to flourish, we must maximize the pleasure we experience and minimize the pain. However, he distinguished between physical and mental pleasures and pains. Physical pleasures and pains come from the senses; they arise from sight, hearing, taste, touch, and smell. Thus, we should speak of pleasurable or painful sensation. Pleasure from smelling a flower, tasting pepperoni pizza, seeing a sunset, and engaging in sex are all physical pleasures. Pain from stepping on a tack, touching a hot pot, and smelling a skunk are examples of physical pains. Many of us tend to think that if the same term is applied to many things, they must have something in common. For example, all things described as red have the same color. However, since we have five senses and therefore at least five entirely different kinds of sensation, such as sensations of touch, visual sensations, and auditory sensations, we should ask Epicurus what all pleasurable sensations have in common and all painful sensations have in common. It may only be a common attitude toward them.

On the other hand, mental pleasures and pains come from using our minds. Mental pleasures could come from playing chess, reading poetry, acquiring knowledge and understanding, and scoring high on a computer game. Mental pains could include fearing some future calamity, having an unsatisfied desire, and feeling depressed, frustrated, or lonely. Mental pleasures and pains are not pleasurable or painful sensations. How, then, are we to understand the pleasure of reading poetry compared to the pleasure from being loved? In what does the pleasure consist? (These are not questions that Epicurus asked.) Again, perhaps the common feature is the attitude one takes toward them.

Pleasures and pains can be mixed, both physical and mental. Consider the pleasure derived from attending the theater or listening to music. Both appeal to the senses and to the mind. Thus, pleasures and pains may be purely physical, purely mental, or a combination of both physical and mental.

Epicurus believed that two sources of mental pain were particularly acute: fear of the gods and fear of death. People fear the gods because they believe that the gods will bring them evils such as poverty and illness or deny them goods such as wealth and health. Then, too, people fear death, and the anticipation of the nothingness of death spoils their happiness. They especially fear being punished for their misdeeds in the afterlife and spending eternity in pain. In Epicurus's view, banishing these twin fears would do much to increase peace of mind, which brings happiness.

Epicurus taught that there's no reason to fear the gods. He didn't deny that the gods exist; rather, he insisted that the gods don't care about Earth and its human inhabitants. Living a blessed life, the gods are indifferent to what happens on Earth. Thus, they don't reward or punish people for their deeds, they don't answer prayers, and they don't intervene in earthly events. The gods don't act to benefit human beings or to harm them; therefore, there's no reason for human beings to fear them (or worship them).

Epicurus also taught that people shouldn't fear death because when a person dies, he or she ceases to exist and all consciousness permanently ceases. We cannot have painful or pleasurable experiences—in fact, any experiences at all—unless we exist and are conscious. It's not as though when we're dead we suffer or feel fear, frustration, or anger knowing that we're dead. We have no thoughts or feelings. There's nothing after death, just as there was nothing before birth. And just as we did not suffer at all before we were born because we did not exist, we will not suffer after we die because we will no longer exist.

Once people stop fearing death and the gods, they can get on with the business of finding happiness here on Earth while they're alive. Like Aristotle, Epicurus taught that true long-term happiness does not come from dedicating our lives to the more obvious physical pleasures such as those afforded by food, drink, and sex. After all, the pleasure of drunkenness leads to the pain of a hangover and can lead to poor health; the pleasure of unprotected sexual intercourse can lead to venereal diseases and AIDS. Rather, Epicurus taught that true happiness comes from a life of simplicity and moderation devoted to health and peace of mind, for he assumed that tranquility and serenity were the greatest pleasures available. We should strive only to supply ourselves with what is necessary for health and contentment. Desire quickly becomes insatiable if not controlled and moderated, leading to frustration and pain. If we desire money, then if we acquire a million dollars, we soon will want two million, then four million. If we desire fame, then if we're well-known to a hundred people, we want to become well-known to a thousand, then a million. Equally important, Epicurus insisted that satisfying our basic needs does not require nearly as much work as does acquiring luxuries and satisfying desires for a mass of material goods. In his view, the more we want, the more work we must do in order to satisfy those wants. According to Epicurus, work is a source of pain, not pleasure. Therefore, the more wants or desires we have, the more we must work, making us slaves of our desires and setting us on a treadmill of work. The fewer wants or desires we have, the less work is required to satisfy them and the more leisure we have for pleasant activities.

Again like Aristotle, Epicurus stressed that other people are an important source of pleasure. He did not mean the pleasures of exploitation and oppression; rather, he meant the pleasures of friendship, which he considered the most important ingredient of happiness. Loving and being loved are fundamental sources of pleasure; being alone and friendless is a fundamental source of pain. To have friends, you must of course be a friend; you must care about others and treat them with respect if they are to be friends. Even if we derive pleasure from harming others, we should not satisfy the desire to injure others, because if we harm others, we risk being harmed in return. He emphasized that committing injustices banishes the calm tranquility that constitutes true happiness because we will always fear exposure and revenge, and the fear and insecurity are very painful.

If Epicureans, like Aristotle, think in terms of virtues and vices, and consider traits that promote our happiness to be virtues and traits that reduce our happiness to be vices, they would probably agree with many of the virtues and vices of commonsense morality. For example, being loyal will make us happier than being disloyal, because if we are disloyal we may be harmed by those whom we have betrayed and we will not be trusted by those whom we betray. Loyalty will make us less fearful and insecure than disloyalty.

STOICISM

Like Epicureans, Stoics claimed that peace of mind and tranquility are central to happiness. It's not pleasure, excitement, or thrills that bring happiness, but rather tranquility, serenity, internal harmony, and peace of mind. And according to Stoicism, these do not come from the things that most people value and pursue: wealth, power, fame, physical pleasure, attractiveness, health, and so on. Why not? Because such externals are not completely under our control. No matter how hard we try, we cannot do anything to guarantee that we will become or remain wealthy, powerful, famous, healthy, or attractive. If our happiness depends on things over which we have little control, we are bound to be unhappy. For example, suppose that your happiness depends on your wealth. If you won't be happy unless you're rich and there's nothing that you can do that will guarantee that you will become rich, then your happiness is jeopardized. Even if you become rich, there's nothing that you can do to guarantee that you'll remain rich, which will breed fear and insecurity. Tranquility and peace of mind come not from pursuing such externals as wealth and fame but from limiting, controlling, and moderating our desires.

Like Epicureans, Stoics saw desire as addictively demanding. The more we satisfy a desire, the more insistent the demand for continued satisfaction becomes. Suppose that we desire power. If we have power over ten people, we want power over twenty-five; if we have power over twenty-five, we want power over fifty. Because desire is insatiable, people spend ever more time and energy satisfying their uncontrolled and uncontrollable desires, while satisfaction becomes ever more elusive. The danger is that desires will control our lives rather than be controlled. Like many Greeks, such as Plato and Aristotle, Stoics believed that reason should be in control of desire. Reason will control desire primarily by moderating desire. Above all, Stoicism preached the importance of self-control; desire should be carefully controlled by reason.

Stoics believed that the universe is governed by divine law—by reason and intelligence—and that everything that occurs is part of a series of events that was preplanned in the far distant past. Because the universe is governed by reason and intelligence, everything that occurs is good, even if it doesn't appear good to us because we're not familiar with the plan. Therefore, a wise person will be content with whatever occurs, recognizing that it is inevitable and part of the master plan of the universe. To feel regret, anger, disappointment, or frustration about the course of events is unreasonable and virtually guarantees unhappiness. We will be happier and have more peace of mind if we simply accept what occurs. A Stoic will face the world with a sense of calm resignation and acceptance and will therefore be happy, come what may.

Stoics use an arresting image. They compare human beings to a dog tied behind a moving cart. The dog has no control over the cart; it must follow where the cart leads. The dog can either resist and be frustrated over where the cart leads it, thus being forever unhappy, or it can make up its mind to follow along without resistance and be resigned to the inevitable, being contented with whatever path and speed the cart takes. That is, it can desire to go someplace other than where the cart will take it, or it can desire to be in harmony with the cart and desire to go wherever the cart takes it. If the dog takes the latter position, it need never be frustrated or unhappy. Like the dog, human beings are carried along by the course of events over which they have no control. People can resist the inevitable course of events and desire what they don't have, or they can resign themselves to accepting without resentment, despair, or discontent whatever fate has in store for them.

HOBBES AND HUME

The English philosopher Thomas Hobbes (1588–1679) maintained that virtues are those characteristics that enable people to live together in peace and harmony. He claimed that virtues such as gratitude, modesty, equity, and mercy "come to be praised, as the means of peaceable, sociable, and comfortable living."[4] For most virtues, there are corresponding vices. For example, justice, the characteristic of keeping our agreements, is a virtue and its opposite a vice; pride is a vice and its opposite, humility, is a virtue. However, the basis of Hobbes's theory is self-interest. Characteristics that are virtues promote social harmony, but in the long run, it is in an individual's self-interest to have such characteristics. Virtues are beneficial both to others and to their possessors, and they are beneficial to their possessors because they are beneficial to others. Virtues enable an individual to live well and be happy in society; vices prevent a person from living well and being happy in society. (Unlike the ancient Greeks, Hobbes spent little time discussing what will make people happy or what will enable us to flourish.)

The Scottish philosopher David Hume (1711–1776) also claimed that at least some traits are considered virtues because they're beneficial to their possessor and other traits are considered vices because they're harmful to their possessor.

> It seems evident, that where a quality or habit [character trait] is subjected to our examination, if it appear in any respect prejudicial to the person possessed of it, or such as incapacitates him for business and action, it is instantly blamed, and ranked among his faults and imperfections. Indolence, negligence, want of order and method, obstinacy, fickleness, rashness, credulity; these qualities were never esteemed by any one as indifferent to a character, much less, extolled as accomplishments or virtues.[5]

Among virtues, he listed: discretion, caution, frugality, good sense, honesty, fidelity, enterprise, industry, prudence, temperance, sobriety, patience, constancy, perseverance, forethought, considerateness, cheerfulness, and philosophical tranquility.

However, Hume noted that people approve of and consider virtuous those traits that are beneficial to their possessor—even when it's other people who have the traits. In such circumstances, the trait may not be beneficial to the person who judges it to be a virtue. Thus, if Jones considers perseverance (the tendency to persist in undertakings despite setbacks) to be a virtue and if Smith has the trait, Jones will consider Smith's perseverance to be a virtue, even though Jones doesn't benefit from Smith's perseverance. In fact, Jones may benefit from no one's perseverance but his own. If Jones considers perseverance to be a virtue, it's a virtue regardless of whose perseverance it is; therefore, his reason for considering perseverance a virtue is not simply that perseverance is in his self-interest. If self-interest were the only reason for considering a trait to be a virtue, Jones would consider his own perseverance to be a virtue but would not consider perseverance in general to be a virtue. As Hume declared, "Now as these advantages are enjoyed by the person possessed of the character, it can never be self-love which renders the prospect of them agreeable to us, the spectators, and prompts our esteem and approbation."[6]

Like Hobbes, Hume also noted that many traits are considered virtues because they are beneficial to others and promote social harmony. "Whatever conduct promotes the good of the community is loved, praised, and esteemed by the community."[7]

Similarly:

> As the mutual shocks, in society, and the opposition of interest and self-love have constrained mankind to establish the laws of Justice,

> in order to preserve the advantages of mutual assistance and protection: in like manner, the eternal contrarieties, in company, of men's pride and self-conceit, have introduced the rules of Good Manners or Politeness, in order to facilitate the intercourse of minds, and an undisturbed commerce and conversation.[8]

Hume maintained that all human beings have at least some benevolence toward their fellows. Without that sympathy, the view that some traits, whoever has them, are virtues and other traits, whoever has them, are vices could not get off the ground.

> Let us suppose a person originally framed so as to have no manner of concern for his fellow-creatures, but to regard the happiness and misery of all sensible beings with greater indifference than even two contiguous shades of the same colour. . . . Such a person, being absolutely uncon-cerned, either for the public good of a community or the private utility of others, would look on every quality [character trait] however perni-cious, or however beneficial, to society, or to its possessor, with . . . indifference.[9]

Given that we do distinguish between virtues and vices, "[t]here seems here a necessity for confessing that the happiness and misery of others are not spectacles entirely indifferent to us."[10]

> It cannot be disputed that there is some benevolence, however small, infused into our bosom; some spark of friendship for human kind; some particle of the dove kneaded into our frame, along with the elements of the wolf and the serpent. Let these generous sentiments be supposed ever so weak; . . . they must still direct the determinations of our mind, and where everything is equal, produce a cool preference of what is useful and serviceable to mankind, above what is pernicious and dangerous.[11]

According to Hume, everyone naturally has some benevolent feelings toward other human beings; no one is completely indifferent to the happiness or suffering of others. This gives everyone a reason for approving of and con-sidering to be virtues those traits that are beneficial to their possessor or to others, and for disapproving of and considering to be vices those traits that are harmful to their possessor or to others. Hume thought that conceptions of virtue and vice are not based on self-interest but rather on the universal characteristics of benevo-lence and sympathy. Whether everyone naturally has (and retains) such charac-teristics of sympathy and benevolence is an open question.

THE SEVEN DEADLY SINS

Jewish educator and psychologist Solomon Schimmel writes that the conception of seven deadly sins in the Jewish and Christian traditions is an important guide to life that is too often overlooked in contemporary Western society. Although from a theological perspective sin is a transgression of God's demands on us, Schimmel points out that these sins are harmful to their possessor.[12] Therefore, we may think of them as seven deadly vices rather than seven deadly sins if we object to a theological perspective.

The seven deadly sins are: pride, envy, anger, lust, gluttony, greed, and sloth. Pride or arrogance often leads to cruelty and harm to others, which often leads to retribution. In our arrogance, we may demean, humiliate, condescend to, and insult people, even if we do not harm them in other ways. Few of us like arrogant people. In fact, we often despise and avoid them. Sometimes we consider them laughable, even pathetic, especially when their views of themselves are unrealistically high. Pride or arrogance is not a trait likely to bring happiness to its possessor.

When we envy others, we believe that their situation is more favorable in some way than ours and we wish that our situation could be more like theirs. We may have negative feelings about ourselves and negative feelings about the person we envy. We may not be contented and satisfied with ourselves and our lives. As Schimmel points out, our envy gives us far more pain than it does the person we're envious of. And others who sense our envy may come to despise or fear us. Envy may cause us to act in spiteful ways. Acts that exemplify envy are almost never admired.

Anger's harms are fairly obvious. When we're angry, we often do things that are contrary to our own interests. Anger causes us to "lose our heads." It can even lead to murder. Then, too, being angry is not a pleasurable state to the angry person. And again, few people genuinely like those who are prone to anger. Instead, most of us tend to avoid them.

Lust is an excessive desire for sex that is often difficult to control. It can lead to the creation of intimate relations with people who are wrong for us when we mistake lust for love. It can break up marriages, lead to sexually transmitted diseases, and create unwanted children. It can lead to incest, rape, and murder.

Gluttony is excessive eating and drinking, and it leads to a variety of health problems. The desire to eat or drink to excess—placing an unreasonably high value on the pleasures of food and drink—can have a variety of causes, but a glutton is rarely happy with his gluttony.

Greed—excessive desire for money and what money can buy—leads to a variety of harms to others, including arson, fraud, environmental pollution, kidnapping, robbery, and murder. And such acts generally have negative consequences for the person doing them. (The toxic pharmacist Robert Courtney's greed landed him in jail and caused him to be despised by those who once respected him.) As with other sins, it is rare that a greedy person is happy. The desires of the greedy person are extreme. The person almost never thinks he or she has enough.

Finally, sloth is a variety of laziness. The slothful person rarely has energy for beginning projects, let alone for pursuing projects to the end. Therefore, he or she fails to do many beneficial things. The slothful person also often fails to fulfill his or her responsibilities.

We should avoid the seven deadly sins both for ourselves and others. We will be happier if we do. Schimmel says that the most important antidote to the seven deadly sins is self-control, control of both our mental states and our behavior.

VIRTUES AS DISPOSITIONS TO OBEY
MORAL RULES

As we have seen, theories about virtue and vice can be divided into two families. One family of theories focuses on the helpfulness or harmfulness of traits, either to their possessor or to others. This family includes theories that claim that moral virtues are those traits that enable their possessor to flourish, whereas moral vices are those that reduce their possessor's likelihood of flourishing. It also includes those theories in which moral virtues or vices are traits that are either beneficial or harmful primarily to others.

Theories in the second family claim instead that virtues are dispositions to obey (true) moral rules, whereas vices are dispositions to disobey (true) moral rules. For these theories, moral rules, laws, or principles come first and are more fundamental than the concepts of virtue and vice. In order to know which traits are moral virtues and vices, we first must know what is morally prohibited and required. However, the differences between these two families of theories should not be exaggerated. It may be that there will be substantial agreement among different theories about which traits are virtues and which are vices, even if they appeal to different principles to justify their claims.

As an example of the second family of theories, we will look at contemporary American philosopher Bernard Gert. He maintains that moral virtues are tendencies to avoid unjustified violations of correct moral rules, whereas vices are tendencies to unjustifiably violate correct moral rules. In his view, virtues and vices cannot be identified independent of or prior to the identification of the correct moral rules. He also distinguishes between moral virtues and personal virtues. Personal virtues—traits primarily or exclusively beneficial to their possessor—are not moral virtues at all. Moral virtues are those traits that are exclusively or primarily beneficial to others.[13]

Consider cruelty, the tendency to deliberately or negligently cause other people pain and suffering. Following Gert, we might say that it's a moral vice because it is a tendency to violate a correct moral rule that prohibits people from deliberately or negligently causing other people pain and suffering. Kindness, on the other hand, is a moral virtue because it is a tendency to conform to a correct moral rule that requires us to avoid causing others to suffer and enjoins us to relieve suffering where we can. Similarly, correct moral rules require us to be merciful, loyal, and honest while prohibiting us from being merciless, disloyal, and dishonest. The former traits are moral virtues and the latter are moral vices.

VIRTUE AND VICE IN HINDUISM: AHIMSA

According to Gavin Flood, the ethics of Hinduism is designed to alleviate human suffering and comprises nonviolence (*ahimsa*), telling the truth, not stealing, celibacy, and not being greedy.[14] Although celibacy admittedly is mainly expected only of the most serious practitioners, the others are expected of all

Hindus. We can think of these in terms of virtuous actions or virtuous character traits. For example, telling the truth is an action, but it also can mean having the character trait of honesty. Refraining from greed obviously refers to a character trait, but as we saw, we also can talk of acts of greed, or acts that exemplify greediness.

According to Hinduism, life is filled with suffering. We face inevitable death, old age, and illness for ourselves and those we love. We experience both physical and psychological pain. It's bad enough to experience this once, but according to Hinduism, we experience these things over and over again because after we die we are reborn again in a different body. Hinduism believes in the transmigration of souls. Our soul is our essence, our Self, what is most essential to who we are. Furthermore, our situation when we are reborn depends on how we lived in previous lives. If we lived well and ethically, our rebirth circumstances will be relatively favorable. We may be born into a higher social class or caste; we may be more physically attractive, healthy, and intelligent than we were in our past life; we may have more worldly success. We may even be reborn as a god. On the other hand, if we lived an unethical life, our rebirth will be less favorable. We may be reborn as a nonhuman animal, such as a dog or a viper. If reborn as a human being, we may be reborn in a lower social class or caste; we may be born into poverty and spend our lives working at backbreaking physical labor from dawn to dusk; we may be illiterate, or blind, or deaf. What determines the nature of our rebirth is the karma we take with us whenever we die, a kind of causal force that acts to determine who or what we will be reborn as and the conditions in which we will live out our next life. Our deeds create our karma. Bad deeds create bad karma, and good deeds create good karma.

According to Hinduism, ultimate happiness comes from ending the cycle of rebirths. To do that, we must achieve enlightenment and accumulate enough good karma. Virtuous acts will benefit us by ensuring a favorable rebirth if we haven't yet achieved an end to rebirth, or they will lead to an end to the cycle of rebirths. Vicious acts will do the reverse. Here we will focus primarily on nonviolence, or *ahimsa*. We will further refine our focus to a well-known modern Hindu, Mohandas K. Gandhi, perhaps better known as Mahatma Gandhi. Gandhi's views on ahimsa are influential with many Hindus and non-Hindus.

Ahimsa as a character trait or virtue is the trait of being nonviolent, while himsa is the trait of being violent. A violent act harms and/or causes suffering. Obviously, someone with the trait of ahimsa will refrain from doing acts of physical violence to people, such as killing, torturing, and assaulting them. But the nonviolence of ahimsa is meant to extend to all living beings, not just to humans. If we can, we should avoid acts of physical violence directed at any living being. Thus, a person with the trait of ahimsa even will avoid stepping on an ant. But because causing psychological suffering is also conceived of as an act of violence, a person with the trait of ahimsa will also avoid causing psychological suffering, and will not betray, scorn, insult, or demean people.

According to Gandhi, true ahimsa involves more than merely not doing certain things. It involves a kind of beneficence—doing good for others:

In its negative form, it means not injuring any living being, whether by body or mind. I may not therefore hurt the person of any wrong-doer, or bear any ill will to him and so cause him mental suffering.... Ahimsa requires deliberate self-suffering, not a deliberate injuring of the supposed wrong-doer.

In its positive form, ahimsa means the largest love, the greatest charity. If I am a follower of ahimsa, I must love my enemy. I must apply the same rule to the wrong-doer who is my enemy or a stranger to me, as I would to my wrong-doing father or son.[15]

Love is at the core of Gandhi's conception of ahimsa. (Many Christians say that love is also at the core of Jesus' moral vision.) Hatred and ill-will are wholly incompatible with it. According to Gandhi, "non-violence implies love, compassion, and forgiveness."[16] The love Gandhi speaks of is a kind of disinterested love that is not like the romantic love between husband and wife, or between people who are in a sexual relationship with each other. In this sense of love, we are capable of loving strangers and enemies, not just family and friends, as well as people of the same sex. This kind of love entails respect, care, and consideration, and excludes both indifference and hate.

Ahimsa also requires compassion and forgiveness. If you lack compassion toward someone, if you are indifferent to or get joy from his or her suffering, you are not really showing love. Similarly, ahimsa requires forgiveness. If someone has wronged us, we can remain angry and bear a grudge; we can plot ways to get revenge. But if we love someone, we must learn to forgive even if that individual wrongs us. Inability to forgive will poison our love and destroy our relationship. Thus, if we have the trait of ahimsa, we will set aside our anger, and forgive those who wrong us.

Gandhi also emphasized that ahimsa requires self-sacrifice. If you have the trait of ahimsa and there is a choice to be made between suffering and someone else suffering, you will choose to suffer over having someone else suffer. Surely that's part of genuine love. We willingly make sacrifices for those we love. Some are big sacrifices, some are small. A mother who loves her children may put money in the bank to pay for their college expenses rather than spend it on herself. In extreme cases, she may give up her life to save her children.

Ahimsa also implies impartiality. We must apply the same rules and standards of conduct to friends and enemies, relatives and strangers. If I apply different standards and rules to friends and enemies, I am not showing love to my enemies or my friends. I am expecting too much of my enemies and perhaps not enough of my friends.

According to the Hindu tradition, violent acts and such negative emotions and feelings as anger and hatred create bad karma. On the other hand, beneficial acts and such positive emotions and feelings as care, compassion, and love create good karma. Therefore, it is in our interest to avoid violent acts and negative emotions and feelings while performing beneficial acts and having positive emotions and feelings.

VIRTUE AND VICE IN BUDDHISM

Buddhism grew out of Hinduism; therefore, there are some common features. Like Hinduism, Buddhism includes a belief in reincarnation and karma. It also views life as filled with suffering and considers ultimate happiness to come only from escaping the cycle of rebirths. According to tradition, Gotama, the Buddha or *enlightened one*, lived in northern India around the fifth century B.C.E. He became enlightened when he discovered or rediscovered the way to end suffering by breaking the cycle of rebirth. His insight was that the suffering we experience while we are alive, and the cycle of rebirths we experience eon after eon, have the same root cause—desire and ignorance. While we are alive, we suffer because we don't get what we want, and do get what we don't want. We all want to live, but inevitably we will die. We want to stay young, but inevitably we will age. We want to be healthy but inevitably we will become injured and/or ill. We want those we love to stay alive, young, and healthy forever, but they won't. We want to be rich, but usually we aren't. We don't want to be betrayed by those close to us, but that often happens.

We can't control our suffering by controlling what happens to us. But if we stop desiring what we can't or don't have, what happens to us will not cause us to suffer. If we can extinguish our desires and attachments—to our lives, our health, our youth and beauty, the opinions others have of us, wealth, fame, and power— we will reduce our suffering in our current life. For example, if you're not attached to your health, youth, and good looks, then you won't be made unhappy when you inevitably lose them. If you're not attached to wealth, you won't be made unhappy if you never acquire it or if you lose it after you do acquire it. If we can even detach from those around us—our family and friends— we will be happier because when those we care about die, age, become ill, desert us, or betray us, we will not be made unhappy. This detachment from other people does not mean that we become indifferent to them. Rather, it is that we do not permit our happiness to be destroyed by what they do to us or by their unhappiness.

The happiness that Buddhists seek seems to be a kind of calmness, serenity, and tranquility; it is not a state of excitement or elation. Perhaps they would say that such a state of calm tranquility and imperturbability is true happiness, whereas other more energetic states are mere counterfeits. High emotional peaks generally lead to deep valleys of depression and disappointment; however, serenity and tranquility can be sustained for long periods.

Another important aspect of Buddhism is commitment to the view that there is no Self. For most Westerners, our souls are the essence of who we are because our souls are the bearers of our mental characteristics: our memories, beliefs, feelings and emotions, likes and dislikes, character and personality traits, values, and preferences. In brief, our souls are the foundations of our consciousness. For example, according to this view, I consider my soul with all my states of consciousness contained in it as my Self—who I am. And I may imagine that there is some unchanging core that is most truly my Self and that persists throughout my whole life to make me the same person at age 2, 21, 50, 75, and so on. But according to Buddhism, there is no unchanging core, because everything is always changing, even the states of consciousness I consider to be my Self. In the sense of a permanent unchanging core of states of consciousness that remains the same from birth to death (and beyond), there is no Self. Compare who you were at age 10 with who you are now. How many states of consciousness have persisted through all those years? The Buddha would say few, if any. Who you are is not a core of states of consciousness that will exist from your birth to your death; rather, at each instant of time there is a collection of states of consciousness that is you at that moment in time and that is related in certain ways to another (different) collection of states of consciousness that existed at earlier moments in time and that was you at those moments.

This doctrine of no permanent Self has important implications. As we will see, according to Buddhism, most of the wrong or harmful things we do to ourselves and others are caused largely by our selfishness. We are too attached to our Selves and that causes us and others a great deal of unhappiness. But if the Self is an illusion, then selfishness does not make sense. And if we can learn to see that the Self is an illusion, we will extinguish our selfishness.

There is another important implication. The ultimate goal for Buddhists is to achieve liberation from the continuous cycle of rebirths and achieve a state called *nirvana* (in Sanskrit) or *nibbana* (in Pali). Until we achieve the state of nirvana, at death some part of our consciousness that was us at the moment of death continues to exist and is ultimately reborn, perhaps as a hell-being, an animal, a human, or even as a god. But it is not a permanent Self that leaves the body at death and is reborn in a different body. It is only a part of the consciousness that was us. (That may be one reason why only the most enlightened people can remember past lives.) Now how are we to understand the ultimate goal of Buddhists—nirvana—which precludes being reborn in a body? It is not a state of nonexistence. Again, after your last or final incarnation, some part of the consciousness that was you at that moment of your last death leaves the body and continues to exist. But it is a completely different form of consciousness. Peter Harvey calls it "objectless consciousness," but admits that hardly helps us understand it.[17] Normal consciousness is consciousness *of* something. I may be conscious of a pain, a tickle, a book in front of me, a desire, and so on. But when we achieve the state of nirvana, our consciousness is not consciousness of anything—there is no object of our consciousness. (But perhaps there is consciousness of feelings of tranquility, serenity, and peace that go beyond human understanding until we have experienced nirvana for ourselves?)

How can we achieve the state of nirvana? We must achieve a state of enlightenment in which we relinquish our attachment to ourselves, our selfishness and self-absorption, our hatred and ill will, and replace these negative traits and feelings with the positive ones of love and compassion. The traits or states of greed and hatred especially prevent us from achieving the state of nirvana and condemn us not only to more rebirths but to bad rebirths. During the period of his enlightenment, Buddha is said to have achieved a state of complete and universal benevolence and compassion so that "Every day in meditation he would deliberately evoke the emotion of love . . . and direct it to each of the four corners of the world. He did not omit a single living thing—plant, animal, demon, friend, or foe—from this radius of benevolence."[18] As his enlightenment progressed, he developed compassion for all living things and a feeling of "sympathetic joy" when he perceived or contemplated the happiness of others. Thus, he suffered when others suffered and felt happiness and joy when others were happy.

The nature of our rebirths is determined by the *law of karma*. Some mental states and acts are intrinsically good while others are harmful. Thus, the states and acts of greed and hatred are bad and create bad karma. On the other hand, the states and acts of love and compassion are good and create good karma. Harming others creates bad karma, helping and serving others creates good karma. At death, the karma accumulated during our life determines the nature of our rebirth. The more bad karma, the worse our rebirth; the more good karma, the better our rebirth.[19]

Buddha preached a path to salvation that included eight requirements, the so-called eight-fold path: right understanding, right thought, right speech, right action, right livelihood, right effort, right mindfulness, and right concentration.[20]

Right understanding is being rid of illusions and delusions. An important illusion is the illusion of a permanent Self. An important delusion is the delusion that harming others won't harm us and that helping and serving others won't benefit us. We must understand these things if we are to achieve enlightenment, happiness in this life, and favorable future rebirths. *Right thought* involves extinguishing the thoughts and desires that prevent us from progressing on the path of enlightenment. We must extinguish hatred, ill-will, and selfishness and cultivate love and compassion. We must extinguish our desires for permanent life, youth, vigor, health, and beauty and see them as trivial. *Right speech* involves avoiding talk that harms others: lying, threats, libel, insults, gossip, and words that demean or humiliate. *Right action* involves not doing actions that harm others and doing what benefits others. *Right livelihood* involves working in professions and occupations that do not cause harm to others and avoiding harm to others if we are working in permitted careers and professions. That probably would forbid us to work for cigarette companies and weapons manufacturers, and forbid us to do things on the job that cause harm, such as pollute the environment or create unsafe and unhealthy work conditions. *Right effort* involves trying hard to live up to the previous requirements and prohibitions.

Mindfulness is somewhat complex. It involves constant attention to the world around us and to ourselves. To be mindful, I must always pay careful attention to how my actions affect others. I must think before I speak or act in order to minimize the possibility that I will cause harm to others. I must constantly search my mind for harmful feelings and thoughts, such as feelings of anger, hatred, greed, arrogance, or lust; prejudiced attitudes such as racism or sexism; or negative thoughts such as that someone is inferior to me. If I find harmful states, I must strive to extinguish them. For example, if I feel anger toward someone, I can focus on the causes and try to see them as not justifying such anger; I can remind myself that the person is doing the best he or she can and is imperfect just as I am. On the other hand, if I find that I lack good states, such as love and compassion, I must strive to acquire them. For example, I can search my memory for instances when I suffered and try to relive it. Then I can more clearly realize what others who suffer are going through. Or I can try to imagine what their suffering is like. As for harmful thoughts, I may have obsessive thoughts about how someone mistreated me or how I made a fool of myself, over and over reliving in memory the painful episode. This just fuels my anger or feelings of humiliation. In such cases I need to push these thoughts out of my mind when they appear. Then, too, I must be aware of my motives in all that I do. If my motive is bad, however good the act, it will create bad karma for me. For example, if I am honest only because I want others to admire and trust me so that I will have a good reputation and success in business, my acts of honesty will not create good karma for me. I must search my mind to see if I harbor any illusions or delusions, or have states that distort my understanding or my perception of reality. Mindfulness requires great self-discipline and self-control. It takes time and practice to achieve.

Finally, *right concentration* involves meditation that enables us to achieve inner peace, calmness, and tranquility, as well as higher or exalted states of consciousness that in turn enable us to see the world and ourselves more clearly and that may even provide us with a glimpse of the state of nirvana.

Following the eight-fold path will create good karma and avoid creation of bad karma, thereby giving us a better rebirth until, if we are strong in our resolve to achieve enlightenment, we end the cycle of rebirths and achieve the state of nirvana.

The Dalai Lama

Can Buddhist ethics appeal to Westerners, most of whom do not believe in reincarnation and the law of karma? The Dalai Lama thinks so. He believes that if we follow the path of Buddhism it can help us achieve more lasting and genuine happiness in this life, regardless of whether there is continued existence after death. In *The Art of Happiness,* the Dalai Lama begins much as Aristotle began, with the claim that the purpose of our lives is to seek happiness. He probably would agree with Aristotle in focusing on happiness over the course of our entire lives rather than on momentary states of temporary happiness. According to the Dalai Lama, happiness is determined not by what we have or what happens to us but rather by our attitude toward what we have and what happens to us. If we feel dissatisfied, deprived, or discontented with our lot in life, we will be unhappy, but if we can feel satisfied and contented instead, we will be happy. True, deep, lasting happiness comes from feelings of contentment, peace, tranquility, and calmness. But suppose I'm poor and obscure. How can I feel contented? I can relinquish my desire for or attachment to riches and fame. I can remind myself that they don't bring happiness, that these aren't things I really need, they're only things I want. We can't take our riches with us when we die, and even the most famous person will someday be forgotten. And most important, I can stop focusing exclusively on myself and how I compare with other people. I can focus more on others. According to the Dalai Lama, true happiness comes from having affection, love, and compassion for others.

The Dalai Lama's collaborator on *The Art of Happiness,* psychiatrist Howard C. Cutler, points out that "[I]n studies . . . examining the risk factors for coronary heart disease, it has been found that the people who were most self-focused . . . were more likely to develop coronary heart disease. . . . Scientists are discovering that those who lack close social ties seem to suffer from poor health, higher levels of unhappiness, and a greater vulnerability to stress."[21] Furthermore, "medical researchers have found that people who have close friendships . . . are more likely to survive health challenges such as heart attacks and major surgery and are less likely to develop diseases such as cancer and respiratory infections."[22]

The Dalai Lama believes that "the basic or underlying nature of human beings is gentleness."[23] As he puts it, "our physical structure seems to be more suited to feelings of love and compassion. We can see how a calm, affectionate, wholesome state of mind has beneficial effects on our health and physical well-being. Conversely, feelings of frustration, fear, agitation, and anger can be destructive to our health."[24] He does not think that selfishness, anger, violence, and aggression are parts of our "most basic, underlying nature." They arise as a result of the misuse of our abilities to reason and imagine, from misperception of reality, as well as from social conditioning.

Compassion is central to the Dalai Lama's vision of the good and happy life. As he puts it, "compassion is the essence of the spiritual life."[25] He also states:

> [G]enuine compassion is based on the rationale that all human beings have an innate desire to be happy and overcome suffering, just like myself. And, just like myself, they have the natural right to fulfill this fundamental aspiration. On the basis of the recognition of this equality and commonality, you develop a sense of affinity and closeness with others. With this as a foundation, you can feel compassion regardless of whether you view the other person as a friend or an enemy.[26]

Anger and hatred are the most important blocks to compassion. "Generally speaking, . . . there are many different kinds of afflictive or negative emotions, such as conceit, arrogance, jealousy, desire, lust, closed-mindedness, and so on. But of all these, hatred and anger are considered to be the greatest evils because they are the greatest obstacles to developing compassion and altruism. . . ."[27] To extinguish hatred and develop compassion, we must also develop tolerance and patience. A product of patience and tolerance is forgiveness. We will be happier if we forgive those who hurt us. If we do not, our own pain will linger and probably intensify, and we may do things that harm others or ourselves.

Paradoxically, the Dalai Lama believes that we will be happier if we think less about ourselves and more about others, if we act more to make others happy and less to make solely ourselves happy. Selfish people are generally less happy than unselfish, altruistic people. People who care about others are generally more happy than people who only care about themselves. Compassion enables us to have the kind of genuine concern for others that in turn enables us to live more for others and less for just ourselves. It is a potent antidote against selfishness and self-absorption. And compassion powerfully motivates us to strive to avoid harming others and to act in ways that benefit others.

CHARACTER AND FREEDOM

Aristotle believed that, to some extent, our character is up to us. He believed that people can change and shape their own character. If we want to be good, we can take effective steps to cultivate the virtues and extinguish the vices. He claimed that "moral excellence comes about as the result of habit,"[28] rather than something innate or inborn. He emphasized that human beings have natures that are to some extent malleable; people have the inborn capacity to acquire a variety of traits. People can be unselfish as well as selfish, temperate as well as self-indulgent, kind as well as cruel. Such character traits are acquired rather than innate. Many of the other thinkers we have looked at also believe that we can change our character, that our character is at least in part up to us.

However, aren't our early environment, training, and conditioning (over which we have no control) decisive in shaping our character? Aren't our character traits acquired very early in life and thereafter quite stable? Aristotle thought not. He believed that we can, in a sense, decondition and recondition ourselves. The potential for acquiring other traits remains after we have been conditioned early in life. Thus, according to Aristotle, "we become just by doing just acts, temperate by doing temperate acts, brave by doing brave acts."[29]

> It is from the same causes and by the same means that every excellence is both produced and destroyed, and similarly every art; for it is from playing the lyre that both good and bad lyre players are produced. And the corresponding statement is true of builders and of all the rest; men will be good or bad builders as a result of building well or badly. For if this were not so, there would have been no need of a teacher, but all men would have been born good or bad at their craft. This, then, is the case with the excellences also; by doing the acts that we do in our transactions with other men we become just or unjust, and by doing the acts that we do in the presence of danger, and being habituated to feel fear or confidence, we become brave or cowardly. The same is true of appetites and feelings of anger; some men become temperate and good tempered, others self-indulgent and irascible, by behaving in one way or the other in the appropriate circumstances. . . . It makes no small difference, then, whether we form habits of one kind or of another in our very youth; it makes a very great difference, or rather all the difference.[30]

If Aristotle is correct, we deceive ourselves if we think that our character is not at all up to us; it is simply an excuse for lack of effort. If we discover that we are cowardly, disloyal, or selfish, we can take steps to perform courageous, loyal, and unselfish actions. If Aristotle is correct, by repeatedly practicing such actions we can eventually extinguish the unwanted trait and acquire the wanted trait.

EXERCISES

1. What kind of person do you think your parents would like you to be? (Alternatively, what kind of character traits do you think your parents would like you to have?) Why do you think they would like you to be that way?

2. What kind of person do you want to be? (Alternatively, what kind of character traits do you want to have?) Why?

3. What kind of person are you? (What character traits do you have or lack?) Do you think you can do anything to change your character?

4. Construct a list of the people you most admire and the people you least admire. What are some of the traits characteristic of the people you most admire? What are some of the traits characteristic of the people you least admire? Why do you admire or deplore these traits?

5. What character traits do you consider moral virtues, and which do you consider to be moral vices? Explain your views.

6. Can virtues such as courage lead one to act wrongly?

7. How are the virtues connected? If we have one, must we have all?

8. Plato wondered whether virtue can be taught. That is, he wondered whether people can be made good through education—whether we can do things to cultivate virtues in children and eradicate vices. In this sense, can virtue be taught? If yes, how?

9. Do you agree with Hinduism that *ahimsa* is a fundamental virtue?

10. Do you agree with Buddhism that the key to happiness and the end of suffering is to follow the noble eight-fold path?

11. Do you agree with the Dalai Lama that compassion is one of the most fundamental virtues and that the vices, such as anger, are negative traits that harm us?

12. Should public schools try to make children good, that is, inculcate virtues and extinguish vices? If yes, what virtues should be inculcated and what vices extinguished?

13. How helpful is it to say that in each situation, we should do what a virtuous person would do? If we're not virtuous ourselves, how can we know what a virtuous person would do?

14. Are the seven deadly sins seven deadly vices?

15. How much control do we have over our own character?

SUGGESTED READINGS

St. Thomas Aquinas. *Introduction to St. Thomas Aquinas*. Edited by Anton Pegis. New York: Modern Library, 1948.

Aristotle. *Nicomachean Ethics*. In *The Complete Works of Aristotle*, vol. 2. Edited by Jonathan Barnes. Princeton, NJ: Princeton University Press, 1984.

Karen Armstrong. *Buddha*. New York: Penguin, 2000.

David Bostock. *Aristotle's Ethics*. New York: Oxford University Press, 2000.

John Cooper. *Reason and Human Good in Aristotle*. Cambridge, MA: Harvard University Press, 1975.

His Holiness the Dalai Lama. *Ethics for the New Millennium*. New York: Riverhead, 1999.

His Holiness the Dalai Lama and Howard C. Cutler, M.D. *The Art of Happiness*. New York: Riverhead, 1998.

Philippa Foot. "Virtues and Vices." In *Virtues and Vices*. Berkeley: University of California Press, 1978.

Mohandas K. Gandhi. *The Penguin Gandhi Reader*. Edited by Rudrangshu Mukherjee. New York: Penguin, 1993.

Peter Harvey. *An Introduction to Buddhism*. Cambridge, England: Cambridge University Press, 1990.

Peter Harvey. *An Introduction to Buddhist Ethics*. Cambridge, England: Cambridge University Press, 2000.

David Hume. *An Enquiry Concerning the Principles of Morals*. LaSalle, IL: Open Court, 1960.

Walpola Rahula. *What the Buddha Taught*. New York: Grove Press, 1974.

Amelie Oksenberg Rorty, ed. *Essays on Aristotle's Ethics*. Berkeley: University of California Press, 1980.

Solomon Schimmel. *The Seven Deadly Sins*. New York: Oxford University Press, 1997.

James Wallace. *Virtues and Vices*. Ithaca, NY: Cornell University Press, 1978.

ENDNOTES

1. "The Toxic Pharmacist," *New York Times* (8 June 2003).
2. His Holiness the Dalai Lama, *Ethics for the New Millennium* (New York: Riverhead, 1999), pp. 27–28.
3. John McDowell, "Virtue and Reason," in *Mind, Value, and Reality* (Cambridge, MA: Harvard University Press, 1998).
4. Thomas Hobbes, *Leviathan* (New York: Collier, 1962), p. 124.
5. David Hume, *An Enquiry Concerning the Principles of Morals* (LaSalle, IL: Open Court, 1960), p. 68. (Originally published in 1777.)
6. Ibid., p. 69.
7. Ibid., p. 79.
8. Ibid., p. 98.
9. Ibid., p. 70.
10. Ibid., p. 79.
11. Ibid., p. 111.
12. Solomon Schimmel, *The Seven Deadly Sins* (New York: Oxford University Press, 1997).

13. Bernard Gert, *Morality* (New York: Oxford University Press, 1988), pp. 182–196.

14. Gavin Flood, *An Introduction to Hinduism* (Cambridge: Cambridge University Press, 1996).

15. *The Penguin Gandhi Reader*, ed. Rudrangshu Mukherjee (Harmondsworth, England: Penguin Books, 1993), pp. 95–96.

16. Ibid., p. 107.

17. Peter Harvey, *An Introduction to Buddhism* (Cambridge: Cambridge University Press, 1990), p. 64

18. Karen Armstrong, *Buddha* (New York: Penguin, 2001), p. 77.

19. Peter Harvey, *An Introduction to Buddhist Ethics*, pp. 11–30.

20. Walpola Rahula, *What the Buddha Taught* (New York: Grove Press, 1959), p. 45.

21. His Holiness the Dalai Lama and Howard C. Cutler, M.D., *The Art of Happiness* (New York: Riverhead Books, 1998), p. 59.

22. Ibid., p. 78.

23. Ibid., p. 52.

24. Ibid., p. 53.

25. Ibid., p. 178.

26. Ibid., p. 115.

27. Ibid., p. 248.

28. Aristotle, *Nicomachean Ethics*, in *The Complete Works of Aristotle*, vol. 2, ed. Jonathan Barnes (Princeton, NJ: Princeton University Press, 1984), p. 1742.

29. Ibid., p. 1743.

30. Ibid., p. 1743.

8

Human Rights

OBJECTIVES

- To understand the concept of a right and its relation to the concept of duty
- To understand how to specify the content of a right by specifying the duties to the right-holder that it imposes on others
- To understand the intellectual foundations of the United Nations Universal Declaration of Human Rights
- To evaluate the plausibility of the rights listed in the United Nations Universal Declaration of Human Rights
- To understand and apply the system of classification of rights in the United Nations Universal Declaration of Human Rights
- To understand and apply John Stuart Mill's Harm Principle
- To understand, apply, and evaluate the plausibility of Feinberg's four liberty-limiting principles

ASSAULTS ON HUMAN DIGNITY

According to Kant, we must treat people with respect because they have a special status—they have dignity or inherent worth. All too often, people are not treated with respect.

"Untouchables" (Dalits) in India

Gandhi called them *Harijans*—children of God. They're the 160 million members of the lowest hereditary caste in Hindu India, comprising about one-sixth of the Indian population. Although this status was abolished in the 1950s under India's constitution, it's still a reality of Indian life. Harijans are shunned and segregated. According to a 1999 Human Rights Watch report, "They may not use the same wells, visit the same temples, drink from the same cups in tea stalls, or lay claim to land that is legally theirs. Dalit children are frequently made to sit in the back of classrooms, and [Dalit] communities as a whole are made to perform degrading rituals...."[1] Furthermore, "[m]ost Dalits continue to live in extreme poverty, without land or opportunities for better employment or education. [Most] are relegated to the most menial of tasks, as manual scavengers, removers of human waste and dead animals, leather workers, street sweepers, and cobblers."[2] "Most live on the brink of destitution, barely able to feed their families and unable to send their children to school.... At the end of the day they return to their hut in their Dalit colony with no electricity, kilometers away from the nearest water source, and segregated from all non-Dalits...."[3]

Dalit leaders are imprisoned and prevented from holding meetings and rallies. Upper-caste landowners have forced Dalit communities into passivity by threatening to throw them off their land. Some Dalits have joined guerrilla organizations using violence to force land reform. Hundreds of Dalits suspected of membership have been murdered by private militias formed by the rich upper-caste land-owners. "In one of the largest such massacres, on the night of December 1, 1997, [a militia group] shot dead sixteen children, twenty-seven women, and eighteen men in the village of Laxmanpur-Bathe...Bihar. Five teenage girls were raped and mutilated before being shot in the chest."[4] In some militia raids on Dalit communities, police were present but stood aside and did nothing to stop them. "Police abuse against the urban poor, slum dwellers, Dalits, and other minorities has included arbitrary detention, torture, extrajudicial executions and forced evictions."[5] In one village, Melavallu in Tamil, a Dalit who won an election for president of the village council was murdered and beheaded for his audacity. Those who attack Dalits are almost never prosecuted.

In southern India, thousands of girls (most of them Dalits) are forced into becoming official prostitutes for the community's upper-caste men, usually before they even reach puberty.... "Once dedicated, the girl is unable to marry...and [is] eventually auctioned off to an urban brothel."[6] Rape of Dalit women, and the threat of rape, has been a potent tool of social control. They are raped as a form of revenge and retaliation against Dalit men who have offended powerful upper-caste men.

Roma (Gypsies)

According to a pamphlet published by the United States Holocaust Memorial Museum entitled "Sinti and Roma," "For centuries Europeans regarded Gypsies (Roma) as social outcasts—a people of foreign appearance, language, and custom."[7] In the twentieth century, like the Jews, they were targets of Nazi Germany's racial hatred and sense of racial superiority. Estimates of the number of Roma who died in the Holocaust range from 220,000 to 500,000. They died in gas chambers, were worked and/or starved to death in concentration camps, and died from diseases rampant in the concentration camps. In Russia, Poland, and the Balkans, they were lined up and mowed down by firing squads. But even before the Nazi seizure of power in Germany in 1933, Roma were discriminated against in Germany. For example, a law was passed in Bavaria in 1926 requiring the registration of all Roma, and any Roma man who couldn't prove he had a job risked a two-year prison sentence at hard labor. By 1929 this law had spread far beyond Bavaria. After the Nazis seized power, a 1933 law called for the involuntary sterilization of Roma women. Roma children were taken from their parents and sent to group homes as wards of the state. In 1941, Roma were excluded from all public schools.

We might imagine that after the overthrow of the Nazi regime in 1945, the position of the surviving Roma would have drastically improved. However, a 1993 report of the United Nations High Commission for National Minorities lays that fond hope to rest. The report estimated that there were a total of 7 to 8 million Roma living in the countries studied, with 5 to 6 million clustered in Central and Southeastern Europe (for example, Poland, Hungary, the Czech Republic, Romania, the former Yugoslavia, and Greece). The report states that anti-Roma prejudice is an important causal factor in their being saddled with "widespread and acute poverty, unemployment, illiteracy, lack of formal education, substandard housing. . . ."[8] In some areas, almost no Roma men have jobs. Roma who do find jobs are clustered in the unskilled low-wage sector. Unemployed Roma often are ineligible for unemployment assistance. With few opportunities, some Roma turn to crime and prostitution, which reinforces negative stereotypes. Children in impoverished Roma families may be too sick or malnourished to go to school, may be needed to work to supplement the family income, or may resist attending school because of taunting and intimidation. Lacking political power, Roma are not easily able to influence government policy, especially when it comes to antidiscrimination measures and protection from the violence of racists, whether semiorganized "skinheads" or the police who are supposed to protect them. There have been numerous episodes since 1945 of mobs attacking Roma while the police just watched, with no efforts made to identify and prosecute the participants. In some cases, Roma have been discouraged or even absolutely forbidden by owners and employees from entering stores, theaters, restaurants, and bars, and the government has done nothing to intervene. In many European countries, Roma are subject to intense and continuous police surveillance.

At the 57th session of the United Nations Committee on the Elimination of Racial Discrimination in August, 2000, the European Roma Rights Center (ERRC) presented an extensive report on treatment of Roma. It was as if a bombshell hit the conference. They told story after story of persecution of Roma. For example, in May 1998, the city council of the Czech city of Usti nad Labem voted to build a wall on Matini Street to separate Romani from non-Romani residents. The central Czech government responded merely by "recommending" that the city not build it. The city built it anyway on October 13, 1999. There were massive demonstrations protesting the wall, but still the Czech government did not order its removal. Finally, public pressure forced the city council to demolish it on November 24, 1999. In May, 2000 in Nea Kios in Greece, municipal authorities voted to evict all Roma from their land because a Roma man got into a dispute over an illegally parked vehicle. The report states, "As of this writing, Roma are not allowed to enter the village, shopkeepers have been instructed not to sell anything to Roma, and Romani children cannot go to school."[9] The ERRC stated that it was unaware of any action being taken by the Greek government. In Italy, the government classifies Roma as "nomads" and its public housing policy puts Roma into "camps" far outside cities where there are few or no public services. Only Roma are subject to such treatment.

Hate speech directed against Roma is common. For example, on April 27, 2000, the mayor of a small town in Hungary said on Hungarian television that Roma "have no place among human beings. Just as in the animal world, parasites must be expelled." There's also violence directed against Roma; governments often just look away.[10] In Romania in the early 1990s, scores of Roma communities were assaulted while police stood aside, but at the time of the ERRC report, not a single police officer had been disciplined. Slovak police frequently refused to even register complaints of Roma that they had been attacked by racist skinheads. To make matters worse, they sometimes are assaulted by the police. Roma in Hajduhadhaz complain that the police harass them, verbally abuse them, and beat them. According to the report, "Police beatings of Roma in detention are also widespread in Albania, Bulgaria, Yugoslavia, and the former Yugoslav republic of Macedonia." In addition, "In a number of countries, law enforcement authorities target Roma communities for special raids—armed assaults in the early morning hours during which homes are searched, contents ransacked, inhabitants, including women, the elderly and children, harassed or subjected to excessive force, and men rounded up for arrest or questioning—often without warrants or other legal safeguards...."[11] Often the goal is intimidation. In Bulgaria, the ERRC found that Roma were usually not given legal counsel when accused of a crime, even though Bulgarian law requires that it be offered, and they generally receive harsher punishment than non-Roma when convicted. Much the same can be said of treatment of Roma in Hungary. When the Czech Republic was created in 1993, Roma living there were denied citizenship, so they are ineligible for a range of rights and government services. About 75 percent of Roma children in the Czech Republic attend special schools for the mentally challenged, primarily because they speak a Roma dialect rather than Czech. In Tiszavasvari in Bulgaria, the public school put Roma children into separate classrooms and dining facilities and even held separate graduation ceremonies for Romani and non-Romani in 1997.

The ERRC found some bars, restaurants, night clubs, swimming pools, and other public places excluding Roma in the Czech Republic, Finland, Hungary, Ireland, Italy, Latvia, Macedonia, Poland, Romania, Slovakia, Spain, Sweden, and Yugoslavia. The ERRC found a cafe in Florence, Italy with a sign posted saying "No Gypsies." "In some countries, advertisements for job openings specifically state that Roma should not apply."

Child Farmworkers in the United States

According to a Human Rights Watch report of 2000, *Fingers to the Bone: United States Failure to Protect Child Farmworkers*, there are hundreds of thousands of children who are hired farm laborers.[12] The Fair Labor Standards Act imposes different rules on farms than on other employers. The minimum age is 12 for farms, as opposed to 14 for nonfarm labor. There are no limits on the hours children farmworkers may work, whereas in nonfarm occupations, children under 16 may work no more than 3 hours per day during the school year. About 85 percent of migrant and seasonal farmworkers are minorities, mainly Latino; in some regions, they're 99 percent of the farm laborers. In 1999, the average income for farm laborers with two income earners was $14,000, well below the poverty level. Many farm laborers do not speak or understand English well enough to communicate with English speakers. Migrant families that follow the crops during the growing season, of course bring their children with them. Most work in the fields alongside their parents to supplement the family's meager income. Children as young as 14 often work 12 to 14 hours a day, six or seven days a week during the growing season. Consequently, they miss so much school that they often drop out. Only 55 percent graduate from high school.

Children in the fields face the prospect of backbreaking labor in extreme weather conditions, including severe heat. Often their employers do not provide them with drinking water, toilet facilities, or hand-washing facilities. They may suffer from dehydration and heat stroke, as well as injury from the labor and the tools and machinery they use. They are almost always exposed to high levels of pesticides. Sometimes, they are sprayed along with the crops. Most farmworkers report that they have not received information and training about handling pesticides and the symptoms of pesticide poisoning, although by law their employers are supposed to provide this. The report cites estimates that about 100,000 children become injured or ill each year in farm-related incidents.

The shelter provided to migrant farmworker families often consists of a single room in a barracks with poor ventilation and sanitation. If farm workers complain, they are generally fired. Federal and local authorities rarely act to ensure that farms are complying with the federal and state regulations that do exist.

RIGHTS

Many people sympathetic to the plight of the Dalits in India, the Roma in Europe, and child farmworkers say that they have rights that are being systematically violated. In the United States, we are familiar with talk of rights. After all, almost all of us are familiar with the Bill of Rights, the first ten amendments to the U.S. Constitution, which says that we have such rights as the rights to freedom of religion, freedom of speech, freedom of the press,, freedom from unreasonable searches and seizures, due process when accused of a crime, and freedom from cruel and unusual punishments. Later amendments specified such additional rights as a right not to be enslaved (Article 13) and a right to equal protection of the laws (Article 14). But while child farmworkers in the United States may have constitutional rights that are being violated, Dalits and Roma don't because they don't live in the United States.

Constitutional rights are not the only rights we have. We also have rights conferred on us by laws passed by a government, called *legal* rights. For example, in most states, people 21 and over have a legal right to drink alcohol, but those under age 21 do not have this right. What legal rights people have depends on what rights their government gives them. For example, Jews in Nazi Germany did not have the same legal rights that so-called "Aryans" had.

We can talk of constitutional and legal rights that people do have, but we also can speak of constitutional and legal rights that they *should* have. Women in the United States did not have a constitutional or legal right to vote until the twentieth century. Suffragists argued that they *should* have this right. Slaves in the United States did not have a constitutional or legal right to be free from enslavement, but abolitionists argued that it was a right that they should have. Centuries ago, people in European countries did not have a legal right to freedom of religion, but we can say that they should have.

We often find it useful to say that when people don't have a legal or constitutional right that they should have, they nevertheless have the right in some sense. For example, we might say that people in a country under a despot whose laws do not give them a right to freedom of speech nevertheless have such a right. But what kind of right are we referring to if it's not a constitutional or legal right?

The rights referred to are generally called *moral* rights. Moral rights are not created by governments, as with constitutional and legal rights. Instead, they are said to exist if there are very strong moral reasons supporting them and few if any strong moral reasons opposing them. Thus, if there are very strong moral reasons for attributing a right to freedom of religion to people and few if any strong moral reasons against it, then we are justified in claiming that people have a moral right to freedom of religion. In order to determine whether people have a specific moral right, we must ask whether there are strong enough moral arguments to support the view that governments *should* confer the right on people and enforce it.

Moral rights may be derived from utilitarian or Kantian reasoning, or from conceptions of virtue and vice. From a utilitarian perspective, we could ask what rights would minimize total harm or maximize total well-being for a society. For each alleged right then, the question to answer would be, Will there be more total well-being (or less total harm) if governments confer this right or instead if they don't confer this right?

From a Kantian perspective, we could ask either what rights we think we should have conferred on us or what rights are most consistent with respect for people, beings who have dignity or inherent moral worth. Thus, if you think that you should have a right to a variety of liberties, such as liberty of thought, then you would be inconsistent if you denied that other people have that same right. Similarly, if you think that a being with dignity and inherent worth should not be tortured merely because it is such a being, then you would be inconsistent if you thought that some people should be tortured.

Applying conceptions of virtue and vice, we could ask how a virtuous person would treat others, and go on to say that people have a right to be treated in that way. For example, we can ask whether a courageous, honest, just, and compassionate person would punish other people for what they believe or try to force people to change their beliefs. If the answer is no, then we could use this as a basis for justifying the claim that people have a right to freedom of thought.

Today, most people refer to moral rights as *human* rights. (At one time, they were called natural rights.) Human rights are called human because they apply to all people regardless of where they live, sex, race, ethnic background, religion, social and economic class, level of education, sexual orientation, and so on. Someone in Russia has the same human rights as someone in France. Women have the same human rights as men. A person of color has the same human rights as a white person. Furthermore, they are called human rights because they are attributed to people solely on the basis of the characteristics that make them human or that make them *people.* (A person is a being that is conscious of itself and its environment. It has the capacity to have a rich network of mental states, such as beliefs, hopes, desires, sensations, feelings, and emotions.)

How do we know what human rights people have? The best place to begin is with what constitutes the world's shared understanding of what human rights people have. This is embodied in the 1948 United Nations Universal Declaration of Human Rights.

THE UNITED NATIONS UNIVERSAL DECLARATION OF HUMAN RIGHTS

After World War II and the Holocaust, the United Nations formed a committee to draft a declaration of human rights. The committee created the following document in 1948, and since then, almost every nation on Earth has ratified it.

The Universal Declaration of Human Rights *(Used with permission.)*

Whereas a recognition of the inherent dignity and of the equal and inalienable rights of all members of the human family is the foundation of freedom, justice, and peace in the world.

Whereas disregard and contempt for human rights have resulted in barbarous acts which have outraged the conscience of mankind, and the advent of a world in which human beings shall enjoy freedom of speech and belief and freedom from fear and want has been proclaimed as the highest aspiration of the common people.

Whereas it is essential, if man is not to be compelled to have a recourse, as a last resort, to rebellion against tyranny and oppression, that human rights should be protected by the rule of law.

Whereas it is essential to promote the development of friendly relations between nations.

Whereas the peoples of the United Nations have in the Charter reaffirmed their faith in fundamental human rights, in the dignity and worth of the human person and in the equal rights of men and women and have determined to promote social progress and better standards of life in larger freedom,

Whereas Member States have pledged themselves to achieve, in cooperation with the United Nations, the promotion of universal respect for and observance of human rights and fundamental freedoms,

Whereas a common understanding of these rights and freedoms is of the greatest importance for the full realization of this pledge,

Now, therefore, THE GENERAL ASSEMBLY *proclaims* This Universal Declaration of Human Rights as a common standard of achievement for all peoples and all nations, to the end that every individual and every organ of society, keeping this Declaration constantly in mind, shall strive by teaching and education to promote respect for these rights and freedoms and by progressive measures, national and international, to secure their universal and effective recognition and observance. . . .

Article 1: All human beings are born free and equal in dignity and rights. They are endowed with reason and should act towards one another in a spirit of brotherhood.

Article 2: Everyone is entitled to all the rights and freedoms set forth in this Declaration, without distinction of any kind, such as race, colour, sex, language, religion, political or other opinion, national or social origin, property, birth, or other status.

Article 3: Everyone has the right to life, liberty and security of person.

Article 4: No one shall be held in slavery or servitude. . . .

Article 5: No one shall be subjected to torture or to cruel, inhuman or degrading treatment or punishment.

Article 6: Everyone has the right to recognition everywhere as a person before the law.

Article 7: All are equal before the law and are entitled without any discrimination to equal protection of the law.

Article 8: Everyone has the right to an effective remedy by the competent national tribunals for acts violating the fundamental rights granted him by the constitution or by law.

Article 9: No one shall be subjected to arbitrary arrest, detention or exile.

Article 10: Everyone is entitled in full equality to a fair and public hearing by an independent and impartial tribunal, in the determination of his rights and obligations and of any criminal charge against him.

Article 11: 1. Everyone charged with a penal offence has the right to be presumed innocent until proved guilty according to law in a public trial at which he has had all the guarantees necessary for his defence. 2. No one shall be held guilty of any penal offence on account of any act or omission which did not constitute a penal offence, under national or international law, at the time when it was committed. Nor shall a heavier penalty be imposed than the one that was applicable at the time the penal offence was committed.

Article 12: No one shall be subjected to arbitrary interference with his privacy, family, home or correspondence, nor to attacks upon his honour and reputation. Everyone has the right to protection of the law against such interference or attacks.

Article 13: 1. Everyone has the right to freedom of movement and residence within the borders of each state. 2. Everyone has the right to leave any country, including his own, and to return to his country.

Article 14: 1. Everyone has the right to seek and enjoy in other countries asylum from persecution. 2. This right may not be invoked in the case of prosecutions genuinely arising from non-political crimes or from acts contrary to the purposes or principles of the United Nations.

Article 15: 1. Everyone has the right to a nationality. 2. No one shall be deprived of his nationality nor denied the right to change his nationality.

Article 16: 1. Men and women of full age, without any limitation due to race, nationality or religion, have the right to marry and found a family. They are entitled to equal rights as to marriage, during marriage and at its dissolution. 2. Marriage shall be entered into only with the free and full consent of the intending spouses. 3. The family is the natural and fundamental group unit of society and is entitled to protection by society and the State.

Article 17: 1. Everyone has the right to own property alone as well as in association with others. 2. No one shall be arbitrarily deprived of his property.

Article 18: Everyone has the right to freedom of thought, conscience and religion; this right includes freedom to change his religion or belief, and freedom, either alone or in community with others and in public or private, to manifest his religion or belief in teaching, practice, worship and observance.

Article 19: Everyone has the right to freedom of opinion and expression; this right includes freedom to hold opinions without interference and to seek, receive and impart information and ideas through any media and regardless of frontiers.

Article 20: 1. Everyone has the right to freedom of peaceful assembly and association. 2. No one may be compelled to belong to an association.

Article 21: 1. Everyone has the right to take part in the government of his country, directly or through freely chosen representatives. 2. Everyone has the right of equal access to public service in his country. 3. The will of the people shall be the basis of authority of government; this shall be expressed in periodic and genuine elections which shall be held by secret vote or by equivalent free voting procedures.

Article 22: Everyone, as a member of society, has the right to social security and is entitled to realization, through national effort and international cooperation and in accordance with the organization and resources of each State, of the economic, social and cultural rights indispensable for his dignity and the free development of his personality.

Article 23: 1. Everyone has the right to work, to free choice of employment, to just and favourable conditions of work and to protection against unemployment. 2. Everyone, without any discrimination, has the right to equal pay for equal work. 3. Everyone who works has the right to just and favourable remuneration ensuring for himself and his family an existence worthy of human dignity, and supplemented, if necessary, by other means of social protection. 4. Everyone has the right to form and to join trade unions for the protection of his interests.

Article 24: Everyone has the right to rest and leisure, including reasonable limitations on working hours and periodic holidays with pay.

Article 25: 1. Everyone has the right to a standard of living adequate for the health and well-being of himself and of his family, including food, clothing, housing and medical care and necessary social services, and the right to security in the event of unemployment, sickness, disability, widowhood, old age or other lack of livelihood in circumstances beyond his control. 2. Motherhood and childhood are entitled to special care and assistance. All children, whether born in or out of wedlock, shall enjoy the same social protection.

Article 26: 1. Everyone has the right to education. Education shall be free, at least in the elementary and fundamental stages. Elementary education shall be compulsory. Technical and professional education shall be made generally available and higher education shall be equally accessible to all on the basis of merit. 2. Education shall be directed to the full development of the human personality and to the strengthening of respect for human rights and fundamental freedoms. It shall promote understanding, tolerance, and friendship among all nations, racial or religious groups, and shall further the activities of the United Nations for the maintenance of peace. 3. Parents have a prior right to choose the kind of education that shall be given to their children.

Article 27: 1. Everyone has the right to freely participate in the cultural life of the community, to enjoy the arts and to share in scientific advancement and its benefits. 2. Everyone has the right to the protection of the moral and material interests resulting from any scientific, literary or artistic production of which he is the author.

Article 28: Everyone is entitled to a social and international order in which the rights and freedoms set forth in this Declaration can be fully realized.

Article 29: 1. Everyone has duties to the community in which alone the free and full development of his personality is possible. 2. In the exercise of his rights and freedoms, everyone shall be subject only to such limits as are determined by law solely for the purpose of securing due recognition and respect for the rights and freedoms of others and of meeting the just requirements of morality, public order and the general welfare in a democratic society. 3. These rights and freedoms may in no case be exercised contrary to the purposes and principles of the United Nations.

Article 30: Nothing in this Declaration may be interpreted as implying for any State, group or person any right to engage in any activity or to perform any act aimed at the destruction of any of the rights and freedoms set forth herein.

The Foundation of the Declaration

The Declaration's preamble refers to the "inherent dignity" and the "dignity and worth" of "all members of the human family." The United Nations Declaration begins with the claim that all people are equal in a fundamental way. Being equal, they deserve equal treatment and equal rights. They are equal in that all have the characteristics that make them human. The most important of these human qualities are the mental capacities we have—consciousness, self-awareness, the capacity to have painful or pleasurable experiences; the beliefs, desires, hopes, dreams, and fears we have; the capacity to love; and the capacity to have a conscience and have our behavior guided by our own preferences, values, and moral principles. People are special because of their mental capacities, which confer on them the dignity and inherent value or worth that demands respectful treatment.

Because of their capacities, because of their status as having dignity and worth, people deserve to have protection from the things under human control that tend to seriously threaten their basic well-being and autonomy, the things that undermine their personhood. (Autonomy can refer to the inherent capacity of people to make decisions and choices that are determined by their own mental states, or to the external conditions that enable people to act on their own choices and decisions.) Because people have inherent worth and dignity, we should not destroy them or their capacities that make them people, and we should not stand aside and let them or the capacities that make them people be destroyed by others. First, of course, to continue to exist as a person, one must continue to live. Therefore, people deserve protection from the common serious threats to their lives that are under human control. This includes most especially the behavior of other people who can do things that will bring about a person's death, such as murdering or starving a person. Therefore, we should not shoot people or stand aside and let them be shot if we can prevent it. But to continue to function as a person, we need a certain level of physical and mental health. Someone may be alive, but if they are in a persistent vegetative state in which all higher level mental functioning has permanently ceased, they can no longer function as a person. Similarly, if someone is mentally retarded, paralyzed, uneducated or poorly educated, or in ill-health, he or she might not be able to function up to his or her full potential as a person. Therefore, people deserve protection from the common serious threats to the capacities that make them people, and they need opportunities to develop and use their mental capacities. In short, simply because they are people, people deserve to live a life appropriate to their personhood.

But how are we to understand the concept of a life appropriate to a human being, and how is that related to the functions or capabilities essential to humans? Amartya Sen emphasizes that human equality and inequality can manifest themselves in many ways: education, intelligence, strength, ambition, income, wealth, power, fame, legal rights, social status, health, and age. From the point of view of social and political theory, what dimensions of equality and inequality count most? According to Sen, basic well-being is most important. But how are we to understand the concept of human well-being? Sen conceptualizes it in terms of human capabilities; that is, what should be equal are our capabilities or opportunities to do the things we value most.

As Sen puts it,

> [Human] Living may be seen as consisting of a set of interrelated "functionings".... The relevant functionings can vary from such elementary things as being adequately nourished, being in good health, avoiding escapable morbidity and premature mortality, etc., to more complex achievements such as being happy, having self-respect, taking part in the life of the community, and so on.[13]

To live well or to achieve well-being is to achieve these functionings.

Achievement requires action on the part of the individual, and many people would object to a government forcing them to take action to achieve a certain level of functioning or well-being. For example, to guarantee that an individual achieves good health, a government would have to require a person to exercise and eat right, as well as to prohibit smoking. Sen claims that a realistic social ideal or goal is not guaranteeing achievement of these functionings, but rather guaranteeing certain levels of (equal) *opportunity* or *capability* to achieve these functionings. That is a role for rights. We say that we have a right to these opportunities for functioning, and an equal right with others.

Martha C. Nussbaum provides a reasonably comprehensive list of the functionings central to human well-being. She agrees with Sen that a primary goal of social policy should be to provide equal opportunities or capabilities for achieving these functions.

1. *Life.* Being able to live to the end of a human life of normal length...

2. *Bodily health and integrity.* Being able to have good health...; being adequately nourished; being able to have adequate shelter

3. *Bodily integrity.* Being able to move freely from place to place; being able to be secure against violent assault...

4. *Sense, imagination, thought.* Being able to use the senses; being able to imagine, to think, and to reason—and to do these in a "truly human" way, a way informed and cultivated by adequate education...; being able to have pleasurable experiences and avoid nonbeneficial pain

5. *Emotions.* Being able to have attachments to things and persons outside ourselves; being able to love ...; not having one's emotional developing blighted by fear or anxiety

6. *Practical reason.* Being able to form a conception of the good and to engage in critical reflection about the planning of one's own life

7. *Affiliation.* (a) Being able to live for and in relations with others, . . . to engage in various forms of social interaction . . . (b) Having the social bases of self-respect and nonhumiliation; being able to be treated as a dignified being whose worth is equal to that of others

8. *Other species.* Being able to live with concern for and in relation to animals, plants, and the world of nature

9. *Play.* Being able to laugh, to play, to enjoy recreational activities

10. *Control over one's environment.* (a) *Political:* being able to participate effectively in political choices that govern one's life; having the rights of political participation, free speech, and freedom of association; (b) *Material:* being able to hold property . . .; having the right to seek employment on an equal basis with others; having the freedom from unwarranted search and seizure. In work, being able to work as a human being, exercising practical reason. . . .[14]

According to Nussbaum, society should guarantee to all its members equal maximum opportunity to actualize these capabilities that are essential to living a fully human life. Rights may be thought of, then, as protecting people's opportunities to exercise these human capabilities.

CLASSIFICATION OF RIGHTS

The United Nations Declaration is a list of rights. Is there any way to bring order to or impose structure and system on it? While no system of classification is likely to be perfect, it seems helpful to divide them into the following. (Note that some rights may fit comfortably into more than one category while others in the Declaration fit into none of the categories.)

1. Rights to Security from Death, Physical Assault, and Physical Abuse
2. Rights to Due Process, Equal Protection, and Equality Before the Law
3. Rights to Political Participation
4. Liberty Rights
5. Welfare Rights

Before examining these categories of rights, however, we need to understand the meaning of rights.

The Meaning of a Right

What do we mean when we say that someone has a specific right, such as a right to life? We can explain the meaning or content of a right by specifying the duties to the right-holder that it imposes on others. If you have a right to life, then others have a duty not to kill you, at least without a morally compelling reason. They may also have a duty to preserve your life when it is seriously threatened (and they can do so at reasonable cost or risk to themselves). Similarly, if you have a right to freedom of speech, then others have a duty to you to not interfere with you when you try to speak. In addition, the government has a duty to provide you with protection from those who would try to prevent you from speaking. To specify the content or meaning of a right, then, we must specify who has the right, who has the duties to the right-holder, and what duties they have to the right-holder.

Duties can be positive or negative. A positive duty is a duty to do something; a negative duty is a duty to not do something. For example, the duty to file an income tax return is a positive duty; the duty not to drive while intoxicated is a negative duty. Rights can entail both positive and negative duties. Those that entail mostly negative duties are called negative rights; those that entail mostly positive duties are called positive rights. The right to life is both positive and negative because it entails a negative right not to be killed and a positive right to have one's life preserved when seriously threatened.

Rights and the duties they entail generally should not be considered absolute. If a right is absolute, then there are no circumstances in which it may legitimately be violated or infringed. Take the right to life. If it's absolute, then there are no circumstances in which we're justified in killing someone. Few people consider even as basic a right as the right to life absolute. Most of us think killing in self-defense or to save the innocent is not wrong. In this situation, the right to life of a murderer is in conflict with the right to life of his victims. (Of course, killing must be necessary to save the innocent victims in order to override the murderer's right to life.) Similarly, few of us think that the right to freedom of speech is absolute. If someone begins giving a speech at the top of his lungs at 3 A.M. outside your bedroom window, you're not likely to think that he has a right to do that even if he has a right to freedom of speech. (Recall that moral principles, which can be expressed in the language of duty and rights, are weighed against each other when making all-things-considered singular moral judgments.)

Let us turn now to an examination of the different categories of human rights.

Rights to Security from Very Serious Physical and Psychological Harm

This category of rights is intended to protect people against various forms of abuse that cause such serious harms as death, injury, and intense pain. This category of rights forbids us to murder, torture, rape, and assault others. (We have a *duty* not to do these things.) It includes Article 3 (the right to life and to security of person) and Article 5 (the right not to be subject to torture or to cruel, inhuman, or degrading treatment). If people have such moral rights, then not only do other individuals have a duty to not kill, rape, torture, or beat them, but governments have a duty to protect the people from these things. Why? Because they are people with inherent worth and dignity, and they and their personhood should not be destroyed, at least without a very compelling moral reason. These rights may be among the most fundamental moral rights, a kind of moral bedrock.

Rights to Equal Protection and Equality Before the Law

This category of rights is intended to protect people from unequal or illegitimate applications of the laws of their community and from various forms of discrimination. What may come to the same thing, they also protect people from arbitrary exercises of power, which can seriously harm people. They require that laws apply to everyone and be applied fairly and consistently. This category includes Articles 1 (equal rights), 2 (right to not be discriminated against on the basis of irrelevant characteristics such as race), 6 (right to recognition as a person before the law), 7 (right to equal protection of the law), 9 (right to be free from arbitrary arrest), 10 (right to a fair public trial), 11 (right to be presumed innocent until proved guilty), 12 (right to be free from arbitrary interference), 15 (right to a nationality), and 17 (right to not be arbitrarily deprived of one's property). Even a superficial acquaintance with history reveals how commonly people and their capacities have been destroyed when they do not enjoy equal protection of the laws and freedom from arbitrary exercises of power.

Rights to Political Participation

This category of rights is intended to protect people from being excluded from government decisions that can have a profound effect on their lives. It is directed against various forms of tyranny and is intended to ensure that government is based on the freely given consent of the governed. In its most general form, it is a right to participate in political decision making. Article 21 (right to take part in the government of his country, directly or through freely chosen representatives) is the primary member of this category, although other articles such as articles 7 (equal protection of the law), 18 (the right to freedom of thought and religion), 19 (the right to freedom of opinion and expression), and 20 (the right to freedom of assembly and association) may be necessary means to the end of effective political participation.

There was a time in the not-so-distant past when almost all ordinary people had no role to play in governing other than to obey. They were subjects of rulers over whom they had little control or influence, rulers they didn't select. Not surprisingly, their governments usually ignored their needs and interests. For example, the twentieth century saw the tyranny of Stalin in the Soviet Union, Hitler in Germany, Mao in China, and Saddam Hussein in Iraq. Yet today, many people think that democracy is the only legitimate form of government, and many argue that democracy is the best protector of people's interests and liberties.

Democracy is a matter of degree. For example, the United States became more democratic when women gained the right to vote. It became even more democratic when the Federal government began to protect the rights of African Americans in the South to vote in the 1960s.

Requirements For Democracy.   What makes a government democratic? Robert A. Dahl lists five general criteria of democratic processes or decision making by groups.

Effective participation. Before a policy is adopted . . ., all the members must have equal and effective opportunities for making their views known to the other members as to what the policy should be.

Voting Equality. [E]very member must have an equal and effective opportunity to vote, and all votes must be counted as equal.

Enlightened understanding. [E]ach member must have equal and effective opportunities for learning about the relevant alternative policies and their likely consequences.

Control of the agenda. The members must have the exclusive opportunity to decide how and, if they choose, what matters are to be placed on the agenda.

Inclusion of adults. All, or at any rate most, adult permanent residents should have the full rights of citizens. . . .[15]

The five general criteria are supplemented by six political institutions needed to make a genuine representative democracy.

1. Elected officials.
2. Free, fair, and frequent elections.
3. Freedom of expression.
4. Access to alternative sources of information.
5. Associational autonomy.
6. Inclusive citizenship.[16] Inclusive citizenship includes, besides the previous list, the rights to vote and to run for office.

On April 27, 1999, the 55th Commission on Human Rights, a body of the United Nations, adopted a Resolution on the Right to Democracy. It expressed an intention to "secure for all people the fundamental democratic rights and freedoms to which they are entitled. . . ." According to Article 2, "the rights of democratic governance include":

a. The rights to freedom of opinion and expression, of thought, conscience and religion, and of peaceful association and assembly;
b. The right to freedom to seek, receive and impart information and ideas through any media;
c. The rule of law, including legal protection of citizens' rights, interests and personal security, and fairness in the administration of justice, and independence of the judiciary;
d. The right of universal and equal suffrage, as well as free voting procedures and periodic and free elections;
e. The right of political participation, including equal opportunity for all citizens to become candidates;
f. Transparent and accountable government institutions;

g. The right of citizens to choose their governmental system through constitutional or other democratic means;

h. The right to equal access to public service in one's own country. . . .[17]

Rights to Liberty or Freedom

This category of rights is intended to protect people's autonomy by protecting certain liberties or freedoms considered basic or fundamental. It includes Articles 3 (right to liberty), 4 (right to not be enslaved), 13 (rights to freedom of movement and residence), 16 (right to freedom regarding marriage and family life), 17 (right to freedom to own property), 18 (rights to freedom of thought and religion), 19 (rights to freedom of thought and expression), and 20 (rights to freedom of assembly and association).

Laws forbid us to do some things and require us to do others. They restrict our liberty. If we live where laws restrict our liberty, are we then unfree? Are we free only if we have a right to do whatever we want whenever we want? If I say I'm free, that doesn't tell you much. Do I mean that I've finally been let out of jail? That my divorce has become final? That I've escaped from my kidnappers? To make sense of the claim, I must explain what constraint I'm free from and what actions I can/may do or not do. Here we'll limit liberty to considerations of being free from government interference to do and not do certain things. For example, if I say I'm free to walk on the grass, I mean that there are no laws forbidding me to do it. If I say I'm not free to smoke marijuana, I mean that there are laws forbidding it.

No one thinks we should be free from government interference to do whatever we want. Surely we all think that the government should forbid some things, whether it's murder, rape, kidnapping, arson, driving while intoxicated, or robbery. The question is what freedoms (note the plural) we should have—we have a right to—and those we shouldn't have. At one time in the South, people were not at liberty to marry whomever they chose. Antimiscegenation laws forbade interracial marriage. Today we think that's a liberty people should have (although many people would deny this unless the couple consists of one male and one female). At one time in the United States, people were not at liberty to terminate unwanted pregnancies by abortion or openly purchase contraceptives. Today many people think these are liberties people should have.

The United Nations Universal Declaration of Human Rights says that everyone has the right to freedom of movement (Article 13); to marry and found a family (Article 16); to own property (Article 17); to freedom of thought, conscience, and religion (Article 18); to freedom of opinion and expression (Article 19); to freedom of peaceful assembly and association (Article 20); to free choice of employment (Article 23); and to form and join trade unions (Article 23). The United Nations Declaration does not pretend to list every liberty we have a right to but rather focuses on the most important liberties.

For Plato, the form of liberty or freedom that is a desirable social ideal lies between the excesses of slavery (too little liberty) and license (too much liberty). When license reigns, law and order are overturned. There is little to restrain people from doing what they want, even if it's to murder or steal. We're not really free if we live where there are no laws, customs, traditions, and public opinion to control people's behavior. If other people's tendencies to harm others in various ways aren't controlled by external forces, we won't be free to do much except cower in our holes. We'll be subject to the force, violence, and coercion of everyone who is stronger than we are. But if people are subject to a variety of social controls, in what sense do they have liberty? In one important sense of liberty, as we saw, someone has liberty if he or she participates in making and enforcing society's rules, and if he or she shares in governing. Second, we're free if the rules that constrain us are not unreasonable, irrational, or arbitrary. The legitimate ideal of liberty is *freedom from arbitrary and unreasonable restrictions and requirements*, not freedom from all social control.

What justifies limitations on liberty or the denial to people of certain liberties, such as the liberty of an adult to engage in sex with a child? How should we decide whether physicians should be free to help their patients commit suicide, or whether people should be free to publicly burn the flag of their country? Should people be free to use marijuana, heroin, and cocaine, or free to buy and sell sex? Should wealthy people be free to contribute as much money as they want to political candidates? Should people of the same sex be free to marry each other? To what principles can we appeal in deciding these questions?

JOHN STUART MILL AND THE HARM PRINCIPLE

In *On Liberty*, John Stuart Mill (1806–1873) claims that governments have the moral right to limit people's liberty only when it is necessary to prevent them from harming others.

> The object of [*On Liberty*] is to assert one very simple principle, as entitled to govern absolutely the dealings of society with the individual in the way of compulsion and control, whether the means used be physical force in the form of legal penalties or the moral coercion of public opinion. The principle is that the sole end for which mankind are warranted, individually or collectively, in interfering with the liberty of action of any of their number is self-protection. That the only purpose for which power can be rightfully exercised over any member of a civilized community, against his will, is to prevent harm to others. His own good, either physical or moral, is not a sufficient warrant. He cannot rightfully be compelled to do or forbear because it will be better for him to do so, because it will make him happier, because, in the opinion of others, to do so would be wise or even right. These are good reasons for remonstrating with him, or reasoning with him, or per-suading him, or entreating him, but not for compelling him or visiting him with any evil in case he do otherwise. To justify that, the conduct from which it is desired to deter him must be calculated to produce evil to someone else. The only part of the conduct of anyone for which he is

amenable to society is that which concerns others. In the part which merely concerns himself, his independence is, of right, absolute. Over himself, over his own body and mind, the individual is sovereign.[18]

According to Mill's Harm Principle, people should be free from social interference to do what they want to do and to not do what they don't want to do unless they are likely to harm others. (Mill remarks that this principle applies only to people who are "in the maturity of their faculties." It does not apply to children or to adults who have serious psychological or mental handicaps. The concept employed today is that of being *competent.*)

Applying Mill's Harm Principle, one can say that people should not be free to commit murder, rape, steal, or drive while intoxicated, because such behaviors obviously harm others or create a serious risk of causing harm to others. On the other hand, people obviously should be free to decide for themselves about smoking, watching television, and exercising because these actions do not harm anyone. According to Mill, laws should not be designed to protect people from themselves. Mountain climbing, motorcycle racing, and smoking cigarettes are dangerous activities, but the government would not be morally justified in prohibiting them. We should be free to act as we see fit, even if our actions might bring harm to ourselves.

FEINBERG: FOUR POSSIBLE PRINCIPLES LEGITIMIZING COERCION

In his four volume work *The Moral Limits of the Criminal Law*, contemporary American philosopher Joel Feinberg provides the most exhaustive treatment available of the Harm Principle and its main competitors. Feinberg identifies four different principles that we might employ in deciding whether it is legitimate for the government to prohibit or require certain behavior.

A. *The Harm Principle.* The government is morally justified in prohibiting actions that will cause serious harm or high risk of serious harm to others and in requiring actions that prevent serious harm to others at small cost or risk to the agent.

B. *The Offense Principle.* The government is morally justified in prohibiting conduct that seriously offends others.

C. *Paternalism.* The government is morally justified in prohibiting actions that will cause serious harm or a high risk of serious harm to the agent himself even if no one else would be harmed.

D. *Legal Moralism.* The government is morally justified in prohibiting immoral behavior even if it will not harm or offend anyone.

Feinberg, in the spirit of Mill, (1) accepts the legitimacy of the Harm Principle, (2) accepts only a heavily qualified version of the Offense Principle, (3) accepts what he calls Soft Paternalism but rejects what he calls Hard Paternalism, and (4) rejects Legal Moralism.

The Harm Principle

According to Feinberg, only actions that cause serious and *unjustified* harms should be forbidden. If I get a job that you needed, I've harmed you. But I should still be free to take the job if the competition was fair because I'm justified in applying for and taking jobs. Then, too, there must be a *high probability* that the action will cause harm to others, not just a possibility, although the more serious the harm, the less probable it must be. And there must be good reasons for thinking that an action will probably cause harm; mere assertion is not enough. Finally, harm that justifies limiting liberty can be to groups of individuals, even society as a whole, not just to single identifiable individuals. For example, if it can be shown that violence on television significantly increases the amount of violence in society, that may justify us in limiting the liberty of broadcasters to broadcast programs with a lot of violence, even if we can't identify the specific individuals likely to be harmed.

Does the Harm Principle justify only prohibiting certain actions, or can it also justify requiring certain actions? Ultimately, Feinberg concludes that a plausible formulation of the Harm Principle should both *prohibit* people from causing harm and *require* them to prevent harm when the harm would be great and the cost of preventing the harm reasonably small. The two types of prohibition—against acting to cause harm and against failing to act to prevent harm—have the same purpose: harm prevention.[19]

The Offense Principle

Feinberg also endorses a restricted and qualified version of the Offense Principle: The government is morally justified in prohibiting conduct that seriously offends others. Offense produces unpleasant or uncomfortable experiences, perhaps disgust, even shock. Feinberg maintains that instances of offense, even serious offense, are less serious than instances of harm. But he provides some hair-raising examples of behavior that, because done in public, would probably offend most people but that would not cause them harm. Consider the following acts likely to cause offense, which are suggested by Feinberg's examples:

A passenger on a bus loudly plays music that most passengers find obnoxious.

A bus passenger uses the American flag as a handkerchief, ostentatiously blowing his nose into it.

Two people on a bus take off their clothes and begin to copulate in the center aisle.

Feinberg's point is that some offensive conduct can be very offensive indeed. He thinks that the government may prohibit some offensive conduct (or prohibit it in certain places or at certain times) but by no means all. Where do we draw the line?

According to Feinberg, only the most seriously offensive conduct should be prohibited, and only if it is difficult to avoid exposure to it. The seriousness of offensive behavior depends on the intensity of the unpleasantness or discomfort of the experience, its duration, and how much inconvenience one would be put through in order to avoid or escape exposure to the offending conduct. The more intense the unpleasantness or discomfort, the longer its duration, and the greater the inconvenience to avoid it, the stronger the case for prohibition. Thus, there's a difference between offensive material being placed in a museum with warnings to potential viewers and placing it in the middle of a well-traveled sidewalk. In the first case, but not the second, we can easily avoid it if we wish to. Finally, the number of offended people is also relevant. The more people who would be offended, the stronger is the case for prohibition. And as with harm, the probability of offense is relevant.

In addition, the reasonableness of the offending conduct and its social utility, if any, must be considered. You may be offended by a business remaining open on the Sabbath, but there may be good reasons for giving its owners the freedom to decide for themselves what days it will be open. On the other hand, you may be offended by the loud profanity and obnoxious music coming from your neighbor's outdoor beer party at 2 A.M. If such behavior is not reasonable and has little social utility, the government may be justified in prohibiting it. Besides its general social utility, the utility or importance of the offending conduct to those who engage in it must also be considered. As Feinberg points out, at one time the sight of interracial couples offended many people. Does the government have the right to prohibit interracial couples from appearing together in public on the grounds that the sight offends people? The cost to the couples would be very great indeed given the importance of friendship and love in people's lives. The *importance to the agents* of the conduct being prohibited counts against the legitimacy of prohibiting it.

In addition to the preceding considerations, the intentions of the agent and the relative inconvenience to which the agent would be put to reduce the offense to others must be considered. If Jones is wearing an offensive T-shirt merely because he wants to offend or intimidate others, then the government would be more justified in prohibiting such conduct than if Jones is wearing an offensive T-shirt in order to educate people or to make a political statement.[20]

Hard and Soft Paternalism

The principle of Paternalism states that it is morally legitimate for the government to employ coercion to protect people from themselves, even when they are competent adults. According to Paternalism, preventing people from harming themselves is as legitimate as preventing them from harming or seriously offending others.

Few would argue that the government may and should pass laws to protect the *incompetent* (for example, children, the mentally handicapped, the mentally ill, and the extremely intoxicated) from harming themselves either deliberately or from their own carelessness or recklessness. But what of adults who are competent, that is, capable of making rational decisions? May the government pass laws designed to protect competent people from themselves?

On the one hand, people may directly and intentionally harm themselves by, for example, committing (or attempting) suicide or mutilating themselves (as by cutting off a hand). On the other hand, people may engage in behavior that creates considerable risk of harm to themselves, although they do not intend to harm themselves. Someone swimming alone at an unguarded beach has a higher probability of drowning than someone swimming with friends at a beach that has a lifeguard on duty. A cigarette smoker may not want to develop lung cancer, but smoking will drastically raise the probability of her developing it. Other risky behaviors include rock climbing, sky diving, auto racing, riding a motorcycle without a helmet, unprotected sex, and handling poisonous snakes during religious ceremonies.

Purely paternalistic laws are those designed solely to prevent people from harming themselves. (If a law is designed both to protect people from themselves and to protect people from others, it is not purely paternalistic.) Paternalistic laws are thus benevolent, motivated by a concern for the agent's own good. But Feinberg distinguishes between hard and soft paternalism.

> Hard paternalism will accept as a reason for criminal legislation that it is necessary to protect competent adults, against their will, from the harmful consequences even of their fully voluntary choices and undertakings.... [I]t imposes its own values and judgments on people "for their own good"....
>
> Soft paternalism holds that the state has the right to prevent self-regarding harmful conduct... *when but only when* that conduct is substantially nonvoluntary, or when temporary intervention is necessary to establish whether it is voluntary or not.[21]

Feinberg accepts the principle of soft paternalism. He believes that the government has a right, perhaps even a duty, to protect the incompetent from harming themselves—for example, an adult who, in the middle of an episode of extreme psychosis, is about to drink poison. Because people who are incompetent are not capable of making rational choices, their actions are not fully voluntary; rather, they are nonvoluntary (as opposed to involuntary). But Feinberg also believes that it is morally legitimate for the government to *temporarily* stop an adult from doing something directly harmful or extremely risky to himself in order to ascertain whether the person is fully competent and understands the risks. If the person is not competent (either temporarily or permanently), then the government may continue to protect him from himself until he becomes competent. However, if the person is competent, then according to Feinberg, it would not be morally legitimate for the government to continue to prevent him from directly harming himself or from engaging in the extremely risky behavior.

Legal Moralism

According to Legal Moralism, it is morally legitimate for the government to prohibit behavior that is considered to be inherently immoral, even if no one is wrongfully harmed or wrongfully seriously offended by it. For example, if a government were to prohibit private homosexual acts between consenting adults solely on the grounds that they are immoral, then it would be applying Legal Moralism.

According to Feinberg, one justification for Legal Moralism appeals to the need to protect and preserve the way of life of a specific community. For example, a community of Puritans might maintain that adultery, divorce, birth control, drinking alcoholic beverages, and dancing are inherently immoral activities that must be prohibited in order to preserve the Puritan way of life. But does the majority of people in a community (or a powerful minority) have a moral right to force other members of the community to conform to rules they disagree with and have not consented to (or no longer consent to)? Surely it would be a serious violation of someone's right to autonomy if the community required him or her to live in strict accordance with the moral code of its rulers or the majority, instead of living (within limits) according to his or her own moral code.

Of course, no community can survive for long if its members seriously and wrongfully harm or offend each other. But Feinberg argues that a community is strengthened if it leaves room for diversity instead of trying to enforce a rigid conformity. Trying to force people to live by rules they no longer accept can lead to an explosion of violent resistance, as happened during the Reformation and Counter-Reformation when communities tried to enforce religious conformity in order to protect the community's way of life. Moral pluralism may be as necessary to social cohesion in the long run as is religious pluralism. Besides, communities naturally change and evolve just as species change and languages evolve. It is futile and probably dangerous to try to block all changes to a community's way of life.[22]

Of course, sometimes changes to a community's way of life may be an improvement rather than the reverse. What a majority in a community believes to be inherently immoral may not be. Some ways of life are oppressive and exploitative. If a community's way of life changes so that it no longer includes a commitment to enslavement of blacks, subordination of women, and strict racial segregation, then surely those changes are for the better. Protection and preservation of a way of life is rather weak justification for coercion of a community's members if the components of the way of life being protected and preserved are morally suspect.

Even if a particular change is considered anything but an improvement—for example, if one thinks that people's engaging in homosexual behavior is a sign of social decay rather than social progress—it does not follow that *tolerating* such behavior will lead to a significant change in the community's way of life, such as transforming it from a mostly heterosexual to a mostly homosexual community. Disapproved forms of behavior are not necessarily "contagious." For example, a person's sexual orientation is highly resistant to change. (What could cause you to change your sexual orientation?) If homosexual behavior is tolerated (not prohibited or punished), most people will still remain heterosexual. Even if adultery and divorce are inherently immoral, tolerating them (not legally prohibiting them) may not have a very profound effect on the community's way of life, leaving substantial parts of it intact.

SEVEN BASIC FREEDOMS

The *Human Development Report 2000* published by the United Nations Development Programme lists seven freedoms that it claims everyone has a right to. The authors believe that these seven freedoms are essential to human dignity and the expansion of choices and alternatives open to people—something at the core of the concept of liberty. They are presented as forms of protecting people from pervasive forces that reduce the fundamental life choices available to them. The seven freedoms are:

Freedom from discrimination—by gender, race, ethnicity, national origin or religion,

Freedom from want—to enjoy a decent standard of living,

Freedom to develop and realize one's human potential,

Freedom from fear—of threats to personal security, from torture, arbitrary arrest and other violent acts,

Freedom from injustice and violations of the rule of law,

Freedom of thought and speech and to participate in decision-making and form associations,

Freedom for decent work—without exploitation.[23]

According to the authors, the amount of liberty we have depends on the number and kinds of obstacles to actualizing and developing our valuable capabilities and on the forces that reduce the choices available to us. Each of the seven freedoms is intended to protect us from these things.

WELFARE RIGHTS

This category of rights is intended to protect people from harm that may befall them because of an inability to meet their basic needs or from their lack of power over their conditions of living and working. They protect the development and maintenance of the capacities identified with personhood. They include Articles 22 (the right to social security), 23 (the right to employment, to favorable conditions of work, etc.), 24 (the right to rest and leisure), 25 (the right to an adequate standard of living), and 26 (the right to education).

The Right to an Adequate Standard of Living

According to Article 25, everyone has a right to a standard of living adequate for their health and well-being. If you have that right, then if you cannot or can barely meet your basic needs, others have a duty to help you get (or provide you with) the things you need in order to survive. The duty does not fall directly on you or me. Rather, it falls on society collectively. Society in general has a duty to help you get or provide you with the things you need in order to survive. The claim that people have a right to a standard of living adequate for their health and well-being is based on the assumption that a person's life, health, and well-being are morally important and deserve social protection.

Does society have a duty to provide things to people who could be self-sufficient but who, perhaps because of laziness, refuse to work to provide themselves with the things they need? Many people say no. They would add the following qualification to the content of the right. Our society has a duty to help us get or provide us with the things we need in order to survive at some level of decency *provided that* we are unable to get these things for ourselves without help. A variety of things beyond our control may make it difficult or impossible to support ourselves: age (too young or too old), poor health, lack of education or job skills, lack of jobs, and low wages. We can build this qualification into the content of all welfare rights in order to overcome the potential objection that their recognition would require society to support people who can but refuse to support themselves.

The Right to Employment

If you have a right to employment and protection against unemployment, it means that others (presumably society collectively through government) have a duty to help you secure employment if you are having difficulty finding work; if the government did nothing to help you get employed or to soften the pain of joblessness, it would violate your rights. Involuntary unemployment is a serious threat to people because of how important employment is in their lives. First and most obviously, employment is the primary or only source of income for most people. If you're unemployed, you can't earn money to pay for the things you need. But work or employment is also important for other reasons. It is often a source of pride, self-respect, and self-esteem; for some it is the core of their identity. Work provides satisfaction for a job well done. It enables people to feel productive and useful and to make a contribution to society that they can feel proud of, however modest the contribution may be. Unemployment can make us feel worthless. Then, too, for better or worse, many people in our society define themselves by their occupation and derive a large part of their identity from it. When others ask us about ourselves, often our first response is to tell them our occupation: a doctor, a teacher, a plumber, an electrician, and so on.

Employment or work also can be an ingredient in the good life. Idleness associated with unemployment can make life boring. We also may find ourselves isolated from other people; work enables us to associate daily with others. If the work is intrinsically interesting or challenging, it can stimulate us. For some people, spending time working is spending time on activities one loves. For example, scientists, teachers, and auto mechanics may love what they do and would feel enormous loss if their work were taken from them.

The Right to Just and Favorable Remuneration

If you have a right to just and favorable remuneration, others (employers) have a duty to not pay you what we could call starvation wages. Paying workers wages or salaries that are so low that workers cannot afford even to meet their basic needs and live a life of reasonable dignity violates the moral rights of workers. If your wages are so low that you can only afford to live in a doghouse and eat dog food, then you do not have just and favorable remuneration for your work. This right imposes on employers a duty to pay adequate wages. It also imposes on governments a duty either to pass minimum wage laws and set the minimum high enough that people can live a life appropriate to human beings rather than beasts, or to subsidize wages to bring a worker's income up to a decent level.

The Right to Rest, Leisure, and Reasonable Working Hours

If you were a factory worker in Victorian England in the 1840s or 1850s, you probably would be forced to work 12–16 hours per day. You also might be forced to work six days per week. If you refused to work such long hours or complained, you would almost certainly be fired. Finding another job would be very difficult because there was a lot of unemployment, and if you were lucky enough to find another job in a reasonable period of time, the hours probably would be no better. If you lost your job, you'd probably be in dire straits because there was no unemployment compensation and few social welfare programs. What social programs that did exist were modest and stingy. Therefore, you would want to hold onto your job even if it meant working 12–16 hours per day six days per week. (Not only were hours long, but pay was paltry.)

What would your life be like if you were working such long hours? For one thing, it would probably be short. You would risk literally working yourself to death at an early age. Then, too, the quality of your life while you lived would be dismal. Imagine always working from 6 A.M. until 8 P.M. at night. You'd always feel tired. You would have no time for anything but work. You would have almost no time for family life or socializing with friends.

Many people think that a life devoted almost exclusively to work, eating, and sleeping is not suitable for a human being or consistent with his or her dignity as a person. They think it especially unsuitable when it is involuntary. Workers in Victorian England did not freely choose to work such long hours. They were forced to by desperation. Being helpless and vulnerable, they faced the choice of working under the conditions dictated to them or starving. The right to rest and leisure is intended to protect people from the threat of being forced to endure working conditions that are incompatible with our dignity as persons. It imposes on employers a duty to limit work hours and provide some time off. The right also imposes on government the duty to protect workers from exploitation by their employers. Laws can limit the hours of work, prohibit compulsory overtime, and require employers to pay workers at a higher rate for overtime.

The Right to Education

For a human being to live a life mired in ignorance and error is not consistent with his or her dignity as a person. Someone who is illiterate and wholly uneducated may not be able to reach his or her full potential as a person. Where knowledge is power, ignorance and error are powerlessness. Someone in an industrial society who is illiterate and without any education is handicapped. Imagine not being able to read street signs, newspapers, or employment applications. Imagine not being able to write to your senator or to a newspaper in order to protest policies that are harmful to your interests. Imagine not being able to count change so that you never know whether you are being cheated when you buy things. Without education, you would have little control over your life and environment.

Article 26 of the Declaration maintains that you have a right to free elementary or "fundamental" education. That means that society has a duty to provide you (and everyone) with basic education at no direct charge. In our country, that right has translated into 12 years of free education up to the senior year of high school. Beyond high school, according to Article 26, higher education is to be made "equally accessible to all on the basis of merit."

Justifying Welfare Rights

If a person is unable to meet his or her basic needs and the society does not do anything—or do enough—to ensure that these needs are met, then that person's welfare rights have been violated.

Some people complain that if people have welfare rights, then that violates other people's liberty rights. In a society where government protects welfare rights, government taxes people to pay for these programs whether or not a taxpayer wants to pay for them. But what precisely are the freedoms or liberties that are in conflict with this? It's not such basic liberties as freedom of religion, thought, speech, or movement. Rather, doesn't it seem that the only freedoms in conflict with implementing welfare rights are the freedoms to not pay taxes and to keep all the money we earn and spend it as we please? (If other liberty rights are violated, which are they?)

One way to look at it is to ask which is more important from a moral point of view: ensuring that people's welfare rights are protected or ensuring that people are free to not pay taxes and to keep all the money they earn. But we also could frame the issue in terms of a clash of freedoms. That is, people's freedom to develop and realize their human potential and freedom from want on the one hand may come into conflict with people's freedom not to pay taxes and to keep all the money they earn. Lack of resources obviously can be a barrier preventing people from realizing and developing their potential, and it equally obviously creates want so that people aren't free from want. To protect people's freedom to realize and develop their potential and to free them from want, we could take resources from those who have more than they need and transfer them to those who have less than they need. If we do not, are we implicitly judging that people's freedom to not pay taxes and keep all they earn is more important from a moral point of view than people's freedom to realize and develop their potential and to be free from want? How might we justify such a judgment?

Finally, another way to look at it is that if a government is democratic, then the decision to tax people in order to pay for government programs to implement people's subsistence rights is made democratically. A commitment to democracy means living with political decisions even if we're on the losing side of the issue.

EXERCISES

1. Some people think that only governments have a duty to respect people's human rights. Giant, Inc. fires all employees accused or suspected of supporting unionization of its work force. There is no hearing or appeals process at which employees can defend themselves. Are any human rights of workers violated? If yes, is it wrong for the company to violate its employees' human rights?

2. Answer the following questions and *defend* your answers.
    - Should physicians ever be free to help their patients commit suicide?
    - Should people ever be free to publicly burn the flag of their country?
    - Should people be free to use marijuana, heroin, and cocaine?
    - Should people be free to buy and sell sex?
    - Should people be free to post pornographic images on the Internet?
    - Should wealthy people be free to contribute as much money as they want to political candidates?
    - Should people of the same sex be free to marry each other?

3. May the government legitimately *require* people to:
    - Wear seatbelts?
    - Serve in the military during war time?
    - Buy automobile insurance?
    - Register all one's firearms?

4. Thompson, who is white, does not want to serve black people in the restaurant he owns. He says that he should be free to serve or refuse to serve whomever he pleases because it is his restaurant. Douglass, a black woman denied service at Thompson's restaurant, maintains that the government should protect her freedom to eat in any public restaurant she wants to eat in by prohibiting Thompson from discriminating against her on the basis of race. In addition, Douglass says that Thompson relies on the government (police and courts) to help him discriminate. If a black person enters Thompson's restaurant and refuses to leave after being ordered to do so, Thompson calls the police to have the patron removed, claiming that the black is trespassing on private property. Would it be morally acceptable for the government to require Thompson to serve blacks as well as whites?

5. Glenburg is an all-white town that has passed an ordinance prohibiting nonwhites from living or owning property in Glenburg. They wish to preserve the "character and charm" of their community and its way of life. An African American couple brings suit in state court to void the law. The inhabitants of Glenburg say that they should be free to exclude nonwhites from their community. The African American couple argues that they should be free to live wherever they want. With whom do you agree? Why?

6. Suppose that someone from a poor community makes the following argument:

Our children have a right to equal education that is being violated.

Wealthy school districts around us have the money to spend twice as much on education per pupil as we can. So they have nice classrooms, small classes, plenty of books, computers, and science laboratories.

Our schools are falling apart and overcrowded. Our class sizes average 38 where class sizes in nearby suburbs average 24. Our school library only has a few hundred books, and it can only stay open 2 hours a day because of staff cutbacks. We don't even have science laboratories or computers. Our kids are not getting an education that's anywhere near equal to what kids in the suburbs around us are getting. This situation is completely unjust. Our childrens' rights are being violated and that's intolerable. Every child should have an education that is equal in quality.

Do people have a human right to equal educational opportunities? If yes, what must be done to implement such a right?

7. After the Japanese bombing of Pearl Harbor that brought the United States into World War II, over 100,000 Japanese Americans on the West coast were rounded up by the United States military and sent to internment camps because they were considered a potential threat to national security. None were accused of any crimes. Many, if not most, were U.S. citizens. Many had been born in the United States. Federal officials feared that they would feel more loyalty to Japan than to the United States, but no evidence was ever presented to prove that they were a threat. None of them received an individual hearing or trial in order to determine whether they were a threat. Being of Japanese ancestry was considered enough. Many of them spent years in concentration camps. However, German Americans and Italian Americans were not similarly interned as threats to our security, although the United States was also at war with Germany and Italy. Did the internment of Japanese Americans during World War II violate anyone's human rights? If yes, which ones?

8. Do people have a human right to medical care? Precisely what duties would such a right entail?

SUGGESTED READINGS

David Copp, Jean Hampton, and John Roemer, eds. *The Idea of Democracy*. Cambridge, England: Cambridge University Press, 1993.

Robert A. Dahl. *On Democracy*. New Haven, CT: Yale University Press, 1998.

Jack Donnelly. *Universal Human Rights in Theory and Practice*. Ithaca, NY: Cornell University Press, 1989.

John Dunn, ed. *Democracy: The Unfinished Journey*. Oxford, England: Oxford University Press, 1992.

Joel Feinberg. *The Moral Limits of the Criminal Law.* Volume 1, *Harm to Others.* New York: Oxford University Press, 1984. Volume 2, *Offense to Others.* New York: Oxford University Press, 1985. Volume 3, *Harm to Self.* New York: Oxford University Press, 1986. Volume 4, *Harmless Wrongdoing.* New York: Oxford University Press, 1988.

Micheline R. Ishay, ed. *The Human Rights Reader: Major Political Essays, Speeches, and Documents From the Bible to the Present.* New York: Routledge, 1997.

David Lyons, ed. *Rights.* Belmont, CA: Wadsworth, 1979.

James Nickel. *Making Sense of Human Rights.* Berkeley: University of California Press, 1987.

Martha C. Nussbaum. *Sex and Social Justice.* New York: Oxford University Press, 1999.

Philip Pettit. *Republicanism: A Theory of Freedom and Government.* Oxford, England: Oxford University Press, 1997.

Amartya Sen. *Inequality Reexamined.* Cambridge, MA: Harvard University Press, 1992.

Henry Shue. *Basic Rights.* Princeton, NJ: Princeton University Press, 1980.

L. W. Sumner. *The Moral Foundation of Rights.* New York: Oxford University Press, 1987.

INTERNET RESOURCES

Human Rights Watch (www.hrw.org).

United Nations—Human Rights (www.un.org/rights/).

U. S. Department of State Human Rights Reports (www.state.gov/global/human_rights/hrp_reports_mainhp.html).

University of Minnesota Human Rights Library (www.l.umn.edu/ humanrts/).

The World Wide Web Virtual Library: Roma/Gypsies (www.geocities.com/Paris/5D1/vlib).

ENDNOTES

1. Human Rights Watch, *Broken People: Caste Violence Against India's "Untouchables"* (New York: Human Rights Watch), p. 2.

2. Ibid., p. 2.

3. Ibid., p. 23.

4. Ibid., pp. 4–5.

5. Ibid., p. 6.

6. Ibid., p. 9.

7. www.holocaust-trc.org/sinti.htm.

8. *1993 Report of UN High Commission for Minorities* (www.riga.lv.minelres/osce/hcnmroma.htm).

9. www.errc.org/publications/legal/cerd_thematic_aug_2000.pdf.

10. ERRC 2000 Report.

11. Ibid.

12. See www.hrw.org/reports/2000/frmwrkr.

13. Amartya Sen, *Inequality Reexamined* (Cambridge, MA: Harvard University Press, 1992), p. 39.

14. Martha C. Nussbaum, *Sex and Social Justice* (New York: Oxford University Press, 1999), pp. 41–42.

15. Robert A. Dahl, *On Democracy* (New Haven, CN: Yale University Press, 1998), pp. 37–38.

16. Ibid., pp. 85–86.

17. See www.humanrights-usa.net/DEMRES.htm.

18. John Stuart Mill, *On Liberty*, ed. Elizabeth Rapaport (Indianapolis, IN: Hackett Publishing Co., 1978), p. 9.

19. Joel Feinberg, *Harm to Others*, vol. I of *The Moral Limits of the Criminal Law* (New York: Oxford University Press, 1984).

20. Joel Feinberg, *Offense to Others*, vol. II of *The Moral Limits of the Criminal Law* (New York: Oxford University Press, 1985).

21. Joel Feinberg, *Harm to Self*, vol. III of *The Moral Limits of the Criminal Law* (New York: Oxford University Press, 1986), p. 12.

22. Joel Feinberg, *Harmless Wrongdoing*, vol. IV of *The Moral Limits of the Criminal Law* (New York: Oxford University Press, 1988).

23. *Human Development Report 2000* (Oxford: Oxford University Press, 2000), p. 1.

9

Feminism and Sexual Equality

OBJECTIVES

- To understand the different conceptions of feminism
- To understand the concept of patriarchy
- To understand the differences between first wave feminism and second wave feminism
- To understand and critically evaluate the position of women in the United States today
- To understand and reach a reasoned opinion on some of the basic issues of interest to contemporary feminism
- To understand some of the international documents on women's rights and evaluate their plausibility
- To understand the care approach to moral decision making and its relation to feminism

PATRIARCHY

Early in the year 2001, a large number of women in the United States came forward to complain of sexual harassment and assaults by police. For example, a Long Island police officer was arrested and charged with having coerced a woman into having sex with him as a condition of not arresting her for drunk driving. Another police officer on Long Island was convicted of using police computers to get information about women that he used in harassing them on the telephone. Some officers were charged with raping women whom they had stopped for traffic violations, while others were charged with forcing women to undress or submit to unwarranted strip searches. In some cases, police officers allegedly ordered young women to stop their cars because the officers wanted to ask them for dates. Often, the women targeted were members of marginalized groups, such as immigrants from Third World countries, that are more vulnerable and less powerful than the average citizen.[1]

Throughout history, women's economic, legal, and social status has been subordinate and inferior to that of men. They have had less power and fewer rights than men. The dominant ideology of every society has claimed that women are inferior to men in a variety of characteristics, which justifies their subordinate status and unequal treatment. A system in which women are subordinate to men is called a patriarchy. Feminism as a political theory is first and foremost committed to the proposition that men and women are equal in all ways relevant to how they should be treated and what rights and responsibilities they have or should have. Among other things, feminist political theorists explore the ways in which women have been subordinated, oppressed, and exploited by patriarchal social systems.

But feminism is not only a matter of theory, or merely evaluating and constructing systems of belief. It aims to guide practice and change society to liberate women from oppression and subordination.

FIRST WAVE FEMINISM IN THE UNITED STATES

Elizabeth Cady Stanton (1815–1902) was one of the earliest and most vigorous champions of women's rights in the United States. When Stanton was growing up in the 1830s, the "cult of true womanhood" was first articulated by ministers, ladies' magazines, and social conservatives. The ideals for women, or more particularly, middle- and upper-class white women, were that they would stay home to take care of the house, the children, and their husbands—often with the help of servants—but otherwise should be physically idle, because exercise and physical exertion were considered too demanding for the delicate, weak female body. In addition, because women were considered weaker than men and because it was believed that their brains were smaller than men's (and therefore less capable of mental exertion), they were excluded from politics, business, and professional life.

When Stanton graduated from high school in 1830, she couldn't go on to college because no colleges accepted women yet. As a wife, Stanton was outraged by the laws of New York, not much different from the laws of any other state, whereby "Wives had no rights to inherit property, keep earnings, sign contracts, initiate suits, establish credit, or claim more than one-third of their husbands' estates. More devastating was their legal inability to have custody or control of their own children."[2] If they divorced, the father automatically got custody of the children. And of course, women, like slaves, were denied the right to vote.

In 1848, Stanton and other feminist activists called a convention on women's rights to meet in Seneca Falls, New York. The convention, attended by over one hundred people, adopted a Declaration of Sentiments and Resolutions, much of it written by Stanton. The Declaration of Sentiments adopted at the Seneca Falls meeting was modeled on the Declaration of Independence:

> We hold these truths to be self-evident; that all men and women are created equal....
>
> > The history of mankind is a history of repeated injuries and usurpations on the part of man toward women, having in direct object the establishment of an absolute tyranny over her.
> >
> > He has never permitted her to exercise her inalienable right to the elective franchise.
> >
> > He has compelled her to submit to laws, in the formation of which she has no voice....
> >
> > He has made her, if married, in the eye of the law, civilly dead.
> >
> > He has taken from her all right in property, even to the wages she earns.
> >
> > ... In the covenant of marriage, she is compelled to promise obedience to her husband, he becoming, to all intents and purposes, her master....
> >
> > He has so framed the law of divorce, as to what shall be the proper cause of divorce; in case of separation, to whom the guardianship of the children shall be given, as to be wholly regardless of the happiness of women....
> >
> > He has monopolized nearly all the profitable employments, and from those she is permitted to follow, she receives but scanty remuneration....
> >
> > He has denied her the facilities for obtaining a thorough education— all colleges being closed to her.
> >
> > He has created a false public sentiment, by giving to the world a different code of morals for men and women....
> >
> > He has endeavored in every way that he could to destroy her confidence in her own powers, to lessen her self-respect, and to make her willing to lead a dependent and abject life.

The resolutions, a selection of which appears below, constitute a call for action.

> Whereas, the great precept of nature is conceded to be that "man shall pursue his own true and substantial happiness."
>
> > *Resolved*, that such laws as conflict, in any way, with the true and substantial happiness of women, are contrary to the great precept of nature and of no validity....

> *Resolved*, that all laws which prevent woman from occupying such station in society as her conscience shall dictate, or which place her in a position inferior to that of man, are contrary to the great precept of nature and therefore of no force or authority.
>
> *Resolved*, that woman is man's equal, was intended to be so by the Creator, and the highest good of the race demands that she shall be recognized as such.
>
> *Resolved*, that the same amount of virtue, delicacy, and refinement of behavior that is required of woman in the social state also be required of man. . . .
>
> *Resolved*, that it is the duty of the women of this country to secure to themselves their sacred right to the elective franchise.
>
> *Resolved*, that the equality of human rights results necessarily from the fact of the identity of the race in capabilities and responsibilities.
>
> *Resolved*, that the speedy success of our cause depends on the zealous and untiring efforts of both men and women for the overthrow of the monopoly of the pulpit, and for the securing to woman an equal participation with men in the various trades, professions, and commerce.[3]

The 1848 Seneca Falls declaration was a guiding light for feminists in the United States in the nineteenth and early twentieth centuries. Unfortunately, Stanton did not live to see the outcome of her struggle for sexual equality. When she died in 1902, women still did not have the right to vote.

But Stanton did live to see some progress. The Married Women's Property Act in New York, amended in 1860, "provided that married women had the right to hold real and personal property without the interference of a husband; [the right] to carry on any trade or perform any service; to collect and use their own earnings; to buy, sell, and contract without the consent of husbands . . .; to sue and be sued; to share joint custody of their children; and to inherit equally with any children on the death of their spouse."[4] These legal rights represented an advance for women, and Stanton campaigned vigorously for passage of the revisions. Of course, the bill only applied to married women in the state of New York. And unfortunately, in the early 1860s, a more conservative New York legislature took back some of the reforms, including "the right of mothers to equal guardianship of their children. . . ."[5]

Stanton also campaigned on behalf of changes in divorce law in New York, which feminists believed harmed women. Stanton wanted to make divorce easier so that women would not be forced to endure marriages marred by "drunkenness, insanity, desertion, cruel and brutal treatment, adultery, or mere incompatibility."[6] Wives at the time could get a divorce from their husband only if they proved that their husband had committed adultery. They could not get a divorce even if their husband had deserted them or was physically abusive. In 1860, the New York State Senate rejected a bill "adding desertion, habitual drunkenness, and cruelty to adultery as grounds for divorce by wives."[7] Enemies denounced Stanton for trying to weaken a bond created by God.

After the Civil War, the issue of the status of freed blacks took precedence over that of the rights of women for most reformers. Stanton pushed without success for votes for women as well as for male African-Americans. To publicize her cause, she maintained that nothing in the Constitution forbade women from running for public office and nominated herself as an independent candidate for the House of Representatives in the eighth district of New York in 1866. She got 24 votes.[8] Voting rights for women was debated in the United States Senate in 1866, and opponents won the day, 37 to 9. According to opponents:

> Women did not need to vote because they were well represented by husbands, fathers, brothers, or sons. Women lacking protective male relatives were ignored. Further, the opponents argued, women were physically and mentally unfit for "the turmoil and battle of public eye." Indeed, female suffrage would create a sexual "state of war."[9]

In the early 1870s, Stanton concluded that the fourteenth amendment to the Constitution, which came into effect in 1868, gave the vote to women. According to section 1, "All persons born or naturalized in the United States, and subject to the jurisdiction thereof, are citizens of the United States and of the State wherein they reside." She thought it obvious that all citizens of a democracy or republic have a right to vote for political office holders. Therefore, she and several other women went to the local polling place to vote in the 1872 presidential election. The dumbfounded poll workers were too surprised to prevent them from voting. Subsequently, Stanton was charged with "'knowingly, wrongfully, and unlawfully voting,' a federal offense."[10] At her trial, she was barred from testifying on her own behalf because she was judged to be incompetent on account of being a woman. She was found guilty and fined $100. In 1874, the United States Supreme Court in *Minor v. Happersett* "held that the Constitution did not automatically confer the right to vote on those who were citizens: suffrage was not 'co-extensive' with citizenship."[11]

As a result of a notorious 1869 Philadelphia case, Stanton championed "an end to the double standard of morality, the right of women to serve as jurors, and the admission of women to law schools."[12] Twenty-year-old Hester Vaughan had been abandoned by her husband and then seduced by her employer. When she became pregnant, she lost her job. Poverty led her to give birth in an unheated attic. The baby died, and Vaughan was charged with infanticide. At her trial she was not represented by an attorney and was forbidden to testify on her own behalf. She was convicted and sentenced to hang. Stanton was active in demanding a pardon for her, but the details of the case highlighted for Stanton the effect of women's second-class status. Women accused of crimes were not judged by their peers; they were judged by all male juries. And women could not be represented by a female attorney because women were excluded from almost all colleges and law schools.

SECOND WAVE FEMINISM IN THE UNITED STATES

The political activities of most first wave feminists concentrated on getting women the legal right to vote. After passage of the twentieth amendment, organized feminist activity became dormant until the 1960s. One event was crucial: the publication in 1963 of Betty Friedan's *The Feminine Mystique*. Friedan expressed the discontent and frustration that many middle-class women experienced; they were highly educated but kept from professional occupations, exhausted from doing all or almost all the housework and child care—even if they worked outside the home—and not taken seriously by men. Many women saw that although they had the right to vote, they had a cornucopia of legitimate grievances against a society that remained thoroughly patriarchal.

For example, in the 1950s Doris Earnshaw graduated from Middlebury College with a degree in French. She taught in France for several years, got married, returned to the United States, and applied to the Ph.D. program in French at the University of California, Berkeley. At her interview, the department chairperson told her that she was "very well qualified, but we do not take married ladies."[13] There were no restrictions on admitting married men. She took a job as a maid to a wealthy family. Earnshaw reports that reading *The Feminine Mystique* "hit me with full force." It wasn't until the 1970s that she entered the Comparative Literature program at the University of California, Berkeley when she was already in her late 40s.

In 1923, feminists submitted to Congress a proposal for an equal rights amendment to the Constitution (ERA). They resubmitted it every year thereafter. It was simply expressed: "Equality of rights under the law shall not be denied or abridged by the United States or by any State on account of sex."[14] It got nowhere in Congress. But the 1960s saw progress in the second wave of feminist concerns. Feminists criticized newly inaugurated President John F. Kennedy in 1961 for not appointing any women to important posts in the executive branch. To mollify them and to avoid having to push for the Equal Rights Amendment, he appointed a Presidential Commission to examine the status of women. It released its findings in 1963 and documented ways that women were discriminated against. Meanwhile, in 1962, the Supreme Court ruled "that states could no longer ban the sale of contraceptives or exclude women from juries." In 1963, the Equal Pay Act was passed, requiring equal pay for the same job, whether the worker is male or female.[15] In 1964, Title VII of the Civil Rights Act was passed, prohibiting discrimination (in education and the workplace) based on sex. Unfortunately, few attempts were made to enforce it. For example, in 1965 the Equal Employment Opportunity Commission (EEOC) ruled that the practice of having separate job advertisements for men and women was legal, a devastating blow to equal employment opportunity. By 1966, women still represented "less than 1 percent of federal judges, less than 4 percent of lawyers, and only 7 percent of doctors."[16] It wasn't until 1968 that the EEOC finally prohibited separate want ads for men and women.

The 1970s saw more progress. In 1970, the Justice Department finally decided to enforce the prohibition on sex discrimination and pursued its first case. In 1972, Congress passed the ERA. However, it died because not enough states ratified it. In 1973, the Supreme Court ruled in *Roe v. Wade* that states may not ban abortions, at least during the first six months of pregnancy. Most feminists saw this as an important victory that increased women's freedom and control over their own bodies. "In 1974, Congress passed the Equal Credit Opportunity Act, which allowed married women, for the first time, to obtain credit in their own names. . . ."[17] But a backlash against feminism had already set in. In 1977, Congress passed the Hyde amendment preventing government funding of abortions for poor women.

In the 1970s, women also publicly questioned the power and practices of the male-dominated medical establishment. They complained that too little research was being done on illnesses that primarily or only affected women, such as breast cancer, and that women were often subjected to medical procedures that were questionable, such as hysterectomies and caesarean sections. They shared experiences of male doctors' dismissive attitudes toward "female" complaints, including problems around menstruation. Health complaints that, if described by a male, routinely would lead doctors to send a patient to the hospital for observation and tests were, if described by a woman, dismissed as "all in her mind." Women also criticized the medical profession for overprescribing tranquilizers and antidepressants for women and for discouraging breast feeding by saying it was unhealthy. Women advocated childbirth in the home rather than in the hospital, complaining that birth in a hospital is treated as a disease. They expressed their outrage at the common policy of requiring poor women to undergo sterilization as a precondition for government payment for an abortion. They urged women to become more knowledgeable about their bodies and health, to become their own experts so they wouldn't be wholly dependent on doctors.

Feminists also criticized the way rape victims were treated. They deplored the coldness with which doctors, nurses, police, and prosecutors treated women who were traumatized. They protested against treating the rape victim as if she was on trial, dredging up her sexual past and requiring her to prove that she had physically resisted her attacker. They insisted that laws be changed so that men could be prosecuted for raping their wives, as well as for raping prostitutes. Both wives and prostitutes, they said, have a right to say no. They also uncovered the hidden crimes of incest and wife battering, long unmentionable in respectable society. They highlighted the way women were sexually harassed at school and work, often coerced into trading sexual favors for grades, jobs, or promotions. In 1980, the EEOC added sexual harassment as a form of illegal discrimination. Some feminists campaigned for decriminalization of prostitution, so that prostitutes would be safer from assault and murder. Other feminists targeted pornography, especially violent pornography, as helping sustain disrespect for and violence against women. Feminists in the 1960s and 1970s hoped to change the world, especially the world of relations between men and women.[18]

THE CURRENT STATE OF WOMEN
IN THE UNITED STATES

In 2005, women made up about 51 percent of the U.S. population, yet no woman had ever been elected President or Vice President. A woman has been on the ticket of a major party only once, in 1984, when Geraldine Ferraro was the Democratic candidate for Vice President. (The Democrats lost that year.) Until 1981, when Ronald Reagan nominated Sandra Day O'Connor, no woman ever served on the Supreme Court. There had been over 100 justices in its history, all of them white males. As of 2001, there were two women on the nine-member Court: Sandra Day O'Connor and Ruth Bader Ginsburg. When Justice O'Connor retired in 2005, President George W. Bush nominated a man to replace her, leaving only one woman on the Supreme Court. As for Congress, in 2005 there were 14 women in the Senate (14 percent) and 70 in the House of Representatives (16 percent). In contrast, in Sweden in 2000 women held 42.7 percent of parliamentary seats, in Norway 36.4 percent, and in Germany 33.6 percent.

Economically, women on average don't fare well if they don't have husbands. In 2004, the median annual family household income was $55,442. If the family consisted of a married couple, however, that figure rose to $64,082. If it consisted of a male householder with no wife present, it declined to $43,087. But if it consisted of a female householder with no husband present, it plunged to a mere $30,095.[19] Women still lag behind men in the world of paid employment. Median annual earnings of full-time workers was $36,476 for males and $26,324 for females.[20]

Median earnings for males working full-time was $40,798 and for females $31,223. Whereas 13.5 percent of families headed by a man were below the poverty level, 28.4 percent of families headed by a woman were below it.[21]

Women, much more than men, also suffer from eating disorders such as bulimia and anorexia, as well as from depression and other psychological disorders. It's obvious that at least part of the cause is the unrealistic cultural expectations about women's bodies that are driven in part by images of women portrayed in the mass media. American men and women are deluged with images of unusually thin, big busted, virtually flawless young women in television commercials and programs, print advertisements, and movies. Many women whose bodies don't match these images feel insecure, perhaps even inferior, and suffer from reduced self-esteem. This may lead them to unhealthy behaviors in order to force their bodies to better match these images. Men, too, are victimized by it. They may feel dissatisfied with their partners if they don't look enough like the models and actresses they see. They may select mates purely on the basis of physical appearance, overlooking the far more important inner person.

WOMEN OUTSIDE THE UNITED STATES

According to the *Human Development Report 2000*, "Around the world on average, one in every three women has experienced violence in an intimate relationship."[22] The forms such violence can take were outlined in a report of the

United Nations Department of Public Information of February 1996 (DPI/1772/ HR), which reflects the research of the Special Rapporteur on violence against women, appointed in 1994. Violence can begin in the womb when female fetuses are aborted because a family wants sons, apparently particularly common in India and China. Women can be victims of incest, rape, and domestic violence committed by male family members. In many countries, a husband cannot be charged with raping his wife because a wife is supposed to submit to all demands for sex from her husband, whether she wants to or not.

In some parts of the world, young girls are subject to what has been called female genital mutilation, called by defenders "female circumcision." According to Martha Nussbaum:

> Three types of genital cutting are commonly practiced:
>
> 1. In *clitoridectomy*, a part or the whole of the clitoris is amputated. . . .
>
> 2. In *excision*, both the clitoris and inner lips are amputated. . . .
>
> 3. In *infibulation*, the clitoris is removed, some or all of the labia minora are cut off, and incisions are made in the labia majora to create raw surface. . . .
>
> Female genital mutilation is linked to extensive and in some cases lifelong health problems. These include infection, hemorrhage, and abscesses at the time of the operation; later difficulties in urination and menstruation; stones in the urethra and bladder due to repeated infections; excessive growth of scar tissue at the site, which may become disfiguring; pain during intercourse; infertility . . .; obstructed labor and damaging rips and tears during childbirth.[23]

According to Nussbaum, "The male equivalent of the clitoridectomy would be the amputation of most of the penis. The male equivalent of infibulation would be 'the removal of the entire penis, its root of soft tissue, and part of the scrotal skin.'"[24] About 2 million young girls are victimized by this procedure every year, primarily but not exclusively in Africa and Asia. The goal is to ensure that women are chaste before marriage and faithful during marriage.

In countries where a bride's family is expected to pay a dowry to the groom and his family upon marriage, dissatisfaction over the size of the dowry often leads to violence against women. There have been many cases where a husband or other family member has thrown acid in the face of the wife or attempted to burn her alive. "In India, an average of five women a day are burned in dowry-related disputes— and many more cases are never reported to the police."[25] Many of the women die. All who survive are scarred for life, some horribly disfigured and crippled.

Women in war zones can be raped, tortured, and murdered to further military and political objectives. This was especially prominent in conflicts in Bosnia, Kosovo, Rwanda, Kuwait, Peru, Somalia, and Colombia, as well as in refugee camps around the world. For example, Human Rights Watch reported an example of rape in Somalia in November 1994, in which a woman "was raped by sixteen men. She couldn't walk and was left for two days until she was discovered."[26] The same report documents cases of Somali refugees raped in camps in Kenya. "Most of the women whose cases we investigated were gang-raped at gunpoint, some by as many as seven men at a time. In the vast majority of cases, female rape survivors were also robbed, severely beaten, knifed or shot."[27]

Inside or outside war zones, women may be forced or lured into prostitution against their will. According to Human Rights Watch, "In any given year, many thousands of young women and girls around the world are lured, abducted or sold into forced prostitution and involuntary marriage." Further, "police officers and other local government officials facilitate and profit from the trade in women and girls."[28] Also, "[i]n Thailand, prostitutes who complain to the police are often arrested and sent back to the brothels. . . ."; "[i]n one incident [in Asia], five young prostitutes burned to death in a brothel fire because they had been chained to their beds."[29] "In the Middle-East and Persian Gulf region, there are an estimated 1.2 million women, mainly Asians, who are employed as domestic servants. [They] often suffer beatings and sexual assaults at the hands of their employers. The police are often of little help. In many cases, women who report being raped by their employers are sent back to the employer—or are even assaulted at the police station."[30]

Women are also particularly vulnerable to AIDS. According to a recent story in the *New York Times*, based on a U.N. study, "The poverty and powerlessness of women in Africa and Asia are combining to make them increasingly vulnerable to AIDS. . . . [I]n many cultures and in the most disadvantaged societies girls and women do not have the power to reject unwanted or unsafe sex."[31] In Africa, more than half of new AIDS cases now are women.

Women suffer from a variety of indignities around the world. For example, in 1990, the Saudi government prohibited women from driving. "When Saudi women demonstrated against the ban on driving, the government responded by prohibiting all future demonstrations by women."[32]

In many parts of the world, women are denied equal access to even the most basic form of education that would guarantee bare literacy.

CONTEMPORARY FEMINIST THEORIES: THE THIRD WAVE

Today, feminism is, if anything, an even more diverse movement and set of ideas than it was during the second wave of the 1960s and 1970s. Our treatment must necessarily be selective.

LIBERAL FEMINISM

Liberal feminists ground their feminism in liberalism. According to Martha Nussbaum:

> At the heart of this tradition is a two-fold intuition about human beings: namely, that all, just by being human, are of equal dignity and worth, no

matter where they are situated in society, and that the primary source of this worth is a power of moral choice within them, a power that consists in the ability to plan a life in accordance with one's own evaluation of ends. To these two intuitions . . . the liberal tradition adds one more . . .: That the moral equality of persons gives them a fair claim to certain types of treatment at the hands of society and politics. [T]he . . . starting point is that this treatment must do two closely related things. It must respect and promote liberty of choice, and it must respect and promote the equal worth of persons as choosers.[33]

She continues: "The choices that get protection will be those deemed to be of crucial importance to the protection and expression of personhood."[34] Her goal as a feminist is to bring women fully within the circle of protection provided by the liberal tradition. When the liberal tradition takes sex seriously, it must be committed to the view that men and women have equal dignity and worth based on the equal capacity for moral choice within them. Men and women also have a fair and equal claim to certain types of treatment—the same treatment. They must have equal liberty of choice. Liberalism is also committed to the flourishing of all persons. Thus, women must be given the same capabilities and opportunities to flourish as men.

What are some of the core issues that contemporary liberal feminists engage with?

Reproductive Rights

For most feminists, reproductive rights for women is one of the most fundamental demands on the feminist agenda. They insist that a woman is not truly free if she cannot control her own reproductive life. Ability to achieve satisfactory levels of bodily health and integrity requires easy access to safe and legal abortions. To the cry of conservatives that abortion is simply murder of innocent children or people, many feminists insist that a fetus, especially in the first few months of its existence, is not yet a person or a child. Liberal feminists generally accept the distinctions enshrined in the Supreme Court decision *Roe v. Wade*: An unborn fetus is not a person with constitutional rights because it is not yet sentient. Thus, in the first trimester of a woman's pregnancy, the state may impose no regulations limiting or forbidding abortion. In the second trimester, when abortion becomes more medically risky, the state may regulate abortions, but only with a view to protecting the mother's health. Finally, in the last trimester when a fetus is much closer to having developed into a person, a state may limit abortions to protect the life of the unborn fetus, but it must permit abortions to protect the life and health of the mother. Even in the third trimester, the interests and rights of the mother take priority over any the fetus may have. Feminists want to preserve *Roe v. Wade* from continual efforts to overturn it and permit states to outlaw abortions.

Many feminists also insist that the government should pay for abortions for poor women who cannot afford them. In their view, a woman cannot exercise the legal right to an abortion if she can't get one because she has no money to pay for it. Then she does not truly have control over her body.

The issue of reproductive rights is further complicated because there must be doctors able and willing to perform abortions if women are to be able to exercise a right to have one. This means that medical schools need to provide adequate training to provide enough doctors to meet the demand. Because of the controversial nature of abortion, some medical schools downplay abortion services in their curricula. An agenda to safeguard reproductive rights needs to focus on medical schools as well as the government. But the state also needs to provide adequate protection to health care providers who perform abortions because some anti-abortion individuals employ or threaten to employ violence to stop abortions.

But abortion is not the only issue of reproductive rights. bell hooks writes that for feminists:

> the overall issue of reproductive rights will take precedence over any single issue. This does not mean that the push for legal, safe, inexpensive abortions will not remain central, it will simply not be the only issue that is centralized. If sex education, preventive health care, and easy access to contraceptives are offered every female, fewer of us will have unwanted pregnancies. As a consequence the need for abortions would diminish.[35]

Reproductive rights include a right to be provided with information about sex, pregnancy, contraception, and abortion. It includes a right to the provision of contraceptives. But it also requires a right to adequate health care for women who choose to remain pregnant.

Equal Opportunity, Care, and the Family

Individuals grow up cared for by adults. Traditionally, the concept of family has been a positive one that is connected to attractive ideas such as nurturing. However, feminists have pointed out that not all families fit the romanticized image of family that is so common in mass culture. Some families are centers of abuse and domination. According to many feminists, it is more likely for women than men to be victimized in some way within the family. And given the importance of family life in shaping an individual, it is important to look critically at families.

Susan Moller Okin stresses the importance of equal opportunity for the feminist agenda, and views the situation and structure of many families in our society as barriers to equal opportunity. Female children growing up in such a family face the danger of becoming damaged in ways that will prevent them from competing on equal terms and achieving the same level of basic human functioning as men. If a girl child sees her mother or sisters constantly denigrated by her father, she may not develop the self-esteem and self-confidence necessary for seeing herself as valuable and as having the same worth and rights as men. She may internalize the view that women should be subordinate to and serve men. She may fail to develop goals and life plans consistent with her abilities and capacities. She may not have the inner strength and drive to achieve her goals. Similarly, if she sees her mother, sisters, or other women in the family psychologically or physically abused, she may fail to develop a healthy emotional attitude toward the world. She may be fearful and feel intimidated. The feeling that the world is a dangerous, unsafe place can be a barrier for women, limiting their freedom of movement, freedom of expression, and so on.

Mona Harrington laments the fact that generally, women have been primarily care givers rather than care receivers, while men have been primarily care receivers rather than care givers. She points out that much of the caregiving in American society has been supplied by women, who received no money for their labor. Society as a whole, especially men, benefit by having women shoulder this responsibility for free. Their home and family responsibilities, from which men were liberated, kept women in a dependent, subordinate position. Even now, when family and work responsibilities conflict, it's usually women rather than men who choose family over work. They may leave paid employment entirely for several years, falling behind their male counterparts in the work world and reducing their chances of future advancement. Or they may choose the newer options of part-time work and flextime. But most employers still think that the best employees, those who merit advancement, place work first. Women who place care of the needs of their family first will lag behind men who put their work first, promoting economic inequality between the sexes.

Okin points out that the "public" worlds of work and politics have been designed as though made solely for men who have women to take care of the day-to-day responsibilities of caring for them, their children, and other "dependents." She asks the question:

> . . . would the structure or practices of the workplace, the market, or the legislature be the same if they had developed with the assumption that their participants had to accommodate to the needs of child-bearing, child-rearing, and the responsibilities of domestic life? Would policy-making or its outcomes be the same if those engaged in them were persons who also had significant day-to-day responsibilities for caring for others, rather than being some of those least likely in the entire society to have such experiences?[36]

To Okin, this is a rhetorical question. She and other feminists would answer, "Of course not!"

Sexual Harassment

Liberal feminists also target sexual harassment in schools and work places. Harrington cites with approval the recommendation of legal scholar Vicki Schultz that government should expand the reach of harassment law beyond literally sexual behavior to any behavior in the workplace that undermines women's equal opportunity. For Schultz this would include, for example, verbal denigration of women, physical sabotage of their work performance, refusal of adequate training or assignments, ostracism, unfair evaluation, physical threats, and false reports of mental instability or physical weakness—all common complaints creating as hostile a work environment as sexual abuse for many women. . . .[37]

According to liberal feminists like Harrington, women's opportunities have been undermined in the workplace in a wide variety of ways, both subtle and not so subtle. It is not just coercion for sexual favors, unwanted touching, and sexualized conversations that create barriers for many women in the workplace. Liberal feminists want stronger legal protections for women against such behaviors.

THE IDEAL OF ANDROGYNY

It is now a commonplace to distinguish between sex and gender. A person's purely physical and biological characteristics, such as having a penis, a clitoris, or a womb, determine sex—traditionally viewed as being either male or female. On the other hand, a person's gender—traditionally viewed as either masculine or feminine—is determined by that person's psychological characteristics, such as ways of thinking, feeling, and behaving. There is considerable controversy over whether gender is a product of biology or the social environment.

Both men and women can be masculine or feminine. Traditionally, men are expected to be masculine and women to be feminine. Feminine men and masculine women have experienced considerable disapproval. Thus, gender is associated with certain human ideals, not just with description. But what traits are associated with masculinity and femininity? According to Ann Ferguson, the conventional stereotypes are as follows:

> A masculine person is active, independent, aggressive (demanding),
> more self-interested than altruistic, competent and interested in physical
> activities, rational, emotionally controlled, and self-disciplined. A feminine
> person, on the other hand, is passive, dependent, nonassertive, more
> altruistic than self-interested (supportive of others), neither physically
> competent nor interested in becoming so, intuitive but not rational,
> emotionally open, and impulsive rather than self-disciplined.[38]

Let's explore these concepts first by focusing on so-called feminine men and masculine women, combinations that many people in our culture disapprove of. Feminine men are widely viewed as weak rather than strong. They're emotional in a way that masculine men aren't. Masculine men get angry and often express their anger and rage orally and physically. But masculine men don't "wallow in," express, or even possess the softer and gentler feelings and emotions, such as rapture over beauty, elation, sadness, tenderness, compassion, and sympathy. Masculine men don't cry at sad movies. They don't ask for a hug because they feel sad or give someone else a hug because they perceive that the person is sad. Masculine men talk about sports, business, and politics, not about their feelings. Masculine men are competent in certain ways that feminine men aren't. Masculine men can make minor repairs on a car or home, and know how to use a variety of tools. They can handle a family's or firm's finances and investments competently. Because of their competence, they're independent. They prefer to do things for themselves rather than depend on others. They are physically active and tough, and they like action. Masculine men would prefer to play sports or watch sports on television rather than read a book or listen to music. They will choose action movies over love stories. If need be, they can fight to defend themselves.

Masculine women are strong rather than weak. They are demanding, assertive, and aggressive. They're strong and competent in the same ways that masculine men are. They can drive a truck, run a business, make home repairs and improvements, give orders to subordinates, and defend themselves from physical attack. Feminine women, on the other hand, are weak. They're more fitted to sew a button than to mow the lawn or shovel snow. They're not competent to repair a car or a leaky faucet, fight off an attacker, or handle family finances. They're dependent on others. They're unassertive and undemanding, givers rather than takers.

Many feminists challenge the ideals of masculinity and femininity, as well as the tradition that men should be masculine and women feminine. First, they point out that some of the ideals of masculinity and femininity aren't very admirable. Weakness and incompetence aren't virtues, either for men or women. Aggressiveness, when taken to extremes, is a vice. But more importantly, some feminists argue that there should be one ideal for all people, one conception of virtue and vice or good and bad character traits, that does not vary by sex. The ideal personality and character should be the same for men and women. That is the ideal of androgyny—one gender ideal for all people rather than two.

A virtue or good character trait enables a person to flourish in his or her society—to meet basic needs, actualize potential, satisfy important desires, form satisfying relationships with others, and achieve autonomy and self-respect. For example, industriousness is more likely than laziness to enable a person to flourish, whether male or female. Thus, industriousness is a virtue for both sexes and should be part of the ideal for both. The same could be said of such virtues as courage, moral or psychological strength, honesty, self-reliance, generosity, patience, loyalty, and kindness. If these traits are virtues, they are characteristics one ought to have regardless of one's sex. As for vices such as cowardice, weakness, dishonesty, undue dependence, selfishness, impatience, disloyalty, and indifference or cruelty, they are undesirable characteristics regardless of one's sex.

One ideal of a person who is androgynous rather than masculine or feminine is of a person who combines the best traits of each of the two mutually exclusive genders without the negative traits. With this ideal, men would be more like the traditional image of women, and women would be more like the traditional image of men. For example, androgynous men would have the conventionally "masculine" traits of being strong, competent, and assertive, along with the conventionally "feminine" traits of being sensitive, caring, and emotionally open. Androgynous women would have the conventionally "feminine" traits of being sensitive, caring, and emotionally open, but they would also have the conventionally "masculine" traits of being strong, competent, and assertive. One ideal would fit both sexes.

Another possibility has been suggested by Joyce Trebilcot. She considers a one-size-fits-all ideal too confining. According to her, people should be free to live by more than one ideal. It's all right for men to be "purely" masculine and women "purely" feminine so long as men may be purely feminine and women purely masculine without facing social disapproval. People should not be forced to live by the gender and sex stereotypes dominant in their society.[39]

CONVENTION ON THE ELIMINATION OF ALL FORMS OF DISCRIMINATION AGAINST WOMEN

It could be argued that the Convention on the Elimination of All Forms of Discrimination Against Women, adopted by the United Nations General Assembly in 1979, reflect the core of liberal feminism. They represent the world's shared understandings about equal rights and responsibilities for men and women.

The United Nations Convention on the Elimination of All Forms of Discrimination Against Women *(1979, used with permission.)*
Article 5. States Parties shall take all appropriate measures:
(a) To modify the social and cultural patterns of men and women, with a view to achieving the elimination of prejudices and customary and other practices which are based on the idea of the inferiority or the superiority of either of the sexes or on stereotyped roles for men and women.

Article 7. States Parties shall take all appropriate measures to eliminate discrimination against women in the political and public life of the country and, in particular, shall ensure to women, on equal terms with men, the right:
(a) To vote in all elections and public referenda and to be eligible for election to all publicly elected bodies;
(b) To participate in the formulation of government policy and the implementation thereof and to hold public office and perform all public functions at all levels of government;
(c) To participate in non-governmental organizations and associations concerned with the public and political life of the country.

Article 10. States Parties shall take all appropriate measures to eliminate discrimination against women in order to ensure them equal rights with men in the field of education and in particular to ensure, on the basis of equality of men and women:
(a) The same conditions for career and vocational guidance, for access to studies and for achievement of diplomas in educational establishments . . .;
(b) Access to the same curricula, the same examinations, teaching staff with qualifications of the same standard and school premises and equipment of the same quality;

(c) The elimination of any stereotyped concept of the roles of men and women at all levels and in all forms of education . . .;

(g) The same opportunities to participate actively in sports and physical education.

Article 11. 1. States Parties shall take all appropriate measures to eliminate discrimination against women in the field of employment in order to ensure, on the basis of equality of men and women, the same rights, in particular:

(a) The right to work as an inalienable right of all human beings;

(b) The right to the same employment opportunities, including the application of the same criteria for selection in matters of employment;

(c) The right to free choice of profession and employment, the right to promotion, job security and all benefits and conditions of service and the right to receive vocational training and retraining . . .;

(d) The right to equal remuneration, including benefits, and to equal treatment in respect to work of equal value, as well as equality of treatment in the evaluation of the quality of work;

2. In order to prevent discrimination against women on the grounds of marriage or maternity and to ensure their effective right to work, States Parties shall take appropriate measures:

(a) To prohibit . . . dismissal on the grounds of pregnancy or maternity leave and discrimination in dismissals on the basis of marital status;

(b) To introduce maternity leave with pay or with comparable social benefits without loss of former employment, seniority or social allowances;

(c) To encourage the provision of the necessary supporting social services to enable parents to combine family obligations with work responsibilities and participation in public life, in particular through promoting the establishment and development of a network of child-care facilities;

(d) To provide special protection to women during pregnancy in types of work proved to be harmful to them.

Article 12. 1. States parties shall take all appropriate measures to eliminate discrimination against women in the field of health care in order to ensure, on a basis of equality of men and women, access to health care services, including those related to family planning;

Article 13. States parties shall take all appropriate measures to eliminate discrimination against women in all other areas of economic and social life in order to ensure, on a basis of equality of men and women, the same rights, in particular:

(b) The right to bank loans, mortgages and other forms of financial credit. . . .

Article 15. 1. States Parties shall accord to women equality with men before the law.

2. States parties shall accord to women, in civil matters, a legal capacity identical to that of men and the same opportunities to exercise

that capacity. In particular, they shall give women equal rights to conclude contracts and to administer property and shall treat them equally in all stages of procedures of courts and tribunals.

Article 16. 1. States parties shall take all appropriate measures to eliminate discrimination against women in all matters relating to marriage and family relations and in particular shall ensure, on a basis of equality of men and women:

(a) The same right to enter into marriage;

(b) The same right freely to choose a spouse and to enter into marriage only with their free and full consent;

(c) The same rights and responsibilities during marriage and at its dissolution;

(d) The same rights and responsibilities as parents, irrespective of their marital status, in matters relating to their children; in all cases the interests of the children shall be paramount;

(e) The same rights to decide freely and responsibly on the number and spacing of their children and to have access to the information, education and means to enable them to exercise these rights;

(h) The same rights for both spouses in respect of the ownership, acquisition, management, administration, enjoyment and disposition of property. . . .[40]

MALE JUSTICE VERSUS FEMALE CARE APPROACHES TO MORAL DECISION MAKING

Many feminists, such as Carol Gilligan and Annette C. Baier, believe that there are different characteristically male and female approaches to moral decision making. Male approaches favor the application of rules and minimize any role for feelings and emotions. Thus, utilitarianism and Kant's Categorical Imperative are viewed as characteristically male. On the other hand, female approaches appeal to emotions such as compassion, sympathy, love, and concern. Women tend to ask such questions as, "What would be the most compassionate thing to do in this circumstance?" or "What act will minimize pain and suffering?" Male patterns of moral decision making have been called a *justice* approach, whereas female patterns have been a called a *care* approach.

Feminists who adopt a care approach point out that caring people are more sensitive to and moved by the sufferings and needs of others than are noncaring people. The perception of suffering or need naturally evokes in caring people a desire to relieve the suffering or satisfy the need. Therefore, caring people can rely on their feelings, emotions, and natural impulses rather than on rules and principles in deciding what is the right thing to do in any given situation. For example, seeing someone starving naturally evokes in caring people a desire to relieve the person's hunger, and a caring person will immediately "feel" that providing food is the right thing to do.

According to many feminists, women tend to be more sensitive than men to the needs and suffering of others, and tend to have more compassion than men. Some feminists hypothesize that the difference between men's and women's perspectives and approaches is rooted in different kinds of experience. Overwhelmingly, women have been the ones to take care of children, the ill, the disabled, and the old. This experience of caring for the weak, helpless, and vulnerable may affect women's point of view, making them more conscious of the need to care and be cared for and readier to act in a caring way. In their view, men are less comfortable than women with having, expressing, and dealing with "tender" feelings and emotions. Men are more comfortable with feelings of anger, hostility, and rage than with feelings of compassion, kindness, love, and sympathy. Also, males tend to value and emphasize independence, competition, and conflict in social life, and are more prone than women to assert themselves and to resort to violence in order to get what they want. Men tend to be primarily self-interested, detached, and relatively indifferent to the well-being of others; they think that an individual's primary task at maturity is to separate from family and society because they value separation more than connection and isolation or solitude more than relationship. Men tend to be loners with few really close attachments. Because they conceptualize people as separate, individual atoms at best loosely connected with others, men also tend to think that the main task facing a society is to contain and limit aggression between individual members caused by conflict over, and competition for, resources and status. From a male perspective, the core of morality is a set of rules designed to limit aggression—rules such as "Thou shalt not kill," and "Thou shalt not steal," as well as a network of negative moral rights to limit interference with a person's life.

According to this theory, women more than men recognize that people are formed by and derive their identity from their place in a network of relationships with other people and that close attachments rather than social isolation and distancing are the core of the good life. Therefore, women find separation and nonattachment threatening rather than liberating. From a woman's perspective, the main task facing an individual at maturity is not to separate from others but to strengthen the web of relationships that to some extent create, nurture, and sustain the individual. Valuing attachment and relationship, women also tend to be more caring, compassionate, nurturing, and sympathetic, and these characteristically female traits guide their moral decision making.

Take people's attitudes toward weakness, for example. It is not unusual for a male to feel contempt and hostility for what he perceives as weakness, especially if another male manifests the weakness. Many males prize strength and despise weakness as a great vice or failing. Consider fathers who feel enraged if their son is a "crybaby." This attitude can lead fathers to behave with remarkable cruelty toward their sons. Perceiving someone as weak, helpless, and vulnerable often leads to aggression and attack, whether verbal or physical. Homophobic males tend to perceive homosexuals as weak, as "sissies," and this perception frequently leads to insults, sometimes to physical attacks, and occasionally to murder. Bullies, who are more likely to be male than female, prey on the weak and vulnerable in a variety of ways. Some subcultures, such as survivalists, white supremacists, and militia movements, practically worship "strength" while deploring "weakness." In contrast, females are more likely than males to feel protective rather than hostile when they perceive weakness, helplessness, and vulnerability. Rather than contempt, many females feel sympathy, pity, and compassion. The perception of weakness is more likely to provoke in a female a desire to provide care and comfort than a desire to attack.

ARE JUSTICE AND CARE APPROACHES INCOMPATIBLE?

The Case of Killing the White Crow

Roger Rigterink uses a striking example to illustrate the difference between the justice approach and the care approach. In 1988, a hunter shot a very rare white crow in Wisconsin. Many people were upset. For example, Jo Ann Munson said, "I was angry about it when I first heard of it and I still am. I don't understand why someone feels the need to shoot a bird like that. It should have been left in the wild for all of us to enjoy."[41] Apparently the bird was well-known and popular with both adults and children in the area. The hunter was unapologetic. When criticized he responded, "I'm a hunter. It's fair game. The opportunity presented itself. People blow these things out of context . . . I had been seeing it for a long time. I wanted it for a trophy."[42] Rigterink points out that there was no law prohibiting hunters from shooting the white crow.

Rigterink asked his students whether the hunter had done anything wrong. Many students claimed that the hunter hadn't done anything wrong; he had a legal right to shoot the crow because there was no law against it, and it was not morally wrong for him to do what he had a legal right to do. Presumably, the hunter thought the same thing. Rigterink believes that this response illustrates a justice approach to moral decision making because it appeals to rules and rights. On the other hand, many students also said that the hunter was "thoughtless, insensitive, a jerk." If they concluded that his killing the white crow was wrong because it was insensitive and thoughtless, they were employing a care approach. Applying the care approach, they might have said that killing the white crow was wrong because a caring person would not have killed it. Even with no law prohibiting shooting the white crow, a caring person would recognize that shooting it in order to have its dead body for a trophy would cause suffering to other people who value the crow as a very special creature. Both children and adults would feel resentment, anger, sadness, and a sense of loss. Only a person who thinks primarily or exclusively of his or her own wants and needs would shoot the crow.

Rigterink claims that the case of the white crow demonstrates a real difference between a justice and a care approach, in part because the two approaches yield incompatible conclusions in this case. He assumes that although the hunter's killing of the white crow was wrong from a care perspective, it was not wrong from a justice perspective. But is he correct that from a justice perspective it was morally acceptable for the hunter to kill the white crow? Rigterink seems to assume that the hunter had a moral right to kill the crow simply because he had a legal right to do so. However, as we've seen, a legal right to do something doesn't entail a moral right to do it. In some societies, men have had a legal right to beat their wives and whites have had a legal right to enslave blacks, but the existence of such laws doesn't require us to concede a moral right to do those things.

Therefore, the fact that the hunter had a legal right to kill the crow does not necessarily show that he had a moral right to shoot it, nor does the fact that he did nothing legally wrong show that he did nothing morally wrong.

In fact, a careful application of such justice approaches as utilitarianism and Kantian moral theory would probably yield the same conclusion as a care approach. For example, an act utilitarian would probably conclude that more total well-being would result if the white crow were not shot than if it were shot and stuffed for the benefit of one hunter. A rule utilitarian would probably conclude that more total well-being would result if people followed a rule prohibiting them from killing rather than permitting them to kill very rare and popular animals in order to stuff them for their own benefit. A Kantian applying the universal law formulation of the Categorical Imperative might maintain that the hunter could not will that a maxim permitting him to destroy for his own benefit things that other people enjoy and value become a universal law. Applying the respect for persons formulation of the Categorical Imperative, a Kantian might maintain that killing the rare and special white crow is incompatible with treating with respect other people who value and enjoy the crow. Thus, the case of the white crow does not demonstrate a significant difference between a justice and a care approach, because either approach would yield the same conclusion.

The Case of the Moles and the Porcupine

Rita Manning uses a different series of examples, based on one of Aesop's fables, to illustrate the difference between a care and a justice approach to moral decision making. A group of moles has spent the summer industriously digging a comfortable burrow. When winter's first icy blasts come, a porcupine begs to be admitted into their burrow for the winter. If the moles admit the porcupine, they'll be less comfortable; the burrow will be overcrowded, and the porcupine's sharp quills will often jab them. In one scenario, the porcupine is homeless because he was lazy and didn't bother to prepare a home for the winter. In another scenario, he's homeless because his burrow was destroyed through no fault of his own. In a third scenario, it's made explicit that the porcupine will die if he's not admitted into the moles' burrow for the winter.

Manning asked her students what the moles should do, and why. She classified her students' justifications in terms of (1) virtues/vices, (2) principles, (3) reciprocity, (4) self-interest, and (5) care:

> The justifications fell into the following categories: Virtue: Laziness should be penalized, hard work rewarded. Principles: P1. You should alleviate suffering. P2. You should honor your commitments. P3. You should protect life. P4. You should honor property rights. P5. You should maximize utility. P6. You should help one another. Reciprocity: You should help those who will be in a position to do the same for you. Self-interest: People should help themselves first. My group is more important than any other group. Care: You should try to construct a compromise that will allow you to accommodate everyone.[43]

Manning identifies the last consideration as exemplifying the care approach. How does this last approach differ from the others? With the other approaches, we either conclude that the moles should let the porcupine spend the winter with them in their burrow or conclude that they would do nothing wrong were they to keep the porcupine out. A person adopting a care approach, however, strives to use her imagination and intelligence to find a way in which the needs and comfort of both the moles and the porcupine can be accommodated. As Manning puts it, the care perspective values "compromise and accommodation." "Those who chose [a care justification] seemed to think it obvious that compromise and accommodation were good things, at least in cases of conflict."[44] Relying on conceptions of virtue and vice or on principles to answer moral questions simply yields an answer of yes/no or right/wrong; it does not encourage us to use our creativity and imagination to expand the alternatives in order to find ways of meeting everyone's needs in a given situation. Rather than focusing simply on the two alternatives of letting the porcupine in or excluding him, a person adopting a care perspective will focus on ways of altering things to limit the moles' discomfort if the porcupine is permitted to live with them for the winter. For example, a person adopting a care perspective might suggest having the porcupine help the moles enlarge their burrow so that the burrow is not so crowded and the moles are less likely to be stuck by the porcupine's quills.

> The importance of intimacy and connection to others is assumed in this [caring] voice. We compromise and accommodate in order to preserve relationships. But this voice needn't be seen as the voice of self-sacrifice. Rather we can see it as motivated by a desire to remain connected, where being connected is seen as a good thing.[45]

A person who adopts a care approach focuses on creating, preserving, and strengthening relationships and attachments, which in turn requires accommodation and compromise. As Manning sees it, one who adopts a care approach focuses less on deciding between given alternatives than on envisioning new alternatives and possibilities that will meet everyone's needs and that will create, preserve, or strengthen relationships.

Manning's analysis deepens our understanding of how a care approach differs from a justice approach. We have a duty to do what a caring person would do, but in some cases at least, a caring person would seek a compromise solution that will guard everyone's interests and well-being. In some cases, no such compromise solution is possible—for example, the case of the white crow. The desires of the hunter and the desires of those who want the white crow preserved are simply incompatible. A caring person who cannot find a suitable compromise alternative would not kill the white crow. But a caring person would at least expend some energy trying to come up with a compromise solution.

However, it is not clear that justice and care approaches are therefore *incompatible*—that we are *forced* to choose between a justice and a care approach to moral decision making. Justice approaches certainly do not forbid or discourage using our intelligence and imagination to search for compromise solutions that will accommodate everyone's needs and interests wherever possible. In fact, a careful and sensitive application of such justice approaches as utilitarianism and Kantian moral theory would probably yield conclusions that encourage compromise and accommodation. Nor do justice approaches necessarily encourage us to be inattentive to the specific details of a situation.

WHY CAN'T A MAN BE MORE LIKE A WOMAN?

In the hit musical *My Fair Lady*, Professor Henry Higgins asks in song, "Why can't a woman be more like a man?" Higgins obviously thought that it would be better if women were more like men. Most contemporary feminists would undoubtedly sing instead, "Why can't a man be more like a woman?", because they believe that the world would be better if men were more like women, more feminine (caring) and less masculine (noncaring). In their view, if men can be socialized to be more like women, then they should be. Many feminists also believe that the world would be better if people adopted the care rather than the justice approach to moral decision making. Assuming that men tend to adopt the justice rather than the care approach to moral decision making *because* they tend to have a masculine (noncaring) personality/character and that women tend to adopt the care approach *because* they tend to have a feminine (caring) personality/character, we can increase the probability that men will adopt the (superior) care approach by socializing men to be more like women.

EXERCISES

1. Are men and women equal in terms of their inherent capacities and abilities? If yes, in what ways? Are there any ways in which they are unequal? What evidence do you have for your views?

2. Is American society patriarchal? Provide evidence for your view.

3. What can or should be done to ensure or achieve greater sexual equality in the United States? (Think of family life, government, the professions, business, and education.)

4. Should society provide enough shelters to meet the needs of women and children who are victims of domestic violence? What can or should society do to reduce the incidence of domestic violence?

5. Most feminists claim that the stereotypical images of masculinity and femininity dominant in U.S. culture harm both men and women. Describe the images of masculinity and femininity that you think are dominant in our culture. What is your view of those images? If there is something objectionable about them, by what means can or should they be changed? What should the ideal images of masculinity and femininity be?

6. How would you describe the dominant ideal of female beauty in our culture? How is it conveyed and expressed? Is it a realistic ideal that is physically and psychologically healthy? If it is problematic, what can or should be done to change it?

7. What, if anything, should the government do about pornography that is violent or that depicts women in degrading ways; for example, pornographic films that show real or fake gang rapes?

8. What constitutes sexual harassment? Should there be laws forbidding it?

9. Try to answer the following questions by applying a care approach to moral decision making:

   a. Is it wrong for a man to lie to a woman in order to get her to have sex with him?

   b. Is it wrong for a man to try to get a woman drunk so that she will have sex with him?

   c. Is it wrong to work for a company that makes cigarettes?

   d. Is it wrong to drive vehicles such as SUVs that use more gasoline and create more pollution than other vehicles?

SUGGESTED READINGS

Annette C. Baier. *Moral Prejudices: Essays in Ethics*. Cambridge, MA: Harvard University Press, 1994.

Claudia Card, ed. *Feminist Ethics*. Lawrence: University Press of Kansas, 1991.

Ann Crittenden. *The Price of Motherhood: Why the Most Important Job in the World Is Still the Least Valued*. New York: Henry Holt, 2001.

Elizabeth Frazer, Jennifer Hornsby, and Sabina Lovibond. *Ethics: A Feminist Reader*. Oxford, England: Blackwell, 1992.

Carol Gilligan. *In a Different Voice*. Cambridge, MA: Harvard University Press, 1982.

Virginia Held. *Feminist Morality*. Chicago: University of Chicago Press, 1993.

Rita Manning. *Speaking from the Heart: A Feminist Perspective on Ethics*. Lanham, MD: Rowman and Littlefield, 1992.

Martha C. Nussbaum. *Sex and Social Justice*. New York: Oxford University Press, 1999.

Susan Moller Okin. *Justice, Gender, and the Family*. New York: Basic Books, 1989.

Ruth Rosen. *The World Split Open: How the Modern Women's Movement Changed America*. Harmondsworth, England: Penguin, 2000.

Miriam Schneir, ed. *Feminism: The Essential Historical Writings*. New York: Vintage Books, 1972.

Miriam Schneir, ed. *Feminism in Our Time: The Essential Writings, World War II to the Present*. New York: Vintage Books, 1994.

Rosemary Tong. *Feminist Thought*. Boulder, CO: Westview Press, 1989.

INTERNET RESOURCE

Feminist Theory Web site (www.cddc.vt.edu/feminism/).

ENDNOTES

1. "Officer Accused of Sexually Assaulting a Woman While on Duty," *New York Times* (27 January 2001), p. A11.
2. Elisabeth Griffith, *In Her Own Right: The Life of Elizabeth Cady Stanton* (New York: Oxford University Press, 1984), p. 31.
3. www.sscnet.ucla.edu/history/dubois/classes/995/98F/doc5.html
4. Griffith, *In Her Own Right*, p. 100.
5. Ibid., p. 109.
6. Ibid., p. 104.
7. Ibid., p. 101.
8. Ibid., p. 125.
9. Ibid., p. 126.
10. Ibid., p. 154.
11. Ibid., p. 155.
12. Ibid., p. 159.
13. Ruth Rosen, *The World Split Open: How the Modern Women's Movement Changed America* (Harmondsworth, England: Penguin, 2000), p. 22.
14. Ibid., p. 66.
15. Ibid., p. 68.
16. Ibid., p. 79.
17. Ibid., p. 90.
18. Much of this information comes from RuthRosen, *The World Split Open*. See especially pages 157–195.

19. U.S. Bureau of the Census, Current Population Reports, *Income, Poverty, and Health Insurance in the U.S.* (Washington, DC: U.S. Government Printing Office, 2005).

20. Ibid.

21. Ibid.

22. *Human Development Report 2000* (Oxford, England: Oxford University Press, 2000), p. 36.

23. Martha C. Nussbaum, *Sex and Social Justice* (New York: Oxford University Press, 1999), p. 120.

24. Ibid., p. 119.

25. "Women and Violence" (www.un.org/rights/dpi1772e.htm).

26. *The Human Rights Watch Global Report on Women's Human Rights* (New York: Human Rights Watch, 1995), p. 27.

27. Ibid., p. 121.

28. Ibid., p. 196.

29. "Women and Violence."

30. Ibid.

31. Barbara Crossette, "In India and Africa, Women's Low Status Worsens Their Risk of AIDS," *New York Times* (26 February 2001).

32. Nussbaum. *Sex and Social Justice,* pp. 94–95.

33. Nussbaum, *Sex and Social Justice,* p. 57.

34. Ibid., p. 58.

35. bell hooks, *Feminism Is for Everybody* (Cambridge, MA: Southend Press, 2000), p. 29.

36. Susan Moller Okin, "Gender, the Public, and the Private" in *Feminism and Politics,* ed. Anne Phillips (New York: Oxford University Press, 1998), p. 130.

37. Harrington. *Care and Equality* (New York: Routledge, 2000), pp. 148–149.

38. Ann Ferguson, "Androgyny as an Ideal for Human Development," in *Feminism and Philosophy,* ed. Mary Vetterling-Braggin, Frederick A. Elliston, and Jane English (Totowa, NJ: Rowman and Allanheld, 1977), p. 46.

39. Trebilcot, "Two Forms of Androgynism," in *Feminism and Philosophy*, pp. 70–73.

40. gopher://gopher.un.org:70/00/ga/cedaw/convention. Used with permission.

41. Roger Rigterink, "Warning: The Surgeon Moralist Has Determined That Claims of Rights Can Be Detrimental to Everyone's Interests," in *Explorations in Feminist Ethics,* ed. Eve Browning Cole and Susan Coultrap-McQuin (Bloomington: Indiana University Press, 1992), p. 38.

42. Ibid.

43. Rita Manning, *Speaking From the Heart: Feminist Perspectives on Ethics* (Lanham, MD: Rowman and Littlefield, 1992), p. 44.

44. Ibid., p. 44.

45. Ibid., pp. 48–49.

10

Morality and Sex

OBJECTIVES

- To understand under what conditions, if any, sex without marriage is immoral
- To understand what moral duties we have to our sexual partners
- To determine if pornography is immoral
- To determine if adultery is immoral
- To determine if prostitution is immoral
- To determine if homosexual sex acts are immoral
- To determine if same-sex marriage is immoral

INTRODUCTION

There was a time when talk of moral issues seemed to focus exclusively on sex, as though morality was only about sexual behavior. Many people are relieved that those days appear to be gone. However, it would be a mistake to embrace the opposite extreme and conclude that morality has nothing to do with sex. Morality is relevant in any situation in which people interact and possibilities of both harm and benefit exist. Moral requirements and prohibitions, virtues and vices, duties and rights that apply in nonsexual matters also apply in sexual matters. For example, if honesty, kindness, and compassion are moral virtues and if dishonesty, callousness, and brutality are moral vices, then they're moral virtues/vices in matters of sex as well as in other areas of life.

In this chapter, we'll examine a number of moral issues relating to sex: sex without marriage, pornography, adultery, prostitution, and homosexual sex acts.

SEX WITHOUT MARRIAGE

Probably the most central issue regarding sex for most people is the issue of sex outside marriage. Many people claim that sexual relations are morally acceptable only within marriage; sex between people who aren't married to each other is immoral. In practice, most of the attention seems to be on the sex lives of teenagers and young adults. However, if this prohibition applies, it applies regardless of age. Most commonly, this prohibition is defended by appealing to God's Law: God forbids us to have sex outside marriage.

It's difficult to say whether a majority of Americans truly believe that sex outside marriage is immoral, or if they do, whether they take it seriously. Many critics of contemporary culture say that it is sex-obsessed. In television programs and movies, unmarried people seem always to be slipping in and out of each other's beds with a great deal of casualness, and people who wish to abstain from sex until marriage are generally portrayed as neurotic and strange. One easily could conclude from watching television and movies that sex is the only thing that makes life worth living. One certainly gets no hint that such behavior might be immoral. Do television and movies reflect the reality of contemporary American attitudes?

Is sex outside marriage morally wrong? If the only reason to think this is theological—that it's contrary to God's Law—then those who do not believe in God won't be persuaded. But even those who do believe in God may not be persuaded. Many theists doubt that God really forbids people to have sex outside marriage. They may ask, "How do we know that God forbids it?" If people point to passages in sacred scriptures such as the Bible or the Koran, some theists may question the interpretation of those who claim that these passages show that God forbids it or they may suggest that these passages aren't God's words but rather reflect the moral beliefs of the human authors. But perhaps more pointedly, they may ask what *reason* God has for forbidding it. If we cannot think of good reasons for forbidding sex outside marriage, we may doubt that God really forbids it.

Marriage today in most of the world is a legal relationship as well as a religious relationship. To be legally valid, a marriage must conform to the laws of the state in which it takes place. For example, there are minimum age limits, and the ceremony must be performed by someone authorized to perform marriages. In the United States, couples do not have to have a religious ceremony; they can be married in a civil ceremony by a Justice of the Peace. Legally, therefore, marriage can be entirely unrelated to religion. Once a valid marriage is created, certain legal rights and duties are created. For example, in some states, each spouse legally owns half of the couple's property. And if it is to be legally dissolved, divorces must also conform to state laws. Therefore, to say that sex without marriage is morally wrong is to say that it is wrong for people to have sex if they are not in a legal relation with each other. But some people will say that what matters is whether people are married to each other "in the eyes of God."

Are there any nontheological reasons to think that sex outside marriage is morally wrong? A utilitarian cannot make generalizations about sex outside marriage; he or she has to make moral judgments on a case-by-case basis. If more total well-being would result if an unmarried couple has sex than if they don't have sex, then according to Act Utilitarianism it is not morally wrong for the couple to have sex. The physical pleasure the couple would experience would be a benefit, but there may be other benefits as well. If they are considering getting married, having sex before marriage would enable them to determine whether they are sexually compatible, which can help them decide whether to get married. One also might maintain that having sex before marriage reduces the probability of marrying purely for sex, thus reducing the probability of making a mistake in one's choice of marriage partner. Potential harms include guilt one or both partners may feel if they believe that it is wrong to have sex outside marriage, sexually transmitted diseases, and unintended pregnancy. Also, when couples have sex, the emotional attachment often becomes stronger and deeper. If the relationship ends without leading to marriage, the pain may be more intense and lasting if they have had sexual relations than if they have not. (Of course, marriage cannot wholly protect us from unintended pregnancy or sexually transmitted diseases, and marriages are not necessarily permanent. Almost half of all marriages end in divorce.)

Whereas an act utilitarian must decide the issue on a case-by-case basis, a rule utilitarian may make generalizations. According to Rule Utilitarianism, if the general practice of unmarried couples having sex would produce more total well-being than the practice of their refraining from having sex, then sex outside marriage is not wrong. On the other hand, if it would produce more harm than benefit, then it is wrong. It is not at all obvious what harms generally are caused by unmarried people having sex, where the harm is wholly the product of their not being married to each other.

What about Kantian moral theory? First, we would ask the question, "Could one, without contradiction, will a universal law permitting unmarried couples to have sex?" It is hard to see how a rational agent would necessarily be contradicting herself by willing such a universal law. (Can you see how a contradiction would arise?) If there is no contradiction, then it passes the test of the universal law formulation of Kant's Categorical Imperative. Second, we would ask whether unmarried couples who have sex are treating each other and themselves with respect. Now if they are merely using each other for sexual gratification, where there is no love or affection or genuine caring, then they are not treating each other with respect. However, that can occur between married people as well as unmarried people, and it surely does not occur between most unmarried couples. So the lack of respectful treatment has little to do with whether they are married to each other. If they are not treating each other or themselves with disrespect, then their behavior passes the test of the respect for persons formulation of Kant's Categorical Imperative.

If we try to apply virtue theories, we must ask whether sex outside marriage exemplifies any vices. Two immediately come to mind: lust and lack of self-control. Lust is excessive sexual desire. But we must ask whether sexual desire that leads to sex is necessarily excessive. Perhaps it depends on the situation. If we are promiscuous and having sex with anyone, even strangers, then the sexual desire motivating our behavior would seem to be excessive. Similarly, if we have sex without protecting ourselves from sexually transmitted diseases and unwanted pregnancies, then the sexual desire seems excessive—it has led us to "lose our heads." As to self-control, we exemplify this vice only if we do something harmful to ourselves or others. But what if sex is motivated by love? Love is a virtue. And sex is a natural expression of romantic love. Of course, people can mistake lust or other emotions and feelings for love. But if we think we love someone and consequently have sex with that person, is it no longer a virtue?

It seems to be difficult to find a thoroughly convincing nontheological reason for a blanket prohibition on sex outside marriage.

SEX AND HAPPINESS

As we mentioned, many critics of contemporary American culture point to a mass media obsessed with sex. There's a lot of bedhopping in movies and television programs. Sex sells a wide variety of products. The message seems to be that sex is the beginning and end of human happiness. The more sex we have with the more partners, the happier we will be. It is appropriate to think critically about what role sex plays (or should play) in a happy human life.

Aristotle focused on eudemonia, a state of happiness that applies to our life as a whole, not just to temporary instants in our lives. Similarly, the Dalai Lama thinks that long-term happiness is much more important than short-term, temporary moments of happiness. Now there's no doubt that sex can produce very intense physical pleasure. However, the pleasure generally lasts only as long as the sex act lasts. Then, if we have had sex with someone we later consider the wrong person or if we failed to take precautions and there is an unwanted pregnancy or a sexually transmitted disease as a consequence, we may bitterly regret the long-term effects of the few moments of intense passion. We may find ourselves emotionally entangled when we don't want to be emotionally entangled.

But even if we've had sex and it isn't someone we come to consider the wrong person, and even if there is no unwanted pregnancy or sexually transmitted disease, and even if we don't find ourselves emotionally entangled where we don't want to be emotionally entangled, there may still be a problem. It could be that sex is more valued and more central to our lives than it deserves to be. As we saw, there are many potential ingredients of a happy life, such as the development and exercise of some of our talents and abilities, achievement, friendship, love, aesthetic experiences, contemplation, and helping others and contributing to their happiness. If we focus too much on sex, we may overlook these other ingredients of happiness. In addition, there is a danger of becoming self-absorbed. We have sex primarily for our own pleasure. If we focus almost exclusively on sex as what will make us happy, we are living almost exclusively for ourselves and not for others. Yet research seems to indicate that those who focus primarily on their own happiness are less likely to find it than those who think more about the happiness of others.

MORAL DUTIES WITHIN SEXUAL RELATIONSHIPS

According to conventional morality, we have duties to minimize the harm we cause others and to help when the need is great and the cost or risk to us is small. This applies to strangers, not just to family and friends. Consider how important it is, then, that we take these duties seriously when it is someone with whom we have a sexual relationship. We are much more vulnerable with them. It is easy to get hurt. Therefore, extra effort must be made to avoid harming the person and to act in ways beneficial to the person.

According to the respect for persons formulation of Kant's Categorical Imperative, we must treat people with respect. One fundamental aspect of treating people with respect centers on ensuring that all our interactions with them are completely voluntary. Obviously, this requirement is incompatible with rape. Thus, the first duty we have toward others regarding our sexual relationships is to ensure that they are completely voluntary. This duty not only prohibits the use of coercion or force, it also prohibits manipulation and deception. Sex is not completely voluntary if a woman has sex with a man only because he got her so drunk that she doesn't know what she's doing and is not capable of giving or withholding consent. (The law in most states now classifies that scenario as rape, and men can go to prison for it.) Similarly, it is not completely voluntary if a woman has sex with a man only because he lied to her. ("I love you," or "I want to marry you.") Lest we think that this is only a problem of men manipulating women, there is also the possibility of a woman having sex with a man in order to "trap" him into marriage. This may be more likely if the man is rich.

When couples have sex, it often reflects or develops into deep emotional attachment. They can hurt each other far more severely and deeply than people they don't care about. They come to need and depend on each other. They trust each other with their secrets, feelings, and thoughts. If they betray one another, show disloyalty, or fail to meet the other person's emotional needs, they may be devastated. Thus, we owe duties of special care to those with whom we are having a sexual relationship. We have a duty to refrain from taking advantage of their vulnerability and trust; we should not exploit, oppress, manipulate, dominate, or betray them. We should ensure that our relationship is mutual, with roughly equal giving and receiving, caring and being cared for. Complete or excessive selfishness is not appropriate.

We also may wonder whether there is anything wrong with the mass media's approach to sex. One question is whether it is harmful to saturate popular culture with sex and to use sex to sell products. Is there a serious possibility that it will encourage young people to experiment with sex and to place undue emphasis on sex in their lives in an unhealthy way? Is it harmful for the young to be bombarded with images of people whose lives seem to revolve around sex or with sexually provocative images in advertising? There seems to be little compelling evidence that it is harmful. Although people point to statistics that show an increase over the last generation in teen pregnancy, single motherhood, abortion, and broken marriages, it's not obvious that sex in the mass media is the most important cause, or even that it's a causal factor.

THE DOUBLE STANDARD

Our society has often applied a double standard: Many people believe that it's far more acceptable for males than for females to have sex outside marriage. A young unmarried male with a lot of sexual experience is often called a *stud*, a term of approval. On the other hand, a young unmarried woman with a lot of sexual experience is often called a *slut*, a term of strong disapproval. Similarly, a man who has a sexual relationship with a woman half his age is not condemned nearly as severely as a woman who has a sexual relationship with a man half her age. Is there any justification for applying different standards of acceptable sexual behavior to males and females? Critics of the double standard say that there is no justification; they maintain that the same standards of sexual conduct should apply to men and to women. They insist that different standards can be justified only if there are relevant differences between men and women; however, they maintain that there are no relevant differences.

Those who endorse a double standard believe that there are relevant differences. They may say that women are psychologically weaker than men—they're more likely than a man to get hurt in a sexual relationship, perhaps because women's emotional lives are deeper than men's. They may be more vulnerable and trusting than men. Many people believe that men's desire for sex is much more intense than a woman's (which may be a myth), so it is easier to ask women to exercise self-control when it comes to sex. The bottom line is that proponents of a double standard believe that women need protection from men, but men don't need protection from women. More stringent moral principles for women regarding sex may be presented as a way to protect women.

Historically, it may be that concern for female "purity" and relative indifference to male purity is related to pregnancy and property. Women, not men, have children. To ensure that they know who the father is, in many societies men strictly regulated women's sex lives. This was especially important where there was property to inherit. Families wanted to make sure that those who inherited its property had the right "blood." Now with more reliable contraceptives and paternity tests, such issues may be less compelling. Certainly the women's movement of the 1960s seriously challenged the legitimacy of different rules of sex for men and women.

PORNOGRAPHY

Material that is sexually explicit is often considered pornographic, and all states have laws controlling the production, sale, purchase, and possession of pornographic material. However, the Internet has unleashed a flood of pornography that is difficult to regulate. Some sexually explicit material is considered tasteful and erotic; some is nasty and vile to a degree going beyond the grotesque. Of course, one serious problem is to define *pornographic*, a notoriously difficult task. We will not attempt that task here.

The production of sexually explicit material that involves children and adolescents is obviously immoral because the children or adolescents participating are too young to give consent and their participation is not fully voluntary. Moreover, youngsters who are forced to participate in this kind of activity are psychologically harmed. Thus, there can be no rational defense for employing children and adolescents in the creation of sexually explicit material. But what of the act of selling, buying, or viewing sexually explicit material that employs children, so-called child pornography? If the material has already been produced, can the seller or buyer defend his conduct by maintaining that he had nothing to do with its production? Critics argue that the consumers of child pornography contribute to the exploitation of these children because the material would not be produced if there were no market for it. Consumers of child pornography thus share the responsibility for its creation. Accepting this reasoning, almost everyone favors laws criminalizing the production, sale, or purchase of child pornography. Almost everyone agrees that people should not be free to produce, sell, or consume child pornography. (A new wrinkle on this problem is the extraordinary realistic depiction of adults having sex with children in animated films that use no live actors.)

However, what of sexually explicit material that employs only adults whose participation is fully voluntary? Clearly, if someone videotapes a real rape, the victim is not participating voluntarily. But what if it is a mock rape that is being videotaped, using adult actors and actresses who are participating voluntarily? What if group sex is videotaped with the consent of the participants, or people having sex with animals? Is it wrong? Should there be laws prohibiting it, or should people be free to produce, sell, and consume such material so long as everyone participating does so voluntarily?

Defenders of such material may deplore the tastes to which it caters, but they maintain that it is not immoral to produce or consume such material. On one hand, defenders probably will say that sexually explicit material, even so-called hard core material, doesn't harm anyone. In fact, they might say that there are benefits: It can increase sexual satisfaction for many couples by providing heightened sexual stimulation and arousal. It can also serve as an outlet for the sexual desires of people who don't have a partner. As for the violence that is often integral to the nastier forms of sexually explicit material, defenders sometimes claim that it reduces the amount of actual violence in society by providing a vicarious experience that can harmlessly release the hostile and violent impulses that many people have. Thus, perhaps it can be defended from a utilitarian perspective. They also maintain that it is wrong to prohibit such material because it unjustifiably interferes with the liberty of those who wish to produce and sell it and those who wish to buy and view it. This justification appeals to people's rights.

Critics reject these claims. They think that many individuals and society in general are harmed by the kind of sexually explicit material, especially material that is violent, degrading, or dehumanizing. First, it can distort the view of sexuality and relationships of those who are frequent consumers of such material. For example, material that depicts women as getting sexual satisfaction from being hurt or degraded can lead men to believe that women want this kind of treatment. It can lead people to think of other people as mere sex objects to be used for their own gratification. It can coarsen, desensitize, and brutalize people, interfering with their capacity to feel love, sympathy, care, and compassion. Material that glorifies brutality and violence and that links violence with sex can precipitate violence, increasing rather than decreasing the amount of violence in our already violence-plagued society. Thus, one can criticize as well as defend pornography from a utilitarian point of view. The stumbling block is probably the question of evidence for assertions of pornography's harms and benefits.

What about Kantian approaches to ethics? Would we necessarily contradict ourselves if we tried to will a universal law stating that people may participate in making sexually explicit material, and buying and selling it, if they are competent adults and their participation is fully voluntary? It's not obvious that we would. What about the requirement to treat people with respect? Here we may have serious doubts that sexually explicit material, at least some of it, treats people with respect. Are we treating someone with respect if we ask him or her to have sex with a nonhuman animal? What about asking them to commit a variety of sex acts with a succession of strangers while their acts are videotaped or photographed to be sold? Are we exploiting people's desperation, weakness, or psychological illness? Are we treating people merely as a means to our own ends? Perhaps. But if competent adults freely consent to do such things because they want to do them, must we conclude that they are desperate, weak, or psychologically ill? So-called workers in the sex industry claim that the condemnation of their activities comes from an irrational and outmoded Puritanism.

What about virtue ethics? What virtues or vices are exemplified in participating in the creation of pornography, selling it, or buying and viewing it? If I create it, I may be motivated by greed. If I watch it, I may be motivated by lust. If I create or watch material that displays hostility towards or disrespect for women, I may be motivated by anger, cruelty, hostility, or hate. On the other hand, it's not easy to think of virtues that would be exemplified.

ADULTERY

Adultery occurs when a person who is married has sex with someone other than his or her spouse. Is adultery immoral?

Our society is a bit split in its thinking about this issue. On the one hand, the institution of marriage in our society seems to include the convention of sexual exclusivity. The expectation and understanding is that when people marry, they commit themselves to having sex only with their spouse. At the same time, adultery appears to be so widespread and, at least in some quarters, so taken for granted that the expectation and understanding of sexual exclusivity is undermined. In a sense, people are and yet are not expected to be "faithful."

According to many people, God forbids adultery. After all, it is one of the Ten Commandments of the Hebrew Bible (Old Testament): "You shall not commit adultery." According to the Divine Command theory of morality, if God forbids adultery then it is immoral. However, as we have seen with other issues, relying solely on religious teachings and alleged revelations of God's Law presents problems. We will focus on nontheological reasons, if any, for thinking that adultery is immoral.

If a marital relationship is built on the explicit or implicit agreement that each partner is committed to sexual fidelity, then adultery involves violating that agreement. Almost every moral theory has a strong presumption against violating agreements or breaking promises (with the possible exception of Act Utilitarianism). Such behavior is justified only if there are strong moral reasons pulling in the other direction. Usually in cases of adultery, it is only our own passion and lust—our own self-interest—that pulls against the anchor of our agreement or promise. A strong reason for condemning adultery, then, is that it constitutes violation of an agreement that we have with our spouse.

Adultery also often involves deception as an adulterous spouse tries to conceal the adultery. Almost every moral theory has a strong presumption against deception (again with the possible exception of Act Utilitarianism). Self-interest alone does not constitute an acceptable moral reason that would justify violating the prohibition against deception. Therefore, if adultery involves deception, it is wrong.

Adultery, if found out, can also cause great pain and suffering. The injured spouse will almost certainly feel betrayed and humiliated, or may take it as a sign that he has lost his spouse's love and affection, or that he has lost his attractiveness and sex appeal. The adulterous spouse, too, is harmed. Discovery of adultery can lead to unwanted divorce, complications, or disruptions of personal life. We may think that we need only be discreet enough to avoid detection, but there is always a significant possibility of detection.

However, what if adultery involves neither the violation of an agreement nor deception? What if a couple freely agrees to have what is called an *open marriage*, where each partner is free to have sexual relationships with other people? They are not violating any agreement, and they have no reason to hide their other sexual relationships from each other. If there is no violation of an agreement and no deception, is adultery morally acceptable?

Many people insist that an open marriage is likely to be a short, unhappy marriage. They maintain that it is very probable that an open marriage will eventually generate such intense jealousy and insecurity on the part of one or both partners that the marriage will dissolve. From a utilitarian point of view, that may be a reason for thinking adultery (or an open marriage) is morally wrong, at least if divorce will reduce rather than increase total well-being. However, sometimes divorce increases rather than decreases total well-being.

Finally, we should once again consider what virtues or vices are exemplified in adultery. Perhaps this varies with the reasons for adultery. Suppose that someone's spouse has been in a coma for several years and he or she begins a relationship with someone else. If it becomes a sexual relationship, she has committed adultery. She probably feels lonely. It wouldn't be surprising if she feels depression from a sense of hopelessness. She may feel sexual frustration. She probably thinks that her spouse cannot ever be hurt by her actions because he will never emerge from the coma. She has needs for human warmth, love, and sexual intimacy. It would be difficult to justify the claim that her actions exemplify vices. She isn't deceiving her husband, because he's not conscious. He can't be led to have false beliefs that she is being faithful. Her new sexual relationship does not deserve to be considered motivated solely by lust. She isn't being cruel or uncaring.

What if someone commits adultery because his or her spouse is conscious but cannot engage in sexual relations? Let's imagine that Brad's wife is paralyzed from the neck down because of a car accident and is incapable of engaging in any kind of sex act. (Of course, I'm not implying that people who are paralyzed can never engage in sexual relations.) Although he loves his wife, he feels intense sexual frustration as the months stretch out into years. Finally, he begins an affair in order to resume having a sex life. (He makes it clear to his new partner that he will never leave his wife.) He keeps it from his wife because he doesn't want to hurt her. His actions exemplify the vices of dishonesty and disloyalty. Is he motivated purely by lust? Perhaps. Is he being unkind or cruel? That's difficult to say. (On the other hand, can you think of any virtues that his actions exemplify?)

Other reasons for having an affair can include revenge, the desire to validate our attractiveness when we are feeling insecure, desire for sexual variety, and pure lust. I leave it to you to consider what virtues and vices adultery may exemplify when one or more of these is the motive.

PROSTITUTION

If sex without marriage is immoral, then obviously prostitution is immoral because it is a form of sex without marriage. However, some people maintain that buying and selling sex is particularly reprehensible.

Not all societies have condemned prostitution as immoral, but today most do. Those who condemn prostitution may assert that while it is morally acceptable to buy and sell objects such as cars and books and even to buy the labor power and services of people such as plumbers, auto mechanics, and athletes, buying and selling sex is different. Of course, some opponents of prostitution will simply maintain that it is contrary to God's Law, but we have seen how problematic such a claim is. Another reason is that they consider the most important aspect of sex to be its connection with love, affection, respect, and trust. Prostitution completely severs that connection. In their view, prostitution degrades sex to the level of a mere animal function. Prostitutes rarely feel even a faint spark of passion for their customers, let alone love, although they may fake passion. In many cases, prostitutes despise their customers. We could also argue that prostitution breeds disease, and that in the age of AIDS the threat to public health is magnified. In addition, prostitution is a dangerous occupation. Many prostitutes are beaten up or murdered.

Some critics of prostitution have a different perspective. They see prostitution as another way that women have been victimized. Prostitutes are generally women who have few economic alternatives to prostitution. (There are male prostitutes, but most prostitutes are female.) Few women turn to prostitution because they enjoy the work and find it exciting; most are driven to it by dire necessity and desperation. In prostitution, women cater to men's desires, whims, and needs because they are driven to it, while the clients of prostitutes are generally not faced with the same kind of dire necessity and desperation. And historically, prostitutes have been treated far more harshly by the law than have their clients. Therefore, prostitution is just another way that men exploit women.

On the other hand, some people believe that just as people should be free to buy and sell their services cleaning houses, repairing cars, and modeling swimsuits, they should be free to buy and sell their services providing sex. In their view, a person's body belongs to that person. If a woman chooses to have sex with someone because of passion, it is her right. Similarly, if she chooses to have sex with someone for money, that, too, is her right. They maintain that many women and men marry for money or for power, ordinarily giving their spouses frequent sexual access to their bodies; they ask how that is different from prostitution.

As for the claim that prostitution severs the connection between sex on the one hand and love and passion on the other, defenders of prostitution might concede that claim and yet deny that it shows that prostitution is immoral. They might agree that sex is more satisfying if it is connected to mutual love and mutual passion, but argue that the absence of mutual love and passion does not make sex immoral. And they might say that if women are driven to prostitution by desperation, then the desperation should be condemned, not prostitution. If women are driven to prostitution by desperation, then that is a reason for taking steps to ensure that they have alternatives and are not desperate.

As for the claim that prostitution constitutes a threat to public health, defenders of prostitution claim that if prostitution were made legal and were regulated by the government, there would be less of a threat to public health. Prostitutes could be licensed and required to undergo regular medical examinations to ensure that they do not have sexually transmissible or other communicable diseases. If they were found to have such diseases, they could be treated, have their licenses revoked, and have their clients warned. Defenders of prostitution maintain that driving prostitution underground because of moral condemnation and legal prohibition increases threats to public health. They could also argue that it makes the occupation more dangerous. Since prostitutes must work secretly because it's illegal, they are more vulnerable to violence.

HOMOSEXUALITY

Many people in the United States today have a strong aversion to homosexuality and to homosexuals. They condemn homosexuals and homosexual acts as immoral. Homosexuals have been discriminated against in a variety of ways, perhaps most obviously in government employment. Homosexuals have been forbidden to serve in the U.S. military and have been unwelcome in certain branches of the federal government such as the Defense Department, FBI, State Department, and Secret Service. Openly acknowledging homosexuality can jeopardize a person's career in many areas of employment. Then, too, homosexuals or people suspected of being homosexuals can become the targets of animosity and violence. People have been verbally harassed, physically abused, and even murdered solely because they are or are thought to be homosexuals.

Homosexual acts are sexual acts between members of the same sex; heterosexual acts are sexual acts between members of the opposite sex. Presumably, homosexuality is objectionable only if homosexual acts are objectionable. Is homosexual sex immoral? This question sidesteps the issue of whether people freely choose their sexual orientation. That can only be relevant to our concerns if homosexual sex acts are immoral or otherwise objectionable.

Homosexuality and God's Law

Many people condemn homosexual sex acts because they believe that such acts are forbidden by God. However, as we have seen, many people find it difficult to justify the claim that God forbids something unless they have some reason independent of God's alleged commands for believing that it is immoral.

Are Homosexual Acts Unnatural?

Some people claim that homosexual acts are immoral because they are unnatural. *Natural* may mean conforming to the physical laws of nature; *unnatural* may mean failing to conform to the physical laws of nature. Thus, according to this conception, it is natural for an unsupported rock to fall to the ground; it is unnatural for it to float in the air or rise. The physical laws of nature include the laws of gravity, which govern the behavior of the rock. Similarly, it is natural for a lion to eat meat and unnatural for it to eat grass; it is natural for a cow to eat grass and unnatural for it to eat meat. In this sense of the words *natural* and *unnatural*, homosexual acts obviously are not unnatural. What is unnatural, in the sense of contrary to the physical laws of nature, *cannot* occur. An unsupported rock cannot simply float in the air or rise. A lion cannot eat grass, and a cow cannot eat meat. The fact that homosexual acts occur proves conclusively that they are not unnatural in the sense of being contrary to the physical laws of nature.

The concept of what's *natural* may also be employed as a statistical concept. If we say that it's natural (or "normal") for dogs to chase cats, we're saying that most dogs will, not necessarily that all dogs will. Similarly, if we say that it's natural for mothers to love their children, we're saying most do, not necessarily that all do. In this sense, because most human sex acts are heterosexual rather than homosexual, heterosexual sex acts are "normal" and natural, whereas homosexual sex acts are "abnormal" and unnatural. However, if we use *natural* and *unnatural* in this statistical sense, it's difficult to see why what is unnatural is immoral. Most humans cannot run a mile in less than 5 minutes, so it is not natural or normal in the statistical sense for humans to run a mile in less than 5 minutes. Since it's not normal or natural, is it immoral to run a mile in under 5 minutes? Therefore, if homosexual acts are unnatural merely in the sense of being statistically rare, that is no reason for thinking that they are immoral.

Another line of argument is that because our sexual organs have the function of procreation, their only natural use is for procreation. In homosexual acts, one's sex organs are used for pleasure rather than for procreation, an unnatural misuse of them. According to this view, it's both unnatural and immoral to use something that has a function in a way that does not make use of its function.

This view has several problems. First, as Burton Leiser points out, something may have more than one function.[1] For example, a book may have the function of both informing and entertaining its reader; an automobile may have the function of both providing transportation and providing status. If something has more than one function, it is not unnatural if we use it for one of its functions but not another—for example, if we read a book for entertainment rather than for information. The mouth can be used for eating, drinking, speaking, whistling, singing, breathing, and kissing. Are all of these its proper functions, or only some? If only some, which ones, and how can we tell what a mouth's *proper* functions are? Do any of these acts constitute an unnatural misuse of the mouth? Is it immoral to use the mouth to whistle? Thus, we might maintain that our sexual organs have the proper functions of both procreation and providing pleasure. If so, then if we are using them in homosexual acts for one of their proper functions, pleasure, they are not being unnaturally misused. (We might insist, they would not provide pleasure unless they have the function of providing pleasure.)

As to the claim that it's immoral to use something contrary to its proper function, we might ask what could justify such a claim. For example, a mug's function is to hold hot liquids such as coffee. If I use a mug to hold pens, have I done something wrong? Surely not.

Probably the most popular argument is that God determines what something's proper function is, and God forbids us to use something in a way that is contrary to its proper function. Let's say that the proper function of a foot is to enable us to walk and run. We would use it in way contrary to its proper function if we used it in a way that prevented us from walking or running. There's nothing wrong with using our foot to kick a soccer ball or hold open a door because that will not render it useless for walking or running.

According to this view, God created our sex organs with the proper function of procreation. If we use them in a way that ensures that we will not procreate, we are misusing them. However, this argument clearly applies to more than homosexual sex acts. It can be used to argue that God forbids contraception, and anal or oral sex between men and women. But this argument relies on controversial theological assumptions that may be asserted, but are difficult to "prove."

Does Homosexuality Threaten the Family?

Another objection is that homosexuality threatens the family. Just how it allegedly threatens the family is rarely made clear, but perhaps the fear is that if enough human beings become homosexuals and engage exclusively in homosexual sex acts, then fewer and fewer children will be conceived and the human race will become threatened with extinction. Those who deny that homosexual sex acts are immoral maintain that the fear is unfounded. First, they could point out that our planet is already overpopulated with human beings. They might argue that if the birthrate declined because of decreased heterosexual sex acts, it would be a blessing rather than a curse. But they would also insist that the probability of a significant decline in the human birthrate to the point where human extinction is threatened because of homosexuality is vanishingly small.

But perhaps the claim that homosexuality undermines the family has a different focus. Perhaps the fear is that if more people become openly homosexual, the traditional family—male husband/father, female wife/mother, and their children—will be supplanted by other versions of the family, such as homosexual couples or extended groups of biologically unrelated people, including children. However, although some people think that this development would be a bad thing, others think that it would be a good thing if people were not, as they view it, forced into the "straightjacket" of the traditional family, but instead had options to construct new forms of the family. We might argue that most people would still choose (and should be free to choose) to create traditional families but that others should be free to develop alternatives. Thus, we might concede that homosexuality would undermine the traditional family, but only in the sense of providing alternative versions of the family. It would not lead to a situation where there are few traditional families left.

Same-Sex Marriages

The issue of same-sex marriage has created deep divisions in some communities. Gay people say that marriage is a legal institution that brings many benefits to the partners, including inheritance rights, rights to make medical decisions if a spouse is unable to, and so on. Some states, such as Hawaii and Vermont, have taken steps to legalize same-sex marriages. The main reason presented is that denying to gay people the right to marry is unjust discrimination. On the other hand, opponents are scandalized. They say that by definition, marriage is a relation between a man and a woman (or a male and a female). They also claim that legalizing same-sex marriage will harm and undermine the institution of marriage, as well as society in general. (Religious opponents generally say also that God intended marriage solely for men and women. Sarcastically, some of them claim that marriage began with Adam and Eve, not Adam and Steve.) Supporters say that marriage is a conventional institution and we can redefine it to include same-sex unions. They also vehemently deny that same-sex marriages would harm any individuals, the institution of marriage, or society.

Recall that marriage is both a legal and a religious relationship. Some people have proposed a compromise. They have suggested that a new legal relationship be created, called something like a "domestic partnership," which would give people the exact same rights and duties as legal marriage. "Domestic partnerships" but not "marriage" would be open to same-sex couples. That way, same-sex couples would have the exact same legal rights and duties as heterosexual couples, so they would not suffer from unjust discrimination, and the concept of "marriage" could remain as a relationship between a man and a woman. Some advocates of same-sex unions protest that this would make same-sex unions a kind of second-class "marriage."

Another proposal has been to let "marriage" remain a purely religious relationship that can only be created within a religious institution such as a church, synagogue, or temple, a relationship that does not automatically confer legal rights or duties on the partners. Given the constitutional requirement of a separation between church and state, supporters of this proposal suggest that the state should not be in the business of "marrying" people. Instead, the state should create a relationship called something like "domestic partnership" that confers the legal rights and duties currently conferred on couples by marriage. If a couple wants to marry, they must find a church or temple that will marry them, but that will have no legal force. If they want to assume the rights and duties traditionally associated with marriage, they must apply to the state to become domestic partners. Thus, the state would treat all couples as equals, whether or not they are same-sex.

EXERCISES

1. Is sex outside marriage always morally wrong? Is it ever morally wrong? Under what conditions, if any, is it morally wrong?

2. Is adultery always morally wrong?

3. Is prostitution morally wrong?

4. Should prostitution be made legally permissible and regulated to protect both prostitutes and their customers?

5. Should pornography on the Internet be forbidden?

6. Is sex between people of the same sex morally wrong?

7. Should the ban on homosexuals in the military be removed?

8. Should the state accept the legitimacy of same-sex marriages?

9. Should the state be in the business of creating domestic partnerships rather than the business of marrying people?

SUGGESTED READINGS

Thomas Mappes and Jane Zembaty, eds. *Social Ethics: Morality and Social Policy,* 3d ed. New York: McGraw-Hill, 1987. (See Chapter 6.)

Jan Narveson, ed. *Moral Issues.* New York: Oxford University Press, 1983. (See Section VI.)

ENDNOTE

1. Burton Leiser, " Homosexuality and the 'Unnaturalness Argument,' " in *Social Ethics.*

11

Life and Death Issues

OBJECTIVES

- To understand the Supreme Court decision *Roe v. Wade*
- To distinguish between the view that abortion is never right and the view that abortion is always right, regardless of circumstances and the stage of development of the fetus
- To understand the continuum of views about abortion that make the rightness or wrongness of abortion depend on the circumstances and the stage of development of the fetus
- To understand the metaphysical concept of a person and distinguish it from the biological concept of a human being
- To distinguish between the judgment that abortion is immoral and the judgment that abortion should be illegal
- To understand the arguments for and against the views that suicide is immoral and that suicide assistance is immoral
- To understand the concept of autonomy
- To understand the concept of euthanasia
- To distinguish among voluntary, involuntary, and non-voluntary euthanasia
- To distinguish between active and passive euthanasia
- To understand the arguments for and against the rightness or wrongness of the various forms of euthanasia

ABORTION

Abortion, the intentional termination of a pregnancy that destroys or kills the embryo or fetus, has been a contentious issue in the United States for decades. It first was made a crime in the nineteenth century, although most states permitted one exception—if it was necessary to save the mother's life. Although it was a crime, women who wanted to terminate an unwanted pregnancy still had abortions. But because it was illegal, abortions were performed in secret. Sometimes women drank a mixture of chemicals that were supposed to initiate a miscarriage, but often they didn't work and sometimes they were deadly. Some women went to "back alley" abortionists, some of whom were doctors or nurses, some of whom weren't. Many abortions were botched because they were performed in unsanitary conditions or because the abortionist lacked the knowledge and skills to perform it safely and effectively. Sometimes a woman tried to perform an abortion on herself. No one knows how many women were injured or killed trying to abort an unwanted pregnancy.

In the 1970s a young woman given the pseudonym "Jane Roe" sued her state's attorney general in order to overturn the laws that made abortion a crime. It came before the U.S. Supreme Court as *Roe v. Wade* and was decided in 1973.

Roe v. Wade

In 1973, the Supreme Court ruled in *Roe v. Wade* that state laws making abortion a crime under almost all circumstances and regardless of the stage of the embryo or fetus are unconstitutional. Writing for the majority, Justice Harry Blackmun maintained that the right of privacy that many jurists claim is implied in the U.S. Constitution "is broad enough to encompass a woman's decision whether or not to terminate her pregnancy."[1] On these grounds, the Supreme Court decided in *Roe v. Wade* that a woman's interest in being free to decide whether to remain pregnant is a private matter. According to Justice Blackmun,

> . . . [t]he detriment that the State would impose upon the pregnant woman by denying this choice altogether is apparent. Specific and direct harm medically diagnosable even in early pregnancy may be involved. Maternity, or additional offspring, may force upon the woman a distressful life and future. Psychological harm may be imminent. Mental and physical health may be taxed by child care. There is also the distress, for all concerned, associated with the unwanted child, and there is the problem of bringing a child into a family already unable, psychologically and otherwise, to care for it. In other cases, as in this one, the additional difficulties and continuing stigma of unwed motherhood may be involved.[2]

Although Justice Blackmun concluded that the constitutional right of privacy gives a woman a right to decide whether to terminate a pregnancy, he did not hold that right to be absolute. Under certain circumstances, the right may be justifiably overridden:

> [The] Court's decisions recognizing a right of privacy also acknowledges that some state regulation in areas protected by that right is appropriate. [A] state may properly assert important interests in safeguarding health, in maintaining medical standards, and in protecting potential life. At

some point in pregnancy, these respective interests become sufficiently compelling to sustain regulation of the factors that govern the abortion decision. The privacy right involved, therefore, cannot be said to be absolute.[3]

Opponents of abortion argued that because a fetus is a "person," abortion violates its constitutional rights. They argued that because the right to life is more important or fundamental than the right of privacy, the government should protect the fetus's right to life rather than its mother's right of privacy. Justice Blackmun denied that a fetus is a "person" as that word is used in the Constitution; "the word 'person,' as used in the 14th Amendment [to the Constitution], does not include the unborn."[4] The implicit conclusion is that because the fetus is not a person, it does not have a constitutionally protected right to life, because only persons (or people) have such a right. Therefore, the mother's constitutional right of privacy does not come into conflict with more fundamental rights of another person that would justify the state in prohibiting abortion.

Opponents of abortion also maintained that because (human) life begins at conception, "the State has a compelling interest in protecting that life from and after conception."[5] Justice Blackmun acknowledged the controversy over when life begins, but he concluded that the Court does not have to resolve that question. Although "there has always been strong support for the view that life does not begin until live birth,"[6] he recognized that some members of the community insist that it begins at conception. Nevertheless, Justice Blackmun implied that even if human life does begin at conception, the question of whether the fetus is a person is the deciding factor, not whether it is alive, and he reiterated that "the unborn have never been recognized in the law as persons in the whole sense."[7]

Roe v. Wade recognizes a woman's *nonabsolute* constitutional right to abortion. According to Justice Blackmun:

> ... the State does have an important and legitimate interest in preserving and protecting the health of the pregnant woman ..., and ... it has still *another* important and legitimate interest in protecting the potentiality of human life. These interests are separate and distinct. Each grows in substantiality as the woman approaches term [birth] and, at a point in pregnancy, each becomes "compelling" [justifying state intervention and regulation].[8]

The Supreme Court majority ruled that the state may not interfere with a woman's decision about whether to continue or terminate a pregnancy during the first trimester (the first three months of pregnancy). However, after that point, the state may impose regulations on abortion *provided that they are reasonably related to protecting the pregnant woman's health*. For example, the state may require that the person performing an abortion be a properly licensed physician or that it be performed only in a certain type of medical facility such as a hospital or clinic. Similarly, the Court majority ruled that the state may not interfere with a woman's decision about abortion *for reasons of protecting potential human life* until the time of viability, when the fetus is capable of surviving outside its mother's womb (with or without medical aid). "If the State is interested in protecting fetal life after viability, it may go so far as to proscribe [forbid] abortion during that period, except when it is necessary to preserve the life or health of the mother."[9] However, prior to the time of viability, roughly the sixth month of pregnancy, the state may not prohibit abortion in order to protect potential human life. *Roe v. Wade's* ruling is summarized in the following chart:

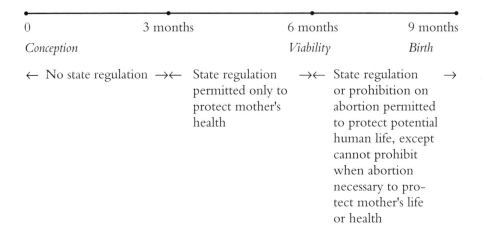

0	3 months	6 months	9 months
Conception		*Viability*	*Birth*

← No state regulation →← State regulation permitted only to protect mother's health →← State regulation or prohibition on abortion permitted to protect potential human life, except cannot prohibit when abortion necessary to protect mother's life or health →

It is important to keep in mind that the Supreme Court decision does not say that a woman's right to an abortion is independent of the stage of development of the fetus or the reasons for state regulation.

Constitutionality and Morality

The Supreme Court decides whether laws are consistent with or violate the U. S. Constitution. The Supreme Court is not a moral court; it does not decide what is morally acceptable and what is immoral. Whether women have a constitutional right to decide whether to continue or to terminate a pregnancy is one question. Whether and under what circumstances abortion is morally acceptable is another question. We will focus on the latter question.

The Right-to-Life Position on Abortion

According to what we will call the right-to-life position, abortion is morally wrong from the moment of conception because at conception, the fertilized egg (called a zygote until the second week, when it is implanted in the woman's uterus, an embryo from the second week until the eighth week when brain waves can be detected, and a fetus from the eighth week until birth) is a living human being with a moral right to life. Thus, John Noonan insists, "If you are conceived by human parents, you are human."[10] He continues:

The positive argument for conception as the decisive moment of
humanization is that at conception the new being receives the genetic
code. It is this genetic information which determines his characteristics. . . .
A being with a human genetic code is [a human being].[11]

Clearly, Noonan is using "human being" in the genetic sense of being a
member of the species *homo sapiens*. Noonan maintains that from the moment of
its conception, every organism that is genetically human has a moral right to life,
presumably because of its potential. A genetically human zygote is a very valuable
organism because it has the potential to develop into a fully functioning human
being that can think, feel, love, hate, laugh, suffer, dream, and plan. A human
being's zygote/embryo/fetus (referred as the fetus hereafter for simplicity) is
genetically human; therefore, at conception it has a moral right to life. Because
the right to life is the most fundamental right, it overrides a mother's right to
decide whether to terminate a pregnancy. (Many opponents of abortion make an
exception if it is necessary to save the mother's life.) They believe that a fetus
should be considered a person within the meaning of the Constitution and should
be granted a constitutionally protected right to life.

According to some right-to-life advocates, anything with a soul has a moral
right to life. In their view, all and only human beings have souls. For them, the
central question is when "ensoulment" occurs—that is, at what point a genetically human organism has a soul. The Roman Catholic Church teaches that a
fetus has a right to life at conception because ensoulment occurs at conception.

In its view, from the moment of conception abortion is immoral and should
be illegal unless it is necessary to preserve the life of the mother.

The Most Liberal View on Abortion

According to the most liberal view on abortion, abortion is always morally
acceptable, regardless of the stage of development of the fetus and the reason
for seeking an abortion. Advocates of the most liberal view claim that women
have a moral right to control their bodies, which entails that they have a right to
decide whether to continue or to terminate a pregnancy. They insist that at no
stage of its development does a fetus have a right to life that overrides a woman's
right to control her body. They agree that a fetus is alive at conception and that it
is genetically human, but they claim that only *people* have moral rights, including
a right to life, and that a fetus is not a person. They maintain that the concept of a
person is not based purely on biology or genetics.

Personhood

According to the liberal view, a fully functioning human being has a right to life
not simply because she is genetically human but because she is a person. Trees,
mosquitoes, frogs, and cows don't lack moral rights simply because of their
species or genes; they lack moral rights because they're not people. What is a
"person"? What criteria enable us to distinguish between persons and nonpersons?

Philosopher Mary Anne Warren asks what traits or characteristics "are most central to the concept of personhood?" She says that they're (roughly) the following:

1. consciousness (of objects and events external and/or internal to the being) and in particular the capacity to feel pain

2. reasoning (the *developed* capacity to solve new and relatively complex problems);

3. self-motivated activity . . .;

4. the capacity to communicate . . .;

5. the presence of self-concepts, and self-awareness.[12]

You're alive, but so is a tree. You're a person, but a tree (presumably) isn't. What are the differences between you and a tree? Unlike a tree, you're conscious, which at least in part involves being aware of your environment by means of perception. You see, hear, feel, smell, and taste things. Because of your perceiving things, you are aware of yourself as a separate entity different from other things. One component of perception, usually associated with the sense of touch, is the phenomenon of sensations such as pain. You have perceptual experiences called sensations that can be painful or pleasurable. Pains can be horrifically intense or fairly mild. Consider the difference between having a tooth drilled without anesthetic and receiving a flu shot. You also have such sensations as itches that are merely irritating. As for pleasurable sensations, those associated with sex are among the most intense. Trees cannot perceive or have sensations that are painful or pleasurable. (We can be fairly confident of this judgment because trees lack the developed brain and central nervous system that seem to be necessary for perception and sensation). Lacking these capacities, trees cannot be considered people or "persons."

However, human beings are not the only living creatures that can perceive and have sensations. As any pet owner knows, dogs and cats can perceive and have painful or pleasurable sensations. Obviously, dogs and cats can see, hear, smell, taste, and feel. Unlike trees, they have brains and nervous systems that are very similar to those of human beings. If you kick a dog, it yelps. The best explanation of its behavior is that it felt pain at the kick. Are dogs, then, persons also? Many people maintain that they should not be considered persons (or at least not full persons) because they do not have the characteristics (to a high enough degree) of being able to reason, communicate, and have self-awareness and self-concepts.

Neither dogs nor cats are capable of constructing or even understanding scientific theories nor of performing even the simplest mathematical calculations, such as adding two and three. They cannot reason at a level of sophistication approaching that of human beings, nor communicate complex messages. Unlike dogs and cats, human beings can design and perform experiments to test scientific theories, write and interpret poetry, build jet airplanes, and manage gigantic business enterprises. These human activities require very sophisticated abilities to reason and communicate that dogs and cats lack. These capacities, too, are integral to the concept of a person. It is because they cannot reason or communicate at a level approaching that of human beings that we do not consider dogs and cats to be persons.

Finally, you are aware of yourself as a being having a past, present, and future. By means of memory you can remember all sorts of past experiences you have undergone, such as birthday parties. You are also aware of yourself in the present and of what you are doing. (Right now you are reading a book. You know where you are as you are reading it, and you may be aware of other things going on or of people in your immediate vicinity.) You are also aware of yourself as a being who will continue to exist into the future. By means of imagination you can project yourself into the future and imagine yourself as you will be ten years from now. Because you are aware of yourself as a being having a future, you make plans and form intentions that affect your present behavior. Presumably, you are in college because of what you think a college degree will mean in the future, a future that you belive will include you. Much of what we do in the present is intended to affect the future, our future. It is doubtful that dogs and cats have such self-awareness—a conception of themselves as beings with a past, present, and future.

Warren's point is that only beings that meet most of these criteria to a high enough degree are persons. The question is whether a fetus meets any of these criteria of personhood.

According to the most liberal view, the mental life definitive of a person requires a certain highly sophisticated, fully functioning brain and central nervous system. In their view, the brain and central nervous system of a fetus, regardless of its stage of development, have not developed to the point where the fetus is conscious and selfaware. Therefore, regardless of its stage of development, a fetus cannot meet any of the criteria of personhood. Because it cannot meet any of the criteria of personhood, it is not a person, and consequently it has no moral rights such as a right to life.

Advocates of the most liberal view rely upon information about fetal development to defend their claim that a fetus's brain and central nervous system are not sufficiently developed to make it conscious, a necessary characteristic of personhood. The brain doesn't even come into existence until roughly the second month. They maintain that until there is a brain there cannot be a person. But the mere existence of the brain is not sufficient for consciousness; the brain has to be functioning at a certain level. Brain functioning relies very much upon connections among brain cells, but these connections develop very gradually. According to advocates of the most liberal view on abortion, there are not enough of these cellular connections essential to consciousness and brain functioning at any period of fetal development.

> In the forty weeks of gestation a human brain grows to a two-thirds-size likeness of the adult brain. Its anatomy at birth is remarkably complete.... But this general impression is misleading in one important respect. The formation of molecular connections, which take up little space but upon which the function of the brain depends, is far from complete.[13]

At no point in fetal development does a fetus have any of the characteristics definitive of personhood, because its brain and central nervous system are not sufficiently developed. Therefore, at no stage of its development is a fetus a person with a right to life.

Warren admits that a human fetus is a potential person; if allowed to develop, it will develop into a person (unless it's severely damaged). But Warren insists that a potential person is not yet a person and therefore it doesn't have a right to life. In her view, only actual people, not potential people, have a right to life.

As for the right-to-life claims that every organism with a soul has a moral right to life and that ensoulment occurs at conception, advocates of the most liberal view such as Warren could either deny that human beings have souls or insist that ensoulment occurs only at birth. Opponents of the right-to-life position would probably maintain that there is no evidence for the claim that human beings have souls or for the claim that a fetus acquires a soul at conception and that therefore such claims are not reasonable and should not be accepted.

Voluntariness

Some philosophers have pointed out that even if a fetus is a person, it does not follow that a pregnant woman has a moral duty to continue a pregnancy that she does not wish to continue. According to them, if a woman is not voluntarily pregnant, then she has no moral obligation or duty to sacrifice herself for the fetus. Judith Jarvis Thomson pursues this point by means of a thought experiment.[14] She asks us to imagine the following situation. A famous violinist is dying from kidney disease. She can be saved only if she is physically attached to you for nine months so that your kidneys can take over the functioning of her kidneys. (Being physically attached means that tubes that carry blood and other bodily fluids will connect the violinist to you. They may be long enough that you can each be in different rooms.) No one else can save her because you are the only person physically compatible with her. (Thomson asks us to ignore the implausibility of the scenario.) Suppose that you have been asked to voluntarily permit your body to be temporarily attached to the violinist for nine months, during which time your freedom will be seriously restricted because you will have to remain in the hospital. Thomson does not think that you have a moral duty to allow yourself to be attached to the violinist, even though she will die if you are not, because the sacrifice required is too great. She also does not think that the violinist has a moral right to the use of your body. (Do you agree? Why or why not?)

Now let us change the scenario a bit. Suppose that no one has asked you whether you will voluntarily lend your body to the ailing violinist for nine months. Instead, while you are in the hospital visiting a friend, you slip and fall, hitting your head so that you lose consciousness. While you are unconscious and cannot give or withhold consent, doctors attach you to the violinist. When you awaken from the temporary coma, you are told that if you are detached from the violinist, she will die. Thomson asks whether you have a moral duty to remain attached to the violinist because she will die if you do not. She answers that you do not. You did not become attached to the violinist voluntarily. (Granted, you did not refuse to be attached to her, but only because you were not asked.) Thomson believes that you have no moral duty to remain attached to the violinist for nine months, or even one day. (Of course, it might be an admirable thing if you decided to remain attached to her in order to save her life, but that is different from saying that you have a duty to remain attached to her.) Thomson believes that you would be doing nothing immoral if you insisted on being detached and the violinist died.

Thomson says that a woman's nonvoluntary pregnancy is like being attached to the violinist nonvoluntarily. She did not choose to become pregnant, did not take actions with the intention of becoming pregnant. True, she may have voluntarily engaged in sexual intercourse, but that is not the same as acting with the intention of getting pregnant. For example, consider a couple who uses contraception during sex but experiences contraceptive failure. They took steps to prevent pregnancy. Surely pregnancy under those circumstances is involuntary. Does the involuntarily pregnant woman have a moral duty to remain "attached" to the fetus? Thomson maintains that if you don't have a moral duty to remain attached to the violinist to whom you have been nonvoluntarily attached, then the pregnant woman in this example does not have a moral duty to remain attached to the fetus and would not be doing anything wrong in having an abortion.

Moreover, not all sexual relations are voluntary. Obviously, rape is not voluntary. Incest is usually not voluntary, especially if the girl is a minor below the age of consent. A young girl below the legal age of consent is, whatever the circumstances, not competent to give her consent to sexual relations. Therefore, a girl who is pregnant and is below the age of consent cannot be considered to have engaged in sexual intercourse voluntarily and therefore cannot be considered to be pregnant voluntarily.

What if a man and a woman, both adults, voluntarily engage in sexual relations without using any form of contraception, but they do not intend pregnancy as an outcome? If the woman becomes pregnant as a result of voluntarily having sex without taking steps to prevent pregnancy, is her pregnancy voluntary? The behavior of the couple may be irresponsible and blameworthy, but it is not obvious that the pregnancy should be considered voluntary. To be fully voluntary, it seems that the behavior should have the intention of producing the outcome. But the couple in our example did not intend to conceive.

Thomson claims that if a woman becomes pregnant and the pregnancy is not voluntary or intentional, then she does not have a moral duty or obligation to remain pregnant any more than you would have a moral duty to remain attached to the violinist if you were nonvoluntarily attached to her. Critics may claim that you do have a moral duty to remain attached to the violinist (and that a woman has a moral duty to remain pregnant), or they may claim that the situation of your being nonvoluntarily attached to the violinist is so different from a woman's being nonvoluntarily pregnant that we can conclude nothing about abortion from reflecting on Thomson's example.

Finally, what if a woman is pregnant voluntarily? Suppose that a woman intentionally becomes pregnant because she wants to have a baby and then changes her mind and wants to terminate her pregnancy? Perhaps her husband or boyfriend has left her. Perhaps she has learned that continuing the pregnancy will harm her health. Perhaps she has learned that the fetus is severely damaged. Does she have an obligation or duty to the fetus to continue the pregnancy? We could reflect on a slight variation in Thomson's example. Suppose that you have agreed voluntarily to be attached to the violinist for nine months in order to save her life. However, after two weeks in the hospital attached to the violinist you discover that it will be far more burdensome than you anticipated when you agreed to be attached to her. Therefore, you decide that you no longer wish to let the violinist use your body. Do you have a duty to remain attached to her? Does the violinist have a moral right to continued use of your body? Would it be immoral for you to change your mind and insist on being disconnected from her, knowing that she will die? We might say that if you have a moral duty to remain attached to the violinist, then the woman has a moral duty to continue with her pregnancy. But if you do not have a moral duty to remain attached, then the woman does not have a moral duty to continue with her pregnancy. Similarly, if the violinist does not have a moral right to continued use of your body, then the fetus does not have a moral right to continued use of the woman's body. Does a fetus have a moral right to the use of its mother's body in order to remain alive, even if its mother does not wish to permit the fetus to use her body to remain alive?

Moderate Positions on Abortion

The right-to-life view and the most liberal view on abortion are extremes. Justice Blackmun's opinion in *Roe v. Wade* may be thought of as suggesting a more moderate view. Whereas a right-to-life advocate maintains that abortion is immoral from the moment of conception and a supporter of the most liberal view maintains that abortion at any stage of development is morally acceptable, *Roe v. Wade* sets a line at viability—the point at which a fetus is capable of living outside the womb. A moderate position on abortion would be that at some stages of fetal development abortion is morally acceptable but that at others it is not. This moderate view could be defended in at least two ways. We might maintain that although a fetus is not a person at conception, it becomes a person at some point before birth. Alternatively, a moderate might maintain that although a fetus is not fully an actual person before birth (the ninth month), the closer it comes to the ninth month, the closer it comes to being transformed from a potential person into an actual person. The more its (mental) potentialities become actualized, the more valuable its life becomes and the more deserving it is of respect and protection. For example, a moderate might maintain, with *Roe v. Wade*, that before viability a fetus is not enough of an actual person to make abortion immoral, but that after viability a fetus is close enough to being an actual person that abortion is immoral except when necessary to preserve the mother's life or physical health.

Stage of Development

Thus, moderates claim that whether abortion is morally acceptable depends on the *stage of development* of the fetus. Although moderates agree that the line should be drawn sometime after conception and before birth, they disagree on precisely where it should be drawn. Most moderates agree that abortion in the early stages of pregnancy (within the first three months) is morally acceptable and that abortion in the late stages of pregnancy (after the sixth month) is immoral unless it is necessary to preserve the mother's life or physical health. However, within the period from the third to the sixth month, they differ on the precise point before which abortion is morally acceptable and beyond which abortion is immoral.

L. W. Summer, for example, maintains that there are degrees or grades of personhood or moral standing. The greater an organism's developed capacities for thought, emotion, and feeling, the higher is its moral standing. The highest moral standing is full personhood, but because organisms can have none, some, or all of the characteristics associated with full personhood and because many of these characteristics are themselves a matter of degree, there are degrees of personhood. According to Sumner, the aspect of consciousness called sentience is the most basic indicator of an organism's moral standing. "Sentience is the capacity for feeling.... In its most primitive form it is the ability to experience sensations of pleasure and pain, and thus the ability to enjoy and suffer."[15] In his view, an organism that is conscious or sentient, unlike one that is not sentient, is sufficiently like a full person to merit substantial protection. What gives an organism moral standing is not necessarily whether it can think, but whether it can feel and suffer.

According to Sumner, the existence of a developed forebrain is necessary for sentience. It does not appear in a human fetus until roughly the end of the first trimester (three months) and is at least *minimally* functional by the beginning of the third trimester. "The threshold of sentience thus appears to fall in the second trimester."[16] Because there is no sudden leap from nonsentience into sentience, no precise line can be drawn. Rather, Sumner refers to an early abortion as one that occurs sometime during the first trimester or early in the second trimester and a late abortion as one that occurs sometime in the third trimester or late in the second trimester. He then concludes, "An early abortion belongs in the same moral category as contraception.... A late abortion belongs in the same category as infanticide.[17] An early abortion does not violate any moral rights of a fetus because the fetus has no moral rights at that stage of development; therefore, abortion is morally acceptable. A late abortion may violate a fetus's moral rights because as it becomes sentient, it gains moral standing. Sumner emphasizes that the earlier an abortion is, the more morally acceptable it is.

According to Summer, late abortions must be evaluated on a case-by-case basis. With early abortions, any reason a woman has justifies abortion; with late abortions, however, only very serious reasons can justify it. Sumner mentions as justifying reasons protecting the life, physical health, or mental health of the mother, as well as fetal deformity. Because a woman can choose to have an abortion early in her pregnancy, Sumner argues, "if a woman freely elects to continue a pregnancy past that stage, she will thereafter need a serious reason to end it."[18] The following diagram summarizes Summer's position:

0	3 months	6 months	9 months
Conception		*Viability*	*Birth*
← Abortion like contraception	→←	Abortion like infanticide	→

Reasons for Wanting an Abortion

According to Sumner, any reason justifies an early abortion, but only very serious reasons can justify late abortions. This distinction introduces another variable: the *reasons for wanting an abortion*. A woman might seek an abortion for many reasons. Pregnancy may be a threat to her life, her physical health, or her mental health. Pregnancy caused by rape or incest, if not terminated, may cause serious psychological damage. Pregnancy for a teenager may cause serious familial, social, or economic hardship. Pregnancy may interfere with a woman's education or career, and may be an economic hardship. Finally, pregnancy may simply be unwanted and unplanned. It may be the result of unprotected sexual intercourse due to carelessness or ignorance, or the result of contraceptive failure. What reasons justify an abortion early or late in pregnancy? An enormous number of answers are possible. For example, a moderate could claim that it would be morally acceptable for a woman to have an abortion at *any* stage of her pregnancy if it's necessary to preserve her life or physical health; that it would be morally acceptable only in the early stages of pregnancy if it's for financial reasons; and that it would not be morally acceptable at any stage of development if it's because one does not like the sex of the fetus. Consider the following list of reasons. In your view, which would be good reasons, and which would not be good reasons for (1) an early abortion, and (2) a late abortion? (How would you defend your judgment?)

teenage pregnancy	badly damaged fetus (severe retardation)
sex selection	mother's physical health
mother's mental health	woman unmarried
family size	money
career	interferes with planned vacation
rape	incest

Infertility Treatments

As if things aren't complicated enough, recent advances in treatment of infertility involve the destruction of embryos. (Remember, a fertilized egg is an embryo during its first eight weeks of existence.) Fertility clinics create many embryos from their clients' eggs and sperm (in vitro fertilization) and grow them outside the woman's womb, in order to place them in the woman's womb, in hopes that they will develop and not spontaneously miscarry. Only a few of the embryos are implanted. Most are stored and then later discarded and destroyed. By conservative estimates, hundreds of thousands of embryos not used in the fertilization process have been destroyed. Not surprisingly, supporters of the practice say that an embryo, although genetically human, is not a person. Therefore, they say that fertility clinics are doing nothing morally wrong in creating and later destroying embryos. In fact, they may apply utilitarian reasoning and say that the practice is part of a process that increases total well-being, because childless couples who are having trouble conceiving are thereby helped. Again, not surprisingly, opponents say that an embryo has the same right to life as a fully developed person.

Sex Selection

In many parts of China and India, boy babies are strongly preferred to girl babies. The reasons are complex. "In many cultures, a boy is particularly valued as a breadwinner who will support his parents in their old age; often only a son can inherit property. A girl is seen as a burden who requires a costly dowry when she marries."[19] Couples who can afford it have tests to determine the sex of the fetus. If it is a girl fetus, they abort it and try again to have a boy. In some cases, couples kill a newborn baby girl. Sex selection is blamed for a drop in the number of girl babies born in India from 962 per 1000 to 927 per 1000 over the last 20 years.[20] The Indian government has tried to discourage such sex selection, but it still occurs.

Applying Moral Theories to Abortion

An act utilitarian would not make blanket generalizations about abortion. Instead, he would say that each instance where a woman wants an abortion must be judged on a case-by-case basis. If total well-being would be greater if a woman has an abortion than it would be if she doesn't, then it's the right thing to do. If total well-being would be less if a woman has an abortion than if she doesn't, then it would be the wrong thing to do. One open question, though, is whether an act utilitarian would count the well-being of a fetus as equal to the well-being of a fully developed person. It has the potential to develop into a person, but it is not yet a person because it does not have the developed capacity to have experiences. And if we count the fetus's well-being, we must figure out or decide by how much its well-being will be reduced if it is destroyed by abortion before having developed into a person.

A rule utilitarian probably would consider a variety of possible rules governing abortion. One pair of contrasting rules is:

A. Women should not have abortion when they want to terminate an unwanted pregnancy.

B. Women should have abortions when they want to terminate an unwanted pregnancy.

The question then is whether following A or B would produce more total well-being. (As with act utilitarianism, there is a question about whether and how much to count the well-being of a fetus.) But there are also qualified rules that a rule utilitarian may consider that would be more sensitive to circumstances. For example:

A. Women should not have abortions when they want to terminate an unwanted pregnancy and the fetus has serious physical defects.

B. Women should have abortions when they want to terminate an unwanted pregnancy and the fetus has serious physical defects.

In such cases, a rule utilitarian would try to answer the same question: which rule will produce more total well-being?

Applying the universal law formulation of Kant's Categorical Imperative also presents some open questions. You might ask yourself, "Would I think it's morally wrong to have an abortion if I were a woman who wants to terminate an unwanted pregnancy?" But we also have to consider it from the other side: "Would I think it's morally wrong to have an abortion if I were a fetus that is going to be aborted?" Alternatively, we might ask ourselves whether we would necessarily contradict ourselves if we willed as a universal law a principle governing abortion, such a "Women who want to terminate an unwanted pregnancy will have abortions." I might be a woman who wants to terminate an unwanted pregnancy, but I also might be a fetus that will be aborted. But this is complicated, because if I were a fetus, I wouldn't be conscious and so I couldn't know that I was going to be aborted. I couldn't experience any suffering as a result of abortion, and I couldn't will anything or contradict myself because I have no beliefs or desires that can come into conflict. Similarly, if I or someone I love suffers from a disease that might be effectively treated by therapies that used embryonic stem cells, I would ask whether I could will without contradiction a universal law permitting research and treatments that require the destruction of human embryos.

As for the repect for persons formulation of the Categorical Imperative, that, too, presents open questions. Kant made it clear that people must treat themselves with respect, not just other people. Does a woman treat herself with respect if she continues a pregnancy that she wants to terminate? On the other hand, it seems fairly clear that in most cases, she is not treating the fetus with respect if she destroys it in the process of undergoing an abortion. But the status of the fetus is problematic. It has the potential to develop into a person, but it is not yet a person. Does the requirement that we treat people with respect apply to fetuses? We also have to ask about other people who might be affected by the woman's decision: the father, relatives, and friends. If the father also wants her to abort the pregnancy, is she treating him with respect if she doesn't? (If he doesn't want her to abort the pregnancy, is she treating him with respect if she does?)

What virtues or vices are exemplified in the decision to have an abortion? In most cases, it's difficult to claim that one is showing compassion for the fetus. However, if the fetus is severely damaged so that it has a high probability of a life filled with suffering or severely diminished capacity, abortion may exemplify compassion for the fetus and the suffering individual it will become. But the fetus is not the only being involved. In some cases an abortion may exemplify a woman's compassion for herself, for example, if the pregnancy is the result of rape or incest. It may also exemplify compassion for others who may be adversely affected by her decision not to end the pregnancy.

A variety of other character traits could be exemplified by the decision to have an abortion. It could exemplify selfishness and callousness. On the other hand, it could exemplify loyalty to a loved one. In order to determine whether a decision to have an abortion exemplifies certain virtues or vices, we need to know the concrete details of the situation and the motives of those who have a role in the decision.

Should Abortion Be Legally Permitted?

Whether and under what circumstances abortion is morally acceptable is one question; whether and under what circumstances abortion should be legally permitted is another question. For example, even if we believe that early abortions are immoral, we may believe that they should be legally permitted. After all, many people believe that not everything that is immoral should be made illegal. We may believe that women should have the legal right to decide for themselves whether to terminate a pregnancy because we place a high value on autonomy and liberty, believe that a woman should be able to control her own body, and believe that it is not appropriate for government to force women to remain pregnant against their wills.

Advocates of the right-to-life position may be what we will call antichoice. The antichoice position advocates making abortion illegal at any stage of development except for certain dire circumstances. Some people in the antichoice camp believe that abortion should be legally permitted only when it is necessary to preserve the life or physical health of the mother. Others believe that abortion should also be legally permitted if there are serious threats to a mother's mental health, such as those that may arise if pregnancy is due to rape or incest. Generally, people are antichoice because they believe that at conception a fetus has a right to life that overrides any less fundamental moral rights of its mother. In their view, the government has a duty to prevent people from violating one another's right to life. They maintain that for the government to permit women to choose abortion for any reason other than self-preservation is equivalent to permitting women to commit murder. They claim that people should not be given such choices. Therefore, the antichoice position generally opposes *Roe v. Wade*.

The most liberal position would presumably make abortion legally permissible at any stage of fetal development, for any reason. Because the fetus is not a person, it has no moral rights that would conflict with a woman's moral right to control her body. Furthermore, government does not have a duty to protect the life of a fetus because it has no moral standing. In their view, a woman's right to choose whether to continue or terminate a pregnancy should be absolute. However, in practice even the most liberal position may not entail that it is morally acceptable to destroy a fetus at any stage of development, even one day prior to birth. At viability a fetus is capable of surviving outside the womb, and then a pregnancy can be terminated without necessarily killing the fetus. An advocate of the most liberal position on abortion could forbid intentionally destroying a healthy, normal fetus after viability while maintaining that a woman's right to terminate a pregnancy at any stage is absolute.

The moderate position is generally that early abortions should be legally permitted for any reason. Because the fetus is not sentient, it has no moral standing that conflicts with the mother's right. However, most moderates would probably agree that late abortions should be legally permitted only under certain very serious circumstances; for example, to preserve the life, physical health, or mental health of the mother or because of severe damage to the fetus—because sometime during the second trimester the fetus becomes sentient and gains moral standing. Because it is very much like a person by this time, it has a moral right to life that only the most serious interests of the mother can justify overriding. Because of its moral standing, the state has a duty to provide it some protection.

Those who believe that abortion should be legally permitted for any reason, at least in the early stages of pregnancy, also offer utilitarian reasons to support their position. In their view, the good consequences outweigh the bad consequences of such a policy. They maintain that in the long run, legalizing abortion saves the lives and health of countless women. They argue that making abortion illegal does not prevent abortion; it only drives it underground. History has shown that many women who don't want to be pregnant will find a way to terminate their pregnancies regardless of the laws. Laws against abortion were not much more effective than prohibition laws against alcoholic beverages. If abortion is illegal, many women will be harmed by unsafe abortions, harm that can be avoided if abortion is legal. Then, too, the social costs of enforcing laws against abortion can be considerable.

Public Funding of Abortion

A final issue involves the question of public funding of abortions for poor women. Abortions cost money, more money than poor women can afford. If a poor woman wants an abortion but can't afford it, should government health care programs pay for it?

Opponents of public funding argue that abortion is immoral and that having the government pay for abortions means paying for and encouraging murder. They also object to having their tax dollars used for purposes of which they strongly disapprove. Proponents of public funding argue that as long as abortion is legally permitted, it should be available to rich and poor alike. They claim that poor women rely upon government funds for their health care because they can't afford to pay for health care on their own. To deny government funds for abortions for poor women denies them an important component of health care readily available to the nonpoor. Proponents of public funding argue that to deny public funding to poor women has the same effect as making abortion legally permissible for the nonpoor but legally prohibited to the poor. That difference, they claim, is unjust.

SUICIDE

Abortion involves causing the death of someone (or something) other than oneself. What about suicide, when it is one's own death that one is causing? Imagine the following situation. Paul Bradley, 64, suffers from bowel cancer. His doctors have informed him that he probably has less than a year to live. Paul knows that bowel cancer causes increasingly intense pain that only larger and larger doses of morphine can control. Large doses of morphine will interfere with his mental functioning and will probably cause other unpleasant side effects. Because of his disease, his body weight will fall rapidly, he will grow progressively weaker, and he will become increasingly helpless. He can expect to be bedridden the last few months of his life.

Before the onset of his illness, Paul was active and healthy. Like almost everyone, he had hoped to die a dignified, swift, and painless death at a ripe old age. Unfortunately, he knows that his death will be neither dignified, swift, nor painless if his illness is allowed to take its course. He does not wish to die in that way, and he does not want his family to suffer from watching him die slowly with their last memories of him being images of a disease-ravaged shadow of his former self. After several days of reflection, Paul decides that he would rather commit suicide than let his disease slowly kill him. Would it be morally acceptable for him to commit suicide?

We may believe (1) that suicide is always immoral, regardless of the circumstances, (2) that suicide is never immoral, again regardless of the circumstances, or (3) that suicide is morally acceptable in some circumstances but not in others. According to (1), it would be immoral for Paul to commit suicide; according to (2), it would be morally acceptable. Whether it would be morally acceptable for him to commit suicide according to (3) depends on the circumstances. If we accept (3), we face the task of specifying both the circumstances in which suicide is morally acceptable and the circumstances in which it is immoral.

Suicide in Ancient Greece and Rome

In his dialogue *Phaedo*, Plato, speaking through Socrates, condemned suicide.

> It probably seems strange that it [suicide] should not be right for those to whom death would be an advantage to benefit themselves.... [However], the allegory which the mystics tell us—that we men are put in a sort of guardpost, from which one must not release oneself or run away—seems to me to be a high doctrine with difficult implications. All the same.... I believe that this much is true, that the gods are our keepers, and we men are one of their possessions.... If one of your possessions were to destroy itself without intimation from you that you wanted it to die, wouldn't you be angry with it and punish it...? So if you look at it in this way I suppose it is not unreasonable to say that we must not put an end to ourselves until God sends some compulsion.[21]

Plato did not consider the prohibition on suicide absolute. It would be at least morally permissible, perhaps even morally required, to commit suicide if the gods wanted us to commit suicide and sent some sign or "compulsion." It is wrong only if we commit suicide without the gods' permission. Plato left open the question of whether, and if so under what circumstances, the gods ever permit or require suicide.

In his much later work, *Laws,* Plato was more equivocal about suicide.

> But what of him who takes [his own life]? I mean the man whose violence frustrates the decree of destiny by *self-slaughter* though no sentence of the state has required this of him, no stress of cruel and inevitable calamity driven him to the act, and he has been involved in no desperate and intolerable disgrace, the man who thus gives unrighteous sentence against himself from mere poltroonery and unmanly cowardice.[22]

Plato clearly disapproved of such suicides, maintaining that they must be buried alone in an isolated, desolate spot. But here Plato's disapproval is limited to a certain kind of suicide. It does not apply to suicide caused by a sentence of the state, cruel calamity, or intolerable disgrace. Rather, it condemns suicide that reflects "unmanly cowardice." The implication is that not all suicides are manifestations of cowardice; those that aren't may not deserve condemnation.

Aristotle also linked suicide with the excellence or virtue of courage.

> Courage is a mean with respect to things that inspire confidence or fear...; and it chooses or endures things because it is noble to do so, or because it is base not to do so. But to die to escape from poverty or love or anything painful is not the mark of a brave man, but rather of a coward; for it is softness to fly from what is troublesome, and such a man endures death not because it is noble but to fly from evil.[23]

Again, the prohibition on suicide does not appear to be absolute. Aristotle condemns suicides that are manifestations of cowardice, but not all suicides are a manifestation of cowardice.

Turning to Stoicism, we find that Stoics considered suicide to be appropriate under certain circumstances. As the Roman writer Cicero put it, "When a man has a preponderance of the things in accordance with nature, it is his proper function to remain alive; when he has or foresees a preponderance of their opposites, it is his proper function to depart from life."[24] Similarly, according to Diogenes Laertius, an important source of information on Stoic doctrine, "They [the Stoics] say that the wise man will commit a well-reasoned suicide both on behalf of his country and on behalf of his friends, and if he falls victim to unduly severe pain or mutilation or incurable illness."[25] The Stoics believed that human beings should do what is "natural" and follow reason. In their view, because suicide can be reasonable, suicide can be morally acceptable. For example, if someone is about to be tortured by the enemy in order to extract information that would harm his country and the only way that he can avoid revealing the information is by committing suicide, then according to the Stoics, suicide would be reasonable and justified. Similarly, if disability, injury, or disease prevents or will prevent us from living a life appropriate to a human being, then ending our life is reasonable and morally acceptable.

There were a number of famous suicides in the ancient world. Cassius and Brutus, the assassins of Julius Caesar, committed suicide when it became clear that their cause was hopeless and that they faced dishonor at the hands of Julius Caesar's successor, Augustus. Similarly, Cleopatra committed suicide rather than fall into Augustus's hands and face the humiliation of being returned to Rome as a slave rather than a queen. Her lover, Marc Antony, also committed suicide. It was not uncommon for people in the Roman world to consider suicide in order to avoid disgrace both noble and courageous rather than a manifestation of cowardice. They believed in the slogan "Death before dishonor."

Suicide and Religion

Many people believe that suicide is always immoral because according to their religious tradition, God sets an absolute prohibition on it. Jews and Christians often appeal to the Ten Commandments, one of which is "You shall not murder." Although some Jews and Christians consider suicide to be a form of murder, namely, selfmurder—and therefore prohibited by God—others disagree. Just as the book of Exodus goes on to endorse capital punishment for a variety of crimes, clearly signaling that its authors do not consider executing certain wrongdoers murder, some may doubt that suicide constitutes murder. Even if we accept the Divine Command theory of morality, discovering whether God absolutely prohibits suicide may be difficult.

Suicide and the Possibility of Error

Some people think that suicide is always immoral because we can never be certain of the future. For example, they point out that medicine is not an exact science and that diagnoses may be mistaken. A patient may commit suicide because he believes that he will die in pain or discomfort, and there is no hope for a cure. However, doctors could be mistaken about the nature or course of a patient's illness. If a patient does not commit suicide, it is possible that he will have a remission or a miraculous cure, or that new treatments will offer new hope. Opponents of suicide may say that we should not commit suicide when our future is uncertain. In fact, our future is never certain.

Although it is possible for physicians to be mistaken about the nature and course of an illness and possible for new therapies to become suddenly available, those who believe that suicide can be morally acceptable deny that such possibilities show that suicide is always immoral. Possible does not mean probable, and they think that it is more reasonable to be guided by probability than by mere possibility. For example, it's possible that a patient will have a fatal reaction to a certain medicine her doctor has prescribed, and possible that she'll regain her health without taking it. However, if the probability of her having such a reaction and the probability of her regaining her health without the medicine are very low, it would be more reasonable for her to take the medicine.

Suppose that a terminally ill man acknowledges that it's possible that new therapies will unexpectedly become available that would extend his life or improve its quality. Nevertheless, suppose that he says that he doesn't want to count on that because it's much more probable that no new therapies will become available before he dies. Why would it be immoral for him to base his decisions on what's most probable?

Suicide and Autonomy

We could maintain that mature, rational human beings have a right to freedom or autonomy and are morally permitted to live their lives according to their own values and preferences, provided that they do not impose unjustified harm on others. It may be a short step from an autonomous person having a right to live in accordance with her values and preferences to her having a right to die in accordance with her values and preferences. We could then conclude that an autonomous person should be able to decide not only how to live her life but also how to die.

Many people think that the right to freedom or autonomy is not absolute; people do not have a moral right to do anything they want to do regardless of its effect on others. We may live or end our life in accordance with our own values and preferences *provided that* we do not impose unjustified harm on others. Committing suicide often imposes unjustified harm on others. Suppose that we have children, a spouse, parents or siblings who love, care about, and are pshychologically dependent on us, and who would be psychologically harmed by our committing suicide. Also, others may be financially dependent and would be harmed by our committing suicide. Therefore, many people argue that we have a moral duty to refrain from committing suicide if it would impose unjustified harm on others.

Good Reasons for Committing Suicide

What might be the circumstances in which suicide would be morally acceptable?

Many people believe that quality of life is more important than quantity of life. They think that if (1) our quality of life has diminished to the point where on careful reflection we judge that continued life is valueless and life is no longer worth living, and (2) there is virtually no chance of recovery, then it would be reasonable to end life. Perhaps the force of this point of view can be better appreciated by first considering it in relation to decisions about taking special steps to prolong life. Suppose that Jones, 75, is crippled with severe and painful arthritis. He is also almost completely blind and partly deaf, and he has no friends or family left alive. Confined to an old age home, he is lonely and has almost no sources of pleasure and happiness left in his life. Doctors now inform him of a new treatment that will probably prolong his life 20 to 30 years, although it will not improve his condition at all. On reflection, Jones decides that 20 to 30 years of additional life have no value for him and that his life is no longer worth living. Therefore, he refuses the new life-prolonging treatment. It seems difficult to deny that it is reasonable to consider quality of life when making decisions about taking special steps to prolong life.

Similarly, we may think that it is reasonable to consider quality of life when making decisions about continuing to live our life. If our quality of life has eroded to the point where we judge that our life is no longer worth living, not only would it be reasonable to do nothing to prolong it, but it would be reasonable to take steps to end it. Good reasons for not taking steps to prolong our life are also good reasons for taking steps to end it. Thus, we may say that if our quality of life has been permanently eroded to a severe enough degree, that situation can outweigh some of the harm that committing suicide can cause.

People sometimes commit suicide as a matter of principle. For example, during the war in Vietnam, many Buddhist monks burned themselves to death in protest against the war. People in other countries have dramatically and publicly committed suicide to draw attention to evil and injustice. Suppose that someone in Nazi Germany committed suicide to draw people's attention to and protest against the policy of exterminating Jews. Suppose further that in doing so she did not impose any unjustified harm on others. She had no dependents relying on her; her action did not jeopardize relatives or friends. Would such principled suicide be irrational? Would it be immoral or blameworthy?

Similarly, suppose that a spy is captured and is about to be interrogated. Because he will be injected with various drugs, he knows that he will divulge information that will jeopardize many of his fellow spies and that will harm his country. Would it be irrational of him to commit suicide in order to ensure that he does not divulge the information? Would it be immoral or blameworthy? Although some people believe that suicide under such circumstances would be blameworthy, others do not.

Bad Reasons for Committing Suicide

Judgements that our quality of life has permanently eroded to the point where our life has become valueless and is no longer worth living can be reasonable. However, such judgements can also be unreasonable. People can believe that their diminished quality of life is permanent when in fact it is only temporary. Similarly, they can falsely and unreasonably believe that their quality of life has sunk so low that they no longer have any sources of pleasure, satisfaction, or happiness.

People can suffer from temporary depression that they believe will be permanent. For example, people who lose loved ones through death or breakup, or who suffer serious financial reverses, sometimes believe that the psychological pain they feel will never diminish. A husband whose wife has just died or a woman whose lover has just left her may believe that the crushing sense of loss and depression they feel will never go away or diminish. A businessperson who has just lost her job may believe that she will never find work again and will be permanently destitute. The belief that our quality of life will be *permanently* diminished by these catastrophic events is hardly ever reasonable. Centuries of human experience have shown that the psychological pain and the catastrophic consequences of such events almost always diminish, and we underestimate the availability of alternative sources of pleasure, happiness, and satisfaction. For example, the woman whose lover leaves her may believe that she can't live without him and that she'll never find anyone to replace him. However, such beliefs are almost always false and unreasonable. Given time, women and men who lose their lovers recover; usually their pain diminishes and they find new loves or new sources of happiness and satisfaction.

Suicide and the Duty to Minimize Harm to Others

We have a duty to minimize the harm that we cause others, and that duty applies to suicide, even when committing suicide would be morally acceptable. There are ways of reducing the harm that suicide may cause. For example, preparing people who will be affected by our suicide rather than committing suicide without warning can reduce the harm it causes. Similarly, some ways of committing suicide can cause more harm than others.

For example, a terminally ill man who has decided to commit suicide could reduce the pain he'll cause others by discussing his intention and preparing those who care about him. He can explain his reasoning to them and try to persuade them that committing suicide is preferable to dying slowly from his illness. Those who care about him may come to support his decision. Even if they disagree with his decision, they may at least understand his reasons and be prepared for what is to come, which will reduce the shock and surprise. Thus, we may argue that those who intend to commit suicide have a duty to those who will probably be harmed by it both to inform them and to prepare them for the event.

Similarly, method and conditions of suicide can matter. A person who unexpectedly finds the body of someone who has committed suicide can suffer severe trauma. To reduce such trauma, we could take steps to ensure that the method used is not too grisly and that the person finding our body is prepared for it. For example, rather than slitting our wrists in a motel bathroom where we may be discovered by a hapless maid, we could take an overdose of sleeping pills in our own bedroom and ensure that our body will be discovered by someone who has been prepared for it.

If we commit suicide without trying to minimize the harm that it will cause others, we have violated our duty to minimize harm to others.

Suicide and Moral Theory

An act utilitarian would maintain that in any circumstance, if committing suicide would produce more total happiness than would refraining from committing suicide, then committing suicide is the right thing to do. For example, an act utilitarian might claim that by committing suicide a cancer patient would avoid pointless suffering, would relieve his family of the suffering of watching his decline, and would save money and scarce medical resources. Since he and his friends and family know that he will almost certainly die within a few months from his illness anyway, there would be an increase in total happiness from his committing suicide. Therefore, it would be the right thing to do.

Rule utilitarians would try to determine whether there would be more total happiness produced from people's following a rule such as "Commit suicide in circumstances C" than if they followed the rule "Don't commit suicide in circumstances C." Each set of rules and the circumstances in which they apply would have to be carefully examined to discover the effect on total happiness of people's following them. Rule utilitarians, like act utilitarians, would rely on experience to answer the question.

A Kantian approach first requires that we identify the maxim that we are following. In the case of a terminally ill patient contemplating suicide, the maxim might be:

> I will commit suicide when I'm terminally ill, I have only a few months to live, I will probably have much intense pain, and I will grow ever weaker and more helpless (call these circumstances C).

According to Kant, acting on this maxim would be morally acceptable only if the individual could consistently will that it become a universal law:

> Everyone will commit suicide in circumstances C.

Kant himself believed that no rational individual could consistently will such a universal law; therefore, he believed that suicide is always immoral. However, not all people find his reasoning persuasive. Many people believe that a rational individual could consistently will such a universal law.

Kant's second formulation of the Categorical Imperative requires us to treat people with respect, including ourselves. Whether treating ourselves with respect is consistent with committing suicide is a difficult question. Some people, including Kant himself, believe that it isn't. Others believe that it can be under certain circumstances. In their view, to undergo pointless suffering and both physical and mental deterioration when terminally ill, rather than prevent it by quickly and painlessly killing ourselves, is not to treat ourselves with respect.

If we applied virtue theories to the issue of suicide, we would ask what virtues or vices are exemplified (or would be exemplified) in a specific instance of suicide. Before we can answer that, we have to know the motive. For example, one person may intend to commit suicide in order to reduce his own suffering and that of those he loves, while another person may intend to commit suicide in order to reduce his own suffering and that of those he loves, while another person may intend to commit suicide in order to increase peoples' suffering, such as those he blames for making him feel miserable. Suicide could be motivated by patriotism and loyalty or by fear and anger. It could exemplify courage or cowardice. It depends on the circumstances and motives.

In an episode of the television program *Law and Order*, a police officer shot an unarmed teenager in a moment of fear. Rather than admit that he had made a mistake in a tense, confusing situation, he planted a gun on the teenager and claimed that he shot the boy in self-defense when he pulled the gun on him. Ultimately, he was exposed and convicted of a crime that would send him to prison. (The prosecutor admitted that if the officer had first told the truth, no jury would have convicted him of any crime.) Before his sentencing, he shot himself to death. Presumably he could not stand the humiliation of going to prison and he found the prospect of serving a lengthy prison sentence intolerable. He considered his life no longer worth living. Perhaps he was trying to get back at the people he thought had betrayed him, to make them feel guilty or remorseful. His action exemplified despair and fear (probably also depression). We might say that a person with the virtues of courage, hopefulness, determination, perseverance, self-control, and patience would have tried to get through the ordeal of prison and rebuild his life when he was released. Lacking these, he ended his life. If we think that his action did not exemplify many virtues and did exemplify a variety of vices, we would say that it was the wrong thing to do.

Rights, Duties, and Suicide Preventions

If someone is competent, mature, rational, and yet wants to commit suicide, many people do not think we have a right to *permanently* prevent him or her from performing the act; permanently preventing suicide would unjustifiably interfere with an individual's right to autonomy. However, many people do think we have a right (perhaps even a duty) to prevent an individual from committing suicide, at least temporarily, if there is a question about the individual's rationality or competence. For example, if someone is not yet an adult, most people think that we have a right to prevent her from committing suicide. They think that individuals who have not yet reached maturity are not competent to decide whether their lives are worth living and should be protected from themselves until they have reached maturity.

If a man suffers from a severe psychological disorder that is the likely cause of his desire to commit suicide, many people think that we have a right to prevent him from committing suicide in order to protect him from himself until he regains his rationality and competence, especially if there are therapies and treatments available that hold promise of relieving the psychological disorder. (We must be careful, however, not to take a suicide attempt or a desire to commit suicide as proof of a severe psychological disorder.) However, if the psychological disturbance turns out to be severe enough and if there is virtually no hope of effective therapy or treatment, we may wonder whether we have a right to permanently prevent him from committing suicide. If the person's future almost surely contains little but suffering, with almost no prospect of relief, it is not obvious that we have a right to force that individual to continue to live such a life.

Supporters of this position could justify on several grounds temporarily preventing someone from committing suicide in order to determine competence. On utilitarian grounds, such temporary prevention probably maximizes total well-being. We might also reach the same conclusion on Kantian principles. We could maintain that we could not consistently will as a universal law a maxim that directs us to do nothing to prevent others from committing suicide, even temporarily. If such a maxim became a universal law, we might ourselves die, or someone we love might die, as a result of temporary self-destructive impulses that could have been prevented but weren't.

EUTHANASIA

My dictionary defines euthanasia as "the act or practice of killing or permitting the death of hopelessly sick or injured individuals ... in a relatively painless way for reasons of mercy."[26] An act of euthanasia may involve killing someone, or it may involve refraining from trying to prevent death (permitting someone to die). However, the condition of the person undergoing euthanasia and the intentions of the person performing euthanasia are crucial for distinguishing between euthanasia and other forms of killing, such as murder or self-defense. According to the dictionary definition, in order for an act to be considered an act of euthanasia, the person undergoing it must be "hopelessly sick or injured," and the motivation of the person(s) performing euthanasia must be mercy. In order to be considered an act of euthanasia, an act must be done in the interests of the person who undergoes euthanasia, and the goal must be to prevent, reduce, or end a patient's suffering, to preserve a patient's dignity, or to respect a patient's autonomy. It is not euthanasia if the person acts or refrains from acting primarily from self-interested motives.

Issues of euthanasia can arise at the beginning of life, the end of life, or any point in between.

Impaired Newborns

Suppose that Mary Jackson gives birth to a baby with physical defects that are almost certain to cause moderate to severe mental retardation and paralysis. Ms. Jackson's physicians tell her that unless they operate as soon as possible to drain the cerebrospinal fluid that has built up in the baby's brain, the baby will very probably die within a year or two and will certainly be profoundly retarded. On the other hand, if the operation is performed without too much delay and the infant receives the best care possible, these is a 50 percent probability that the baby will live 10 to 15 years and will be only slightly retarded. Unfortunately, regardless of what they do, the baby will be crippled or paralyzed because of irreparable spinal damage, and there is a high probability that the child will not be able to control its bladder or bowels and will suffer from chronic urinary infections.

The Jacksons recognize that even if their baby has the operation, there is a high probability that it will have a relatively short, unhappy life. If it doesn't have the operation, its quality of life may be even lower, but its life will be much shorter. Therefore, they wonder whether it would be more merciful and compassionate to refuse rather than permit the operation.

Pamela Ross has given birth to an infant with exactly the same physical disabilities and probable future as the Jacksons' infant. However, her baby also has a heart defect that, if uncorrected, will almost certainly kill the infant in a matter of days or weeks. She and her husband wonder whether it would be best to refuse permission for the operation and let their infant die quickly.

Tina Velasquez gave birth to an infant suffering from anencephaly; it was born without a complete brain. Her doctors have informed her that although her infant may live for several months, it will not be conscious in any recognizably human sense; it will not be self-aware or aware of its environment, nor will it be capable of thought, feeling, or emotion. It also has an intestinal blockage that prevents it from absorbing any nutrients; if the blockage is not corrected, the baby will starve to death over a one- to two-week period. Tina and her husband wonder whether to let the infant die by refusing to permit the operation. However, they also wonder whether it would be more merciful to give it a lethal injection in order to kill it swiftly and painlessly rather than let it die slowly from dehydration and starvation.

Irreversible Comas

In 1975, 21-year-old Karen Quinlan suffered severe brain damage and became comatose when she stopped breathing after mixing alcohol and barbiturates. She was placed on a respirator. After several months doctors concluded that she was in a "persistent vegetative state"—an almost always irreversible state characterized by the absence of all higher-level mental functioning, such as awareness of environment, self-awareness, thought, and emotion.

> Over the next five months, Karen's posture began to show . . . neurological damage. . . . Her left wrist cocked at a right angle to her hand so that it looked as if her fingernails were digging into her wrist; her left foot twisted inward; her left elbow drew into her body. These positions were held rigidly. . . . Karen's weight dropped [to 70–80 pounds], and because her muscles were so rigid that IV [intravenous] feeding couldn't be used, a naso-gastric (N-G) feeding tube [through the nose] was used.[27]

Karen did not just lie in bed peacefully. She suffered from spasms that were like convulsions, and often her head would thrash about wildly. Because doctors told them that there was no hope of recovery, the Quinlans requested that the hospital take Karen off the respirator so that she could be permitted to die. However, the hospital refused their request and went to court to prevent the Quinlans from taking Karen off the respirator.

The case dragged on through New Jersey courts for months, but the New Jersey Supreme Court finally ruled in the Quinlans' favor. During this time, however, doctors at the hospital went to great lengths to wean Karen from the respirator so that she would be able to breathe without it. They succeeded. When Karen was finally taken off the respirator (more than a year after her parents' initial request), she did not die. In 1976 Karen was placed in a nursing home, where she lingered for another ten years without regaining consciousness until she died from pneumonia. Many people wonder whether the Quinlans should have been permitted to have Karen's respirator removed earlier to let her die. Other people wonder whether it was morally acceptable for the hospital to work to ensure that Karen could live without the respirator once it was removed.

End-of-Life Cases

Brad Felton had always been an active, healthy outdoorsman; his greatest passions were hiking and climbing in the Sierra Nevada mountains of California. At age 76 he had more energy and vigor than most men half his age. Now he has had a stroke that has left him severely brain damaged. Like Karen Quinlan, he is in a persistent vegetative state with virtually no hope of recovery. Doctors have told his family that he can live another five to ten years in this condition. Although Brad rarely talked about such possibilities, his family believes that he would not want to continue to live in this condition. Brad receives nourishment and fluids through a feeding tube. If the feeding tube is disconnected, Brad will die in one to two weeks from dehydration and starvation. Doctors assure the family that he will feel no pain during this process because of the damage to his brain. The family is considering requesting that feeding be discontinued so that Brad can be permitted to die.

Frank Barker, age 52, has malignant mesothelioma, a cancer of the chest lining that is untreatable and invariably fatal. He has been slowly wasting away. His weight has dropped from 180 to 125 pounds, and he is so weak that he cannot stand or walk without assistance. He is receiving large doses of morphine to control the pain and discomfort, so that his mind is perpetually dulled. His medications are causing bouts of constipation followed by diarrhea. Frank is now bedridden in the hospital awaiting death. Several times Frank has privately asked his physician, Dr. Nora Trent, for a lethal injection to put him out of his misery, telling her that he would prefer to die swiftly and painlessly rather than wait for his illness to kill him slowly over a period of three to six months. Dr. Trent has informed Frank's wife and children of Frank's request and they have endorsed it, assuring her that no one outside of the family would know. Dr. Trent wonders whether she should comply with the request and give Frank a lethal injection to end what he and his family consider to be his pointless suffering.

Active and Passive Euthanasia

Is euthanasia ever morally acceptable? To answer that question, we need to make a number of important distinctions.

Passive euthanasia occurs when someone intentionally withholds treatment or care from a patient, letting the patient die; active euthanasia occurs when someone intentionally kills a patient. For example, if the conditions for an act of euthanasia are met and a patient dies because he or she has been disconnected from a respirator or has had needed surgery or medication withheld, it is a case of passive rather than active euthanasia. However, if the patient dies because someone has deliberately given him or her a lethal injection; or the patient has been shot, stabbed, drowned, smothered, or strangled, it would be a case of active euthanasia.

Many people maintain that although passive euthanasia is sometimes morally acceptable, active euthanasia is always immoral. However, it's not easy to provide precise criteria for distinguishing between active and passive euthanasia. We may be tempted to think that we can distinguish between active and passive euthanasia simply on the basis of the difference between acting and not acting—that active euthanasia requires doing something whereas passive euthanasia simply requires not doing something. For example, consider the difference between *giving* a patient a lethal dose of morphine and *not giving* a patient an injection of antibiotics needed to cure pneumonia. However, passive euthanasia can require that tubes providing medication, oxygen, or nourishment be removed or that switches on medical equipment be flipped, all of which are actions, not merely omissions.

Perhaps we could say that unlike active euthanasia, passive euthanasia involves a certain kind of inaction in that we cease to act or refrain from acting so as to prevent or delay death. We might also add a difference of intention: In active euthanasia we intend to directly cause the patient to die; in passive euthanasia we intend to refrain from taking steps to delay or prevent death. Finally, we might maintain that the direct cause of death differs in active and passive euthanasia: In passive euthanasia, it is the illness or injury that directly causes the patient's death, but if someone gives a patient a lethal injection of morphine or smothers a patient, it is the injection or smothering that directly causes the patient's death. However, if we withhold food or fluid from a patient in passive euthanasia, it seems difficult to deny that the agent directly caused the patient's death (and intended to cause the patient's death). The starvation that caused the death is a condition that the agent directly causes, unlike the situation in which an injury or illness caused the death.

Extraordinary Treatment and Ordinary Care

Many people claim that although it may be morally acceptable to withhold extraordinary treatment in passive euthanasia, it is never morally acceptable to withhold ordinary care. Extraordinary treatment (an unfortunate term) may include surgery and the provision of medications (oral or intravenous) and medical services such as CPR (cardiopulmonary resuscitation), kidney dialysis, blood plasma, and oxygen. Ordinary care is generally limited to things that all people need regardless of their state of health, such as food and water, or to comfort-oriented care such as bathing, massage, and pain-relief therapies. The question is whether one can be as morally justified in withholding ordinary care that is necessary for a patient's survival, such as food and water, as in withholding extraordinary treatment.

Voluntary, Nonvoluntary, and Involuntary Euthanasia

If a fully informed, competent patient has freely requested or freely consented to undergo euthanasia, it is voluntary euthanasia. If a patient who is not competent to give or withhold consent undergoes euthanasia, it is nonvoluntary euthanasia. If a competent patient undergoes euthanasia without having freely consented, it is involuntary euthanasia. (Free consent means that the patient has not been coerced into giving consent.)

Thus, if a competent patient were given a lethal injection at his or her own request, it would be voluntary (active) euthanasia. It would also be voluntary euthanasia if treatment were withheld from a comatose patient who had, before becoming comatose, clearly requested or expressed a desire that treatment or care be withheld in such circumstances. Euthanasia of impaired newborn infants or of comatose patients who had never expressed a desire for or against euthanasia would be nonvoluntary euthanasia. Finally, euthanasia of a competent patient who has not requested it would be involuntary euthanasia.

There are, then, six different forms that euthanasia can take: voluntary active, voluntary passive, nonvoluntary active, nonvoluntary passive, involuntary active, involuntary passive. There is also the withholding of ordinary care and of extraordinary treatment. Our question is whether any of these forms of euthanasia can be morally acceptable.

Involuntary Euthanasia

Involuntary euthanasia, in almost all conceivable circumstances, whether active or passive, seems clearly immoral. To kill people or let them die against their will when death is preventable unjustifiably violates their right to life and their right to autonomy. People don't have a right to override other people's decisions about their own lives and deaths, or to substitute their judgment for another's about whether that person's life is worth living. This judgement can be easily justified by appeal to Utilitarianism or Kantian moral theory. Involuntary euthanasia is rationally indefensible.[28]

Voluntary Passive Euthanasia

Frank Barker, the 52-year-old man slowly dying from mesothelioma, has come down with pneumonia. His doctors have told him that the pneumonia will kill him within a few days unless he is given injections of antibiotics to combat it. After discussing it with his wife, Frank refuses to consent to have the antibiotics because he wants to die sooner from pneumonia rather than later from the cancer. If he dies from pneumonia because he refused to accept medical treatment for it, it will be a case of voluntary passive euthanasia. Doctors face a choice. They can comply with Frank's request, withhold the antibiotics, and let him die from pneumonia, or they can give Frank antibiotics against his will and cure the pneumonia. What's the right thing to do?

In the United States, competent patients may not be forced to undergo medical treatment against their will; medical treatment may be provided to a competent patient only with the patient's consent. The law reflects our society's commitment to autonomy and to the fundamental importance of bodily integrity. Others may not handle our property without permission; how much more important that others be forbidden to handle our bodies, the center of our being, without permission. It also reflects our society's commitment to personal freedom. The law also may reflect recognition that sometimes the most merciful and compassionate thing to do is to let someone die. It can be senseless and cruel to take energetic measures to prolong someone's life against his or her will if that life promises to contain little but suffering. We do not treat people with respect if we force them to continue to endure a life of suffering against their will.

There are good moral reasons for believing that voluntary passive euthanasia can be morally acceptable. Considerations of individual autonomy or freedom; appeal to virtues such as kindness, compassion, and mercy; and appeal to the requirement to treat people with respect favor the view that voluntary passive euthanasia is morally acceptable, sometimes perhaps morally obligatory. We could also justify it on utilitarian and Kantian grounds. In some situations, taking steps to delay or prevent death is harmful because delayed death simply means additional suffering.

However, suppose that Frank does not contract pneumonia; instead of refusing antibiotics he refuses food, intending to starve himself to death. Would it be morally acceptable to comply with a competent patient's request to starve himself to death? Doctors can either comply with his request and let him die from starvation, or they can forcibly keep him supplied with nourishment and fluids— either by forcing Frank to swallow food and liquid or by forcibly installing a feeding tube into his veins or stomach and restraining or sedating him to prevent him from removing them.

Although many people would probably agree that Frank's doctors should not force him to take antibiotics against his will, many people would be less certain about whether doctors should force food and fluids into Frank if he refuses to eat and drink. We could argue that the same moral considerations that justify the prohibition on forcing medical treatment on a patient against his will also justify a prohibition on forcing care such as food and water on a patient against his will.

Voluntary Active Euthanasia

Many people insist that although passive euthanasia can be morally acceptable, even morally obligatory, active euthanasia is always immoral. For example, suppose that rather than refusing food and water, Frank Barker asked his doctor for a lethal injection to end his life swiftly and painlessly. Many people belive that it is immoral for doctors to give patients lethal injections even if they have requested it. In their view, although it can be permissible to let someone die, it can never be permissible to kill someone.

This view appears to be based on the assumption that it's always worse to kill someone than to let someone die. However, James Rachels challenges that assumption. In his view, letting someone die is often no better from a moral point of view than killing someone. For example, suppose that a child's evil uncle comes into the bathroom with the intention of drowning her in the bathtub because he stands to inherit a million dollars. As he enters, the child slips and hits her head, loses consciousness, and slides under the water. Her uncle does nothing; he lets her drown, waiting in the bathroom for five minutes until he is certain that she is dead. According to Rachels, letting her drown is no better than drowning her.[29] Similarly, suppose that the child dies as a result of her evil uncle's starving her to death or withholding her asthma medication. Is that really better than her uncle's shooting or smothering her? Not according to Rachels. In his view, these examples show that it's not always worse to kill someone than to let someone die.

In fact, according to Rachels, letting someone die may be worse than killing him if letting him die produces far more suffering. Usually a person will die more slowly and painfully from having treatment withheld than from receiving a lethal injection that swiftly and painlessly ends his life. In Rachels's view, the moral considerations that justify passive euthanasia (autonomy and freedom; virtues such as compassion, mercy, and kindness; treating people with respect; the balance of harm and benefit) also sometimes justify active euthanasia.

Then, too, many people believe that the moral prohibition on killing other people is not absolute. For example, most people seem to believe that it is morally acceptable to kill people in self-defense, in war, and as punishment for serious crimes. Unless we take the position that it is always immoral to kill someone regardless of the circumstances, the mere fact that active euthanasia involves killing someone does not automatically show that it is immoral. We might argue that like self-defense (or perhaps capital punishment), active euthanasia can be justified as a legitimate exception to the moral prohibition on killing other people.

However, many opponents of active euthanasia fear that if we permit or legalize active voluntary euthanasia, it will inevitably lead to a kind of moral corruption. In their view, it would undermine respect for life and would act as the opening wedge for nonvoluntary and involuntary euthanasia—for example, killing people who are old or mentally handicapped. However, supporters of voluntary active euthanasia maintain that such fears are exaggerated. They claim that if the intention is to minimize suffering and if the patient's desires are scrupulously respected, then the likelihood of moral corruption and decreased respect for human life is minimal.

Nonvoluntary Passive Euthanasia

Issues of nonvoluntary euthanasia arise when a patient is not competent to give or withhold consent for care or treatment, as in the case of a defective newborn infant or a comatose adult patient. In such cases, someone else must make decisions. Can it be morally acceptable for someone to make life-and-death decisions about treatment and care for another person? Is it morally acceptable for the relatives of a patient who is in a persistent vegetative state or for the parents of a defective newborn infant to decide to withhold medical treatment and let the patient die?

There is no way to avoid having others make life-and-death decisions for incompetent patients. Someone must decide between the two alternatives of providing or withholding medical treatment. However, we might claim that if we do not know what the patient wants or would want under the circumstances, we should always err on the side of caution and life-providing, rather than withdraw or withhold treatment or care. On this view, it would be wrong for others to decide to withhold or discontinue treatment of an incompetent patient, but not wrong for others to decide to provide medical treatment to an incompetent patient.

Nonetheless, many people believe that nonvoluntary passive euthanasia can be morally acceptable for much the same reasons, under much the same conditions as voluntary passive euthanasia. Provided that the good of the patient is the only or primary consideration, minimizing and preventing suffering for the patient or respecting the patient's dignity and autonomy can justify someone's deciding to withhold treatment or care. However, extreme caution is required in evaluating the life prospects of an incompetent patient. In order to be justified in withholding treatment or care from an incompetent patient, we must have strong evidence that there is a very high probability either that the patient's life will contain little but intense suffering, or that the patient's capacity for higher level mental functioning associated with being a person has been permanently lost. We might require that, given the patient's life prospects, virtually no reasonable person would act energetically to delay death.

Nonvoluntary Active Euthanasia

If it would be morally acceptable to withhold treatment or care from an incompetent patient, would it also be morally acceptable to kill a patient? For example, is it worse to give a lethal injection to a patient in a persistent vegetative state than to disconnect his respirator or feeding tube? Is it worse to withhold surgery from an anencephalic infant with a bowel obstruction, letting him or her die from dehydration or starvation over a period of days, than to give him or her a lethal injection that will swiftly and painlessly kill him or her?

Advocates of nonvoluntary active euthanasia can appeal to the duty to minimize suffering. Letting someone die can easily produce far more suffering than would killing the person. Considerations that would justify letting someone die—such as a concern to prevent or minimize suffering and virtues such as kindness and compassion—might also justify killing someone, if killing would produce less suffering and would preserve the patient's autonomy and dignity more than would letting the person die. Of course, anyone who believes that active euthanasia is always immoral would reject this line of argument.

EXERCISES

1. At what stage of development, if any, and for what reasons, if any, is abortion morally acceptable? Defend your answer.

2. Suppose that an advocate of the right-to-life position maintains that because a woman can always choose to give up an unwanted infant for adoption, abortion is morally wrong except when it's necessary to save the mother's life. Do you agree?

3. In the United States, there is a high demand for white babies for adoption but a very low demand for nonwhite babies. What effect would that situation have on your answer to question 2? Why?

4. At what point in its development, if any, does a fetus become a person? Does that matter to the question of the rightness or wrongness of abortion? Is its potential to develop into a person sufficient to ground the judgment that a fetus has a right to life?

5. Should abortion be legal? If yes, under what conditions? Defend your answer.

6. Should there be public funding of abortions for poor women? Defend your answer.

7. Should minors have to have one or both parents' consent before they can legally undergo an abortion?

8. Is suicide always morally wrong? If not, under what conditions is it not morally wrong?

9. Tom is a spy who has been apprehended. He has knowledge that would enable his captors to arrest an entire spy network that includes dozens of people. He is fairly certain that he will not be able to withstand the torture he can expect under interrogation and that he will reveal his knowledge to his captors. He has a cyanide capsule secreted in a false tooth. When he became a spy, he took an oath promising to use the cyanide capsule to commit suicide if he was ever captured. Would it be morally right for him to commit suicide? Does he have a moral duty to commit suicide?

10. Paula Finn has Alzheimer's disease. Sometimes she is lucid, but at other times she is not. When she is not, she is wholly unable to care for herself. She cannot remember who she is or where she lives; she cannot recognize her family; she cannot fully control her bodily functions. When she is lucid, she knows what is happening to her. She has reached the point where she is lucid about 70 percent of the time, but her condition will continue to worsen and the periods during which she is lucid will grow ever briefer. Right now Paula is lucid. She does not wish to live in a state of mental deterioration; she judges that her life is no longer worth living. Would it be irrational for her to commit suicide? Would it be morally wrong for her to commit suicide? If her family or doctors know that she intends to commit suicide, should they have the legal right to stop her? Would it be morally wrong for a doctor to prescribe drugs that will enable her to end her life quickly and painlessly? Should the laws forbid doctors to help patients in any way to commit suicide, even to provide them with information about how to kill themselves quickly and painlessly?

11. Should active voluntary euthanasia or doctor-assisted suicide be legally permitted? If yes, under what circumstances? If yes, what safeguards should there be to minimize the chance of someone being killed against her will?

12. In Shakespeare's play *Romeo and Juliet*, Romeo and Juliet, two teenagers, fall in love, but their families are deadly enemies. They marry in secret, but Romeo must leave the city after he kills a kinsman of Juliet. Juliet's family thereupon intends to force her to marry a man of their choice, not knowing of her prior marriage to Romeo. In order to avoid the marriage and permit

her to escape from her family, Juliet drinks a potion that makes her appear to be dead. The plan is for Romeo to revive her in her tomb so they can run away without anyone following. Unfortunately, Romeo doesn't get the message informing him of the plan. He thinks Juliet is really dead. He comes to her tomb at night before she has revived and kills himself in despair over Juliet's death. When Juliet awakens and discovers that Romeo has killed himself, she commits suicide. Neither wanted to live without the other. Was it morally wrong of Romeo to kill himself because he believed that Juliet was dead? Was it morally wrong of Juliet to kill herself when she discovered that Romeo was dead?

13. Dr. Jack Kevorkian has assisted in several suicides and has constructed a socalled suicide machine to enable patients who want to kill themselves to do so swiftly and painlessly. Is he doing anything morally wrong?

SUGGESTED READINGS

Jane English. "Abortion and the Concept of a Person." In *Social Ethics: Morality and Social Policy*, 3d ed. Edited by Thomas Mappes and Jane Zembaty. New York: McGraw-Hill, 1987.

Jonathan Glover. *Causing Death and Saving Lives*. Harmondsworth, England: Penguin, 1977.

David Hume. "Of Suicide." In *Essays Moral, Political, and Literary*. Edited by Eugene Miller. Indianapolis, IN: Liberty Classics, 1985.

Immanuel Kant. "Doctrine of Virtue," Book 1, Article 1, "On Killing Oneself." In *The Metaphysics of Morals*. Edited by Mary Gregor. Cambridge, England: Cambridge University Press, 1991, pp. 218–220.

Ronald Munson. *Intervention and Reflection: Basic Issues in Medical Ethics*, 4th ed. Belmont, CA: Wadsworth, 1992. (See Chapters 2 and 3.)

John T. Noonan, Jr. "An Almost Absolute Value in History". *In Social Ethics: Morality and Social Policy*.

Gregory Pence. *Classic Cases in Medical Ethics*. New York: McGraw-Hill, 1990.

Plato. "Phaedo." *In the Collected Dialogues of Plato*. Edited by Edith Hamilton and Huntington Cairns eds.. Princeton, NJ: Princeton University Press, 1961.

L. W. Summer. *Abortion and Moral Theory*. Princeton, NJ: Princeton University Press, 1981.

Mary Anne Warren. "On the Moral and Legal Status of Abortion." In *Social Ethics: Morality and Social Policy*.

ENDNOTES

1. *Roe v. Wade* in *Constitutional Law*, 10th, ed., ed. Gerald Gunther (Mineola, NY: Foundation Press, 1980), p. 591.

2. Ibid., p. 591.

3. Ibid., pp. 591–592.

4. Ibid., p. 593.

5. Ibid., p. 593.

6. Ibid., p. 593.

7. Ibid., p. 594.

8. Ibid., p. 594.

9. Ibid., p. 595.

10. John T. Noonan, Jr, "An Almost Absolute Value in History," in *Social Ethics: Marality and Social Policy*, 3d, ed., ed. by Thomas Mappes and Jane Zembary (New York: McGraw-Hill, 1987), p. 9.

11. Ibid., p. 12.

12. Mary Anne Warren, "On the Moral and Legal Status of Abortion," in *Social Ethics: Morality and Social Policy*, p. 16.

13. "Brain Development," in *The Oxford Companion to the Mind*, R. L. Gregory (New York: Oxford University Press, 1987), p. 104.

14. Judith Jarvis Thomson, "A Defense of Abortion," in *Social Ethics: Morality and Social Policy*.

15. L. W. Summer, *Abortion and Moral Theory* (Princeton, NJ: Princeton University Press, 1981), p. 142.

16. Ibid., p. 149.

17. Ibid., p. 151.

18. Ibid., p. 153.

19. Susan Sachs, "Indians Abroad Get Pitch on Gender Choice," *New York Times* (15 August 2001).

20. Ibid.

21. Plato, "Phaedo," in *The Collected Dialogues of Plato*, ed. Edith Hamilton and Huntington Cairns (Princeton, NJ: Princeton University Press, 1961), pp. 44–45 (62a–c).

22. Plato, "Laws," in *The Collected Dialogues of Plato*, p. 1432 (IX: 873 c–d).

23. Aristotle, "Nichomachean Ethics," in *The Complete Works of Aristotle*, vol. 2, Jonathan Barnes (Princeton, NJ: Princeton University Press, 1984), p. 1762 (1116a 10–15).

24. Cicero, "On Ends," in *The Hellenistic Philosophers*, vol. 1, A. A. Long and D. N. Sedley (Cambridge, England: Cambridge University Press, 1987), p. 425.

25. Diogenes Laertius, in *The Hellenistic Philosophers*, p. 425.

26. *Merriam-Webster's Collegiate Dictionary*, 10th. ed. (Springfield, MA: Merriam-Webster, 1994)

27. Gregory Pence, *Classic Cases in Medical Ethics* (New York: McGraw-Hill, 1990), pp. 5–6.

28. For simplicity, I ignore situations in which medical treatment is not provided because of high cost and limited economic resources.

29. James Rachels, "Active and Passive Euthanasia," and "More Impertinent Distinctions and a Defense of Active Euthanasia," both in *Social Ethics: Morality and Social Policy*.

12

Economic Inequality, Poverty, and Equal Opportunity

OBJECTIVES

- To understand egalitarianism and the arguments for and against more economic equality
- To distinguish between inequality and poverty, and between comparative and noncomparative concepts of poverty
- To apply Rawls's decision procedure to issues of economic inequality and poverty
- To understand the arguments for and against government action to alleviate poverty
- To understand the concept of equal opportunity, what is required for genuine equality of opportunity, and the arguments for and against equal opportunity
- To understand the concepts of a graduated income tax and a flat tax, and to understand the arguments for and against a flat tax.

INTRODUCTION

It seems that the world has always been divided between rich and poor. Wealth and income have rarely, if ever, been equally distributed among the members of a community. Economic inequality has been the norm both between and within nations. For example, the United States is far wealthier than Ghana. Within the United States, there are billionaires who can satisfy their every whim as well as paupers who can't afford life's basic necessities, such as food, shelter, clothing, and medical care.

Let's look at some statistics from the U.S. Bureau of the Census. In 2004, median annual household income of non-Hispanic whites was $48,977. (The median point is where 50 percent are above the figure and 50 percent are below it.) However, the median for black households was $30,134, and for Hispanic households it was $34,241. No household in the bottom 20 percent had an annual income exceeding $18,500, whereas no household in the richest 5 percent had an annual income below $157,185. The poorest 20 percent received only 3.6 percent of total U.S. income, while the richest 20 percent received 50.1 percent. In 1970, the poorest 20 percent received 4.1 percent and the richest 20 percent received 43.3 percent. Income inequality is correlated with both race and gender.

In non-Hispanic white households, 25.1 percent had an annual income below $25,000 compared with 42.3 percent of black households and 35.9 percent of Hispanic. On the other hand, whereas 18 percent of non-Hispanic white households had an annual income of $100,000 or higher, only 6.7 percent of black households and 8 percent of Hispanic households did. Statistics also show that only 8.6 percent of non-Hispanic whites were below the official poverty level, compared with 24.7 percent of blacks and 21.9 percent of Hispanics. Additionally, 45.8 million people were without health insurance, 15.7 percent of the population; however, whereas 11.3 percent of non-Hispanic whites were without health insurance, 19.7 percent of blacks and 32.7 percent of Hispanics were without health insurance.[1]

Statistics can be pretty dry. What is life like for people near the bottom? Poor people sometimes go to bed hungry. Sometimes they can't pay their rent, and they get evicted. Sometimes their homes have leaky roofs, faulty plumbing, and rats. In cities, their apartments can be stifling in summer and freezing in winter. Some neighborhoods where they live and try to bring up children are infested with drugs and crime. The schools in poor neighborhoods and towns often are overcrowded, dilapidated, and lacking in many of the things taken for granted in schools in middle-class and rich neighborhoods and towns. Sometimes poor people can't pay their utility bills, and their utilities are shut off. Sometimes they can't afford to pay for prescriptions they need. They either go without the medication, or if it's a prescription they regularly take, they dilute the doses to make the prescription last longer. Tens of millions of Americans lack health insurance, so they delay seeking medical care; they sometimes delay until their health has significantly deteriorated. Often they go to crowded emergency rooms of local public hospitals rather than to the offices of private physicians because they will not be required to pay for the care they receive. They're always worried about money.

People are poor for many reasons. Obviously, children who are poor are poor because they grow up in poor families. As for adults who are poor, some work full time but their jobs pay very little and don't include benefits. In 2006, the federal minimum wage was $5.15 per hour. Someone working 40 hours per week would earn $10,712 in a year if he or she earned only the minimum wage. Even if she earned $7.50 per hour, a full-time job would pay only $15,600 per year. These usually are people with knowledge or skills that are not highly valued, and most grew up in poor families and poor neighborhoods. (It's far more rare for someone growing up in a middle- or upper-class family to be in this plight.) Many economists say that both sexism and racism play at least some causal role in poverty. Some adults can only find part-time work. Others are poor because they can't work; they're too ill, disabled, or elderly. Some adults are poor because of addictions, such as alcoholism. Some are mentally ill. The point is that while many of us may think that it's their own fault if people are poor or near the bottom of the economic ladder, in many cases it's because of things over which people have little control.

IS TOO MUCH ECONOMIC INEQUALITY MORALLY WRONG?

Egalitarians believe that economic and social inequalities should be kept to a reasonable minimum. Different egalitarians may have different conceptions of what constitutes a reasonable minimum, but all egalitarians agree that virtually all societies today have too much inequality. Economic inequality is a matter of degree. For example, the highest income earners in a society may receive 10 times what the lowest income earners receive, or they may receive 10,000 times what the lowest income earners receive. There is much greater inequality in the second situation.

The Case for Equality

According to John Rawls, there is a presumption in favor of economic equality. Given that the moral point of view is supposed to be an impartial point of view, Rawls asks us to imagine that we are in a situation where we don't have any of the information that would allow us to be influenced by our biases, whether conscious or unconscious. He claims that a particular principle is justified if everyone who lacks this information would freely accept it.

Consider the various named biases, such as racism and sexism. A male may be biased in favor of males. A white person may be biased in favor of white people. Similarly, someone who is elderly may be biased in favor of the elderly. A Christian may be biased in favor of Christians. That is, because of self-interest, we tend to be biased in favor of people who have characteristics we have. How can we prevent such biases from influencing our judgments and behavior? Rawls points out that if we don't know what characteristics we have—whether we're a man or a woman, black or white, Christian or non-Christian, young or old—self-interest cannot bias us in favor of people who have the same characteristics we have.

Therefore, Rawls asks us to imagine that we're in what he calls the *original position* behind a *veil of ignorance*. We enter the original position before we have accepted any principles of justice. It is while we are in the original position that we will choose the principles of justice we will incorporate into our moral code. The principles of justice we would accept in the original position are the "correct" principles. The veil of ignorance hides us from ourselves, preventing us from having any information about ourselves that can lead to bias. Thus, one doesn't know such things as one's sex, age, race, ethnicity, economic class, intelligence, health, religion, and sexual orientation

We ask, for example, If you were in the original position behind the veil of ignorance, would you accept the principle that it is just to discriminate against blacks? According to Rawls, because you don't know whether you're black, you would not accept the principle that it is just to discriminate against blacks. No one in the original position would. Thus, that principle is "incorrect" or unjustified. Similarly, we ask whether you would accept the principle that it is just for men to have more rights than women. Because you don't know whether you're a man or a woman, you would not accept that principle.

There is no original position with a veil of ignorance. However, Rawls thinks that we have powerful enough imaginations that we can imagine ourselves in such a situation. He also thinks that we can know what principles we would accept or reject if we were in such a situation. For example, I know that if I were ignorant of what my religion is, I would not accept the principle that it is just to discriminate against Muslims.

In Rawls's view, people in the original position behind the veil of ignorance would insist on a relatively equal distribution of the product of their social cooperation, unless some inequality would be advantageous for all. People behind the veil of ignorance do not know whether they will be healthy or ill, of high or low intelligence, skilled or unskilled, educated or uneducated, highly motivated or poorly motivated. Therefore, they will refuse to accept principles of justice for economic distribution that say, for example, that it's just that the more educated have more than the less educated, or the skilled than the unskilled. They will reject such principles because they don't know whether they will be among the more privileged (educated and skilled) or the less privileged (uneducated and unskilled). They will try to ensure that the worst that can happen to them is at least tolerable. Demanding an equal distribution of income and wealth, unless an unequal distribution will clearly benefit them, gives them the maximum protection from disaster if they wind up having characteristics that would put them at the bottom of the economic ladder.

According to Rawls, people in the original position behind the veil of ignorance would accept the principle that "All social values—liberty and opportunities, income and wealth, and the bases of self-respect—are to be distributed equally unless an unequal distribution . . . is to everyone's advantage."[2]

Economic inequality can have a number of bad effects. Some people may have so much that there isn't enough left over to meet even the basic needs for food, clothing, shelter, medical care, and education of many people at or near the bottom. Often, political and social power comes with greater income and wealth. Great economic inequality can give some people the resources to dominate and oppress others, and to gain undue influence over government and public policy. This enables them to amass and protect a variety of privileges. Great economic inequality can produce envy and an erosion of self-respect among those left behind as well as arrogance and callousness among those who surge ahead.

Therefore, Rawls maintains that rational self-interested individuals in the original position behind the veil of ignorance, knowing all this, would accept this principle: Social and economic inequalities are to be arranged so that they are both (1) to the greatest benefit of the least advantaged, and (2) attached to offices and positions open to all under conditions of fair equality of opportunity.[3]

"Injustice," according to Rawls, "is simply inequalities that are not to the benefit of all."[4] (Rawls makes several assumptions that lead to the conclusion that all are benefited if and only if the least advantaged are benefited.)

Rawls's presumption of equality means that economic *inequality* must be justified as benefiting everyone—most specifically, the least advantaged—if it is to be just or morally acceptable. Inequality benefits everyone if, for example, it is both sufficient and necessary as an incentive for greater production. If a certain degree of inequality is required in order to get people to be more productive and if their greater productivity increases the size of the economic pie so that everyone gets a bigger slice with the inequality than they would get without the inequality, then the equality is just and morally acceptable. However, if the inequality is more than is required to increase productivity, then it is unjust and morally unacceptable. For example, if people would be motivated to go to medical school and become good doctors only if the average income for doctors were three times the national average, then it would be just for doctors to have average incomes that were three times the national average. We would agree to this in the original position because whatever our situation, we are likely to benefit if there are enough doctors to meet society's needs whereas we may be harmed if there aren't. However, if receiving an income three times the national average is sufficient to motivate enough people to go to medical school and become good doctors, then it would be unjust for doctors to have annual incomes five times the national average. (Rawls implies that there is a far greater degree of economic inequality in U.S. society than is necessary as an incentive for production and that there is too much economic inequality resulting from this.)

Other egalitarians reach conclusions similar to Rawls's on other grounds. Contemporary U.S. philosopher Gregory Vlastos maintains that "the human worth of all persons is equal however unequal may be their merit."[5] As a corollary of this basic assumption, Vlastos claims that "*one man's well-being is as valuable as any other's.*"[6]

Therefore, "one man's prima facie right to well-being is equal to that of any other."[7]He then argues, "Since men have an equal right to well-being..., they have an equal right to the means of well-being."[8] Therefore, he concludes, people have a right to an "equal distribution [of economic resources] at the highest obtainable level."[9]According to Vlastos, because people have equal inherent worth simply because they are people, they have an equal moral right to economic resources, one of the primary means of well-being. If some people have many more economic resources than others, they have a much greater ability to achieve happiness or a satisfactory level of well-being. Too much economic inequality thus violates people's moral right to equal resources for pursuing and achieving happiness or well-being.

Some philosophers justify greater equality in the name of liberty. According to Rousseau (1712–1778), freedom cannot survive without a certain degree of equality. Too much inequality destroys or undermines freedom. Equality, argues Rousseau, "must not be taken to imply that degrees of power and wealth should be absolutely the same for all, but rather that power shall stop short of violence and never be exercised except by virtue of authority and law, and, where wealth is concerned, that no citizen shall be rich enough to buy another and none so poor as to be forced to sell himself."[10] If some people are enormously wealthy, they can use their wealth to tyrannize over others, destroying freedom; if some people are terribly poor, they become so dependent on others for their very lives that they are no longer free. Both extremes are bad for society, according to Rousseau.

Utilitarians would favor greater economic equality if it would increase total well-being, but oppose it if it reduced total well-being. In any given situation, then, a utilitarian would ask what would be the effect on total well-being if there were more equality or less equality. It seems undeniable that in many situations of great inequality, there would be more total well-being if there were more equality. For example, consider a situation where a rich person has two mansions and 20 poor people are homeless. If one mansion were taken from the rich person and sold to provide housing for the 20 homeless people, it seems clear that total well-being would increase. The question is what would be the effect on total well-being of decreasing economic inequality by taxing the rich in this country at this time.

Arguments Against Equality

Some people argue that economic equality means that everyone will be the same. In their view, if everyone has roughly equal amounts of wealth and income, all individuality will be lost. Everyone will act in the same way, dress identically, drive the same car, live in identical houses, and think the same thoughts. These opponents of economic equality maintain that human diversity is extremely valuable; the world of human beings would be terribly boring and monotonous if everyone were the same. Because economic equality would destroy human diversity, they argue, economic equality is undesirable.

Egalitarians, however, deny that people would be pretty much identical to one another if they had equal amounts of wealth and income. Suppose we know only that A and B have the same amount of wealth ($65,000 in assets) and income ($50,000 per year). Can we confidently predict that they are pretty much alike? Egalitarians say that we cannot. A may wear suits, listen to classical music, play golf, drink wine, go to the opera, and read philosophy; B may wear jeans, listen to rock and roll, climb mountains, jog and lift weights, drink beer, play cards, and watch televised sports. Egalitarians insist that having equal wealth and income cannot make people the same or similar in other areas, such as their religion, political beliefs, behavior, interests, tastes, and preferences. Egalitarians maintain that greater economic equality would not lead to the dreary uniformity that opponents of egalitarianism fear.

Probably the most important argument against reducing economic inequality is that achieving it requires economic redistribution, which violates the rights and freedoms of those from whom resources are taken. Economic redistribution occurs when economic resources (wealth or income) are taken from those who have a lot and redistributed to or given to those who have little. For example, a government may tax the nonpoor in order to give to the poor, Robin Hood style. People opposed to economic equality object that the freedom of people to spend their earnings as they wish or to keep all the money and resources that they have legitimately acquired is violated if they are taxed in order to reduce economic inequality—that is, to close the gap between rich and poor. They consider such taxation a form of theft. Contemporary U.S. philosopher Robert Nozick maintains, "Taxation of earnings from labor is on a par with forced labor."[11] Nozick appears to assume that people have a more or less absolute moral right not to be taxed in order to reduce economic inequality—a right that cannot justifiably be overridden in order to increase total happiness or to respect the moral rights of other people, such as a right to equal life prospects or welfare rights. (Egalitarians deny that people have a right not to be taxed.)

Let's assume that taxes are fair and just, so that a rich person won't be impoverished by taxation. We might ask what people in the original position behind the veil of ignorance would accept. If you didn't know whether you were a rich person being taxed to pay for services to meet the needs of poor people or a poor person dependent on such tax-supported social programs, would you think that taxation to pay for social services for the poor is just or unjust?

IS POVERTY IN THE MIDST OF AFFLUENCE MORALLY WRONG?

Is poverty in the midst of affluence immoral? It could only be morally wrong if poverty is subject to human control. If people can't do anything to reduce or eliminate poverty, then they cannot be blamed or morally condemned for it. It would be like asking whether gravity is immoral. Gravity is not under anyone's control; therefore, it doesn't make sense to say that gravity is immoral. However, poverty isn't like gravity; in an affluent society, poverty is under people's control. Poverty is a condition of having too little money to afford life's necessities; it can be cured by providing job opportunities, training, money, or life's necessities to the poor person.

Is poverty in the midst of affluence morally wrong if we believe that poor people are poor through their own fault? For example, we might claim that poor people are poor because they freely choose not to work hard enough to lift themselves from poverty; therefore, they're poor voluntarily rather than involuntarily. We might go on to claim that voluntary poverty is not immoral, and that all poverty is voluntary. But as we saw previously, that is simply not true of many poor people, especially children, who make up a large majority of the poor.

Arguments for Relieving Poverty

According to both Act and Rule Utilitarianism, total happiness or well-being should be maximized, whether by acting directly to accomplish that end or by following rules that, if followed, will accomplish that end. A utilitarian could claim that total well-being is not maximized when poverty exists amidst affluence because total well-being would be greater if the rich had less and the poor had more—that is, if the basic needs of the poor were met rather than the desires of the rich for luxuries. Therefore, on utilitarian grounds we could say that poverty amidst affluence is immoral because it violates the utilitarian requirement that total well-being be maximized.

We might also appeal to Kant's Categorical Imperative. According to the universal law formulation, we should only act on maxims that we can consistently will to be universal laws. Those who believe that poverty should be reduced or eliminated when it is possible to do so might maintain that no one can consistently will a maxim recommending that one ignore the suffering of the poor and refrain from relieving poverty. Kant himself took this position:

> A...man, for whom things are going well, sees that others (whom he could help) have to struggle with great hardships, and he asks, "What concern of mine is it? Let each one be as happy as heaven wills, or as he can make himself: I will not take anything from him or even envy him; but to his welfare or his assistance in time of need I have no desire to contribute." If such a way of thinking were a universal law of nature, certainly the human race could exist.... It is nevertheless impossible to will that such a principle should hold everywhere as a law of nature. For a will which resolved this would conflict with itself, since instances can often arise in which he would need the love and sympathy of others, and in which he would have robbed himself, by such a law of nature springing from his own will, of all hope of the aid he desires.[12]

For example, imagine a man who naturally wants to have help if he needs it. If he wills as a universal law a maxim that permits him to ignore the needs of others in distress, his will is in conflict because he simultaneously wills that he be helped and yet not be helped when he is in distress and requires aid. Therefore, actions according to such a maxim are morally unacceptable. People should help those in need and relieve the sufferings of the poor.

Similarly, according to the respect for persons formulation of the Categorical Imperative, we should always treat other people with respect. We do not treat people with respect if we allow them to suffer or die or leave them unable to secure life's necessities because of poverty. A person is not being treated with respect if he or she is left homeless, hungry, or ill and bereft of medical care. Respecting people involves caring about them and taking effective steps to promote or sustain their well-being.

We might also claim that a person's right to life is violated if he is left without life's necessities in the midst of affluence. Killing someone without sufficient justification (such as self-protection) would certainly violate a person's right to life;

having a right to life entails that others have a duty not to kill without sufficient justification. Some people maintain that the right to life also entails that others have a duty to save a person's life when they can do so at relatively little cost to themselves. According to this view, letting someone die when the death is preventable also violates that person's right to life. Suppose that you're choking because you've inhaled food and I could save your life by applying the Heimlich maneuver. Many people maintain that I would be violating your right to life were I to walk away and let you die. Poverty can be just as deadly as choking on food if a person does not get assistance. Thus, we might claim that leaving people in poverty when poverty is preventable and remediable violates their right to life.

We might also appeal to Rawls's theory. We could maintain that individuals in the original position behind the veil of ignorance would not agree to accept principles that would permit the rich to ignore the plight and suffering of the poor. In the original position, a person does not know whether he or she will emerge rich or poor. If he or she agrees to accept principles that permit the nonpoor to escape from having to help the poor or that permit the poor to remain poor when it is preventable, he or she may be consigned to the sufferings of poverty.

Many people claim that people have welfare rights. According to the United Nations Universal Declaration of Human Rights, every person has a right to social security (Article 22), to work and protection against unemployment (Article 23), and "to a standard of living adequate for the health and well-being of himself and of his family, including food, clothing, housing, and medical care and necessary social services" (Article 25). If someone cannot afford life's necessities and is left without them to die in a society affluent enough to meet those needs, that person's moral rights are being violated. The nonpoor have a duty of nonmaleficence and of beneficence—a duty to *minimize* harm to others and to relieve suffering caused by poverty. The question is whether we can provide adequate justification for the claim that people have these welfare rights.

Finally, those who support policies to reduce or eliminate poverty might appeal to considerations of virtue and vice, as well as to a care approach. They may claim that a good or caring person would not ignore the sufferings of the poor. The virtues of generosity, kindness, compassion, concern, sympathy, benevolence, and beneficence would lead people to work to reduce or eliminate poverty; only the vices of selfishness, greed, and callousness would make them indifferent to the sufferings of the poor.

EQUAL OPPORTUNITY

Besides poverty and economic inequality, equal opportunity may also be a moral concern. For example, John Rawls's egalitarian principle of justice, cited previously, includes a requirement of equal opportunity Social and economic inequalities are to be arranged so that they are both (1) to the greatest benefit of the least advantaged and (2) attached to offices and positions open to all under conditions of fair equality of opportunity.[13]

According to Rawls, equality of opportunity means:

> ... that those with similar abilities and skills should have similar life chances. More specifically, assuming that there is a distribution of natural assets [innate abilities and capacities], those who are at the same level of talent and ability, and have the same willingness to use them, should have the same prospects of success regardless of their initial place in the social system, that is, irrespective of the income class into which they are born.[14]

Equal opportunity means that people with roughly the same genetic endowment have a roughly equal probability of rising to the same level in society. To the extent that people are either advantaged or disadvantaged by their environment, equal opportunity is compromised.

People can be advantaged or disadvantaged by their social environment in a variety of ways. If some people receive better nutrition and health care than most others while in the womb or in infancy, they have an advantage. If they receive better education or live in a more secure and nurturing environment than most others, they have an advantage. If they have family connections that enable them to get into desirable professional schools or career positions, they have an advantage. Conversely, if some people receive worse nutrition and health care than most others while in the womb or in infancy, they have a disadvantage. If they receive worse education or live in a less secure and nurturing environment than others, they have a disadvantage.

We might compare competition in society for income, wealth, status, education, and jobs to a huge marathon. Those who finish in the lead get the best things society has to offer; those who finish at the back get what's left over, if anything; those who don't finish may get nothing. If some people are running a rough uphill course, others are running a smooth level course, and still others are running a smooth downhill course, opportunity isn't equal—the race isn't fair.

Rawls maintains that people in the original position behind the veil of ignorance would insist on equal opportunity. Because they do not know what social class they are in, they will not want members of the upper classes having special advantages because they know that they may not be members of the upper classes. Similarly, they will not want members of the lower classes having special disadvantages because they may emerge as members of the lower classes. Because people in the original position would demand equal opportunity, unequal opportunity is unjust and morally unacceptable.

A Kantian would probably reach the same conclusion for similar reasons. A Kantian might maintain that rational agents could not consistently will as a universal law a maxim tolerating unequal opportunity because the willer of the maxim could be disadvantaged by it as well as advantaged. A rational agent would want inherent intelligence, skills, talents, and abilities to determine life prospects and position in society, rather than have his or her place in society determine her life prospects.

A utilitarian might claim that equal opportunity will enable people to rise to the appropriate level in society so that society's human resources will be used with maximum efficiency, maximizing total well-being. With unequal opportunity, someone with the innate ability to be a nuclear physicist, engineer, brain surgeon, or conductor might be washing dishes in a diner or sweeping floors in a factory, a terrible waste of human potential.

JUSTICE, FAIRNESS, AND TAXES

In recent presidential elections, some candidates have endorsed a so-called flat tax, maintaining that it is fairer and simpler than a graduated income tax. With a flat tax, all people pay the same percentage of their income in taxes, whether their annual income is $25,000 or $2.5 million. With a graduated income tax, on the other hand, higher income taxpayers are taxed at a higher rate.

For example, if we had a flat tax of 20 percent, then all income taxpayers would be taxed at a rate of 20 percent. Someone with a taxable income of $25,000 would pay $5,000 in taxes, leaving her with $20,000; someone with a taxable income of $2.5 million would pay $500,000 in taxes, leaving her with $2 million. Now suppose instead that we had a graduated income tax with three tax brackets: Income under $30,000 is taxed at a rate of 15 percent, income from $30,000 to $100,000 is taxed at a rate of 30 percent, and income over $100,000 is taxed at a rate of 35 percent. In that case, someone with a taxable income of $25,000 would pay $3,750 in taxes, whereas someone with a taxable income of $2.5 million would pay $865,500 (15 percent of the first $30,000 [$4,500], plus 30 percent of the next $70,000 [$21,000], plus 35 percent of the remaining $2,400,000 [$840,000]). Someone with a taxable income of $25,000 would have $21,250 in after-tax income, and someone with a taxable income of $2.5 million would have an after-tax income of $1,635,000. Which is fairer?

Proponents of the flat tax maintain that it would be fairer than the graduated income tax because, unlike a graduated income tax, a flat tax treats all taxpayers *equally*. But as we saw, Aristotle said that justice requires treating people who are equal in relevant respects in the same way and people who are unequal in relevant respects differently. Supporters of a flat tax seem to imply that all taxpayers are equal in the ways relevant to paying taxes and that therefore they should be treated equally by being taxed at the same rate.

Opponents of the flat tax, however, claim that not all taxpayers are equal in the ways relevant to paying taxes. They claim that someone with an annual income of $25,000 is not equal in relevant respects to someone with an annual income of $2.5 million. If both are taxed at 20 percent, the individual with an income of $25,000 pays $5,000, leaving only $20,000 on which to live. This person will find it difficult to afford life's basic necessities, let alone afford luxuries, on the money left after taxes. Paying 20 percent is a real hardship for him. On the other hand, the individual with an annual income of $2.5 million pays $500,000 but has $2 million left after taxes. Not only can she easily afford necessities, but she has ample money left over for a variety of luxuries. The 20 percent tax is no hardship for her. Thus, the two taxpayers are not equal in their *ability to pay*. Because they are not equal in all respects relevant to paying taxes, it would be unjust and unfair to treat them as if they were equal. Therefore, opponents of the flat tax claim that people with higher incomes who can afford to pay more should be taxed at a higher rate. But note that both the richer and poorer taxpayers pay the same tax rate on the first $25,000 of income.

Interestingly, one common tax actually has the opposite structure: Those with *higher* incomes are taxed at a *lower* rate. Under the Social Security tax, income is taxed at a flat rate of 7.65 percent—but for 2005 only the first $90,000 of income is taxed at all. As a result, everyone with a taxable income under $90,000 is taxed at a rate of 7.65 percent, but everyone with taxable income over $90,000 is taxed at less than 7.65 percent. Their rate is lower because no matter how much they earn, they still pay only $6,885 in Social Security tax. Thus, for example, someone with a taxable income of $500,000 is taxed at a rate of slightly more than 1 percent.

EXERCISES

1. Review the economic data provided at the beginning of this chapter. Do you believe that there is too much economic inequality in the United States? Defend your answer. If you believe that there is too much economic inequality, what do you believe should be done to reduce it? Why?

2. Is economic redistribution to reduce economic inequality morally wrong?

3. Should the United States pursue policies to reduce or eliminate poverty? What should be done?

4. Do we have genuine equal opportunity in the United States? If not, does it matter from a moral point of view? If it does matter, what can or should be done to increase equality of opportunity?

5. Consider two people, Jim and Tom. Jim was born into a poor family. When he was in the womb, his mother suffered from malnutrition because of her poverty, and as a result, Jim's brain was affected during its early development. After he was born, he continued to suffer from malnutrition and hunger. He often went without medical attention when he was ill because his family could not afford to pay for it. He has lived all his life in slums, and he went to substandard schools in the inner city that were overcrowded, dilapidated, and dangerous. During junior high school and high school he worked at least 20 hours a week in a grocery store to help his family, which took him away from his studies. He had a C average in high school, has received no encouragement to further his education, has no money for college, but has thought about college. Jim took the SAT and achieved a combined score of 900.

    Tom was born into an affluent family. He has never known hunger. He has lived in a large, comfortable, suburban house; he was sent to preschool; he attended superior suburban schools. He never had to work, and if he had trouble with a subject, his family hired private tutors. Tom had a B average in high school. Since he was 10 years old, he has been encouraged to attend college, and the family has the money to pay for even the most expensive private college. He plays sports, takes music lessons, and skis. Tom took an expensive SAT preparation course and achieved a combined score of 950 the first time he took it. He retook the SAT preparation course, retook the SAT, and achieved a combined score of 1020. His mother has connections among her business associates who can use their influence to help him get accepted into a good college or university.

Jim and Tom are both 18. Are they now able to compete on equal terms for admission to college? If they both go to college and are both accepted by the same college, will they be able to compete on equal terms? If their circumstances violate the requirement of equal opportunity, what can or should be done?

SUGGESTED READINGS

John Arthur and William Shaw. *Justice and Economic Distribution*, 2d ed. Englewood Cliffs, NJ: Prentice-Hall, 1991.

Robert Goodin. *Reasons for Welfare: The Political Theory of the Welfare State*. Princeton, NJ: Princeton University Press, 1988.

Immanuel Kant. *Foundations of the Metaphysics of Morals*, 2d ed. Translated by Lewis White Beck. New York: Macmillan, 1990.

Louis Pojman and Robert Westmoreland, eds. *Equality*. New York: Oxford University Press, 1997.

John Rawls. *A Theory of Justice*. Cambridge, MA: Harvard University Press, 1971.

James Sterba. *Justice: Alternative Political Perspectives*, 2d ed. Belmont, CA: Wadsworth, 1992.

INTERNET RESOURCE

Current economic statistics are available on the U.S. Bureau of the Census website (www.census.gov/).

ENDNOTES

1. Carmin DeNavas-Walt, Bernadette D. Proctor, and Cheryl Hill Lee, U.S. Census Bureau, *Income, Poverty, and Health Insurance Coverage in the United States: 2004*, Current Population Reports, P60–229 (Washington, DC: U.S. Government Printing Office, 2005).

2. John Rawls, *A Theory of Justice* (Cambridge, MA: Harvard University Press, 1971), p. 62.

3. Ibid., p. 83.

4. Ibid., p. 62.

5. Gregory Vlastos, "Justice and Equality," in *Social Justice,* ed. Richard Brandt (Englewood Cliffs, NJ: Prentice-Hall, 1962), p. 43.

6. Ibid., p. 43.

7. Ibid., p. 51.

8. Ibid., p. 52.

9. Ibid., p. 59.

10. Jean Jacques Rousseau, *The Social Contract,* trans. Maurice Cranston (Harmondsworth, England: Penguin, 1968), p. 96.

11. Robert Nozick, *Anarchy, State, and Utopia* (New York: Basic Books, 1974), p. 169.

12. Immanuel Kant, *Foundations of the Metaphysics of Morals,* 2d ed., trans. Lewis White Beck (New York: Macmillan, 1990), p. 40.

13. Rawls, *A Theory of Justice,* p. 83.

14. Ibid., p. 73.

13

Racism and Affirmative Action

OBJECTIVES

- To be acquainted with the history of racism in the United States
- To distinguish between affirmative action and preferential treatment
- To distinguish between the various forms of preferential treatment
- To understand the arguments for and against the rightness or wrongness of the various forms of preferential treatment

INTRODUCTION

Today many of us think that there are different human races rather than one human race. Nineteenth-century anthropologists in Europe and the United States created a three-fold classification of the human family based on such easily observable physical differences as skin color. Put in a way that most people today find offensive, there is the white race, the black race, and the yellow race. The division was not evaluatively neutral. Those anthropologists had no doubt that the white race is superior to the "colored" races. It should come as no surprise that the anthropologists were white. In part, the motive was to provide a "scientific" foundation to justify slavery, which was based on "race."

Before the invention of the categories of race, people cared more about differences of geography, income and wealth, religion, social class, and language. The ancient Greeks divided the human family between people from Greece who spoke Greek, and everyone else. Those who didn't speak Greek were labeled "barbarians" because to the Greek ear, their language sounded like a meaningless string of sounds—Bar Bar Bar. Of course, the Greeks considered themselves superior to those barbarians.

The ancient Romans initially divided themselves between patricians and plebeians, based on "noble" versus "common" birth or blood. Patricians were

273

not just wealthier, more politically powerful, and more highly educated and cultured than plebeians; the gods also loved patricians more than they loved plebeians. Slavery existed in Rome, but it was not based on anything approximating race. Anyone could become a slave if unlucky enough. Most slaves were peoples defeated by the Roman army.

The problem of the category of race is complicated, and in part depends on technical issues in the philosophy of language, one of which is the "reality" of what are called "natural kinds." A "natural" kind is discovered rather than invented. It "exists" in nature. A natural kind is a group of things that have a fundamental similarity. An example may be species in biology. Roughly, if two organisms can reproduce and create a replica of themselves that in turn can reproduce, they are members of the same species. If they cannot reproduce, they are not. Thus, because a cat and a chihuahua cannot reproduce, they are not members of the same species. However, because a black lab and a German shepherd can reproduce, they are members of the same species. In order to be capable of reproducing, there must be fundamental physical similarities. Obviously, a rose bush cannot reproduce with a rat, and a rat cannot reproduce with a crocodile.

Dogs and cats are natural kinds. Some would say that the division between the physical and the mental also is a division between two natural kinds. So what kinds aren't natural? Well, we could divide the world into things that make sounds and things that don't. Bricks and fence posts would be among the things that don't make sounds, birds and lawnmowers would be among the things that do make sounds, and trees would be among the things that make sounds when it's windy but among the things that don't make sounds when it's still. Now unlike black labs and German shepherds that have many "deep" similarities in virtue of which they can reproduce and thus are members of the same species, things that make sounds don't necessarily have any similarities other than making sounds. The category of things that make sounds isn't a natural kind, it's something I invented.

I suspect that "weed" is another example of a kind of thing that isn't a natural kind. What do all weeds have in common other than there being called weeds because we humans don't like them? Granted that they are all plants, but not all plants are weeds. A dandelion is a weed, but a tulip isn't. Why?

Because we can reproduce, we are members of the same biological species—homo sapiens. (Biologists tell us that the differences among and between "races" on the genetic level is very slight.) Because we have so many physical characteristics in common with chimps and gorillas, we humans are members of the same genus—primates. Because primates have so many fundamental characteristics in common with such beings as dogs, cats, deer, and bears, we are members of a wider class that includes them called *mammals*. We really are different from, say, chimps and gorillas. The differences are fundamental. But how fundamental are the differences used to distinguish between races, such as skin color, hair texture, and the shape of nose and lips?

We can divide the human family into the tall and short, the right handed and left handed, the bald and the non-bald, the old and the young, men and women, the blind and the sighted, those with big feet (or noses) and those with small feet (or noses), the fat and the thin, the skeptical and the credulous. Why aren't all these differences the basis of a category as important as that based on differences in skin color? In part, it's because we believe that there are no important or fundamental differences between, say, those with big feet and those with small feet. We believe that the size of one's feet does not affect one's intelligence, character, personality, or emotional make-up. Therefore, it's not important to us. However, we, or at least most self-described "whites," have been conditioned to believe that skin color, hair texture, and the shape of one's nose and lips do affect these important features, although the evidence shows that they do not. The point is that the category of "race" should be no more an important natural kind that can justify judgments about one's superiority or inferiority or justify unequal treatment than is being left handed or right handed, or having big feet as opposed to small feet.

Tragically, the category of race has been used to justify terrible atrocities and injustices, for example apartheid in South Africa and the internment of Japanese-Americans in American concentration camps during World War II (neither German-Americans nor Italian-Americans were sent to concentration camps, although we were at war with Germany and Italy, as well as Japan.) Another is the monumental injustice of generations of black slavery and segregation in the United States.

RACISM AND BLACKS

Unlike the vast majority of whites, blacks did not come to North America from their homelands voluntarily. They were brought against their will as slaves. It is difficult to convey the horrors of slavery to people today who are unacquainted with it. Transportation from Africa on slave ships was as hellish as the human mind can imagine. If they survived and reached America, slaves, especially field hands, were often worked mercilessly and poorly fed, clothed, and housed. As children, they were often sold away from their parents at an early age and put to work. Laws in the South forbade educating a slave or teaching a slave to read. Slaves were frequently whipped and beaten, and the beatings left terrible scars. Female slaves were routinely raped by their masters and male relatives of their masters. Parents often had to face having their children sold away from them.

After slavery ended, blacks who had been slaves were free, but they were poverty stricken. Despite the obvious demand of justice to compensate them for their decades and centuries of unpaid labor that helped make whites in the South and elsewhere prosperous, they were freed with few resources. They remained an underclass in the South, oppressed economically, socially, and politically. Up to 1915, about 90 percent of blacks continued to live in the South, where they were cheated, terrorized, murdered, and dehumanized by white racists. For example, "Martin Luther King Sr. [Martin Luther King Jr.'s father], born in 1899, spent his youth in rural Georgia, where he witnessed drunken white men beat a black man to death for being 'sassy'...."[1] What makes it worse is that the murderers in such cases would almost never even be prosecuted. If they were, there was no chance of a conviction, since juries were all white. Similarly, "[s]ix-year-old Pauli Murray would never forget the sight of John Henry Corniggin's body lying out in the field, where he had been shot to death for walking across a white man's watermelon patch."[2] And, "[e]ight-year-old Lucy Miller stood in her front yard in Daytona Beach in 1907, watching white residents parade through the black community the body of a black man they had just lynched. The victim, Lucy learned, 'had dared to stand up for his rights'...."[3]

> The violence turned the American dream of hard work leading to increased prosperity into a nightmare. The violence inflicted on black people was often selective, aimed at educated and successful blacks, those in positions of leadership, those determined to improve themselves, those who owned the best farm in the county and the largest store in town, those suspected of having saved their earnings, those who had just made a crop—that is, black men and women perceived by whites as having stepped out of their place.[4]

For example, around 1910:

> ...[n]ear Savannah, Tennessee, white tenants objected to blacks operating successfully on land they owned. Ben Pettigrew, accompanied by his two young daughters, was driving a load of cotton from his farm to town. Several miles from his place, four white men appeared on the road, shot the black farmer to death as he sat in the seat of his wagon, and dragged his two daughters from the top of the load and hanged them from a nearby tree. While their bodies dangled from a limb, the mob drove the wagon loaded with cotton under them and set fire to it. The message sent to enterprising black farmers in the region could not have been clearer.[5]

In another horrifying example of the depths of depravity of many whites, there is the case of Sam Hose, who killed his white employer in self-defense in Georgia in 1899. Local newspapers distorted the story, accusing Hose of murdering his employer unprovoked and raping his wife while the victim lay dying. What follows requires a strong stomach to read. There were public announcements of a lynching. About 2,000 men and women came to watch, some from nearby Atlanta. Hose was taken out before the crowd.

> After stripping Hose of his clothes and chaining him to a tree, the self-appointed executioners stacked kerosene-soaked wood high around him. Before saturating Hose with oil and applying the torch, they cut off his ears, fingers, and genitals, and skinned his face. While some in the crowd plunged knives into the victim's flesh, others watched with "unfeigned satisfaction" (as one reporter noted) the contortions of Sam Hose's body as the flames rose, distorting his features, causing his eyes to bulge out of their sockets, and rupturing his veins. When in Hose's

agony he almost managed to unloosen his bonds, the executioners quenched the flames, retied him, and applied more oil to his body before relighting the fire. "Such suffering," reported one newspaper, "has seldom been witnessed." The only sounds that came from the victim's lips, even as his blood sizzled in the fire, were "Oh, my God! Oh Jesus."[6]

Spectators fought over pieces of his body to save as souvenirs. The names of various prominent white citizens who attended were reported in the newspapers. The participants were well-known. No one was indicted or tried for the crime of murder. A similar thing happened to Luther Holbert and his wife in Mississippi in 1904. Holbert was accused of killing his employer. His wife was not accused of anything. Nevertheless, she shared his horrible fate while about a thousand spectators watched. Before killing them, members of the mob used a large corkscrew that was "bored into the flesh of the man and woman, in the arms, legs and body, and then pulled out, the spirals tearing out big pieces of raw, quivering flesh every time it was withdrawn."[7] In another case, a mob decided to torture and kill the mother of a black man suspected of burning down a white man's barn when they couldn't find him. According to conservative estimates, there were nearly 3,000 lynchings in the South from 1890 to World War I, including many public acts of sadistic torture attended by hundreds or thousands of "respectable" whites, such as happened to Sam Hose. Generally, there was public praise rather than condemnation of lynchings.

Beginning in the 1890s, whites in the South stole the right to vote from blacks. For example, "In Louisiana, as late as 1896, there were 130,000 registered black voters; eight years later, the number had been reduced to 1,342." In Alabama in 1906, 83 percent of white adult males were registered to vote, but only 2 percent of black adult males.[8] By 1940, things hadn't changed much for the better. "In the eleven states of the former Confederacy, fewer than 5 percent of eligible African Americans were registered to vote. . . ."[9] And of course, public accommodations were strictly segregated. In addition, the justice system provided no protection to blacks. "In administering justice, the courts regularly excluded blacks from juries, disregarded black testimony, sometimes denied counsel to black accused, and meted out disproportionately severe sentences to black defendants."[10] Black lawyers were very scarce, and white lawyers generally didn't want to spend much time defending black clients. There were no black judges. Many blacks wound up on chain gangs for minor crimes, which, if it was a long sentence, was not much different than a death sentence. In 1884 in Tennessee, nearly 15 percent of prisoners died. The figures don't count those who were near death, but were released to go home to die.

Every effort was made by the white community to limit blacks' access to education. For example, in Atlanta in 1903, there were 20 schools for the 14,465 whites and 5 for the 8,118 blacks.[11] Black teachers in Atlanta earned two-thirds the salary of white teachers. But things could have been worse. Across the South on average, "The minimum salary for white teachers was nearly twice as high as the maximum salary paid black teachers."[12] The education they received praised the superiority of the white race and denigrated their own race. The 1896

Supreme Court decision *Plessy v. Ferguson* declared educational segregation constitutional, and thus enshrined the "separate but equal" ideal. Of course, schools were separate, but no one even pretended that they were equal. Black schools had "the largest classes, the poorest paid teachers, the shortest school year, and an acute shortage of books, paper, pencils, blackboards, and maps."[13] In 1900 in South Carolina, the state spent more than four times more educating white children than it spent on educating black children. In 1915, that ratio rose to over 10:1.[14] Even as late as 1940, 75 years after the end of the Civil War, "Three-quarters of adult blacks had not finished high school. One in ten had no schooling whatever, and many more were functionally illiterate."[15]

Although the Southern economy was based principally on agriculture well into the twentieth century, few blacks owned their own land. Instead, they were sharecroppers, renting their land from white property owners for a quarter to a third of the crops they grew. They generally had to buy their supplies from white store owners on credit at exorbitant interest rates. After working hard for 30, 40, or 50 years, they often found themselves with nothing but debts. In fact, whites did not want blacks to own their own land and be economically independent. "In 1900, an estimated 75.3 percent of black farmers in the South were sharecroppers or tenants."[16] In the 1920s in the Delta region, only about 2 percent of blacks owned and worked their own land. In 1940, "[t]hey earned, on the average, 39 percent of what whites made. Almost nine of ten black families eked out a living on incomes below the federal poverty threshold. . . . One third were sharecroppers or tenant farmers."[17]

As for black women in the farm economy, they did not conform to white stereotypes of female fragility, helplessness, and incompetence.

> Up at dawn, she cooked breakfast for the family, after which she joined her husband and the grown children in the fields, plowing or chopping cotton. She would return to the cabin in midmorning to cook dinner, clean up, and return to the fields in the early afternoon and work until sundown. In the evening, she might also be expected to milk the cows and feed the chickens before preparing supper, after which she performed the household chores, such as mending, making, washing, and ironing clothes and scrubbing floors. "Plenty of times," a North Carolina woman recalled, "I've been to bed at three or four o'clock and get up at five the first one in the morning."[18]

During World War II, military units were segregated. All black units were led by white officers, and until near the end of the war, many black units performed only menial tasks. After the war, African American soldiers from the South returned there, convinced that they had earned the rights of full citizenship only to find that their sacrifice and heroism meant nothing.

Meanwhile, federal housing policies, based on segregation, helped create ghettoes to entrap African Americans in Northern cities. The housing division of the Public Works Administration built segregated public housing, for whites in predominantly white neighborhoods and for blacks in predominantly black neighborhoods. The Federal Housing Administration—which furnished low-cost mortgages to millions of people, thereby helping to fuel the runaway expansion of suburbs and the consequent deterioration of inner cities—discriminated against African Americans by providing loans mainly to whites, which helped keep blacks from owning their own homes or moving to the suburbs, trapping them in cities. To add insult to injury, "For the dubious privilege of living in... crowded areas, blacks in Chicago, lacking market options, faced rents ranging between 10 and 25 percent higher than those paid by whites for comparable shelter."[19] Chicago was not unique in that respect. Violence in the North helped keep the doors of the trap shut on African Americans. For example, there was a race riot in Chicago in 1947 that injured 35 African Americans. A white mob attacked blacks to keep them out of all-white public housing projects.[20]

African Americans in the North faced other forms of discrimination that kept them poverty stricken. From the 1940s through most of the 1950s, many unions that had managed to improve the wages and work conditions of their members refused to admit blacks, keeping them out of the better paying jobs. Residential segregation, promoted by federal agencies and private lenders, as well as white violence, kept most schools segregated and vastly inferior to white schools. In 1954, the Supreme Court outlawed racial segregation in schools in *Brown v. Board of Education,* but President Eisenhower was less than thrilled with the decision and did almost nothing to enforce it. White Southerners made it clear that they would resist school desegregation, violently if necessary. The *Brown* decision was rather tentative anyway because it did not set a timetable for compliance, nor did it define acceptable levels of integration.[21] In fact, 10 years later in 1964, "fewer than 2 percent of blacks attended multiracial schools in the eleven states of the old Confederacy. Many southern colleges and universities excluded blacks until the 1960s or accepted only a token few. Very few black teachers were allowed to work in white or desegregated schools."[22] *Brown* only attacked laws requiring school segregation, not school segregation per se. School segregation persists to this day, with many students of color in public schools that have a very small percentage of whites.

African Americans in the South began to organize to demand their rights in the 1950s. For example, there was the Montgomery, Alabama, bus boycott of the mid-1950s. "The bus company in Montgomery hired no black bus drivers. Its white drivers enforced rules that required blacks to pay at the front of the bus, enter toward the back, and sit in the rear. Drivers often insulted and demeaned black passengers."[23] On December 1, 1955, Rosa Parks was arrested for refusing to move to the back of the bus when ordered to by the bus driver. Under the leadership of the Reverend Martin Luther King Jr. and others, such as E. D. Nixon, a Pullman porter, and Jo Ann Robinson, an English teacher, African Americans organized a boycott of the buses that lasted for more than a year. The boycott led to jailings of black leaders and the bombing of the homes of some of them. It ended in November 1956 when the Supreme Court decided that the bus seating laws violated the Fourteenth Amendment. It was a narrowly focused decision.

African Americans generally are angered and bewildered by the response of many whites to this history of racism in America. Some whites say, "Many people faced discrimination when they came to the United States, even whites: Irish, Italians, Poles, Slovaks. They overcame it in a generation or two. Why can't blacks?" Racist attitudes and discriminatory behavior toward African Americans in North America span about 15 generations. It is so deep in our culture that it is very difficult to root out. Second, it's easier to visually identify someone who is "black" than someone who is a second or third generation Italian American or Irish American. Thus, it's easier to enforce rigid discrimination on the basis of a few characteristics, such as darker skin color and texture of hair. Third, every aspect of their lives was determined by their race. Finally, the intensity and scope of violence used to keep African Americans subordinate was unique, except for what happened to Native Americans. It's difficult to find examples of public torture and lynching of Irish or Italians in America.

If we review the comparative economic data from the previous chapter, we can see that by most measures, race still affects one's life chances. People with dark skin are far less likely to flourish than people with white skin. Many observers say that it is because of the lingering effects of past discrimination and the on-going (perhaps more subtle) present discrimination based on skin color.

There is no doubt that African Americans (and Hispanics) are not flourishing as well as whites. We have not yet achieved racial equality and genuine equality of opportunity unaffected by race. The ethical question is whether anything should be done about it, especially by government, and if so, what. There are several possibilities.

SOLUTIONS TO RACISM

Prohibit Discrimination

The United States government has passed a variety of laws prohibiting racial discrimination in areas such as schooling, employment, home buying, renting, and lending. It requires that decisions be made on the basis of race-neutral criteria. Many people maintain that our society can achieve racial justice and African Americans can achieve political, social, and economic equality provided that we simply rigorously enforce laws prohibiting racial discrimination.

Other people believe that more is needed. Although they agree on the need for laws prohibiting racial discrimination, they maintain that we must go further to achieve racial equality and equal opportunity. Our society is based on competition—competition for high-quality education, good jobs, decent housing, adequate health care, and so on. There simply aren't enough of the good and best things in life to go around. Not everyone can attend an Ivy League university, be a CEO of a *Fortune 500* company, a doctor, or a lawyer.

Many people maintain that because of past and present racial discrimination, African Americans have a variety of disadvantages that slow them up in the race for economic and social goods. The competition isn't fair because the participants don't compete on equal terms. Although some whites are also disadvantaged or poor, their disadvantage or poverty is not based on race, and they probably have benefited from racism, however small the benefit. Many more African Americans than whites are victims of poverty, childhood malnutrition, crime- and drug-plagued neighborhoods, substandard schools, low self-esteem, and serious family problems.

Let me reflect on my own circumstances. My father, who was white, began as a blue-collar shipyard worker after graduating from high school at the start of World War II. When he left the Navy at the end of the war, he became a white-collar employee for insurance companies. He didn't have to compete for these jobs with women or blacks, because they would not even be considered for such jobs due to racial and sexual discrimination. If he had, he might have remained a blue-collar worker. He became a supervisor and rose into the ranks of the middle class. Again, he didn't have to compete with women or African Americans for supervisory positions. If he had, he might not have become a supervisor, because a woman or an African American might have bested him if the competition had been open and fair. We'll never know because he didn't have to compete against them.

I benefited from my father's successes in the biased competition. My family was able to afford to move to an affluent suburb with excellent schools. We could afford to have my mother stay home to care for the house and my sister and me. There was no crime in my neighborhood or my high school. I never went to bed hungry, cold, or afraid. I did not attend a school that was overcrowded or understaffed. There were always ample books, science laboratories, libraries, and other school supplies. The school building was always in good repair. I was not bombarded by messages from the culture telling me in subtle and unsubtle ways that I was inferior because I'm white. I always saw people like me in positions of authority and status, whether in front of the classroom, on television, or in movies, including political leaders from the President on down. My family could afford to send me to college, and I was always strongly encouraged to go to college. I had ample self-confidence that no unfair barriers to achievement would get in my way.

When I applied for college, I had to compete with very few African American high school graduates. If I had, I might not have been accepted by my first choice college. After I graduated from college, my first job was in the insurance industry. Like my father, I didn't have much competition from women or blacks. My life would have almost certainly been much different if I had been born black and had grown up in an inner-city ghetto in the North or in a poor rural district of the South. It probably would not have gone nearly as well for me.

There is another problem I never had to face. Bias is often unconscious. The problem is that someone in authority whose conscious or unconscious bias has affected his decision to reject an applicant for a job, promotion, or school may believe, or falsely maintain, that he judged the rejected applicant solely on her qualifications. He may say that the applicant did not present herself well in the interview or that, in his judgment, she would not "fit" in the organization. It is not easy to prove that discrimination on the basis of race has occurred in any given situation. Therefore, merely prohibiting racial discrimination may not eliminate it.

Affirmative Action and Preferential Treatment

Some people support policies of *affirmative action*. Affirmative action covers a wide variety of policies and programs. One modest form of affirmative action has the goal of simply increasing the number of people of color who apply for jobs or school admissions. Sometimes people of color are underrepresented in a pool of applicants for a job. Why? It may be that most people of color did not know about the job opening because the job was not advertised and applicants learned of it by word of mouth, perhaps from employees of the company who are friends. Perhaps the job was advertised in a place that is not well-known or popular with people of color. Perhaps few applied because they were discouraged by the company's history of discriminating against black applicants. Perhaps the job wasn't even advertised, and someone got it because of the right "connections."

In order to increase the number of applicants of color, an employer may first off ensure that the position is advertised. The company may then change the way jobs are advertised—for example, by listing a position with career resource centers that specialize in working with people of color or advertising in media (newspapers and magazines) that are widely circulated in communities of people of color. A company may also publicly announce that it does not tolerate discrimination as a way of encouraging people of color to apply. These are forms of affirmative action—acts undertaken to increase the pool of minority applicants.

Similarly, a college, in order to increase the number of applicants of color, may advertise in media popular with people of color or have special open houses or luncheons for people of color in order to show them how much the college has to offer them. A college may try to ensure that its admissions brochures include pictures of students and faculty of color in order to send the message that the college is hospitable to and values diversity. These types of affirmative action do not involve preferential treatment for people of color in hiring or admission.

Affirmative action can also take the form of preferential treatment. In the ideal model of decision making, decision makers select the applicant or candidate they perceive as most highly qualified on the basis of objective criteria that are completely relevant to the requirements of the position. But with preferential treatment, that is not the case. Instead, someone is selected who the decision makers do not perceive to be most highly qualified.

For example, take college and university admissions. Ideally, applicants should be judged solely on such objective criteria as high school grades and scores on standardized tests, which will be reliable indicators of how well they will handle the academic demands of college classes. Letters of recommendation should not be given great weight because they are notoriously unreliable. (Few submit bad letters of recommendation, however weak a student may be.) Now suppose there are two applicants for admission to a certain college. One, call him A, has a 3.2 high school GPA and a combined score of 1150 on the SAT. He also has done a lot of volunteer work in the community and has been a leader in several high school organizations, including student government. The other, call him B, has a 3.4 GPA and a combined SAT score of 1200. Unlike A, he has not been at all active in his community or his school. If the only thing that matters is the ability to handle the academic demands of college classes, shouldn't B be preferred to A? If A is admitted rather than B, then shouldn't we say that the college is practicing a form of preferential treatment, because the characteristics that are decisive are not purely academic?

Similarly, suppose that there's a third applicant, C. C has a 2.2 high school GPA and a combined SAT score of 980, but C is the highest scoring basketball player in his high school's history. If C is admitted rather than B, then shouldn't we call that preferential treatment? (If the answer is yes, then preferential treatment for athletes is very widespread in American universities and colleges, though it does not evoke the same passions as preferential treatment for minorities.) Further, suppose that there's a fourth applicant, D, who has a 3.1 GPA and a combined score of 1100 on the SAT. D also has a father and an aunt who graduated from the college. If D is accepted while B is rejected, shouldn't we call that preferential treatment for relatives of alumni and alumnae? (If the answer is yes, then preferential treatment for relatives of alumni is widespread in American colleges and universities, although it too does not evoke the passions of preferential treatment for minorities.) Finally, suppose that positions are distributed largely on the basis of performance on a test, for example, positions in the civil service, or in fire and police departments. If veterans automatically have a certain number of extra points added to their scores, isn't that preferential treatment for veterans? (Veterans do receive extra points.)

Preferential treatment for blacks involves selecting a black applicant over a white applicant when the applicants are perceived to be equally qualified on the basis of purely job related or academic criteria or when the black applicant is perceived to be less highly qualified in terms of purely job related or academic criteria. But preferential treatment for blacks is highly controversial. First, opponents say it's unfair to whites, a form of reverse discrimination and a denial to whites of equal opportunity and equal treatment. Second, it departs from the ideal model of decision making where the decision makers choose the most highly qualified person on the basis of objective criteria purely relevant to the position selected. Opponents often say it leads to selection of the unqualified rather than the most highly qualified.

Supporters of preferential treatment for blacks believe that it is justified. First, they maintain that virtually all African Americans have been harmed and handicapped in competition with whites by past racial discrimination. They say that the status quo denies equal opportunity and equal treatment to blacks and that preferential treatment for blacks is needed to right that wrong. From inferior segregated schools to inferior segregated housing, from lack of access to mortgages to lack of access to capital for business ventures, from inferior health care to inferior job prospects, most African Americans have been kept from the table of American abundance. Then, too, the psychological damage of living in a racist society that brands and treats African Americans as inferior is virtually inescapable. It reduces self-esteem and self-confidence; it reduces motivation; it breeds hopelessness and despair. Therefore, advocates of preferential treatment maintain, African Americans deserve preference over those who have not been harmed and handicapped by racism, but instead have benefited; such preferences will enable them to compete on more equal terms with people who have not been victimized and oppressed.

Second, supporters say that the ideal model of decision making that preferential treatment for blacks is measured against simply has never existed in the real world. Therefore, the fact that preferential treatment for blacks does not conform to it isn't a strong objection because no real life decision making has ever conformed to it. It's not as though preferential treatment for blacks departs from fairer practices we've been following in the past. It departs from practices that were even less fair. It's an improvement, not the reverse.

Third, supporters say that as long as imperfect humans are the decision makers, the ideal model of decision making will be unattainable. The model depends on the decision makers' *perception* of who is most highly qualified. There's a root element of subjectivity involved, and as long as humans have biases, those biases will affect their judgment of qualifications. Even if a black applicant is the most highly qualified, studies show that white decision makers are not likely to perceive him or her to be the most highly qualified.[24] Knowing that white decision makers are likely to have conscious and unconscious racial biases, preferential treatment for blacks may be seen as a corrective to distorted perceptions.

Opponents of preferential treatment for blacks maintain that such programs entail hiring the unqualified for jobs, promoting the unqualified, or accepting the unqualified into colleges, universities, and professional schools. But supporters deny this. They point out that preferential treatment for blacks does not prohibit establishing a set of genuinely relevant and objective criteria that all applicants must meet in order to be considered qualified and limiting selection to those who meet all the criteria. Only then would preferential treatment kick in. Among the qualified applicants, a black whom decision makers perceive to be less highly qualified than other white applicants could be selected. That individual would certainly not be unqualified, nor would she necessarily be perceived as the least qualified. And, given the element of subjectivity and the likelihood of conscious or unconscious bias if the decision makers are white, that individual may in fact really be the most highly qualified, even if she is not perceived to be the most highly qualified by the decision makers.[25]

For example, suppose that a city is seeking to desegregate its police and fire departments. In order to be hired, an applicant must score at least 70 on a departmental civil service examination. Suppose that in fact almost no one who has scored below 90 has been hired, and suppose further that because of the segregated, inferior education to which they have been consigned, very few African Americans have scored 90 or above on the examination. If the departments were to select some African American applicants with scores in the 80s over white applicants with scores in the 90s, they would not be hiring the unqualified. Advocates of preferential treatment for blacks also say that we may have too narrow a view of relevant qualifications. Race may be relevant in a positive way, given the goals of decision makers. If a college has very few blacks among the faculty, staff, or students, diversifying may be a legitimate educational goal, more legitimate, for example, than the goal of increasing the number of talented athletes. Students need to learn how to improve their interactions with people of different races, religions, and cultural backgrounds. If students rarely encounter people different from themselves in classrooms, offices, campus centers, and dormitories, they're losing out on an important part of the educational experience. A college may have a need for black faculty as much as a need for someone to teach history classes. Being black may be a relevant positive characteristic for a job, just as skill at oral and written communication might be.

However, Gertrude Ezorsky recognizes that there is a serious problem here: If less qualified African American applicants are selected over more qualified white applicants, the white applicants are harmed. These white applicants may not be the most privileged members of our society. Suppose that in desegregating a city's police and fire departments, high-scoring white applicants are harmed by not being hired. Should they bear the total cost of compensating African Americans for past discrimination and the cost of desegregating economic and social life? They may not have benefited personally from past discrimination nearly as much as other whites in society. Those who may have benefited most from past discrimination escape having to share the cost of rectifying it. The outcome seems unjust: In benefiting members of one group, we are harming members of another group.

Ezorsky advocates compensating the white victims of preferential treatment programs. For example, suppose that six people are hired for the fire department, three whites and three African Americans. However, several white applicants scored higher than the African American applicants. If the department did not have a program of preferential treatment, they would have been hired instead of the three African American applicants. Because we can reliably identify those whites who have been harmed—that is, those whites who very probably would have been hired if there were no program of preferential treatment—we can and should compensate them for the harm that has been done to them. (In reality it probably is rarely the case that we know who would have gotten the job or college offer of acceptance if there were no preferential treatment.) The fairest way is to use tax dollars in order to spread the burden of affirmative action. The three white applicants might receive extra unemployment compensation if they are unemployed or some other monetary compensation.[26]

But supporters of preferential treatment for blacks say that many whites indulge in mythologizing and demonizing preferential treatment. Opponents say that in general, preferential treatment makes whites, especially white males, practically a new disadvantaged class. According to them, preferential treatment for blacks is taking away the good things from whites and giving them to blacks. There are two problems with this from the point of view of supporters of preferential treatment for blacks. First, data show that blacks still lag behind whites in almost every measure. If whites were now disadvantaged and blacks advantaged by preferential treatment programs, surely the data would reflect that. Second, many complaints about preferential treatment rely on inflammatory tales of highly qualified white applicants losing out to less qualified or unqualified black applicants. But these stories are questionable. Suppose that a white applicant claims to have lost out in competition to a black applicant who he says was less qualified. He claims that he would have been selected if it hadn't been for preferential treatment for the black applicant. But how can he know that of all white applicants, he would have been selected? How can he know that he is, or was perceived to be by the decision makers, the most qualified white applicant? He probably can't. Second, how does he know that the black applicant who was selected is less qualified than he is? He may merely be assuming that the decision makers did not perceive the black applicant to be the most qualified. (Why would he assume that? Could unconscious racism be influencing his perceptions?)

Supporters of preferential treatment also maintain that the motivation and attitudes underlying these programs make them significantly different from unjust reverse discrimination. The motive underlying discrimination was racism. African Americans were discriminated against because they were despised and judged to be inferior to whites; the discrimination was pervasive, occurring in all areas and at all levels of society. It was not a question of one African American losing one good job to one white applicant; economic and educational opportunities were severely restricted everywhere but at the bottom.

If an African American is selected over a more qualified white applicant because of a program of preferential treatment, prejudice has nothing to do with it. The decision is not based on the assumption that whites are despicable or are inferior to African Americans. The purpose of selecting the African American is not to exclude a white from a social benefit solely because of his or her race, and it is not part of a pervasive pattern of exclusion based on race. It does not consign individual whites or whites as a group to the cellar of economic life or globally deny them equal opportunity everywhere they turn. If a white applicant who is more qualified than an African American is passed over in one situation in favor of the African American, he or she will not necessarily be excluded from other opportunities.

Thomas E. Hill Jr. argues that discrimination is generally thought unjust when it is arbitrary discrimination. Discrimination that gives preference to African Americans, however, is not arbitrary. It is based, first, on the fact that in the past not only were blacks treated differently from whites but they were treated "*as no human beings should be treated,*"[27] and second, on the claim, which some whites deny, that African Americans continue to be treated as no human beings should be treated. Justice requires that whites not be *arbitrarily* discriminated against in school admissions, hiring, and promotions. Supporters of preferential treatment for African Americans maintain that the discrimination that these programs embody is not arbitrary and not unjustified, and therefore not unjust.

Hill points out that "the values that give affirmative action its point … include … the ideals of mutual respect, trust, and fair opportunity for all."[28] He claims that what is needed is "a message to counter the deep insult inherent in racism."[29] To be believed, the message must include deeds as well as words. Inaction or passivity would send the message that our society and its (white) power structure are not very concerned about the fact that African Americans continue to lag far behind whites on almost every front. Failure to employ preferential treatment sends a message of indifference. Furthermore, it sends the message that our society is more concerned with protecting whites who have not suffered from past discrimination than it is in helping African Americans who have suffered and probably continue to suffer from racist discrimination. As Hill puts it, the message would be, "We would rather let the majority of white males enjoy the advantages of their unfair headstart than to risk compensating one of you who [might] not deserve it."[30]

On the other hand, according to Hill, if our society does employ affirmative action programs, including programs of preferential treatment, in order to help African Americans improve their economic condition, we would be sending the following message:

> We acknowledge that you have been wronged . . . by humiliating and debilitating attitudes prevalent in our country and our institutions. We deplore and denounce these attitudes and the wrongs that spring from them. We acknowledge that, so far, most of you have had your opportunities in life diminished by the effects of these attitudes, and we want no one's prospects to be diminished by injustice.[31]

The message of affirmative action to those who have been disadvantaged by racist discrimination is that of concern, care, respect, and welcome into the mainstream of American life. It is important that we send this message.

What message does affirmative action send to whites? Does it send the message that they are inferior and not worthy of respect? No. Hill thinks that we should try to send the following message to whites:

> Our policy [preferential treatment for African Americans] in no way implies the view that your opportunities are less important than others', but we estimate (roughly, as we must) that as a white male you have probably had advantages and encouragement that for a long time have been systematically, unfairly, and insultingly unavailable to most . . . minorities. . . . We appeal to you to share the historical values of fair opportunity and mutual respect that underlie this policy and hope that, even though its effects may be personally disappointing, you can see the policy as an appropriate response to the current situation.[32]

White resistance to affirmative action and preferential treatment for African Americans suggests that few whites today accept this message.

EXERCISES

1. Jefferson City is 40 percent white and 40 percent African American, but its police force is 95 percent white. Community leaders believe that it's important to increase the number of African American police officers, believing that they are more effective than white officers in African American neighborhoods. In order to qualify for the police force, applicants must score at least 70 on the police exam. In practice, the force selects applicants with

the highest scores on the exam. Ninety-five percent of the highest scorers have been white. Some community leaders claim that whites score higher because the schools they attend are much better than those that most African Americans attend. They also question using the scores on this test as the only criterion for selection. They are proposing that the department set a goal of having 50 percent of the *new* police officers it hires over the next five years be African Americans. To reach that goal, they recommend that African Americans be hired over whites even if they score lower on the test; however, they recommend maintaining the minimum score requirement of 70. Thus, an African American who scored 71 could be selected over a white applicant who scored 93. Would this program of preferential treatment be acceptable?

2. Blacks make up only 3 percent of the student population of Holmes School of Law, even though they are 12 percent of the general population in the United States and 14 percent of the population of the state where Holmes is located. The faculty and administration believe that more African American lawyers are needed and that white law students need to rub shoulders with more African American law students; therefore, they propose that the school accept more African American applicants who meet the minimum qualifications for admission—at least a 3.0 GPA and a score on the LSAT at least in the 60th percentile—even if it means rejecting some white applicants who have higher grades and LSAT scores. The goal is to have 10 percent of the class African American within six years. Would this program of preferential treatment be acceptable?

3. Ted, a white male, graduated from college with a B.A. in economics, a minor in business administration, and a 3.4 GPA. He applied to the management training program at Summa Corporation. He was not hired. However, he learned that Summa has an affirmative action plan that includes a program of preferential treatment because the company has so few African Americans in management. Although Summa rejected Ted's application, the company hired an African American applicant to the management training program who has a B.A. in government and a 2.9 GPA. Ted believes that he was discriminated against because he's white, and that Summa's program of preferential treatment is morally unacceptable. Do you agree with him?

4. Sheila, an African American female, grew up in a poor urban ghetto and attended segregated, inferior schools. Her neighborhood was infested with crime and drugs. She had to work about 20 hours weekly in order to help support her family. Her family gave her no encouragement to finish high school, let alone attend college. Despite all this, she earned a 2.6 GPA and scored 1020 on the SAT and applied to XYZ University. Brad, on the other hand, grew up in a wealthy suburb and attended excellent schools. He never had to work. He got tutoring when he had trouble with a course. He took an SAT preparation course. He got strong encouragement from everyone around him to do well in high school and go on to college. He earned a 2.9 GPA in high school and got 1060 on his SAT. He, too applied to XYZ

University. Sheila was rejected, and Brad was accepted. Sheila believes that it's unfair that XYZ University selected Brad over her. Do you agree?

SUGGESTED READINGS

Barbara Bergmann. *In Defense of Affirmative Action*. New York: Basic Books, 1996.

Bernard Boxill. *Blacks and Social Justice*. Totowa, NJ: Rowman & Littlefield, 1982.

George Curry, ed. *The Affirmative Action Debate*. Reading, MA: Addison-Wesley, 1996.

Gertrude Ezorsky. *Racism and Justice*. Ithaca, NY: Cornell University Press, 1991.

Alan Goldman. *Justice and Reverse Discrimination*. Princeton, NJ: Princeton University Press, 1979.

Beverly Daniel Tatum. *Why Are All the Black Kids Sitting Together in the Cafeteria?* New York: Basic Books, 1997.

ENDNOTES

1. Leon F. Litwack, *Trouble in Mind: Black Southerners in the Age of Jim Crow* (New York: Vintage Books, 1998), p. 13.
2. Ibid., p. 13.
3. Ibid., p. 13.
4. Ibid., p. 151.
5. Ibid., p. 157.
6. Ibid., pp. 280–281.
7. Ibid., p. 289.
8. Ibid., pp. 225.
9. David M. Kennedy, *Freedom from Fear: The American People in Depression and War, 1929–1945* (Oxford, England: Oxford University Press, 1999), p. 18.
10. Litwack, *Trouble in Mind*, p. 249.
11. Ibid., p. 63.
12. Ibid., p. 107.
13. Ibid., p. 106.
14. Ibid., p. 107.
15. Kennedy, *Freedom from Fear*, p. 765.
16. Litwack, *Trouble in Mind*, p. 122.
17. Kennedy, *Freedom from Fear*, p. 765.
18. Litwack, *Trouble in Mind*, p. 126.
19. James T. Patterson. *Grand Expectations: The United States, 1945–1974* (Oxford, England: Oxford University Press, 1996), p. 27.
20. Ibid., p. 29.

21. Ibid., pp. 393–394.

22. Ibid., pp. 398–399.

23. Ibid., p. 400.

24. Studies show similar results for men's perception of women's qualifications.

25. Having served on many search committees, I have seen firsthand how subjective the process is when applications from scores of highly qualified applicants must be reviewed to find the one person who is "most highly qualified." In my experience, the best that can be done is to identify the 10 or 20 applicants who all seem to be roughly equally qualified. Anyone who confidently believes that he's identified the one person who is most highly qualified is almost certainly deluding himself.

26. Gertrude Ezorsky, *Racism and Justice* (New York: Cornell University Press, 1991), pp. 84–88.

27. Thomas E. Hill, Jr., "The Message of Affirmative Action," in *Autonomy and Self-Respect* (Cambridge, England: Cambridge University Press, 1991), p. 195.

28. Ibid., p. 205.

29. Ibid., p. 206.

30. Ibid., p. 208.

31. Ibid., p. 209.

32. Ibid., p. 210.

14

Capital Punishment

OBJECTIVES

- To understand the arguments for and against capital punishment and to form a well-reasoned view about the moral acceptability of capital punishment
- To understand the concept of desert and the criteria of being morally responsible and deserving punishment
- To understand and apply the concept of competence when it comes to someone deserving the penalty of death

INTRODUCTION

The men who dragged James Byrd to his death and the toxic pharmacist Robert Courtney, who killed an unknown number of people by diluting their medications, surely should be punished for their actions. The question we will address here is what form that punishment should take. Speaking practically, there are two alternatives when it comes to first degree murder: death or prison. Imprisonment can be for a specified time, for example, 25 years, or for life with no chance of parole.

Punishment serves several purposes. Perhaps most fundamental is social protection: We want punishment to make society safer. We assume that the threat of punishment will deter people from committing crimes, that is, if people believe there is a high probability of being caught, convicted, and punished for committing crimes, they will be less likely to commit them. And, we want to protect people from those who have already broken the law, that is, when it comes to murder, we want to make sure that murderers don't commit more murders.

Of course, punishment is not the only way to reduce crime. If we can gain knowledge about the causes of crime, we might be able to use this knowledge for crime prevention. If substance abuse, such as alcoholism or drug use, increases the incidence of crime, then perhaps substance abuse programs can reduce crime. If poverty increases crime, programs to fight poverty might be effective. If mental health problems increase crime, then mental health programs might help.

Finally, punishment has at least one more purpose or function. Often we punish people not only because we think it will deter others and protect society from the criminal but also because we think that they simply deserve to be punished. One way of looking at it is that a crime such as murder creates a kind of moral imbalance that must be righted by harming the criminal. Criminals are said to have a "debt" to society that they must pay. Probably the desire for revenge plays a role in the idea of a moral imbalance that must be righted. We want to hurt people who have hurt us, to "pay back" people in their own coin. This may be part of the reason behind the idea that punishment should fit or be proportional to the crime, that, for example, we should take an eye for an eye. If the punishment is too light or too heavy, we still have a moral imbalance.

Because most people think that we have a right to life, we will start with the presumption that the burden of proof or justification falls on those who favor capital punishment, and we will assume that today the only crimes eligible for capital punishment are such crimes as premeditated murder, terrorism, and treason. Supporters of capital punishment need to provide reasons for thinking that capital punishment is not wrong.

Supporters of capital punishment generally argue that murderers have forfeited their right to life because of their actions. This is a very difficult issue to come to grips with. The basic questions are: How do we know that the right to life is forfeitable? And how do we know that your right to life is forfeited if you commit murder? What evidence can we look for that will tell us whether the right to life is or isn't forfeitable? Is this a matter of the discovery of a truth about the nature of the right to life, or instead a decision we make about what we will accept? This seems to be one of those issues where all we can appeal to are our "intuitions," our strong pre-theoretical convictions. In essence, there seems to be no way to prove who is right about whether the right to life is forfeitable, and more specifically, forfeitable for murder, nor prove that if it calls for a decision, the decision to make the right forfeitable is the most reasonable one. Perhaps the only way to come to grips with this question is to ask someone, "If the person you most love committed murder, do you think that he would have forfeited his right to life?" If the answer is yes, it's difficult to see what else can be said by someone who disagrees.

That said, let's look first at justifications that are based on the idea of social protection. In effect, these are utilitarian justifications of capital punishment, justification based on good consequences.

SOCIAL PROTECTION

Probably the primary justification for capital punishment is based on the idea that of social protection. It saves lives. Supporters say that one way it saves lives is through deterrence.

Deterrence

It surely is reasonable to say that we should deter people from committing crimes and protect people from further harm by those who have already committed crimes. We must be clear, though, that in order to justify capital punishment in this way, it's not enough to show, if we can, that it reduces, say, the murder rate. What we must show is that it does *a better job of reducing the murder rate than alternative forms of punishment*, such as life in prison without parole. At least, we must show this if we accept the principle that we should use the least harmful means that will enable us to achieve our objectives. According to this principle, for example, if we can achieve our objectives without killing anyone, we should not employ means that will kill people; if we can achieve our objectives by killing one person, then we should not employ means that will kill two. This is a principle that applies well beyond the issue of capital punishment. It may be based on the more general principle that we should minimize the harm we cause. (Alternatively, thinking in terms of reasons for all-things-considered singular moral judgments, the fact that A will cause more harm than B is a reason to choose B over A.) For example, we might say that if we can achieve the objective of building a road by destroying three houses, we should not follow a plan that will destroy four or five. Therefore, applying this principle, if we can achieve the same degree of deterrence by imprisoning someone for life as we can by killing him, we should choose imprisonment over killing.

Does capital punishment do a better job of deterring than less harmful alternatives, such as life in prison without parole, and does it do a better job of preventing murderers from murdering again? One can make these claims, but their truth or plausibility must be assessed in light of the available evidence and arguments.

Opponents of capital punishment claim that the threat of death is no more effective a deterrent than the threat of a long prison sentence. Many studies have compared the incidence of murder in similar jurisdictions that have capital punishment with the incidence of murder in jurisdictions that don't have capital punishment. If capital punishment is the most effective deterrent, we would expect to find that the incidence of murder in jurisdictions *with* capital punishment would be lower than the incidence of murder in jurisdictions *without* capital punishment. However, years of social science research have failed to provide much evidence that the death penalty is a more effective deterrent than other forms of punishment. For example, the authors of a study of murder rates between 1976 and 1987 concluded:

> We find no consistent evidence that the availability of capital punishment, the number of executions, the amount of television coverage they receive.... is associated significantly with rates for total and different types of felony murder. These findings are consistent with the vast majority of studies of capital punishment.[1]

Why wouldn't the threat of death be a greater deterrent than the threat of a long prison sentence? Research on deterrence suggests that the probability of being apprehended, convicted, and punished is more important in deterring crime than is the severity of the punishment. If people believe that the probability of being apprehended, convicted, and punished is low, crime rises; if people believe that the probability of being apprehended, convicted, and punished is high, crime declines.[2] No threatened punishment, however severe, will deter people who believe that there's a high probability that they can escape it. However, studies suggest that less severe forms of punishment such as imprisonment will be as effective in deterring crime as more severe forms of punishment such as death if people believe that there is a high probability of their not being able to escape punishment. Therefore, increasing the probability of detection and conviction will do more to deter crime than will increasing the severity of the punishment threatened.

The people most likely to commit violent crimes such as murder are also the least likely to be deterred by the threat of punishment, even if the punishment is death. British psychiatrist Anthony Storr claims that a certain very small minority of individuals is responsible for most of the violent crime in Western societies. A combination of genetic and environmental influences makes some people "antisocial" and predisposes them to violence; alcohol and drug use makes matters worse, suppressing ordinary inhibitions against violence. Storr believes that whereas the ordinary individual will be deterred from violence by the threat of relatively moderate punishment, antisocial people will not easily be deterred by any threatened punishment, even death. Many antisocial people have poor impulse control, low self-esteem, and a sense of grievance and an excess of rage for the damage done to them by family or society—characteristics that reduce the probability that threats of severe punishment will prevent them from violent behavior. An individual under the influence of alcohol or drugs is even less likely to have self-control or be able to rationally consider the probable consequences of violent behavior, regardless of the potential punishment. For people under such conditions, the threat of death will be no more effective than any other threatened punishment.[3]

Social science research does not seem to support the claim that the death penalty is a better deterrent than alternatives, such as life in prison without parole. But what of the idea that it is better than alternatives at guaranteeing that murderers will not murder again? After all, the dead cannot kill anyone. Opponents of capital punishment cannot deny that only death will guarantee that a murderer will not murder again. However, they can say that asking for 100 percent guarantees is asking too much, especially, as we will see, because there is a risk of executing the innocent. They concede that prison without parole cannot guarantee that a murderer will not murder again, but they think that it provides a sufficiently high probability that a murderer will not murder again.

Some supporters of capital punishment argue that it is acceptable because it is cheaper than keeping a murderer imprisoned for life. Opponents object to this for two reasons. One is that studies show that it is not cheaper, because the cost of the system of appeals put in place to reduce the probability of executing the innocent is so costly. Second, opponents say that the value of a human life, even the life of a murderer, is not commensurable with the value of money. In their view, even if it were cheaper to kill rather than imprison a murderer, the fact that it would be cheaper is no reason at all to take the life of a murderer. The value of a human life is on a far higher plane than the value of money.

The Probability of Executing the Innocent

In May 2005, it was announced that Virginia's central crime laboratory had made a mistake in DNA testing in a major murder case; it required a careful review of over 150 other cases processed by the crime lab, including over 24 cases of prisoners on death row. Among other things, the outside evaluators said that there may have been pressure on lab personnel to testify that their conclusions were far more certain than they were. The main case involved a mildly retarded man convicted of raping and murdering a 19-year-old woman in 1982. DNA testing undertaken in 1993 that would have identified the real killer was supposedly "botched" by the lab. He was released in 2000 after new re-testing because the results raised serious doubts about his guilt.[4]

As of November 25, 2005, the Innocence Project at the Benjamin N. Cardozo School of Law of Yeshiva University in New York, an organization that examines the evidence and pays for new DNA testing in capital murder cases, has found new evidence that has exonerated 163 people on death row since 1992. (See http://www.innocenceproject.org.) This has occurred even in cases where the defendant confessed to the crime! According to the Innocence Project,

> These cases demonstrate that a confession or admission is not always prompted by internal knowledge or guilt, but may be motivated by external influences. Many factors arise from interrogation that may lead to a false confession, including: duress, coercion, intoxication, diminished capacity, ignorance of the law, mental impairment. Fear of violence (threatened or performed) and threats of extreme sentences have also led innocent people to confess to crimes they did not perpetrate. . . .

Further,

> Even absent those factors, adults also give false confessions due to a variety of factors like the length of interrogation, exhaustion, or a belief that they can be released after confessing and prove their innocence afterward.

In another shocking case, Oklahoma City's top forensic chemist, Joyce Gilchrist, was removed from her position in 2001 because of evidence that she falsified and bungled tests and knowingly gave false testimony in order to get convictions. For example, in one trial she testified that DNA tests were "inconclusive" when in fact the tests showed that the accused's DNA was definitely not present. It was also found that she often misidentified DNA, hairs, and fibers found at crime scenes, as well as exaggerated the degree of certainty of her conclusions and tests. However, because she was good at getting convictions, her shoddy work was passed over by her superiors for years.[5]

The point is that we are fallible. We make mistakes, some of them intentional. It is notorious that eyewitnesses are unreliable, yet juries often convict based solely on the testimony of eyewitnesses. People may make false confessions, yet juries often convict based solely on the basis of a confession. Witnesses can lie. Forensic scientists can make mistakes or falsify test results. In short, it is all too possible for innocent people to be convicted and sentenced to death. Opponents of capital punishment maintain that it is wrong and irresponsible to put people to death when there is the risk that we are killing an innocent person. Supporters of capital punishment maintain that the risk is low enough and worth it because of the benefits to society. Opponents of capital punishment surely would ask rhetorically whether they would still think the risk worth it if they or someone they loved were executed, though innocent.

Discrimination Based on Race and Class

Justice requires that we treat people equal in relevant respects equally. A corollary of this principle is that people should receive the same punishment for the same crime. However, it is notorious that not all suspected murderers or convicted murderers are treated equally. The reality is that the criminal justice system suffers from systematic bias based on race and class. From 1930 to 1990, 4,002 people were executed in the United States.[6] More than 50 percent of them (2,122) were black, although blacks have never made up more than roughly 12 percent of the total population. In 2005, the Associated Press found that in Ohio, a person was twice as likely to be sentenced to death if the victim was white than if the victim was black. People convicted of murder were far more likely to be sentenced to death if they were tried in a conservative county than if they were tried in a liberal county.[7]

A middle- or upper-class white person is far less likely to be sentenced to death than a poor person—black, white, or Hispanic—even if their crimes are identical. Opponents of capital punishment claim that the death penalty is inherently discriminatory because police, prosecutors, judges, and juries cannot wholly escape the taint of racism and bias. African Americans, Hispanics, and the poor in general will always be far more likely than anyone else to be sentenced to death.

There is also the fact that thousands of murders are committed each year in the United States, but only a tiny fraction of those convicted of murder are sentenced to death. Critics of the death penalty see it as a huge lottery where the unlucky few, no different from the lucky many, lose purely based on luck. Critics think that a penalty as severe and final as death should not be the outcome of a lottery that is so much a matter of mere luck. Because it is so sensitive to racism and other forms of illegitimate discrimination and because it is so governed by the vagaries of luck, opponents think that capital punishment is immoral.

Supporters of capital punishment, on the other hand, may admit that discrimination is unjust, but they might insist that the criminal justice system can be reformed in such a way as to minimize the effect of racism and prejudice on death sentences. They may insist that the death penalty is not *inherently* discriminatory.

Utilitarian Justifications May Legitimize Punishing the Innocent

A notorious problem with utilitarian justifications of capital punishment is that such arguments need not distinguish between the guilty and the innocent if all that matters is the outcome. Critics of utilitarianism ask, What if we could deter murder more effectively by making sure that someone is convicted and executed for every murder, even if the police and district attorneys know that some of them are innocent? From the point of view of the public whose members we are trying to deter, it will look as though no one ever gets away with murder, which will be a more effective deterrent than if they think that some can. (We probably think that such a scenario is almost impossible because such a secret could not be kept indefinitely, but the theoretical point remains.) Most people surely think that only the guilty should be executed. The guilty deserve punishment, the innocent don't, and we should punish only those who deserve punishment.

DESERT

Do murders deserve to die, at least those who committed premeditated murder? We said above that there seems to be no way to prove whether murderers have forfeited their right to life. A similar problem emerges with the claim that murderers *deserve* death. Can we prove it? There are some perplexing problems that complicate the issue of whether murderers deserve death. For example, we may feel confident that an unrepentant murderer who shows no guilt or remorse deserves death, but what if the murderer feels genuine remorse and guilt? And what about situations where a murderer's character undergoes a significant transformation between the time of the crime and the time of execution, which generally is many years? What if a cold-blooded killer, cruel and callous, becomes kind and compassionate? In a sense, he may not be the same person he was when he committed the crime. It may be that the person he was before the transformation deserved death, but does the different person he became still deserve death?

Consider the case of Karla Faye Tucker in Texas. In 1983, at age 23, she hacked two people to death during a robbery. While in prison, she became a born-again Christian. (At least, most people who had personal contact with her were thoroughly convinced that her conversion was genuine.) Those who met her after her transformation spoke of her remorse over what she had done, her gentleness, and her sincere desire to help others. They considered her a very loving person. At the time of the murders, she had been a prostitute addicted to drugs since her early teens. From a hopelessly broken family, her mother a prostitute, she had begun taking heroin by age 13 and become a prostitute by age 14. Not surprisingly, she committed the horrific murders while high on drugs.[8] Despite a world wide outcry, she was executed in 1998 at age 38. The woman executed at age 38 was a far different person than who she was at age 23 when she committed the murders.

Many supporters of capital punishment invoke the Biblical injunction of "an eye for an eye." The corollary is a life for a life. But Christians, at least, must consider the words of Jesus, who explicitly repudiated this principle of justice:

> You have heard that it was said, "An eye for an eye and a tooth for a tooth." But I say to you, Do not resist an evildoer. But if anyone strikes you on the right cheek, turn the other also; and if anyone wants to sue you and take your coat, give your cloak as well; and if anyone forces you to go one mile, go also the second mile. Give to everyone who begs from you, and do not refuse anyone who wants to borrow from you. You have heard that it was said, "You shall love your neighbor and hate your enemy." But I say to you, Love your enemies and pray for those who persecute you. . . . (Matthew 5: 38–44)

Long before Jesus, Socrates questioned the common view among the ancient Greeks that justice requires us to help our friends and harm our enemies. Socrates was convinced that a good person would not intentionally harm anyone, whether friend or enemy.

COMPETENCE: AGE, MENTAL HEALTH, AND INTELLIGENCE

One deserves punishment only if he is morally responsible for his actions. An important requirement of moral responsibility is competence. Competence is a function of rationality. Someone is competent only if her beliefs and actions are under the control of her reason, and her reason must be sufficiently developed. This is a function of age, mental health, and intelligence. It is uncontroversial that a 5-year-old is not morally responsible for his actions. If a 5-year-old killed someone, virtually no one would think that he deserves the death penalty. Similarly, if someone is severely mentally ill, suffering from an acute psychosis, few people would hold her morally responsible, deserving death, if she committed a murder Finally, if someone is severely mentally handicapped, with an IQ, say, of 50, the same thing applies. Almost all of us think that a 5-year-old, someone seriously psychotic, and someone severely mentally handicapped are not competent, and therefore not morally responsible and deserving of death if they kill someone.

But all these are matters of degree. A 10-year-old is generally more mature and competent than a 5-year-old, and a 15-year-old even more mature and competent. At what age do people deserve death if they commit murder: 10, 15, 16, 18, 21? It seems that most nations in the West now agree that no one who committed a murder before age 18 deserves the death penalty, but in the United States, many people seem to disagree. Some seem to think that anyone even as young as age 15 or 16 who commits murder deserves the penalty of death. What age should be the minimum age for deserving death? How competent must one be to deserve death, and how competent are people at the various ages mentioned?

Mental health, too, is a matter of degree. Neuroses shade into psychoses, and some psychoses are more serious than others and do more to undermine one's competence. Where should the line be drawn between deserving and not deserving the punishment of death when it comes to mental illness?

Finally, there is the issue of "intelligence," generally as measured by an IQ test. A score from 90 to 110 is average. What if a murderer has an IQ of 80, or 70, or 60? Below what score would they not deserve death, even if they murdered someone? That is, below what IQ score would one be considered insufficiently competent to be fully morally responsible and therefore not deserving of death?

EXERCISES

1. Construct an argument to try to persuade an opponent of capital punishment that it is morally acceptable.

2. Construct an argument to try to persuade a supporter of capital punishment that it is immoral.

3. Do you think that capital punishment is morally right?

4. Would a virtuous person be in favor of capital punishment? What specific character traits would lead one to support it? What specific character traits would lead one to oppose it?

5. If the person you love most committed murder, would you think that he or she deserved the penalty of death? Convert your answer into an argument applying the universal law formulation of Kant's Categorical Imperative.

6. If you had been governor of Texas, would you have commuted Karla Faye Tucker's sentence of death to life in prison?

7. How would you define or characterize the concept of competence that is required for moral responsibility?

8. Suppose that you know that a murderer had suffered horrible abuse and deprivation as a child. Would this affect your view of whether he deserved the penalty of death?

9. At what age do people deserve the penalty of death if they commit murder?

10. Where would you draw the line between deserving and not deserving the penalty of death in terms of mental illness and mental handicap?

SUGGESTED READINGS

Hugo Adam Bedau ed. *The Death Penalty in America*, 3d ed. New York: Oxford University Press, 1982.

Joseph Dillon Davey. *The New Social Contract: America's Journey from Welfare State to Police State*. New York: Praeger, 1995.

Lawrence M. Friedman. *Crime and Punishment in American History*. New York: Basic Books, 1993.

Jonathan Glover. *Causing Death and Saving Lives*. Harmondsworth, England: Penguin, 1977. (See Chapter 18.)

Thomas Mappes and Jane Zembaty eds. *Social Ethics: Morality and Social Policy*, 3d ed. New York: McGraw-Hill, 1987. (See Chapter 3.)

Jeffrie G. Murphy ed. *Punishment and Rehabilitation*, 3d ed. Belmont, CA: Wadsworth, 1995.

Jan Narveson ed., *Moral Issues*. New York: Oxford University Press, 1983. (See Section 111.)

Neil Weiner, Margaret Zahn, and Rita Sagi eds. *Violence: Patterns, Causes, Public Policy*. Orlando, FL: Harcourt Brace Jovanovich, 1990.

INTERNET RESOURCE

Catholic Bishops of the United States, *Responsibility, Rehabilitation, and Restoration: A Catholic Perspective on Crime and Criminal Justice* (http://www.nccbuscc.org/sdwp /criminal.htm).

ENDNOTES

1. Ruth Peterson and William Bailey, "Felony Murder and Capital Punishment: An Examination of the Deterrence Question," *Criminology* (August 1991), p. 388.

2. Peter Greenwood, "The Violent Offender in the Criminal Justice System," in *Violence: Patterns, Causes, Public Policy*, ed. Neil Weiner, Margaret Zalln, and Rita Sagi (Orlando, FL: Harcourt Brace Jovanovich, 1990), pp. 339–340.

3. Anthony Storr, *Human Destructiveness* (New York: Ballantine, 1991).

4. *New York Times* (7 May 2005).

5. "Oklahoma Inquiry Focuses on Scientist Used by Prosecutors," *New York Times* (2 May 2001).

6. *American Almanac: 1992–1993* (Austin, TX: Reference Press, 1992), p. 200.

7. *Associated Press* (7 May 2005).

8. Sister Helen Prejean, "Death in Texas," *New York Review of Books* (13 January 2005).

15

War and Peace

OBJECTIVES

- To understand the concept of peace and the views of pacifists
- To understand and apply the concept of a just cause of war
- To understand and apply the concept of authorization of war by a competent authority
- To understand and apply the concepts of last resort and proportional response
- To understand and apply the criteria for justice in waging war
- To understand and apply the criteria for justice in the aftermath of war
- To understand the difference between conventional and unconventional weapons and reach a reasonable conclusion about the moral status of unconventional weapons
- To understand the concept of deterrence and the forms it may take, and reach a reasonable conclusion about the moral acceptability and limits of deterrence

INTRODUCTION

The world has had a long and sorry history of war. The United States was born in war, the American Revolution. Expanding European settlement precipitated a series of wars with Native Americans, including the Black Hawk War of 1832, the Seminole wars of the 1830s, and the Sioux wars of the 1870s. In 1846, the United States fought a war with Mexico in order to seize parts of what is now Texas. From 1861 to 1865, Americans fought the Civil War as the Southern states attempted to secede from the Union and the Northern states sought to prevent it. In 1898, the United States fought Spain. In 1917, we entered World War I; in 1941, we entered World War II. In the 1950s, the United States fought in Korea; in the 1960s and 1970s, we fought in Indochina (Vietnam, Laos, and

Cambodia); in the 1980s, we invaded Grenada and Panama. In 1991, we fought in the Middle East in order to liberate Kuwait from Iraqi occupation, in 2001–2002 we fought the Taliban in Afghanistan, and in 2003 we invaded Iraq.

No one knows precisely how many wars have been fought in human history nor how many people have died as a result of war, but the numbers must be enormous. Major wars in the twentieth century killed tens of millions of people, both combatants and noncombatants, injured tens of millions of others, and destroyed uncountable amounts of property. The victims range from infants to men and women in their nineties. Some people, fed on sanitized images of war from television and movies, view war as heroic, romantic, and exciting. Compared to flipping burgers at a fast-food restaurant, bagging groceries at the food store, or shuffling papers at an office desk, war may seem a thrilling, adventurous relief from the often boring routine of peacetime existence. But however glorious, thrilling, or exciting war may seem to some people, for most people it brings nothing but death, destruction, injury, and suffering, often on a gargantuan scale. People die from being blown apart, crushed, burned, stabbed, and shot, as in the Nazi air attacks on London and the Japanese pillaging of the Chinese city of Nanking; they sometimes are burned alive or asphyxiated by fire, as in the, fire bombing of Dresden in World War II; they died vaporized by atomic bombs, as in Hiroshima and Nagasaki; they died from starvation due to destruction of food supplies and infrastructure or enemy blockades; they died from diseases unleashed by war, exacerbated by the destruction of hospitals, medicines, and medical personnel. Some died quickly and painlessly, others slowly and painfully. If they do not lose their lives, they may lose limbs, eyes, or internal organs; they may be permanently crippled, disabled, or disfigured. In addition to destroying people, war destroys property that people need to survive and creates intense emotional suffering and anguish from the loss of possessions and loved ones.

Even when nations are not fighting wars, they are preparing for war, spending money to pay and equip armies, navies, and air forces. If we just confine ourselves to the end of the twentieth century, the numbers are breathtaking. Estimates are that from 1970 to 1990, the world spent $17 trillion on the military. By 1990, annual world military spending totaled about $1 trillion. About 5 percent of the world's GNP goes to the military—money that could be spent for other purposes.[1] According to the United Nations *Human Development Report 2000,* in 1998 the United States spent 3.2 percent of its GDP on the military, over $325 billion. Money spent on battleships, tanks, bombers, missiles, military installations, and soldiers could have been spent on education, health care, housing, child care, transportation, and other civilian-oriented goods and services.

Wars have been fought for all kinds of reasons. Sometimes they're purely defensive, sometimes purely aggressive. Nations may defend themselves from attack, but they may also attack other nations to acquire territory or economic resources, to enhance their prestige, to settle disputes, or to protect important interests. Wars can be fought in all sorts of ways. An army can assault and massacre civilians; execute prisoners of war; besiege, starve, and bomb cities with conventional, chemical, biological, or nuclear weapons; poison water supplies; spray an enemy's land with defoliants that kill vegetation; or assassinate an enemy's leaders.

Two fundamental moral issues thus arise regarding war and peace. First, under what conditions, if any, is it morally acceptable to resort to the organized violence of war? Secondly, is everything morally acceptable in war, or are there moral limits to what is permissible in waging war?

These questions are vital not only for national leaders who must decide whether to and how to fight a war but also for ordinary citizens, especially in a democracy. Ordinary citizens have to decide whether to vote for or against political candidates who favor war, and whether to publicly support or oppose a war that their leaders have entered or threaten to enter. They may have to decide whether to volunteer to fight, consent to conscription, remain in the military, or work in military-related industries. If they are fighting in a war, they may have to decide whether to obey the orders of superiors who demand that they massacre defenseless civilians or bomb cities filled with civilians. If there are moral limits to whether and how war may be fought, they apply to ordinary citizens as well as to national leaders.

PEACE

The opposite of war is peace. But peace comes in different forms. In one sense, peace is merely the absence of fighting. But that's not a very robust form of peace. After all, there is the "peace of the grave." The dead don't fight. There is also the peace of a "cold war," such as existed between the United States and the Soviet Union from 1945–1989. They were at "peace," but they always kept nuclear weapons pointed at each other, and came extremely close to using them in the Cuban missile crisis of 1962. Consider also the relations between Israel and its neighbors when they aren't actually fighting. That's a fairly fragile and unfriendly peace. So the intentions and attitudes of leaders (and people) are relevant to whether there is "true" peace.

A better kind of peace is when there is no enmity and fear between people, not merely when there is no fighting. But even that does not reach the full vision of peace of most religious traditions. People can be at peace but wholly indifferent to each other. For example, what if the United States has no intention of attacking a neighboring country, but also is unwilling to provide even the smallest crumb of assistance no matter what catastrophe may befall it? That's better than animosity, but it still doesn't rise to the vision of "true" peace. That peace flows from a spirit of brotherhood, friendship, and love rather than hostility or indifference. That peace is not merely negative—the absence of fighting—but also positive—the doing of acts of mercy, compassion, and justice.

Pacifism

According to many thinkers, peace should be the overriding goal, both within and among nations. Some people believe that however tragic it may be, the only way to preserve peace is to be prepared for war, and sometimes the only way to regain peace is to fight for it. Pacifists, on the other hand, believe that war is never justified for two reasons: First, it is an immoral means for achieving goals, even if the goals are legitimate. Second, it is ultimately ineffective; violence always breeds nothing but more violence in the long run rather than peace. Pacifists live their principles by refusing to participate in any way in war. They will not serve in the military, and they will not work in war-related industries, such as a company that produces tanks or bombers. Many campaign actively against war and in favor of the deepest visions of peace. Some refuse to pay taxes that go to support the military.

Many pacifists appeal to religious precepts, such as the Hebrew Bible commandment "You shall not murder," claiming that war is nothing but organized murder. Pacifists in the Christian tradition point to the words of Jesus in the Sermon on the Mount:

> Blessed are the peacemakers, for they will be called children of God. You have heard that it was said, "An eye for an eye and a tooth for a tooth." But I say to you, Do not resist an evildoer. But if anyone strikes you on the right cheek, turn the other also. . . . (Matthew 5:38–40)

Pacifists argue that war violates the most fundamental moral right of innocent people, the right to life. In their view, no cause, however good, can outweigh the evil of war. Then, too, the virtues seem to be on the side of peace, and the vices on the side of war. Kindness, compassion, sympathy, and love must lead one to deplore war; cruelty, callousness, brutality, indifference to suffering, greed, arrogance, and hate weigh in on the side of war.

Pacifists also point to the dubious record of war in achieving a sustained and lasting peace. For example, World War I laid the foundation for World War II. World War II laid the foundation for the Cold War between the United States and the Soviet Union, which led to numerous smaller scale wars, such as those in Indochina, Central America, and South America, as well as repression in Eastern Europe. Wars in the Middle East have not created peace; they simply led to more wars and perpetual hostility and insecurity. The NATO bombing of Serbia led to increased Serbian atrocities against Albanians in Kosovo. Palestinian violence against Israelis and Israeli violence against Palestinians have not led to peace between them. War and violence breed hate and enmity, not love and friendship. Pacifists believe that lasting "true" peace can be achieved only by replacing violence and hatred with nonviolence and friendship.

It's important to stress that thoughtful pacifists do not abandon the struggle against evil. It's not as though they counsel passivity in the face of tyranny or massive human rights violations. Rather, like Mohandas K. Gandhi and Martin Luther King Jr., they insist on active struggle. It's just that the struggle is nonviolent rather than violent.

Mohandas K. Gandhi

Gandhi (1869–1948) first came to the world's attention when he led the struggle for equal rights for Indians and other "colored" races in South Africa from 1893 to 1914. He was a well-educated lawyer from India doing business in South

Africa when he became radicalized. He had a ticket for a first-class railway carriage, but a conductor ordered him to the third-class carriages reserved for "coloreds." When he refused to relocate, he was removed from the train. The humiliating experience opened his eyes to the reality of prejudice and discrimination, and he became a leader of the Indian community in its efforts to overturn racist laws. In 1906, the Transvaal province required Indians and other Asiatics to register with the authorities and carry an identity card. Gandhi began a campaign of nonviolent resistance to the law, refusing to register and urging others to do the same, even if it meant jail. He organized picketing of permit offices to discourage Indians from complying with the odious laws. But he warned the picketers not to assault anyone who might choose to register, insisting that their tactics remain nonviolent. In 1907, Gandhi was arrested, tried, and imprisoned. He urged his followers to fill South Africa's jails. The laws weren't repealed until 1911. Gandhi called his technique of nonviolent resistance *satyagraha*. Satyagraha pits soul force, the force of love and truth, against physical force.

In 1913, Gandhi led another satyagraha campaign against an unjust immigration bill in South Africa, once again urging his followers to resist the laws and fill the jails. He was arrested and jailed once more, but his campaign was successful. The hated laws were repealed. Gandhi then left South Africa to return home to India.

At the time, India was ruled by the British. Gandhi soon became a leader of the forces striving to cast out the British to win self-determination and liberty for India as well as a tireless campaigner for uplifting India's downtrodden poor, eliminating the Hindu caste bias against Untouchables, and creating Hindu-Muslim unity. His satyagraha campaigns were always nonviolent, depending on civil disobedience. Sometimes he broke laws and cheerfully went to jail. Sometimes he held fasts, often potentially life-threatening, in order to change people's hearts and minds, both those of his adversaries and those of his followers. Sometimes he led boycotts, for example, of British cloth. Often, he was successful. Sometimes he wasn't. But ultimately, his campaigns forced Britain to give up control of India. Tragically, he was not able to prevent Hindu-Muslim violence. When Britain left the subcontinent, hundreds of thousands of people were murdered as Hindus and Muslims killed each other. The land was torn apart, with millions of Hindu refugees fleeing to Hindu India and millions of Muslim refugees fleeing to the newly created Muslim Pakistan.

Gandhi, the man of peace, was murdered in 1948 by a Hindu militant who especially objected to his efforts to eliminate the ancient Hindu caste of Untouchability as well as to his efforts to eliminate the enmity between Hindus and Muslims. But his legacy and lessons live on.

Gandhi based his nonviolent philosophy on the Hindu virtue of *ahimsa*. As he put it:

> In its negative form, it means not injuring any living being, whether by body or mind. I may not therefore hurt the person of any wrong-doer, or bear any ill will to him and so cause him mental suffering. . . . Ahimsa requires deliberate self-suffering, not a deliberate injuring of the

supposed wrong-doer. In its positive form, ahimsa means the largest love, the greatest charity. If I am a follower of ahimsa, I must love my enemy. I must apply the same rule to the wrong-doer who is my enemy or a stranger to me, as I would to my wrong-doing father or son. The active ahimsa necessarily includes truth and fearlessness.[2]

Love is at the core of ahimsa. Hatred and ill-will are wholly incompatible with it. He stated that "[n]on-violence implies love, compassion, and forgiveness"[3] and that "[w]e have no right to destroy life we cannot create...."[4]

Furthermore, Gandhi insists that "the practice of ahimsa calls forth the greatest courage," because the practitioner is willing to give her life to fight evil or injustice. Victory in the struggle for peace and justice requires strength, but according to Gandhi, "Strength does not come from physical capacity. It comes from an indomitable will."[5] "Non-violence . . . does not mean weak submission to the will of the evil-doer, but it means the putting of one's whole soul against the will of the tyrant."[6] The strength of nonviolence also calls for the most difficult virtue—self-restraint. It's very difficult to resist the searing temptation to retaliate in kind against those who hurt us. Restraining ourselves from retaliating requires more strength than does succumbing to the temptation to strike out at our foes.

Gandhi believed passionately that nonviolence is more effective in the long-run than violence. Accepting suffering rather than causing suffering will inevitably change the hearts and minds of our foes if we are in the right. His goal was "conversion, not coercion."[7] In 1922, writing about the British who refused to give India its independence, Gandhi said, "Let no one blame the unbending English nature. The hardest 'fibre' must melt in the fire of love. . . . When British or other nature does not respond, the fire is not burning strong enough, if it is there at all."[8] If we practice true ahimsa and have love rather than hate in our hearts, the foe will respond. If we fail to reach the foe, it's because we haven't filled our hearts with enough love and emptied them of hatred. Gandhi believed that virtually no human being is so corrupt and depraved as to be unmoved by the satyagraha's courageous willingness to suffer rather than make others suffer.

Consider the civil rights movement in the United States. It swept into public consciousness when television showed scores of innocent blacks accepting suffering without retaliating. People's hearts and minds were changed when they saw blacks bitten by attack dogs and bowled over with fire hoses. On one interpretation, their acceptance of suffering led to the end of Jim Crow laws and denial of rights. Another real life example is that of the Danes in World War II. When the Nazis ordered all Jews to wear a yellow star of David, the Danish king appeared in public with a yellow star of David sewn to his coat. Almost all Danes followed suit. And unlike many French citizens who cooperated with Nazi authorities in identifying and aiding in the deportation of Jews to concentration camps, virtually no Danish citizen cooperated. Consequently, whereas many French Jews were victims of the Nazi mass murder, almost no Danish Jews were. In Denmark, nonviolent resistance worked, even against Nazis.

Hate and violence breed nothing but more hate and violence. "Our non-violence must not breed violence, hatred, and ill-will." They are no firm foundation for peace and justice.[9] But violence also breeds fear in the foe. The foe will change behavior only so long as he or she continues to feel the fear. When the fear is gone, he or she will revert back to his original behavior. The heart and mind haven't been changed by fear. "[W]hat is granted by fear can be retained only so long as the fear lasts."[10] Gandhi points out that nonviolence has shown its effectiveness throughout history if we'd only look. For example, if we try to solve conflicts in family life through violence, it never has succeeded. Only nonviolent solutions that all parties willingly accept due to negotiation and compromise are permanent solutions. Violent solutions tear a family apart. Thus, Gandhi says, "I object to violence because, when it appears to do good, the good is only temporary, the evil it does is permanent. . . ."[11]

Gandhi recognizes that people can make mistakes about what is right and just. He thinks it is abominable to make other people suffer for our mistaken beliefs. If we practice nonviolence, we are the only people who suffer for our mistakes. Consider white southerners who lynched African Americans in order to maintain segregation and white supremacy. Theirs was an unjust cause. If they believed so passionately in it, they should have been willing to die for it rather than kill for it. Instead, they made others suffer horribly to further their mistaken cause. "If this kind of force (satyagraha) is used in a cause that is unjust, only the person using it suffers. He does not make others suffer for his mistakes."[12]

While some individuals and groups strive to follow Gandhi in commitment to ahimsa and satyagraha in the face of injustice or what is thought to be injustice, many do not. Martin Luther King Jr. in the United States and Bishop Desmond Tutu in South Africa followed in Gandhi's footsteps. However, the conflicts between the Palestinians and the Israeli Jews, the Irish and the English, the Albanians and the Serbs, the Hutu and the Tutsi, have all been violent. No nation seems willing to forgo violence, even Gandhi's own India. India and Pakistan have fought three wars, primarily over Kashmir, since their independence in 1948. They both acquired nuclear weapons and continue to threaten violence toward each other. They still engage in periodic border skirmishes that lead to death and injury, and in 2002 they came perilously close to another war.

Nations still rely on armies for security. Some, like the United States, rely on nuclear weapons. While many leaders and ordinary people deplore war and violence for the same reasons Gandhi did, virtually every national leader on Earth believes that violence is sometimes necessary to protect important interests, and justified because it is necessary. None of them believe that they can always protect their vital interests and get what they most want employing only non-violent means.

For example, Gandhi urged satyagraha rather than violence to resist the Nazi invaders in Europe during World War II. He said that it would be better to die nonviolently resisting and refusing to cooperate than to kill Nazi soldiers. (Notoriously, Gandhi recommended that Europe's Jews either kill themselves or let themselves be killed during the Holocaust as a way of resisting and protesting the Nazi genocide. He thought that was preferable to resisting violently or letting oneself be carted off to a concentration camp to be gassed.) But many people believe that that would have guaranteed a Nazi victory and the absolute extermination of all of Europe's Jews. They do not have Gandhi's faith in the human heart and the power of love. They do not think that Nazi hearts and minds could be transformed by witnessing willing suffering.

THE JUST WAR TRADITION

The United Nations Charter proscribes aggressive war. Aggression is the first use of force or violence. According to Article 2, "[a]ll Members shall refrain in their international relations from the threat or use of force against the territorial integrity or political independence of any state. . . ." Article 33 states that "[t]he parties to any dispute, the continuance of which is likely to endanger the maintenance of international peace and security, shall, first, seek a solution by negotiation, enquiry, mediation, conciliation, arbitration, judicial settlement, resort to regional agencies or arrangements, or other peaceful means of their own choice."[13] But what about using force and violence defensively to repel aggression?

In the Roman Catholic tradition, not all wars are unjust. For example, according to St. Thomas Aquinas, a war is just if it is: (1) declared by competent authority, (2) for a just cause, and (3) fought with the right intentions. The right intention is to regain peace and deliver the world from evil. However, there are other requirements. The war must have a reasonable chance of success. Shedding innocent blood on behalf of an obviously lost cause is wrong. War must also be the last resort rather than a first resort. Finally, there are moral limits on how wars may be fought, even if the cause is just and there is a reasonable chance of success. We must employ just means and avoid unjust means, and the response must be proportional to the provocation. The just war tradition rejects the slogan "All's fair in love and war."

Declaration by Competent Authority

Under the United States Constitution, only Congress, not the President, can declare war. Presidents got around that in the twentieth century by waging war without actually declaring war. For example, Presidents Johnson and Nixon used their powers as commander in chief of the United States military to order troops into combat in Indochina, but never went to Congress for a declaration of war against North Vietnam or any other foe. In 2001, President George W. Bush ordered a military attack on Afghanistan because the Islamic fundamentalist Taliban apparently was shielding some of the plotters of the World Trade Center bombing of 9/11, and in 2003 he ordered an invasion of Iraq without a Congressional declaration of war. Before the invasion of Iraq, however, President Bush sent a resolution to the U.S. Senate requesting authorization to use whatever means he thought appropriate to disarm Iraq. During the time leading up to the invasion, most well-informed observers believed that the regime of Saddam Hussein was stockpiling chemical and biological weapons, and was trying to build nuclear weapons. The Bush administration was not satisfied that the U.N. weapons inspectors that had returned to Iraq would be able to find the weapons and prevent them from being used. It sought direct authorization from the U.N. Security Council for an invasion, based on its claims that the evidence for Saddam Hussein's weapons program was certain. The Security Council did not vote to authorize an invasion, but the Bush administration invaded anyway, claiming that it had sufficient authority based on prior U.N. resolutions.

As of this writing (December 2005), no weapons of mass destruction have been found. Now, almost all knowledgeable observers have concluded that Iraq did not have stockpiles of chemical and biological weapons, nor was it actively engaged in a program to develop nuclear weapons. Controversy swirls over whether the Bush administration intentionally exaggerated the danger of Saddam Hussein's regime and intentionally exaggerated the certainty of the evidence.

Despite the fact that the original justification of the invasion was to eliminate the threat of Saddam Hussein's weapons of mass destruction, the Bush administration later emphasized the importance of "regime change," removing Saddam Hussein from power because he was a tyrant guilty of massive violations of the human rights of his own people.

One question for the United States, then, was whether the President alone should have the authority to wage war, and if not, what short of a declaration of war constitute authorization from the U.S. Senate. A question for the world is: Should one nation alone have the authority to wage war, or should that be a collective decision? Should war be waged only if a competent international authority, most obviously the United Nations, has authorized it?

Some thinkers maintain that unless a nation is defending itself against an actual invasion or military attack, it should only resort to military violence if it has received authorization from an international or regional body. Many look to the United Nations, but others are willing to look at lower level regional alliances, such as NATO, the European Union, and the Organization of African Unity. But if the locus of authority is to be the United Nations, should it be in the 15-member Security Council where the United States has a veto, or should it be in the General Assembly, where almost every nation on Earth is represented and gets one vote?

If a nation brings a request to use violence to the United Nations or a regional body, the issues can be carefully debated and all sides of the question can be examined, including whether peaceful alternatives are available. The likelihood of war being waged in an unjust cause or in unjust ways is reduced. In the view of supporters, issues of war and peace are fit candidates for international democratic deliberation. But other thinkers are skeptical about the feasibility of such approaches. It's often difficult to get agreement, especially if the locus of authority is to be the General Assembly of the United Nations. And most people in the United States are very reluctant to give an international or regional body veto power over U.S. policy. When United States leaders have wanted to resort to violence and been confident that they will get approval from an organization outside the United States, they have brought the issue forward. In part, this is to reassure U.S. opinion as to the justice of the cause. But if leaders have wanted to use violence, as in Indochina, and doubt they'll get authorization from an organization outside the United States, they act unilaterally and don't seek authorization.

Just Cause, Self-Defense, and Aggression

According to the just war tradition, war is justified if it is necessary to protect innocent people from harm and to protect a nation or people from unjust aggression. Wars of aggression initiated to conquer or subjugate a nation's neighbors are illegitimate and immoral. As the National Council of Catholic Bishops expressed in their 1983 pastoral letter on war and peace, "War is permissible only to confront 'a real and certain danger,' i.e., to protect innocent life, to preserve conditions necessary for a decent human existence, and to secure basic human rights."[14]

According to the just war tradition, nations have a right to self-defense, just as individuals do. Self-defense for a nation means defending the lives, health, freedom, and property of its citizens, as well as defending its territorial integrity and political independence. We might justify the claim that nations have a right of self-defense by pointing out that in many cases a nation-state protects (and is the only entity that can and does protect) its citizens' well-being and way of life. Note, though, that in the cases of the U.S. invasions of Afghanistan and Iraq, neither nation was waging a war of aggression against the United States or its friends or allies.

In addition to military attacks and invasions, a nation can face a variety of nonmilitary threats. For example, other nations may refuse to sell it resources it needs, such as oil or wheat, or refuse to admit its exports into their markets, jeopardizing its standard of living. In extreme cases, the lives and health of a nation's inhabitants may be jeopardized. For example, if nation X can't grow enough food to feed its population and other nations refuse to sell it the grain and meat it needs, its people may face widespread starvation and malnutrition. Can nonmilitary threats to a nation's economic well being constitute a just cause?

For example, suppose that a nation faces widespread starvation because of drought, but a neighboring nation with plenty of food refuses to sell it any. Would it be wrong to invade and seize the food? Or suppose that a nation needs oil to sustain its economy, and other nations refuse to provide it. Would it be wrong to invade (or threaten to invade) to get the oil it needs?

What about a situation as in Afghanistan, where the Taliban leadership for several weeks refused to turn over the men suspected of masterminding the 9/11 attack on the World Trade Center? If a nation is harboring suspected terrorists or aiding them in any way, would that constitute a just cause?

Proving Strength and Determination

During the Vietnam War, President Nixon insisted that he would not permit the United States to appear to be a "pitiful, helpless giant." At least one reason for continuing the war, then, was to prove to the world that the United States was militarily strong and determined to use its strength to protect its vital national interests. Similarly, many people believe that President Reagan ordered the U.S. invasion of the tiny island of Grenada in 1983 primarily to enhance the image of

U.S. power and determination. Is the desire to prove a nation's military strength and determination a good enough reason to go to war? Some people maintain that proving a nation's power and determination cannot outweigh the losses of war. Even if a war is kept limited and controlled (a difficult task), people will die and be injured. (From a moral point of view, we must include the losses of our adversaries as well as our own losses.) However, others maintain that to prove a nation's power and resolve may be worth at least some deaths because a nation's image of power and resolve is vital to its well-being. They claim that powerlessness (or the image of powerlessness) leaves a nation vulnerable to economic, political, and military threats from aggressive neighbors. In their view, an image of declining power and resolve invites attack, increasing the probability that a nation will be faced with a choice of resisting or surrendering. However, if aggressive neighbors believe that a nation is militarily powerful and willing to use that power to protect its vital national interests, they will be much less likely to threaten those national interests. Therefore, sometimes initiating "small" wars to prove a nation's power and resolve can prevent large wars, paradoxically saving lives.

Unfortunately, political leaders (and their people) are sometimes prone to exaggerate, intentionally or unintentionally, the extent to which their nation's image of power and resolve is threatened and the extent to which war will enhance that image. Similarly, political leaders sometimes tend to overestimate their ability to control and limit the level of conflict and to underestimate the losses (to themselves and others) that a war will bring. Therefore, it is often difficult to determine whether a war to enhance or protect a nation's image of power and resolve is necessary (and sufficient) to protect a nation from aggression. Often such wars of prestige simply make diplomacy easier, or enable a nation to more easily protect its standard of living and economic interests, or enable it to get its way in the international arena more frequently.

One problem, of course, is that wars of prestige to deter aggression are often fought not against the nation that threatens the aggression but against other nations. For example, if the United States wars against Vietnam and Grenada were for the sake of prestige, the message of undiminished power and resolve that U.S. leaders wanted to communicate was directed not toward those small nations but toward the Soviet Union. It's difficult to imagine how a nation can rationally defend attacking a (relatively) innocent third party in order to deter an attack from another nation. If nation X wants to show nation Y that its power and resolve remain undiminished in order to deter aggression from Y, it may be acceptable for it to attack Y, but surely it would be immoral for it to attack nation Z. It's even problematic whether X would be justified in attacking Y for reasons of prestige. Therefore, it is at least questionable whether projecting an image of strength and resolve constitutes just cause.

Preemption

If a nation appears to face imminent military attack, it may have a choice: wait to be attacked before responding or attack first. Preemption is the act of attacking first in self-defense. For example, in 1967, Israel launched a preemptive military first strike against Egypt. According to Michael Walzer, for several weeks preceding the Israeli attack, Egypt had engaged in actions that almost any reasonable observer would have considered preparation for war. Egypt and the other Arab nations had been extremely hostile to Israel since its creation in 1948 and had already fought several wars with Israel with the publicly expressed intention of destroying and eliminating it. Believing that an Egyptian military attack was imminent and that Israel would be more likely to survive, win, and limit its casualties if it attacked before being attacked, Israel struck first. Although in hindsight Walzer thinks that Egypt's leaders intended to humiliate rather than actually attack Israel, he thinks that it was perfectly reasonable for Israel's leaders to expect an attack.[15]

Walzer suggests that a first strike is justified by the right of self-defense and morally acceptable if there is "a manifest intent to injure, a degree of active preparation that makes that intent a positive danger, and a general situation in which waiting, or doing anything other than fighting, greatly magnifies the risk."[16] To insist that a nation wait to be attacked before acting can, in some circumstances, seriously jeopardize a nation's ability to protect itself, especially in an age when there are huge stockpiles of weapons of mass destruction. If we have a right of self-defense, then a high probability of imminent attack may therefore constitute a just cause for war. To justify attacking first, however, there must be very strong evidence that an attack is imminent and that waiting to be attacked would make self-defense far more costly or uncertain. These judgments are always uncertain. The case of the mistaken intelligence about Iraq's weapons of mass destruction is a case in point. But even if the intelligence had been correct, would the mere possession of weapons of mass destruction be a sufficient threat to justify preemption, or must there be weighty reasons to think that the possessor intends to use them in the very near future? If their possession alone justifies preemption, then it seems to follow that the United States would be justified in invading such nations as China or India to disarm them, because they have nuclear weapons, and other nations would be justified in invading the United States because we possess nuclear weapons.

Revolution and Civil War

In the 1770s, the American colonies turned to war to secure their political independence from England. In 1861, the Southern states turned to war to gain their political independence from the Federal Union. From the 1950s through the early 1970s, nationalist and communist forces in Vietnam fought to overthrow the U.S.-backed government in the South and to reunify North and South Vietnam. Is it morally acceptable to wage war to gain political independence or to seize control of the government of one's own country?

Few people find it plausible to maintain that revolution or civil war is never justified. Governments can be unjust and oppressive and can violate fundamental moral rights of all or some of their people. They can exclude members of some groups from political participation, or they can exploit, oppress, and even systematically massacre people (for example, the Nazi government's policy of exterminating Jews in Europe and the Khmer Rouge's genocidal policies in Cambodia in the 1970s that led to the death of perhaps 15 to 25 percent of Cambodia's population). According to many people, a government's systematically violating fundamental moral rights of a large number of its members can constitute a just cause for war, whether civil war, revolution, or international intervention. In such cases, we are striving to protect the innocent. The more oppressive and unjust the government, the more justified we are in resorting to violence to resist or overthrow it; the less oppressive and unjust the government, the less justified we are. Certainly this can sometimes be justified on utilitarian grounds. It may also be justified by appeal to Kant's Categorical Imperative.

Most people probably also accept that securing a region's or people's political independence or autonomy can be a just cause. For example, few people today condemn the leaders of the American Revolution for resorting to war to secure American independence from England. However, some people do not consider violence in order to gain political independence ever acceptable. As we saw, Gandhi in India insisted that the campaign for Indian independence be nonviolent. Certainly, war to gain political independence in some cases will be *wrong* according to utilitarian principles. Sometimes, the losses will exceed the gains in total well being. The outcome of Kantian deliberations is less clear. Partly it may depend on whether a group has a right to political independence, and often that's not easily known. But even if violence to achieve political independence is sometimes justified, it must be necessary and a last, rather than a first, resort.

Humanitarian Intervention

What of intervening in order to protect allies or friends or to protect oppressed minorities within a country? Even if a nation is not itself attacked, may it wage war to protect its allies and friends from unjust aggression or to protect the innocent from massive evil or violations of their fundamental moral rights? Many people in the United States during the Cold War were ready to attack the Soviet Union if it invaded Western Europe. The United States participated in the Korean War in the 1950s, even though North Korea had invaded South Korea, not the United States. Similarly, Operation Desert Storm of 1991 ejected Saddam Hussein's Iraqi troops from Kuwaiti territory, not from U.S. territory. Is protecting allies, friends, or innocent people a just cause?

Such wars can sometimes be justified on the basis of self-defense. A nation's security depends at least in part on having friends and allies in the world who are ready and willing to come to its aid. If an aggressor conquers all of a nation's friends and allies, its position may become hopeless. It will be alone in a hostile sea. However, as before, a nation must beware of intentional or unintentional exaggeration. Nations may overestimate the justice of a friend's cause and underestimate the justice of an adversary's. They may also exaggerate a friendly nation's contribution to their security.

Although some interventions may be based on self-defense, others may be based on humanitarian considerations. A nation may wish to protect a weak nation from a strong and aggressive one simply because the aggressive nation will oppress, exploit, enslave, or exterminate the people it conquers. A nation may wish to protect a people from its own government, not an invader, for the same reason. At least some people maintain that it would have been morally acceptable for the United States to overthrow Castro's government to "liberate" the people of Cuba. Similarly, many people maintain that it would have been morally acceptable for other nations to wage war to overthrow the genocidal Khmer Rouge government of Cambodia in the 1970s or that it was morally acceptable to wage war against the Nazi government pursuing its policy of exterminating Jews and other "subhumans" in Germany in the 1940s.

World leaders have been harshly criticized for not intervening to stop the genocide in Rwanda that led to the murder of between 800,000 and 1 million people. On the other hand, some have criticized the Bush administration for following a policy of regime change to protect the Iraqis from their own government. Do such humanitarian reasons constitute just cause? Many people find it difficult to rationally defend the claim that however massive the violation of basic human rights may be, even if it constitutes genocide, other nations must stand aside and do nothing so long as their own interests are not threatened. But how can we justify that claim? Admittedly, a crusading mentality can be profoundly dangerous, and could lead to perpetual wars to right every conceivable wrong. However, the opposite mentality seems equally dangerous. Duties to minimize suffering, to resist or prevent evil, and to protect the weak and helpless do not lapse at a nation's borders.

Other Conditions of a Just War

Last Resort   According to just war theory, war is justified only as a last resort, never as a first resort. Nations must first make a good faith effort to resolve issues peacefully through genuine diplomacy, negotiations, bargaining, or compromise. A resort to war can be morally acceptable only if all peaceful means of achieving a nation's (just) objectives or resolving a conflict have been exhausted. Part of the controversy surrounding the U.S. invasion of Iraq in 2003 centers on whether the United States gave sufficient time for more peaceful means to achieve the stated objective of disarming Iraq of its weapons of mass destruction. U.N. inspectors in Iraq searching for weapons of mass destruction were given only a few months to complete their mission. This is a perplexing problem. "Last resort" can in effect be "never," because no matter what step you take, you can always take another step, even if it's to repeat an earlier step. Where to draw the line between enough time and too much time, or too few peaceful steps and too many peaceful steps, is a matter of judgment. There probably is no precise rule we can cite that will tell us when we have tried enough nonviolent means and must resort to violence.

Reasonable Chance of Success   According to just war theory, a nation (or people) is justified in resorting to war only if it has a reasonable chance of achieving its (just) objectives. To initiate violence that will kill thousands or tens of thousands of innocent people for a cause that has virtually no chance of success is immoral. For example, if violent resistance to an invader would be futile and would create far more casualties than would not resisting, it would not be morally acceptable to violently resist. (Nonviolent resistance would be a different matter.) Similarly, if a revolution has no chance of success, it would be wrong to revolt and throw lives away in what is obviously a lost cause.

Proportional Response   According to just war theory, any violent response must be proportional to the provocation. For example, if a nation is invaded, a legitimate response would be to repel the attack and perhaps to punish the aggressor to the extent required to discourage further attacks. It would not be legitimate to exterminate every citizen of the attacking nation, enslave all of its inhabitants, or destroy its economy. Self-defense permits only what is actually necessary to protect the lives and health of a nation's citizens, defend its territorial integrity, and preserve its political independence. The duty to minimize harm entails that a nation should cause as little harm as possible in defending itself.

JUSTICE IN WAGING WAR

General Sherman, who left a trail of devastation in Georgia and torched Atlanta during the Civil War, said that "war is hell," and implied that anything done to win or shorten a war is morally acceptable. Just war theory rejects this view. According to its theorists, some ways of waging war are immoral, even if one is fighting in a just cause. This understanding has been incorporated into international law, the Geneva Conventions, which prohibit some forms of warfare as too cruel to be acceptable. These international agreements prohibit the use of certain weapons, as well as mistreatment of prisoners of war and civilian populations under military control, and demand extreme caution in protecting civilian populations in war zones.

Consider the 1907 Hague Convention governing war:

Article 22: The right of belligerents to adopt means of injuring the enemy is not unlimited.

Article 33: [I]t is especially forbidden: (a) To employ poison or poisoned weapons; . . .

(e) To employ arms, projectiles, or material calculated to cause unnecessary suffering. . . .[17]

It also prohibits the use of bullets that "expand or flatten easily in the human body," and "projectiles the object of which is the diffusion of asphyxiating or deleterious gases."

The distinction between combatants and noncombatants is fundamental to the moral evaluation of warfare. Combatants are regular and irregular military or paramilitary personnel (for example, members of the armed forces, guerrilla bands, and active terrorist organizations) who participate in the fighting. Noncombatants are nonparticipants and usually include children, women, the ill, the aged, and ordinary workers. According to just war theory, combatants pose a military threat and therefore may be attacked in a just cause; noncombatants are innocent victims who do not pose a military threat and therefore may not be attacked even in a just cause. Not only may they not be attacked, but strong measures must be taken to avoid harming them.

The distinction between combatants and noncombatants has often been ignored. Even when battles between soldiers could be clearly limited in space and time, enabling each side to clearly recognize who was a combatant and who was not, the victor sometimes killed all or most of the inhabitants of the area captured. For example, according to the Hebrew Bible, Joshua and the Israelites slaughtered all the people of Jericho, Ai, Makkedah, Hazor, and other towns after defeating their armies. The ancient Greeks and Romans, too, sometimes slaughtered all the inhabitants of towns that they conquered. Similarly, the U.S. cavalry in the nineteenth century indiscriminately slaughtered the inhabitants of Indian camps: children, women, and the aged, as well as able-bodied men.

The distinction between combatants and noncombatants has become increasingly blurred as human beings have invented weapons of mass destruction and engaged in a kind of total warfare. Bombing cities has become a commonplace tactic of war, in part because things of military value are often in or near major cities: communication and transportation systems, energy sources, military installations, and factories producing war-related items such as guns, ammunition, tanks, bombs, airplanes, and ships. Sometimes, however, a city is targeted simply to demoralize or terrorize the enemy, as Hitler tried to beat Britain into submission by bombing London and the Allies tried to cow Germans through the February 1945 bombing of Dresden. The firebombing of Dresden was designed to maximize civilian casualties. The bombing raids created a (foreseen) firestorm that "killed more than sixty thousand people and left most of the city's population homeless."[18]

Even if the goal is not explicitly to kill noncombatants, it is foreseeable that large numbers of noncombatants will be killed. Nuclear, chemical, and biological weapons have made this problem even more acute. Because of their terrible destructiveness, a single weapon can literally destroy an entire city, killing and injuring millions of people, most of whom are noncombatants.

Almost everyone now agrees that it is immoral to intentionally attack defenseless noncombatants. Although such behavior still occurs in wartime, when it does occur virtually every nation condemns it. However, there is sharp disagreement about whether it is morally acceptable to attack military targets if such attacks will inevitably and foreseeably lead to numerous casualties among noncombatants. In such cases the goal is not to kill noncombatants but to destroy targets of military value; the noncombatant casualties are an unavoidable by-product, now referred to as "collateral damage."

Many people claim that a nation's interest in winning or shortening a war, or in limiting its own casualties, justifies attacking targets with important military value even if a large number of noncombatant casualties is inevitable. In their view, the right of self-defense permits a nation to harm or kill innocent people, if necessary, to limit its own injuries or to save itself. For example, if a nation can win or significantly shorten a war only by destroying an enemy's fuel supplies, it may do so even though destroying them requires destroying large parts of the cities in which refineries and storage facilities are located, killing tens of thousands of noncombatants.

However, some people believe that morality places limits on what we may do in furthering our own self-interest, whether as individuals or nations. We cannot harm innocent people just because it is in our self-interest. First, critics maintain, we must show beyond reasonable doubt that attacks that will cause noncombatant casualties are directed at targets of military value whose destruction is absolutely necessary for winning or significantly shortening a war. Second, we must make every effort to *minimize* noncombatant casualties in such attacks, even if it means additional risks to the attackers. Finally, if the likely cost in noncombatant injury and death is too high, we should refrain from attacking, even if it makes defeat highly probable. In their view, a nation's or individual's right of self-defense does not entail a right to inflict limitless harm on innocent people.

But are noncombatants of an enemy nation innocent? What if our own cause is just and our enemy's cause is unjust? In that case, wouldn't all citizens of the enemy's country be in some sense guilty rather than innocent? That view is difficult to justify. Not all people have influence over their government's policies, most obviously children; they cannot be held responsible for the misdeeds of their government. Some people may disapprove of or actively resist rather than support their government's policies; they, too, cannot be held responsible. Thus, many people will be innocent, even if they inhabit the country of our enemy and the enemy's cause is unjust.

JUSTICE IN THE AFTERMATH OF WAR

So far, we have talked of conduct before a war and during a war. What about after a war, when, presumably, one side has won and the other has lost? The ancient Romans sometimes annihilated or enslaved every survivor of a defeated enemy, men, women, and children. When the Greeks finally breached the walls of Troy, they burnt the city to the ground, killed most of the men, and enslaved the women and children. When Rome defeated Carthage in the Third Punic War, not only did it destroy the city and enslave the survivors, it sowed the ground around it with salt so that it could not be rebuilt and would be uninhabitable for generations.

Contrast that with how the United States and its allies treated their defeated enemies in World War II: Germany, Italy and Japan. The United States helped these nations rebuild and transform their political systems into democracies. Turning to the 2003 invasion and subsequent occupation of Iraq, the swift victory and subsequent overthrow of the regime of Saddam Hussein highlights the difficulty this may cause. The United States occupied Iraq with the intention of helping it rebuild its economy and transform its political system. But U.S. soldiers were not exactly treated as liberators. Hundreds continued to die, and thousands of Iraqi civilians died as the occupation dragged on because the invasion created so much turmoil and animosity among different groups in Iraq. Hundreds of billions of dollars were being spent by the United States to try to establish and maintain order and stability, create new political institutions, and promote industrial recovery. It would have been far cheaper in money and U.S. lives if the United States simply withdrew from Iraq after overthrowing Saddam Hussein, but then-Secretary of State Colin Powell enunciated a theory of responsibility: If we broke it, we have the responsibility to fix it.

What obligations does the winner have to the loser? People in the modern world do not think it is acceptable to enslave or annihilate defeated enemies, but the Nuremberg trials of Nazi leaders established a precedent that leaders of defeated nations guilty of a war of aggression or of committing atrocities may be put on trial and in some cases executed. May the victors simply walk away if there is turmoil and devastation in its wake? How much sacrifice is called for on the part of the victor to bring order where there is chaos or to rebuild what has been destroyed? It's difficult to believe that any of the moral theories we have examined could be used to justify a policy of ignoring the suffering of the survivors of a war, most of whom will be innocent of any wrongdoing.

UNCONVENTIONAL WEAPONS

The duty to minimize the harm that we cause to innocent people makes questionable any use of unconventional weapons, whether nuclear, chemical, or biological. Weapons capable of destroying most living things within a wide radius are incapable of discriminating between combatants and noncombatants. Many people are convinced that any use of unconventional weapons would be immoral. In their view, recourse to such weapons not only indiscriminately destroys innocent noncombatants but significantly increases the likelihood of escalation to all-out nuclear war that could exterminate all of humanity.

DETERRENCE

Even if using unconventional weapons—nuclear, chemical, or biological—would be immoral, is *threatening* to use them immoral? The threat to use unconventional weapons is an essential element of a policy called deterrence: threatening to retaliate and inflict unacceptable damage on an adversary in order to discourage attack. Rational adversaries are expected to calculate that because of such retaliation, the costs of aggression would be far greater than any conceivable benefits; therefore, they will avoid aggression that could lead to such retaliation. Thus, during the Cold War, the United States threatened to use nuclear weapons against the Soviet Union if it attacked Western Europe or the United States, whether with conventional or unconventional weapons. The threat was intended to deter such an attack, much as the threat of capital punishment is intended, in part, to deter violent crime.

Let's assume for the sake of argument that to actually use unconventional weapons in attacking the Soviet Union, even in retaliation for aggression, would be immoral because of the horrific number of innocent people who would be killed. Is it immoral to threaten to do what it would be immoral to actually do? Many people think not. From a utilitarian perspective, if the threat is effective in deterring attack, many lives are saved, making the gains far greater than the losses. And if deterrence fails and a nation is attacked anyway, it need not carry out the threat. Therefore, deterrence may be morally acceptable.

TORTURE AND INTERROGATION

During its occupation of Iraq, the United States was accused of mistreating numerous detainees who were being interrogated as part of the war on terror. Official investigations confirmed that several prisoners died as a result of the mistreatment. (See the torture information in the case studies.) Some observers maintained that the mistreatment constituted torture. Others denied that and said it only rose to the level of what is called "cruel, inhuman (or inhumane), and degrading" treatment. Both torture and "cruel, inhuman, and degrading" (CID) treatment are prohibited by U.S. and international law. (For example, according to the United Nations Universal Declaration of Human Rights, people have a right not to be tortured.)

The definitions or criteria of what constitutes torture or CID treatment are contested, but generally, part of the definition of both is that the victim experiences serious suffering, whether physical or psychological. Torture and CID treatment are considered especially heinous because of the intensity or seriousness of suffering and because causing suffering is the intended objective. So why at the beginning of the twenty-first century has the issue of whether to torture or impose CID treatment become a subject of serious discussion? Many people thought that the idea that torture could ever be acceptable and respectable had died out. The war on terror brought the issue back because of concerns about interrogating suspects. People who think that torture and CID treatment are sometimes justified claim that some prisoners may have important information that might avert further terrorist attacks or help capture terrorists, but may be resistant to less "robust" forms of interrogation. There are two issues here. One is whether torture is ever justified (right rather than wrong). The second is whether there should be laws imposing an absolute prohibition on torture.

The famous case of the ticking bomb is said to prove that torture is not always wrong. In this scenario, terrorists have planted a nuclear bomb in a major city. It will kill tens of thousands of innocent people. It is set to go off in an hour. We have in our custody someone who helped plant it. The only way to get him to reveal the information that will enable us to defuse the bomb is to torture him.

Many if not most people say it would be right to torture him. It may be a tragic dilemma, but when we weigh the loss of thousands or tens of thousands of innocent lives against the pain and suffering imposed on someone who can prevent the catastrophe but won't, most of us think that the innocent lives should be saved even at the cost of torture. If an interrogator makes the opposite choice and permits all those innocent people to die to avoid torturing the terrorist, most people would think the wrong choice was made.

But this leaves us with a number of troubling questions. How certain must we be that there is a bomb set to go off, and that the person we contemplate torturing actually has the information that will enable us to prevent it from detonating? How certain must we be that less-cruel methods will fail to elicit the information in time? Are we justified in torturing him if we merely *suspect* that there is a bomb and *suspect* that he has the information? In the theoretical examples of the ticking bomb case that are usually discussed, we assume we *know* all these things to be true. In real life, we're not likely to *know* that these things are true.

To alter the case, suppose we are certain that there is a bomb, and certain that one (but only one) of twenty prisoners we hold has information that will enable us to prevent it from detonating, but we don't know which one. Would we be justified in torturing all twenty, knowing that we will be torturing nineteen who don't have the information we seek? We may say yes assuming that all are terrorists who, because they are terrorists, are not merely innocent bystanders. But what if we are not certain that all or even most really are terrorists? What if there is a risk of unknown magnitude that some of the people we torture not only don't have the information, but are innocent people unconnected to terrorism?

It is easier to advocate torture if we *know* the person to be tortured is a terrorist who refuses to divulge his knowledge of how to defuse the bomb, but cases like this are likely to be exceedingly rare. If we reflect on the actual situation that seemed to confront U. S. interrogators, the case was not that close to a ticking bomb case. First, interrogators did not seem to have reason to think that a ticking bomb was already planted some place where it would kill many innocent people. Rather, they had good reason to think it highly likely that terrorists would continue to carry out attacks that would kill many innocent people, and they thought it likely that *some* of the detainees had information that would enable the U.S. to prevent some of those attacks. The situation was more like mistreating a hundred prisoners because some of them *might* have information that would prevent a terrorist attack. The question is whether torture would be justified in situations like this that depart from the conventional ticking bomb cases.

Another issue is connected to the fact that torture, as well as cruel, inhumane, and degrading treatment, comes in degrees. In a ticking bomb case, how much violence or suffering is permissible or justifiable? Perhaps it would be all right to slap the prisoner, but would it be all right to stick needles under the prisoner's fingernails? Break his legs? Rape her or sodomize him? Burn him with cigarettes? Jolt her with electric shocks to the genitals? Cut off his fingers one finger at a time? Cut or pour acid on her face? Gouge out one of his eyes? Dangle her by the feet outside the window on the seventh floor and threaten to drop her? Threaten to kill or torture her family? Actually torture a family member in front of the prisoner? Is there a level of violence or threat beyond which we many not go, regardless of the stakes? If we connect the issue of degrees of intensity of violence with degrees of certainty, we must ask how certain we must be that the prisoner has information that will save many innocent lives before violence of a certain intensity is justified.

The second issue is whether there should be an absolute prohibition in law on torture and CID treatment, even in ticking bomb cases, or instead whether there should be exceptions. Those who argue for exceptions say it's necessary in case we are ever in a ticking bomb situation. Opponents say that even one loophole will lead to torture becoming a more regular interrogation technique even when it's not a ticking bomb case.

If there is an absolute legal prohibition on torture, does that mean that interrogators cannot and will not torture even in ticking bomb cases, where most people probably would approve of torture? Will it mean allowing hundreds, thousands, tens of thousands of innocent people to die in order to "keep our hands clean" from torture? Supporters of an absolute legal prohibition point out that people do break laws. For example, the law prohibits murder, but some people still commit murders. If you're an interrogator in a ticking bomb case, you face the choice of obeying the law and letting many innocent people die, or disobeying the law, thereby saving all those innocent lives. It is up to the interrogator (actually, the interrogator's superiors) to decide what to do. It is likely that many interrogators would choose to disobey the law and torture the prisoner to save the innocent lives. Therefore, an absolute legal prohibition will not necessarily force us always to choose to keep our hands clean and let the bomb explode.

What's the likely outcome if an interrogator violates the law that prohibits torture but thereby saves many innocent lives? First, a prosecutor has to decide whether to prosecute her for the violation of the law. If she is prosecuted and tried, a jury has to find her guilty. If a jury finds her guilty, a judge has to impose what he considers the appropriate penalty. If the interrogator thinks the verdict is mistaken or the penalty too harsh, she may appeal. The point is that there is no guarantee that the interrogator will be severely punished even though she broke the law. If she can show that it really was a ticking bomb case, that less violent methods of interrogation failed, and that the torture resulted in the saving of many innocent lives, she probably will not be punished. She may even be rewarded. (Philosopher Henry Shue likens this to the way civil disobedience is handled. People sometimes break the law for moral reasons. The law doesn't admit of exceptions for civil disobedience, but if a judge and jury are convinced that the civil disobedience was justified, the person will often be either acquitted or given a very lenient sentence.) The attraction of this for some supporters of an absolute legal prohibition on torture is that everyone who commits torture must justify it after the fact, which in their view will deter people from resorting to torture too casually.

Others, such as Harvard Law School Professor Alan Dershowitz, suggest that instead of an absolute legal prohibition, which requires after-the fact justification, the law should permit torture, but only if the torturer has first received authorization (a torture warrant) from a court, similar to the way courts must approve searches and wiretaps (search warrants) before the fact. He thinks this will provide as much protection from unjustified torture as the absolute legal prohibition, with its requirement that torturers face indictment and trial.

EXERCISES

1. First, try to construct a defense for pacifism. Next, try to construct a defense for the rejection of pacifism. What are your real views on pacifism?

2. You have just been elected President of the United States. Write a message you will deliver to Congress and the American people about your plans for maintaining world peace.

3. You have just been elected President of the United States. Write a message you will deliver to Congress and the American people about your policies regarding weapons of mass destruction.

4. Suppose that Germany didn't begin World War II. Instead, it kept within its borders and began to exterminate its Jewish population. Would Britain and France have been justified in employing force or the threat of force in order to halt the annihilation of Germany's Jewish population?

5. If the Soviet Union had invaded Western Europe during the Cold War, would it have been morally acceptable for the United States to use nuclear weapons to drive it back to its borders?

6. About 800,000 Rwandans were massacred in the mid-1990s. Many people say that if the United States had threatened to intervene militarily and had supported deployment of a regional peacekeeping force, perhaps under the authority of the United Nations, the massacre could have been prevented. What, if anything, do you think the United States should have done?

7. The United States is the only nation in the world that has actually used nuclear weapons. U.S. leaders knew that dropping atomic bombs on Hiroshima and Nagasaki in 1945 was not necessary to win the war, but they (apparently) believed that it was the only or the best way to shorten it and save lives. Critics of the bombing insist that there were other alternatives that would have led to a swift Japanese surrender, that there were virtually no targets of military value in these cities, and that one important reason for dropping the bomb was to impress and intimidate the Soviet Union. Construct an argument defending the dropping of atomic bombs on these Japanese cities. Construct an argument condemning the bombing. What is your true opinion about the moral acceptability of the atomic bombing of Hiroshima and Nagasaki? Why?

8. Write a speech to deliver to the Israelis and Palestinians comparing the likely effects of violent and nonviolent struggle.

9. The United States has had an embargo on doing business with Cuba since 1961. The United States has even tried to prevent other nations from doing business with Cuba. If Cuba were more powerful than the United States, would U.S. policy be a just cause for Cuba to wage war against the United States?

10. Was the United States justified in invading Iraq in 2003?

11. If you knew that a terrorist in custody had information that, if divulged, would prevent the deaths of many innocent people, including members of your family, and that although the terrorist refuses to divulge the information under ordinary methods of interrogation, there is a high probability that he would divulge it under torture, would you think that it would be wrong to torture him?

12. If you knew that one of ten prisoners was the terrorist in question 11, but you don't know which one is the terrorist, would you think it wrong to torture the ten prisoners?

13. If you answered no to questions 11 and/or 12, what forms of torture would you consider justified?

14. Should the legal prohibition on torture and "cruel, inhuman, and degrading" treatment be absolute?

SUGGESTED READINGS

St. Thomas Aquinas. *On Law, Morality, and Politics*. Edited by William Baumgarth and Richard Regan. Indianapolis, IN: Hackett, 1988.

Avner Cohen and Steven Lee eds. *Nuclear Weapons and the Future of Humanity*. Totowa, NJ: Rowman and Allanheld, 1986.

Marshall Cohen, Thomas Nagel, and Thomas Scanlon eds. *War and Moral Responsibility*. Princeton, NJ: Princeton University Press, 1974.

The Essential Gandhi. Edited by Louis Fischer. New York: Vintage, 1962.

David J. Garrow. *Bearing the Cross: Martin Luther King, Jr. and the Southern Christian Leadership Conference*. New York: William Morrow, 1986.

Karen J. Greenberg ed. *The Torture Debate in America*. New York: Cambridge University Press, 2006.

Martin Luther King Jr. *A Testament of Hope: The Essential Writings and Speeches of Martin Luther King, Jr.* Edited by James W. Washington. San Francisco: Harper, 1986.

Robert W. McElroy. *Morality and American Foreign Policy*. Princeton, NJ: Princeton University Press, 1992.

National Conference of Catholic Bishops. *The Challenge of Peace: God's Promise and Our Response*. Washington, DC: United States Catholic Conference, 1983.

The Penguin Gandhi Reader. Edited by Rudrangshu Mukherjee. New York: Penguin, 1993.

W. Michael Reisman and Chris T. Antonious eds. *The Laws of War*. New York: Vintage, 1994.

Michael Walzer. *Arguing About War*. New Haven: Yale University Press, 2004.

Michael Walzer. *Just and Unjust Wars*. New York: Basic Books, 1977.

Stanley Wolpert. *Gandhi's Passion: The Life and Legacy of Mahatma Gandhi*. Oxford: Oxford University Press, 2001.

ENDNOTES

1. Mostafa K. Tolba, *Saving Our Planet* (London: Chapman & Hall, 1993), pp. 210–211.
2. *The Penguin Gandhi Reader*, ed. Rudrangshu Mukherjee (New York: Penguin, 1993), pp. 95–96.
3. Ibid., p. 107.
4. *The Essential Gandhi*, ed. Louis Fischer (New York: Vintage, 1962), p. 211.
5. *The Penguin Gandhi Reader*, p. 99.
6. Ibid., p. 100.
7. Ibid., p. 74.
8. Ibid., p. 103.
9. Ibid., p. 105.
10. Ibid., p. 41.
11. *The Essential Gandhi*, p. 201.
12. *The Penguin Gandhi Reader*, p. 48.
13. *The Laws of War*, ed. W. Michael Reisman and Chris T. Antoniou (New York: Vintage, 1994), pp. 5–11.
14. National Council of Catholic Bishops, *The Challenge of Peace: God's Promise and Our Response* (Washington, DC: United States Catholic Conference, 1983), paragraph 8C.
15. Michael Walzer, *Just and Unjust Wars* (New York: Basic Books, 1977), pp. 82–85.
16. Ibid., p. 81.
17. *The Laws of War*, p. 47.
18. Robert W. McElroy, *Morality and American Foreign Policy* (Princeton, NJ: Princeton University Press, 1992), p. 163.

16

Ethics and the Environment

OBJECTIVES

- To understand and be able to evaluate the seriousness of a variety of threats to the environment
- To understand and apply the concept of sustainable development
- To formulate a well-informed view of a morally acceptable environmental policy
- To understand the concept of environmental racism and evaluate its moral status
- To understand the difference between a life-centered and a human-centered environmental ethic
- To formulate a well-reasoned view about the obligations we have to future people and nonhuman forms of life

INTRODUCTION

Some people maintain that we face an environmental crisis of potentially catastrophic proportions. In their view, human activities are altering Earth so dramatically that much of the planet's life, including human life, is in great danger. They insist that in order to avert these potential environmental catastrophes, human beings must significantly change their ways. Others dismiss these dire warnings as the deliberate exaggerations of "environmental extremists" who are exploiting the issue in order to advance their own economic and political agendas.

Although scientists are uncertain about the exact nature and extent of the threats to the environment posed by human activity, what they do know is not comforting.

ENVIRONMENTAL THREATS

In manufacturing products, generating energy, growing food, and transporting people and things, highly industrialized societies spew a variety of harmful substances into the air, water, and soil. Such substances adversely affect human health by causing diseases such as cancer and emphysema, neurological damage, and birth defects. In addition, some substances affect human life and health more directly by altering the environment.

The Greenhouse Effect and Global Warming

On November 26, 2005, a report emanating from Rutgers University in New Jersey revealed that sea levels are rising twice as fast as they did 150 years ago, before the huge increase in the use of fossil fuels. For the last 5,000 years before the start of the Industrial Revolution, sea levels rose about 1 mm per year. Since the Industrial Revolution, they have been rising at the rate of 2 mm per year. The research team constructed a record of sea level changes going back 100 million years.[1]

In early 2005, it was reported that the meltdown of glaciers in Antarctica had accelerated over the last 50 years because over that period air temperature increased by 2 degrees Celsius.[2] Glaciers were only half as thick as they were 30 years ago.

Report after report since 2000 has revealed evidence of the reality of global warming. Most climate experts think it probable that the effects will generally be quite harmful to human interests. And most climate experts believe that human activity is the primary cause of global warming.

Atmospheric levels of greenhouse gases (most importantly carbon dioxide but also methane, ozone, nitrous oxide, and chlorofluorides) have increased significantly in the past 200 years, primarily because of the burning of fossil fuels. Greenhouse gases trap infrared rays from the sun that would otherwise be reflected out into space, raising the surface temperature of Earth. Without the trapped infrared sunlight, Earth's surface would be too cold to sustain life. However, human activity now is almost universally blamed for part of the roughly 0.6 degree Celsius increase in the average temperature of Earth during the twentieth century. According to the Intergovernmental Panel on Climate Change (IPCC), organized by the United Nations, "it is very likely that the 1990s was the warmest decade and 1998 the warmest year in the instrumental record, since 1861."[3] Furthermore, "New analyses . . . indicate that the increase in temperature in the 20th century is likely . . . to have been the largest of any century during the past 1000 years."[4] The report notes that mountain glaciers have been retreating precipitately, sea levels have been rising, and arctic sea-ice has been thinning significantly during the twentieth century. Small changes in some variables can lead to large changes in other variables. It is worth noting that during the most recent Ice Age, when a lot of North America was buried under ice, the average global temperature was only about 5 degrees Celsius lower than it is now.

The IPCC report also notes that atmospheric levels of CO_2 have increased 31 percent since 1750, and the level probably has not been higher in the past 20 million years. The concentration of methane has increased 151 percent since 1750. Although it is difficult to state how much of the rise in global temperatures and of greenhouse gases are due to human activity, most climate scientists believe it is substantial. The best computer modeling studies available in 2000 predict that by 2100, CO_2 concentrations will be 90 to 250 percent higher than they were in 1750, assuming that strong action is not taken to control and reduce greenhouse gas emissions. Ominously, the models predict a rise in global average temperatures by 2100 of 1.4–5.8 degrees Celsius.

The likely consequences include higher maximum and minimum temperatures all over the world, and more hot days and fewer cold days. In addition, there probably will be many more extreme weather conditions, including heavy rain storms with attendant flooding, droughts, and a larger number of more intense hurricanes. Sea levels will rise 0.09 to 0.88 meters (roughly 3.5 to 35 inches), leading to potentially catastrophic flooding along the coasts, where the majority of the world's population lives (53 percent of the U.S. population). It may lead to changes in precipitation. Regions that are dry may become wetter, and regions that are wet may become drier. These changes, in turn, would affect agriculture, perhaps reducing the world's food supply. If the food supply drops, food prices will rise, increasing the cost of living for virtually everyone and increasing the incidence of malnutrition and starvation in poor countries of the world.

When the Bush administration entered office in 2001, it asked the National Academy of Sciences (NAS) to review the work of the IPCC. Its 2001 report, *Climate Change Science*, supported the IPCC claim that most of the global warming that occurred over the course of the nineteenth and twentieth centuries was probably caused by human activity and its predictions about the extent and likely consequences of global warming that will continue throughout the twenty-first century. For example, the NAS report stated that the IPCC midrange estimate of an increase in global temperature of nearly 6 degrees Fahrenheit is a reasonable prediction. The report pointed out that according to ice core records going back 400,000 years, until the Industrial Revolution atmospheric CO_2 was never above 280 parts per million by volume (ppmv), but since the Industrial Revolution, it has risen to around 370 ppmv. It agreed with the IPCC that global warming probably will lead to "increases in rainfall rates and increased susceptibility of semi-arid regions to drought."[5] Semi-arid regions include the Great Plains in the United States. In addition, "heat stress and smog induced respiratory illnesses in major urban areas would increase, if no adaption occurred."[6]

According to the *United Nations Human Development Report 2000*, in 1996 the developed nations accounted for nearly half of the carbon dioxide emitted into the atmosphere. The United States alone, with only about 4 percent of the world's population, accounted for 22.2 percent of the carbon dioxide released. China accounted for 14.1 percent, and India 4.2 percent.[7]

In December 2000, the Clinton administration signed the Kyoto Protocol to the United Nations Framework Convention on Climate Change, which entails a commitment to reduce carbon dioxide emissions 5 percent below 1990 levels in the period 2008 to 2012. It did not submit the Kyoto Protocol to the Senate for ratification because it knew it would be defeated by the Republican majority. One important component of the program to limit carbon dioxide was a plan to regulate emissions from power plants. On March 13, 2001, the new Bush administration announced that it would not follow through on George W. Bush's campaign pledge to regulate CO_2 emissions from coal-burning power plants because it interfered with the administration's priorities of increasing domestic energy production and keeping energy prices low. The administration said that requiring reductions in carbon dioxide emissions would raise the price of electricity to consumers. Furthermore, the administration cited what it said is the uncertainty about causes of and solutions to global warming. This decision was considered by many to be a rejection of the Kyoto Protocol. According to newspaper accounts, heavy pressure for this move came from lobbyists for utilities dependent on coal and coal companies, and conservative Republicans in Congress. Instead of regulations, the Bush administration will rely on "incentives to encourage voluntary moves by industry to reduce emissions."[8]

Ozone Depletion

The sun's rays include potentially destructive ultraviolet radiation. Ultraviolet radiation causes sunburn and skin cancer in human beings. Too much ultraviolet radiation reaching the surface of Earth would practically fry many living things, both plants and animals. Most of the sun's ultraviolet radiation is screened out by a chemical called *ozone* (O_3) that exists in the stratosphere, a band that stretches from about 9 to 22 miles above Earth's surface. Without that screen of ozone, life as we know it could not exist on Earth. Scientists have discovered that atoms of chlorine and bromine, called halogens, destroy atoms of ozone. One chlorine atom in the stratosphere can destroy up to 100,000 atoms of ozone. One bromine atom can destroy even more atoms of ozone. Scientists have discovered that certain human-made chemicals that include halogen atoms have risen to the stratosphere and seem to be destroying some of the ozone there. (Scientists have been viewing with alarm the large and growing "ozone hole" that has developed above the Northern Hemisphere.) As a result of the thinning of the ozone layer, more ultraviolet radiation is reaching Earth's surface.

The probable effects include an increase in the incidence of skin cancer and cataracts among humans; suppression of both human and animal immune systems, leading to lowered resistance to infection and disease; reduction in crop yields, reducing the food supply; and a reduction in phyloplankton in the ocean, the small organism that lies at the base of the ocean's food chain, which would reduce the amount of fish in the ocean at every level of the food chain.

Air Pollution

The list of common air pollutants includes sulfur oxides, nitrogen oxides, suspended particulate matter, carbon monoxide, a variety of trace metals (for example, lead, mercury, and zinc), ground-level ozone (smog), and a veritable zoo of volatile organic materials (the Environmental Protection Agency lists 189). The primary sources are fossil fuel energy sources and industrial production.

One form of air pollution that has gotten special attention is acid precipitation. As a result primarily of sulfur and nitrogen oxides, rain, fog, and snow have far greater acidity than normal. This acidity, in turn, has increased the acidity of streams, rivers, and lakes, reducing their capacity to sustain plant and fish life. Acid precipitation damages plants, buildings, bridges, and human health. The effects of this and other forms of air pollution on human health include lung damage and disease (lung cancer, emphysema, pneumonia, bronchitis, and asthma), birth defects, cancer of vital organs, nervous system damage, immune system suppression, and aggravation of heart disease.

Water Pollution

We do not have (and probably never will have) the technology to create large amounts of water. The water supply that now exists on Earth is all the water we are likely to ever have. According to recent estimates, 94 percent of it is salt water in the oceans. Thus, only 6 percent of the world's water supply is fresh water that can be used by human beings. Of that amount, 27 percent is frozen in glaciers and 72 percent is underground, leaving a mere 1 percent of the world's freshwater in the atmosphere, streams, rivers, and lakes.[9] Humans use freshwater for domestic purposes (drinking, cooking, washing), agriculture, and industry. Globally, 69 percent of freshwater is used for agriculture, 23 percent for industry, and 8 percent in the home. Contaminated water cannot be used for these purposes.

The chief sources of water pollution are untreated or inadequately treated sewage; discharge of volatile organic compounds, trace metals, and nitrogen and sulfur oxides by industry; and the runoff of fertilizers and pesticides used in agriculture. The consequences include human illness and disease, water shortages, and reductions in aquatic life. The same pollutants also affect the salt water in the oceans, leading to human illness and infection from bathing in contaminated water and eating contaminated fish, and to reductions in a variety of fish species.

Energy Consumption

Global energy consumption continues to grow as world population grows and more poor countries try to increase their standards of living. The average annual rate of growth in energy consumption has been estimated at 2.2 percent for the period 1900–1950, 5.2 percent for 1950–1970, and 2.3 percent for 1971–1990. The slowdown in energy consumption after 1970 resulted from several factors, including higher energy prices, economic slowdowns in many parts of the world, and explicit policies of energy conservation. Predicted annual growth rates after the year 2000 are 1.9 percent for developed countries, 3 percent for Russia and Eastern Europe, and 4.5 percent in the developing nations.[10]

In 1990, 32 percent of the world's commercial energy came from coal and 36 percent from oil. This dependence on fossil fuels creates two problems. First is the depletion of fossil fuels. The question is not whether we will run out of these nonrenewable energy sources, but when. Estimates are that, based on known supplies, at 1990 levels of consumption the world will run out of oil around 2040, natural gas around 2060, and coal around 2200.[11] The second problem is the variety of pollutants emitted in the mining, transportation, and combustion of fossil fuels. The use of nuclear energy creates the additional problem of safe disposal of radioactive waste, which will remain radioactive for tens of thousands of years. Can we find cleaner sources of energy? Can we perfect technologies for "renewable" sources of energy such as sun, wind, and tides?

Both pollution and the depletion of natural resources are attributable largely to the developed world. Most of the world's pollution has been generated by the United States, Canada, Western Europe, and Japan, which do the lion's share of producing and consuming the world's goods. The developed world, with 22 percent of the world's population, uses 82 percent of the world's energy while the developing world, which contains the other 78 percent of humanity, uses only 18 percent of the world's energy.[12] As with so many indicators, the United States is near the top. For example, in 1997 the per capita energy use in kilograms of oil equivalency was over 8,000 for the United States, while ranging from roughly 3,500 to 6,000 for such countries as Australia, Sweden, the Netherlands, Japan, the United Kingdom, France, and Germany. (Canada's was 7,930.) In contrast, it was 1,501 for Mexico, 769 for Costa Rica, 1,140 for Turkey, 907 for China, 479 for India, and 197 for Bangladesh.[13]

Deforestation and Species Loss

Roughly 95 percent of the species that ever existed on Earth since life emerged about 3.5 billion years ago are now extinct, almost all from natural causes rather than from human activity. Now, however, the speed of extinction is vastly accelerating because human activity has destroyed and is destroying natural habitats at an increasing rate.

More than half the species of plants and animals currently on Earth are located in (and only in) tropical rainforests. Poor, overpopulated countries have felt compelled to overexploit their rainforests in order to meet their immediate needs. They export timber and clear the forests for agriculture and animal grazing. Additionally, global warming and ozone depletion may adversely affect the world's forests.

Some people estimate that human activity has increased the rate of species extinction as much as 10,000-fold. From a purely human point of view, such accelerated extinction is unfortunate because various species (and varieties within species) of plants and animals constitute important sources of food, energy, and medicine. They are also a fundamental and irreplaceable source of the gene pool of Earth. The National Academy of Sciences notes: "Commercial species are continuously crossbred with their wild relatives to improve yield, nutritional quality, responsiveness to different soils and climate, and resistance to pests and diseases."[14] Similarly, the World Commission on Environment and Development, established by the United Nations in 1983, points out, "Vast stocks of biological diversity are in danger of disappearing just as science is learning how to exploit genetic variability through the advances of genetic engineering."[15]

Besides causing species extinction, destruction of tropical rainforests affects Earth's climate. As the wood decays or is burned, it releases carbon dioxide, which accelerates the greenhouse effect. The rainforests also affect the patterns of rainfall and protect soil from erosion. Forest loss can bring drought or flooding to vast areas.

Wilderness Preservation

A very large part of the Earth's surface has been altered by humans to meet their needs. Land has been cleared to plant crops, graze animals, construct buildings, and pave roads. The landscape is crammed with cities and shopping malls. Even leaving behind cities and suburbs for "the country," we generally travel on paved roads, and almost everywhere we look we're liable to see fields or pastures. Sometimes we come across power plants with huge smokestacks belching black smoke. There aren't many places left that are pretty much unaltered and undisturbed by humans.

Many people wish to leave the few remaining wilderness areas untouched. They don't want loggers to cut down the trees or developers to build ski resorts; they don't want vacation homes built there; they don't want corporations to explore for coal, gas, or oil, or to mine for precious metals or coal. They don't even want roads built. They want snow mobiles and motorboats that pollute and shatter the placid stillness excluded. Why?

Many people today appreciate natural beauty and have deep feelings about and responses to mountains, forests, streams, and the flora and fauna living there. They value such experiences as camping, hiking, rock and mountain climbing, and fishing. Some people find it spiritually nourishing to get as far away as possible from human alterations of the landscape. They may have a religious experience, feel closer to God, or find it easier to develop and deepen their self-knowledge. Experiencing nature unaltered by human activity may nurture people's imagination and creativity, and make them feel a unity with all things. Max Oelschlaeger says that, "wild nature . . . offers opportunity for contemplative encounters, occasions for human beings to reflect on life and cosmos, on meaning and significance that transcends the culturally relative categories of modern existence."[16] To such people, wild nature should not be looked at as merely a resource to be exploited or "tamed" but as something having intrinsic value or worth for its own sake.

Other people find little value in wilderness and have little interest in preserving it. In some areas, such as the Tongass National Forest in Alaska, they want to permit exploration for and extraction of energy sources such as oil, natural gas, and coal, to permit logging, and to construct roads. They think it is folly to leave valuable natural resources in the ground if they can be extracted, and to leave valuable timber to die a natural death and lie rotting on the earth.

In reply, those in favor of leaving wilderness untouched say that once a wilderness area is altered by humans, it ceases to be wilderness for at least centuries. There's so little genuine wilderness left on Earth that we should set aside some of that little that remains and say it's out of bounds to the kind of development that will transform it even a little. In their view, it's difficult to preserve any of wilderness untouched unless there's an absolute prohibition on development.

But others point out that if left untouched, wilderness areas are inaccessible to most people. For example, relatively few people will ever visit or penetrate deep into the Tongass National Forest if there are no roads or trails. So why preserve wilderness if it's only going to benefit a small number of people?

People who will never visit a wilderness area may nevertheless value it. They may want it preserved for their children, grandchildren, or great-grandchildren; perhaps even other people's children, grandchildren, and great-grandchildren, who may desire to visit it. They don't wish to have people from future generations condemn them for leaving no wilderness areas left for them to enjoy. They ask themselves what they would think and feel if past generations had not taken steps to preserve such natural wonders as Yellowstone National Park or Yosemite. They value wilderness in part because of its rareness, not just its natural beauty.

Some religious people point out that humans didn't create the natural world, God did. They say that when God created the natural world, it was wilderness, and God saw that it was good and beautiful. Only afterwards did God create humans. God didn't create Earth and its wilderness areas intending to have humans destroy or degrade all of it. God didn't give humans the right to treat Earth as their sewer or to take whatever they want from it without regard to its effects. Instead, God gave humans the responsibility to be stewards of the Earth. Stewardship requires care and concern to conserve and preserve what's valuable. God-created wilderness must have value and worth, or God wouldn't have created it and considered it good and beautiful. Thus, we have a God-given duty to preserve what wilderness we can in the state God created it.

Human Population Growth

The human population has been growing at an alarming rate. Estimates are that around 6,000 B.C.E. there were probably about 5 million human beings on the entire Earth. Then, with the agricultural revolution, human populations began to soar. Here are growth estimates:

1 C.E.	250 million
1600	500 million
1850	1 billion
1930	2 billion
1960	3 billion
1974	4 billion
1986	5 billion
2000	6.1 billion
2005	6.45 billion

It took tens of thousands of years for the human population to reach the one billion mark. It took about a century to double and add another billion by 1930. The next billion were added in only 30 years. The fourth billion were added in only 14 years, and the fifth billion in 12. Then population growth slowed a bit, and it took about 14 years to add the sixth billion. Much of the recent population growth has occurred in the developing world, whose share of world population has risen from 64 percent in 1930 to 77 percent in 1990.[17]

Human population is still growing. The projections as of 2004 are that the world's population will increase to 9.1 billion people by 2050. Most of that growth will occur in the less and least developed nations. According to the United Nations Population Division, six nations account for half of this annual growth: India, China, Pakistan, Nigeria, Bangladesh, and Indonesia. Reducing the number of births in these nations would do much to significantly reduce world population growth.

The more human beings there are on Earth, the greater the strain on the environment. More human beings means more energy consumed, more pollution emitted, more water used, and more land cleared. The world's poor people are less and less content to have their standard of living lag far behind that of the developed world, and they are demanding economic growth to close the enormous gap between rich and poor. But the disparity between poor and rich countries is growing rather than shrinking. In 1960, the richest 20 percent of the world's population had an annual income 30 times that of the poorest 20 percent; in 1991, it was 59 times that of the poorest 20 percent.[18] If poor people achieve a higher standard of living approaching that of middle-class Americans, it will mean that there will be more environmental degradation.

As paradoxical as it may seem, however, many experts believe that increasing living standards of poor people will lead to a reduction in their fertility. Recent history shows an inverse relationship between income and family size: As a society becomes more affluent, family size falls. Thus, economic development is considered one way to control population. In addition, experts call for a global campaign to promote contraception and to make it affordable and accessible. Also, empowering women and educating both men and women about the value of small families will help women gain greater control over their own fertility.

During the 1980s and early 1990s, the Reagan and Bush administrations stopped contributing to international family planning organizations that informed women about the option of abortion or that provided abortions. The Clinton administration resumed financing from 1992 to 2000, but the administration of George W. Bush, elected in 2000, reinstated the prohibition in its first weeks in office. America has also been less generous than most developed nations in providing foreign aid for economic development to combat poverty. According to the *Human Development Report 2000*, the United States spent 0.10 percent of its GDP in 1998 for official development assistance as compared to 0.99 for Denmark, 0.91 for Norway, 0.40 for France, 0.29 for Canada, 0.28 for Japan, 0.27 for the United Kingdom, and 0.26 for Germany. As a percentage of the central government's budget, the figures were 0.3 for the United States, 1.8 for

Denmark, 2.0 for Norway, 0.9 for France, 0.7 for Canada, 0.9 for Japan, 0.7 for the United Kingdom, and 0.6 for Germany. The amount of official development assistance provided by the United States was $29 per U.S. citizen; for Denmark it was $316, for Norway it was $309, for France it was $103, for Canada it was $64, for Japan it was $82, for the United Kingdom it was $61, and for Germany it was $70.[19]

INTERNATIONAL DECLARATIONS AND AGREEMENTS ON THE ENVIRONMENT

Under the auspices of the United Nations, many international agreements about the environment have been adopted. Excerpts from some follow.

1972 Declaration of the United Nations Conference on the Human Environment

In 1972, representatives of many nations met in Stockholm under the auspices of the United Nations to forge a consensus about principles that should govern humanity's interactions with the environment. The resulting document was called the Stockholm Declaration.

Principle 1   Man has the fundamental right to freedom, equality, and adequate conditions of life, in an environment of a quality that permits a life of dignity and well-being, and he bears a solemn responsibility to protect and improve the environment for present and future generations. . . .

Principle 2   The natural resources of the earth, including the air, water, land, flora, and fauna . . . must be safeguarded for the benefit of present and future generations. . . .

Principle 3   The capacity of the earth to produce vital renewable resources must be maintained and, wherever practicable, restored or improved.

Principle 4   Man has a special responsibility to safeguard and wisely manage the heritage of wildlife and its habitat. . . .

Principle 5   The non-renewable resources of the earth must be employed in such a way as to guard against the danger of their future exhaustion and to ensure that benefits from such employment are shared by all mankind.

Principle 6   The discharge of toxic substances . . . and the release of heat, in such quantities or concentrations as to exceed the capacity of the environment to render them harmless, must be halted in order to ensure that serious or irreversible damage is not inflicted upon ecosystems. The just struggle of the people of all countries against pollution should be supported.

Principle 11   The environmental policies of all States should enhance and not adversely affect the present or future development potential of developing countries, nor should they hamper the attainment of better living conditions for all. . . .

Principle 21   States have . . . the sovereign right to exploit their own resources pursuant to their own environment policies, and the responsibility to ensure that activities within their jurisdiction or control do not cause damage to the environment of other States or of areas beyond the limits of national jurisdiction.

Principle 26   Man and his environment must be spared the effects of nuclear weapons and all other means of mass destruction. States must strive to reach prompt agreement . . . on the elimination and complete destruction of such weapons.[20]

As with all international declarations and agreements, this declaration is the result of hard bargaining and compromise among states with different and conflicting interests. In particular, there has been conflict between the developed and the developing nations. Many people in the developed nations worry that the environment can't sustain a level of economic growth that would enable a large part of the population of the developing world to enjoy a middle-class lifestyle. Developing nations, on the other hand, want economic growth to lift more of their people out of poverty. They are calling on the developed nations to transfer more resources and technology to them so that they can achieve sufficient levels of growth. And they are asking people in the developed world to consume less so that there will be more available for their people to consume. The difficult task is to balance economic development with environmental protection.

The 1992 Rio Declaration on Environment and Development

In 1992, the United Nations Conference on Environment and Development met in Rio de Janeiro and agreed to the set of principles called the Rio Declaration. The Rio Declaration is considered a follow-up to the 1972 Stockholm Declaration. The concept of sustainable development had not yet evolved in 1972. In 1992 it was the center of attention.

Principle 1   Human beings are the centre of concerns for sustainable development. They are entitled to a healthy and productive life in harmony with nature.

Principle 3   The right to development must be fulfilled so as to equitably meet the developmental and environmental needs of present and future generations.

Principle 4   In order to achieve sustainable development, environmental protection shall constitute an integral part of the development process. . . .

Principle 5   All States and all people shall cooperate in the essential task of eradicating poverty as an indispensable requirement for sustainable development, in order to decrease the disparities in standards of living and better meet the needs of the majority of the people of the world. . . .

Principle 7   States shall cooperate in a spirit of global partnership to conserve, protect, and restore the health and integrity of the Earth's ecosystem. . . . The developed countries acknowledge the responsibility that they bear in the international pursuit of sustainable development in view of the pressures their societies place on the global environment and of the technologies and financial resources they command.

Principle 24   Warfare is inherently destructive of sustainable development. States shall therefore respect international law providing protection for the environment in times of armed conflict and cooperate in its further development, as necessary.

Principle 25   Peace, development, and environmental protection are interdependent and indivisible.

The Rio Declaration recognizes the vital importance of economic development for the poorer nations. Poverty-stricken people overexploit their environment. Therefore, economic development to alleviate poverty must be an integral part of environmental policy. In addition, the Declaration recognizes the role that women must play if the environment is to be saved from overexploitation and destruction. Unless women gain the power to control their fertility, population growth will probably remain at unsustainable levels in poor countries. In countries where men have a lot of control over women, birth rates are higher. Studies have shown that women are more likely than men to use the economic resources they control to benefit their children and families rather than themselves. For example, on average poor men spend a lot more of their income on cigarettes and alcohol for themselves than women do.

CREATING A SUSTAINABLE SOCIETY

What, if anything, can be done? What, if anything, should be done? Many environmentalists say that we now have a global economic system that is "unsustainable." In their view, because the global system of industrial capitalism creates huge amounts of waste and pollution that poison the planet and depletes scarce nonrenewable resources, it is destroying its own foundations. The system may be able to function in this way for several decades, but eventually it will cease to function. The currently unsustainable system must be transformed into a "sustainable" society—an economic system that can continue to meet the needs of people into the foreseeable future without destroying its own foundations.

Creating a sustainable society requires many changes. Production processes must be redesigned and made more efficient so that more is produced with less. Where possible, renewable clean sources of energy would replace the nonrenewable fossil fuels that pollute the planet. It also would mean design changes in production processes to reduce or eliminate waste, whether hazardous or nonhazardous. Where waste is generated, every effort would be made to recycle—to find a way of using that waste in some other production process. Hazardous waste, if it could not be eliminated, would be stored safely. The agricultural sector of the economy would have to reduce its reliance on human-made pesticides and fertilizers, and rely more on organic farming. Pesticides and fertilizers harm the environment in many ways that are now clearly recognized. Their use must be minimized. Products would be redesigned so that they operate more efficiently, especially in their use of energy. For example, motor vehicles would be redesigned to be more fuel efficient and electric appliances redesigned to use less electricity. Products should also be designed to be reusable or recyclable rather than disposable.

Consumers would need to be more environmentally responsible and sensitive in their purchases. First, we would need to refrain from buying things we don't need, especially products that use energy. We would need to stop discarding things because they are "out of style." We would need to refrain from buying disposable items. Second, people would need to buy and use more environmentally friendly products and refrain from buying and using environmentally unfriendly products. For example, we would need to buy vehicles that are fuel efficient rather than gas guzzlers. Third, we could refrain from buying the products of companies that behave in an environmentally irresponsible way, voting with our dollars, and organize boycotts and public criticism. We can refrain from investing in companies that do not meet our standards of environmental responsibility.

People would also need to change their habits. More reliance on mass transportation or carpooling, or on alternatives such as bicycling or walking, and less reliance on the private automobile would help preserve the environment. We need to keep our homes cooler in winter and warmer in summer. We must insulate our homes and make them more energy efficient. We must recycle and reuse products while avoiding disposable items.

Government also could help increase sustainability. It could raise taxes on energy to encourage conservation. It could provide subsidies for consumers to insulate their homes or purchase energy saving technology. It could provide money for research and development of alternative energy sources and for mass transportation. It could provide tax incentives for companies to invest in pollution control technology, pass laws regulating waste and pollution, mandate fuel efficiency minimums for motor vehicles, and provide funds for population control, on both a national and a global level. It could provide education to sensitize people to the necessity of being more environmentally responsible. It could provide economic assistance to poor countries to help them protect their environments.

Some environmentalists claim that many companies have few incentives to reduce the pollution and waste they generate as long as they don't have to pay the full cost of the environmental damage they cause. Companies that pollute are not charged for the human illnesses and damage to flora and fauna that their pollution causes. If companies that pollute were charged the full cost of their pollution, then they would have a great incentive to change the way they do things.

Opposition to Sustainability

If sustainability were cost free, there would be no resistance to it. In fact, however, many industries and individual companies will have increased costs because of the expense of controlling the amount of pollution they emit or of safely disposing of hazardous wastes they generate. Owners of polluting sources of energy such as oil and coal may see the value of their investments decline if alternative sources of energy are developed. A company may lose profits or go out of business if its products are replaced by less polluting alternatives.

Because they believe that they face economic loss if sustainable economies are implemented, many business and political leaders have criticized as "environmental extremists" those who want to create sustainable economies, which they say will harm the industrialized countries by dramatically lowering their standards of living. Jobs will be lost, salaries and wages will decline, prices and taxes will rise, and government regulation will increase.

Although some industries, individual businesses, and individual people will indeed face economic losses if sustainable economies are created, it's far less clear that industrialized societies as a whole will lose out. Some people will gain. If pollution is reduced, the lives of some people will be saved and the health of many people will be improved. Similarly, if new technologies and new resources are developed, the owners of and workers in these new industries will be economic winners even if older industries and companies are economic losers.

Applying Moral Theories

If we apply moral theories to the question of sustainable economies, we cannot limit our gaze to its effects on just one country, such as the United States, or one social class. The moral point of view is impartial. In order to evaluate environmental policy and sustainable economies from an impartial point of view, we must consider the interests of all people on the planet. (Whether we can limit our view to our own species is discussed later in this chapter.)

For example, if we apply utilitarianism to questions of environmental policy, we must consider not only the gains and losses of people in the industrialized countries but also the gains and losses of people around the world. A utilitarian could thus defend creating a sustainable economy by claiming that shifting to it would increase the total happiness or well-being of the human race.

If we apply the universal law formulation of Kant's Categorical Imperative, we will ask whether a maxim such as the following could consistently be willed a universal law:

> I will use up the world's nonrenewable resources and pollute the environment when it benefits me.

If a rational agent could not will such a universal law without contradiction, then acting in accordance with such a maxim is immoral. A Kantian could then maintain that no rational agent could will such a maxim without contradicting himself or herself. If we apply the respect for persons formulation of the Categorical Imperative, we must ask whether we are treating everyone with respect if we follow policies of "unsustainable" development. A Kantian might maintain that if we pollute and deplete resources, we are not treating other people with respect because some people are harmed by it when harm to them is avoidable. We are not making their ends our own.

Present Versus Future People

According to many environmentalists, unless we change our ways, our industrial civilization will break down within a few generations. But why should we care about the future? Why should we sacrifice now in order to benefit people who haven't even been born?

Suppose that some form of pollution will not affect any presently existing people. For example, suppose that highly toxic wastes could be dumped into the ocean encased in concrete that will last a hundred years. When the concrete cases finally disintegrate and release the toxic waste, no presently existing people will be harmed. Do presently existing people have moral duties only to other presently existing people, or do they also have moral duties to future people? Do only presently existing people have moral rights, or do future people also have moral rights?

We could argue that from a moral point of view, the time during which people exist is irrelevant; as long as they can be harmed or benefited by an action, their interests must be considered. Thus, for example, from a utilitarian perspective, the interests of future people are no less important than the interests of presently existing people. Similarly, we could argue that it's irrelevant, from a Kantian or hypothetical social contract perspective, that people would be harmed who have not yet come into existence. In adopting a moral point of view, we are supposed to be impartial. Impartiality requires not only that we shouldn't be influenced by differences of race, sex, national origin, religion, and sexual orientation, but also by our location in space and time. Therefore, we could argue that presently existing people have the same moral duties toward future people as they have toward other presently existing people and that future people have the same moral rights as presently existing people.

ENVIRONMENTAL RACISM AND JUSTICE

As paradoxical as it may seem, environmental degradation provides benefits as well as burdens. Industries that pollute, deplete resources, and consume energy also make profits for their owners, generate high salaries for their managers, and provide wages for their workers—all clearly benefits. The burdens, of course, are pollution and depleted resources. Balancing the burdens and benefits of environmental degradation is complicated by the fact that these benefits and burdens are not fairly distributed. Often the people who benefit most are able to escape shouldering the burdens while the people who bear most of the burdens receive few of the benefits.

Studies have shown that in the United States an unusually high percentage of polluting industries and hazardous waste facilities are located in communities of poor people of color, particularly African Americans, Latinos, and Native Americans. The people who own the industries and benefit most from them do not live in the communities where they are located; the people who live in the communities where they are located generally do not benefit much from them.

The reason is power. Communities that are predominantly white and middle or upper class don't want pollutants and hazardous wastes in their communities, and they have the political influence to keep them out. Communities that are predominantly African American, Latino, or Native American usually don't have the same kind of political influence, and they get stuck with them.

For example, in 1970 the Harris County (Texas) Board of Supervisors forbade placement of a municipal solid waste landfill in Northwood Manor, a subdivision of the city of Houston. At the time, Northwood Manor was predominantly white. By 1979 Northwood Manor had become predominantly African American. In that year, the Board of Supervisors approved placement of the landfill there. Robert D. Bullard writes:

> Houston has a long history of locating its solid waste facilities in communities of color, especially in African American neighborhoods. From the early 1920s through the late 1970s, all five of the city-owned sanitary landfills and six of the eight municipal solid waste incinerators were located in mostly African American neighborhoods. Similarly, three of the four privately owned solid waste landfills were located in mostly African American communities during this period. African Americans, however, made up only 28 percent of the city's population.[21]

Similarly, in 1982, 30,000 cubic yards of soil was contaminated in North Carolina as a result of illegal dumping of toxic compounds known as PCBs. The site selected for burying the toxic soil was in Warren County, North Carolina, a mostly African American county. Opponents maintained that the site was not chosen because of scientific evidence showing that it was the most appropriate location. Rather, they claimed, the decision was purely political. Counties that were predominantly white were able to use their influence to keep it out of their communities.[22]

A 1983 report by the General Accounting Office of the United States government "found a strong relationship between the location of off-site hazardous waste landfills and the race and socioeconomic status of the surrounding communities."[23] For example, in EPA region IV, comprising Alabama, Florida, Georgia, Kentucky, Mississippi, North Carolina, South Carolina, and Tennessee, three of the four hazardous waste landfills were located in predominantly African-American communities, although African Americans made up only 20 percent of the population of region IV.

Similarly, a 1992 study by staff writers from the *National Law Journal* concluded that "there is a racial divide in the way the U.S. government cleans up toxic waste sites and punishes polluters. White communities see faster action, better results and stiffer penalties than communities where blacks, Hispanics and other minorities live."[24] In addition, Bullard claims that "African Americans and Latino Americans are more likely than whites to live in areas with reduced air quality." He quotes a report by researchers from the National Argonne Laboratory who found that "a total of 33 percent of whites, 50 percent of African Americans, and 60 percent of Hispanics live in the 136 counties in which two or more air pollutants exceed standards."[25] Bullard points to Chicago's Southeast neighborhood around Altgeld

Gardens, a housing project. The neighborhood is 70 percent African American and 11 percent Latino; it is "encircled by municipal and hazardous waste landfills, toxic waste incinerators, grain elevators, sewer treatment facilities, smelters, steel mills, and a host of other polluting industries."[26]

Regina Austin and Michael Schill summarize the imbalance:

> People of color throughout the United States are receiving more than their fair share of the poisonous fruits of industrial production. They live cheek by jowl with waste dumps, incinerators, landfills, smelters, factories, chemical plants, and oil refineries whose operations make them sick and kill them young. They are poisoned by the air they breathe, the water they drink, the fish they catch, the vegetables they grow, and in the case of children, the very ground they play on.[27]

If they and Bullard are right, then our country faces a situation that is unjust. People in our country are not receiving equal protection from environmental degradation. The burdens of that degradation are being shifted to the shoulders of the least powerful and most vulnerable of our citizens, people of color—precisely those people who, from an economic point of view, benefit least from that degradation. Something needs to be done to ensure that middle- and upper-class whites, who benefit the most, shoulder their fair share of the burdens of environmental degradation. What might be some morally acceptable solutions to the problem?

One solution might be to export polluting industries and the pollution they cause to Third World countries in Latin America, Africa, and Asia. For example, chemical manufacturing plants can be moved to nations such as India so that they will pollute those nations rather than ours. An added benefit is that most developing countries have far less stringent laws protecting their environments, so factories can spend less on safety and pollution control. (Consider the environmental disaster in Bhopal, India, where a chemical plant exploded, leaking out a highly toxic substance that killed and injured several thousand people living near it.) We could also build hazardous waste landfills and incinerators in these nations and send them our toxic wastes. (We are already exporting some toxic wastes in this way) But the question is, "Would it be just? Would it be morally acceptable?" Given the moral requirement of impartiality, the answer is obvious.

LIFE-CENTERED VERSUS HUMAN-CENTERED
ENVIRONMENTAL ETHICS

So far we have discussed environmental ethics as though only human well-being counts from a moral point of view. However, we should keep in mind that human beings constitute only one species out of the tens of millions that exist on Earth. Many environmentalists claim that it is arbitrary to think that only human beings have moral standing. They think that we should consider the effects of our behavior not only on other human beings but on all living creatures.

We use nonhuman living things in a variety of ways. We kill and eat many of them, for example, cows, pigs, deer, sheep, rabbits, and fish. We hunt and kill them for sport. We kill them for their fur or skin. We use them in medical experiments to test new drugs or new forms of surgery. We use them in schools, where they are dissected by students or observed and conditioned in psychology laboratories. We test cosmetics on them. We confine them in zoos, circuses, and aquariums and sometimes train them to behave in ways that are not natural to them, such as training a seal to balance a ball on its nose or a whale to leap over a net. We keep them as pets. We encourage them to fight and kill each other for our entertainment, as in rooster or dog fights. We may sacrifice them to our gods or fight and kill them for entertainment, as in bullfighting. Is our treatment of nonhuman animals morally acceptable? May we use them in any way we please, ignoring their well-being?

Many environmentalists claim that nonhuman living things count from a moral point of view. In contrast to a human-centered ethics that assumes that only human beings have moral worth and that takes account only of human harm and benefit in moral deliberation, many environmentalists recommend a life-centered ethics that assumes that all living things have some moral worth and that takes account of the harm and benefit to all living things.

Peter Singer maintains that when we limit moral worth and status to human beings, it is parallel to whites who limit moral worth and status to other whites (racism) and males who limit moral worth and status to other males (sexism). Singer calls it "speciesism."[28] In his view, speciesism is as morally objectionable as other forms of arbitrary and unjust discrimination.

Paul W. Taylor has presented a theoretical defense of a life-centered ethics. He argues that all living things have what he calls "inherent worth" and should be treated with respect. According to him, human beings are superior to other creatures only from a human-centered point of view. But if humans are not superior according to any objective standard, then there is no justification for treating humans better than we treat nonhuman animals. That is not an invitation to treat human beings with as little respect as we treat nonhuman animals. Rather, it is an invitation to treat nonhuman animals with the same kind of respect that we treat (or should treat) human beings.

Why should we treat human beings with respect? According to Taylor, it is because human beings have intrinsic worth. We have intrinsic worth because we are alive and conscious and because we are the product of billions of years of evolution. But we cannot prove that we have intrinsic worth. We can only say that it is an assumption that is reasonable given a clear understanding of our nature. Similarly, according to Taylor, we cannot prove that nonhuman animals have intrinsic worth. But according to him, it is an assumption that is reasonable given a clear understanding of the facts. Human beings are related to all other living things. We are part of a family of life. The differences between us and other living things are only a matter of degree. All other living things are as alive as we are. Many of them are conscious. Many of them have a form of intelligence akin to our own. All forms of life are interdependent in a variety of ways. All are the product of evolution that occurred over billions of years. As a result, Taylor claims, not only do all living things have inherent worth, they have equal inherent worth, whether an oak tree, an insect, a fish, a cow, an elephant, or a human being all have equal inherent worth.

Does this mean that it is never morally acceptable for us to use or harm nonhuman living things? Is it wrong to cut down a tree to build a house? To kill a cow and eat it? To test drugs and surgical procedures on animals? To hunt? To place animals in zoos and use them in circuses and rodeos? To kill insects that carry bacteria or viruses that cause human diseases? Human life would be impossible if we did not use other living things. Accepting this reality, Taylor does not advocate behavior that would lead to human extinction or mass misery. However, he does say that a commitment to the equal inherent worth of all living things requires change. "In order to share the Earth with other species," he states, "we humans must impose limits on our population, our habits of consumption, and our technology."[29]

According to Taylor, all living creatures—including human beings—have a right of self-defense. Thus, "it is permissible for [human beings] to protect themselves against dangerous or harmful organisms by destroying them."[30] If a mad dog or a lion is threatening to attack you, it is morally acceptable to kill it if that is the only way to protect yourself. The right of self-defense also justifies us in killing bacteria and viruses that threaten our health, as well as other living things that may carry such bacteria and viruses, such as mosquitoes, fleas, and rats.

Taylor also makes a distinction between basic and nonbasic interests:

> The interests of an organism can be of different degrees of comparative importance to it. One of its interests is of greater importance to it than another, either if the occurrence of the first makes a more substantial contribution to the realization of its good than the second, or if the occurrence of the first is a necessary condition of the preservation of its existence, while the occurrence of the second is not. We might say that one interest is of greater importance than another to the extent that the nonfulfillment of the first will constitute a more serious deprivation or loss than the nonfulfillment of the second. The most important interests are those whose fulfillment is needed by an organism if it is to remain alive.[31]

When the interests of human beings and nonhuman living organisms conflict, the basic interests of human beings may prevail. However, if a nonbasic interest of human beings conflicts with a basic interest of a nonhuman living organism, then the basic interest of the nonhuman living organism should prevail.

For example, if we human beings need to kill and eat other living creatures in order to survive, then it is morally acceptable for us to do so because life is our most basic interest and we need not sacrifice our own lives or existence as a species in order to preserve the lives of other organisms. We are not morally required to commit suicide. However, our desire for entertainment is a nonbasic interest. If we are entertained by watching bullfights or by hunting and killing deer, then the basic interest of bulls and deer in continued life should prevail over our nonbasic interest in mere entertainment. Taylor gives examples of other instances where, because the interests of humans are nonbasic while the interests of the other living things are basic, a kind of action is not morally acceptable:

> Slaughtering elephants so the ivory of their tusks can be used to carve items of the tourist trade. Killing rhinoceros so that their horns can be used as dagger handles. Trapping and killing reptiles, such as snakes, crocodiles, alligators, and turtles, for their skins and shells to be used in making expensive shoes, handbags, and other "fashion" products. Hunting and killing rare wild mammals, such as leopards and jaguars, for the luxury fur trade.[32]

However, some nonbasic interests may be so important for human well-being that even the basic interests of living organisms may be sacrificed for them if the interests can be protected in no other way. Taylor gives the following examples:

> Building an art museum or library where natural habitat must be destroyed. Constructing an airport, railroad, harbor, or highway involving the serious disturbance of a natural ecosystem. Damming a free-flowing river for a hydro-electric power project.[33]

Although these projects are not essential for continued human existence or health, they may be so important for ensuring a meaningful, satisfying human life that we are justified in sacrificing the basic interests of other living things.

However, Taylor maintains that just as commonsense, human-centered ethics assumes that we have a duty to minimize the harm we cause other humans, life-centered ethics assumes that we have a duty to minimize the harm that we cause other nonhuman living things. When basic or important human interests are in conflict with the basic interests of other living things, we should take concrete steps to ensure that we require the smallest possible sacrifice of their interests. We should harm as few living things as possible, minimize the destruction or disruption of ecosystems and habitats, and take special steps and assume substantial costs to avoid causing the extinction of an organism.

EXERCISES

1. Do you believe that threats to the environment are serious? Defend your answer. (Specify particular kinds of alleged environmental threats and the basis for your evaluation of their seriousness.)

2. How would shifting to policies of sustainable development affect the lives of individuals in the United States among (1) the rich, (2) the middle class, and (3) the poor? How would it affect business and government? Defend your answer.

3. You have been elected President of the United States. One of your first tasks is to draft a statement of principles and a detailed policy agenda for dealing with both national and international environmental problems. What would your statement say?

4. A certain region of the country that depends on logging for its prosperity has a dilemma. Major sections of forest in that region are the last natural habitats of several varieties of insect and one bird species. If logging is permitted, the insect varieties and bird species will almost certainly become extinct. However, unemployment in the region is high. If logging is permitted, many unemployed workers in the region will be employed again; if it remains forbidden, they will remain unemployed. Should logging be permitted?

5. Toxins-R-Us has submitted an application to the state to build a solid waste incinerator. They have chosen a site in a community that is 70 percent African American and Latino because they believe that primarily white communities have enough political influence to put up a long, hard, expensive fight over the application. Because the community has a very high unemployment rate and Toxics-R-Us promises to provide more than 100 new jobs, many of the community's political leaders have decided not to oppose the application. However, environmental activists are opposing the application, calling it a case of environmental racism and injustice. Opponents have pointed out that three of the four solid waste incinerators are in primarily minority communities in a state that has an African American and Latino population of about 20 percent. If the new incinerator is built in this community, then four of the five solid waste incinerators in the state will be located in primarily minority communities. Should something be done to prevent the building of the incinerator in this community? Why or why not? If something should be done, what precisely could be done?

6. Bug-Away is selling in Third World countries a pesticide that it manufactures in the United States. The EPA has banned its use in the United States because it is considered too toxic and long-lasting. The pesticide is not prohibited by the laws of the Third World countries in which it is sold. Is there anything wrong with Bug-Away's activities?

7. Is it morally acceptable to capture wild animals, such as lions, elephants, tigers, whales, dolphins, and seals, and use them in circuses and aquariums?

8. A high school student has petitioned the local school board to stop the practice of dissecting dead animals in biology class. She maintains that students can learn from computer simulations everything they now learn by dissection. If you were on the school board, would you vote for or against her petition? How would you defend your decision?

SUGGESTED READINGS

National Academy of Sciences. *One Earth, One Future*. Washington, DC: National Academy Press, 1990.

National Academy of Sciences. *Climate Change Science*. Washington, DC: National Academy Press, 2001.

Max Oelschlaeger, *The Idea of Wilderness*. New Haven Press: Yale University, 1991.

Mostafa K. Tolba. *Saving Our Planet*. London: Chapman & Hall, 1992.

United Nations Human Development Report. New York: Oxford University Press, Annual Editions.

Donald VanDeVeer and Christine Pierce, eds. *The Environmental Ethics and Policy Book*. Belmont, CA: Wadsworth, 1994.

World Commission on Environment and Development. *Our Common Future*. New York: Oxford University Press, 1987.

INTERNET RESOURCES

Intergovernmental Panel on Climate Change (IPCC) (http://www. ipcc.ch).

Rio Declaration on Environment and Development (1992) (http://www .greenpeace.org/%7Eintlaw/rio1.html).

Stockholm Declaration on the Environment (1972) (http://www.tufts.edu/departments /fletcher/multi/texts/STOCKHOLM-DECL.txt).

U.N. Framework Convention on Climate Change (1992) (http://www.unfcc.de/text /resource/conv/conv.html).

U.S. Clean Air Act, Summary (http://www.epa.gov/region5/defs/html/caa.htm).

ENDNOTES

1. "Rate of Oceans' Rise Doubles over 150 Years," *The Australian* (26 November 2005).
2. Fiona Harvey, "Retreat of Antarctic Ice Gathers Pace," *Financial Times*, London: (21 April 2005).
3. IPCC Working Group I, *Third Assessment Report* (February 2001), p. 1. (http://www.ipcc.ch).
4. Ibid.
5. National Academy of Sciences, *Climate Change Science* (Washington: DC: National Academy Press, 2001), p. 1.
6. Ibid., p. 4.
7. *Human Development Report 2000* (New York: Oxford University Press, 2000), pp. 231–234.
8. "Bush, in Reversal, Won't Seek Cut in Emissions of Carbon Dioxide," *New York Times* (14 March 2001).
9. Mostafa K. Tolba, *Saving Our Planet* (London: Chapman & Hall, 1992), p. 46. (This book is a product of the United Nations Environmental Programme, of which Tolba is executive director.)
10. Ibid., pp. 150–152.
11. Ibid., pp. 150–152.
12. Ibid., pp. 150–151.

13. *Human Development Report 2000*, pp. 227–230.

14. National Academy of Sciences, *One Earth*, p. 128.

15. World Commission on Environment and Development, *Our Common Future* (New York: Oxford University Press, 1987), p. 148.

16. Max Oelschlaeger, *The Idea of Wilderness* (New Haven: Yale University Press, 1991), p. 2.

17. Joel E. Cohen, *How Many People Can the Earth Support?* (New York: Norton, 1995).

18. Ibid., p. 53.

19. *Human Development Report 2000*, p. 218.

20. http://www.tufts.edu/departments/fletcher/multi/texts/STOCKHOLM-DECL.txt.

21. Robert D. Bullard, "Environmental Justice for All," in *Unequal Protection: Environmental Justice and Communities of Color*, ed. Robert D. Bullard (San Francisco: Sierra Club Books, 1994), p. 4.

22. Ibid., p. 5.

23. Ibid., p. 6.

24. Ibid., p. 9.

25. Ibid., p. 12.

26. Ibid., p. 14.

27. Regina Austin and Michael Schill, "Black, Brown, Red, and Poisoned," in Bullard, *Unequal Protection*, p. 53.

28. Peter Singer, *Practical Ethics* (Cambridge, England: Cambridge University Press, 1979), Chapters 2 and 3.

29. Paul W. Taylor, *Respect for Nature* (Princeton: Princeton University Press, 1986), p. 258.

30. Ibid., pp. 264–265.

31. Ibid., p. 271.

32. Ibid., p. 274.

33. Ibid., p. 276.

Appendix A
Moral Decision Making

We can now try to pull together the material on moral theories to provide an informal blueprint for making moral decisions about right and wrong. We will present them as a series of questions to ask ourselves.

1. What are all the relevant facts about this situation? Specifically:
   What do I know? What do I have good reason to believe? What do I merely suspect? What information is missing? What individuals will be affected and how will they be affected?

   How will the social environment be affected?

   How will the physical environment be affected?

   How will nonhuman sentient creatures be affected?

   Has anyone created obligations by his or her acts? If so, what are they?

2. What action will produce the least total harm? (We should not do something if there are alternative actions that will produce less harm.)

3. What actions probably will produce the most overall or total benefit? (That an act would increase total well-being is a good moral reason to do it.)

4. How will the action affect my well-being? If it will reduce it, are the sacrifices too great or unreasonable? (If the sacrifices to the agent are too great, that is a reason for not doing it.)

5. What justified moral principles or rules apply in this situation? (That my action would violate a justified moral principle is a good moral reason not to do it.)

6. How would I want others to treat me in this situation if I were the acted upon rather than the agent? (That I wouldn't want others to treat me the way I will treat others is a good moral reason not to do it.)

7. If I act in this way, would I be treating everyone with respect? (That I would not be treating all people with respect is a good moral reason not to do something.)

8. What virtues or vices would be exemplified in my action? What would a virtuous person do in this situation? (That an act would exemplify a vice or that a virtuous person would not do it is a good moral reason not to do it.)

9. What rights do people have that are relevant in this situation? What rights would I probably violate? What rights would I probably respect? If people's rights conflict, which rights should take priority because they're more important? (That an act would violate people's rights is a good moral reason not to do it.)

10. What would be the caring, compassionate thing to do in these circumstances? (That an act would exemplify compassion is a good moral reason for doing it.)

11. Do these moral reasons conflict? That is, do the different questions yield different answers in this situation? If yes, which way of deciding should take priority?

Appendix B
Thinking About Case Studies

In thinking about the case studies that follow, try to answer the following questions to help guide your reasoning.

1. What did people do? Why did they behave as they did?

2. What are the relevant facts about the context or circumstances?

3. How did their behavior affect other people, the social environment, other sentient beings, and the physical environment?

4. If people's behavior caused harm, were they justified in acting as they did? If yes, what justified their actions?

5. If people's behavior caused harm, did they have alternatives that would have caused less harm? If yes, how much of a sacrifice of their own interests would have been required?

6. Was any good done? If yes, what good and to whom?

7. Were any justified moral principles or rules violated? If yes, were the violations justified? If yes, what justifies? If yes, what justifies them?

8. How would I want others to treat me if I were in this situation? (This may require thinking about the question from the perspective of the different people in the situation, both those acting and the people acted upon.) Which perspective takes priority? Why?

9. Was everyone treated with respect?

10. What virtues or vices were exemplified in people's behavior?

11. Were anyone's rights violated? If yes, what rights? Were the violations justified? If yes, what justified the violations? If people's rights were in conflict, which should take priority? Why?

Overall Evaluations:

12. Did anyone do anything that was morally wrong? If yes, what acts or omissions were morally wrong? What should they have done? Why?

13. Did anyone do anything that was morally right or good? If yes, what acts or omissions were right or good? Why was it morally right or good? Is what they did praiseworthy? If yes, why?

14. What would you have done if you were the decision maker? Why?

Case Studies

McWANE, INC.

If the claims made in a series of articles that appeared in the *New York Times* in January 2003 are true, and there are ample reasons to believe that they are, then the words that Dante said are inscribed over the door to hell apply to workers unfortunate enough to be employed by McWane, Inc., of Birmingham, Alabama—Abandon All Hope, You Who Enter Here.[1] According to the series, the results of a nine-month investigation undertaken by the *New York Times*, PBS's *Front Line*, and the Canadian Broadcasting Corporation, McWane, Inc., one of the biggest makers of sewer and water pipe, at that time was among the most egregious violators of laws governing environmental protection and worker health and safety. McWane pipe plants, located in many different states, employed about 5,000 workers. From 1995 to 2002, there were at least 4,600 injuries and 9 deaths. McWane's injury rate was four times greater than the injury rates of its four major competitors COMBINED! The company had over 400 citations for violations of Federal health and safety laws.

For example, Rolan Hoskins, a master electrician employed by McWane's Tyler Pipe in Tyler, Texas, was killed on June 29, 2000, after less than two months on the job. He was repairing a conveyor belt. Federal law requires that conveyor belts be shut down when maintenance is performed on them. The belt had not been shut down. Federal law requires that there be safety guards to protect workers from being caught in the apparatus and pulled into it. There were no safety guards. Rolan Hoskins had been trained to repair the belt while it was still running, even though it was a violation of Federal law. When did he receive the training? The night he was killed by the conveyor belt, he was trying to repair it while it was running. His left arm got caught in the conveyor belt, which pulled him into the machinery, first crushing his arm and shoulder and then crushing his skull.

McWane systematically violated worker health and safety laws in order to keep churning out more pipe at the lowest possible cost. Executives calculated that it was cheaper to violate the laws and pay the fines and penalties than to conform to the laws. Workers were forced to work 12–16 hours per day, sometimes six or seven days per week. Tired workers are at greater risk in a place as dangerous as a pipe foundry. Supervisors were rewarded only for producing more pipe and penalized if they took actions that reduced the amount of pipe churned out, even if it was action to protect workers. Supervisors were not penalized if a worker was injured or killed during their shift. Thus, Rolan Hoskins's supervisor would have been penalized if he shut down the conveyor while Rolan repaired it; he was not penalized for getting Rolan killed.

In April 1996, Juan Jimenez fell 55 feet to his death after stepping on a skylight as he and other members of his crew cleaned gutters on the roof of a McWane building. Federal law requires that there be guard rails around skylights. There were none. On January 22, 1997, Ira Cofer crawled down into a machine pit alone in order to make repairs. Although written company policy forbade workers to work alone in the pits, the practice of working with someone else had proved too costly, so that the rule was systematically ignored by workers and supervisors. Like other conveyor belts, the one that Mr. Cofer was working on lacked the required safety guards. While working alone in the pit, Mr. Ofer's arm got caught in the conveyor belt. He was luckier than Rolan Hoskins. Over a three-hour period, the conveyor belt sanded away the flesh and bone from his fingertips to above his elbow. He lost an arm, not his life. During his three-hour ordeal, he screamed for help, but because of all the noise, no one heard him. Plant mangers blamed Mr. Cofer for his injuries. After all, written company policy explicitly stated that workers are to keep their hands and arms away from moving conveyor belts and are not to work alone in the pits. Within months of Mr. Ofer's injury, four other workers suffered similar injuries. By 2000, 60 percent of maintenance workers had been injured, and management was fully aware of that fact. Senior managers knew that required safety features were missing and that workers were routinely violating the supposed company policy not to work alone in the pits, but they never added the missing safety features or ordered workers to comply with written policy.

In 1998, 19-year-old Shane Shaw came close to dying from arsenic poisoning from removing material from a casting machine without a respirator. He wasn't told that the material was laced with arsenic and therefore highly toxic. He wasn't told that he was supposed to wear a respirator.

McWane is also accused of doctoring the evidence to get itself off the hook. On March 24, 2000, Alfred Coxe was run over and killed by a forklift. Before investigators showed up, the forklift was taken to the repair shop to have its defective brakes repaired. Police tried to preserve the crime scene for the detectives. Before the detectives arrived, McWane workers drove a street sweeper over the area many times, obliterating chalk and tire marks. The driver of the forklift said that the brakes had failed and that supervisors knew that most of the forklifts had defective brakes and horns, which was later confirmed by OSHA inspectors. OSHA inspectors also discovered that many forklift drivers, including the driver of the forklift that killed Alfred Coxe, were not certified to run forklifts.

The question is often asked, Why do bad things happen to good people? A variation on this question is, Why are bad things done by good people? Top management, middle management, and line supervisors at McWane plants turned a blind eye to what is happening as a result of their decisions and orders. We surely are tempted to ask what happened to people's conscience?

Michelle Sankowsky, a nurse, worked for only four months for McWane's Tyler Pipe as an occupational health and compensation manager. Her conscience forced her to quit. She discovered that her job primarily was to save the company money by reducing the number of injuries reported to OSHA. One way to reduce the number of reported injuries, obviously, is to reduce the actual number of injuries by making the work environment safer. Another way is to manipulate the numbers. McWane management had a blame-the-victim mentality, so it assumed that most workers who claimed that they were injured were lying or exaggerating. To detect fraud, all workers who claimed to be injured were required to report to the company's own physicians at a company hired by Tyler Pipe called Occu-Safe. Occu-Safe got the contract to provide medical care and evaluation because it promised to reduce the amount of money Tyler paid in worker's compensation. Michelle Sankowsky recognized a conflict of interest when she saw it. She knew that there was no way that Occu-Safe would provide unbiased diagnoses and health care to Tyler workers who were injured on the job.

On March 2, 2002, Marcos Lopez suffered a severe spinal compression fracture. When he was transported to Occu-Safe, the doctors didn't bother to order an x-ray or order him to go to a hospital. Instead, after a cursory examination, their diagnosis was back strain; he was given pain medication, sent home, and told to stay home for three days. In excruciating pain, Mr. Lopez returned to the Occu-Safe clinic twice. On his third visit, 12 days after he was injured, Occu-Safe physicians finally ordered an x-ray, which revealed the severity of his injuries. Incredibly, the clinic sent him home and did not inform him that the x-ray showed that he had a severe spinal compression fracture. Finally, after more than three weeks had passed since his injury, Mr. Lopez was sent to a surgeon. The surgeon noted that his injury had gotten worse since the accident because it had not been treated and Mr. Lopez was very close to being paralyzed for the rest of his life because of it. Cases such as this troubled Michelle Sankowsky's conscience so much that after only four months, she quit her job rather than participate in such conduct. Why did so few people follow Michelle Sankowsky's example?

Robert Rester, who worked for McWane for 24 years and rose to be a plant manager, didn't begin to question McWane's policies and practices until he found himself on the receiving end of them. He admits that he became like a robot, insensitive to the deaths and injuries. He didn't question the propriety of what he was doing until he was on the receiving end. He was on sick leave for a heart problem. McWane claimed that he had an alcohol problem that he refused to have treated and fired him. Robert Rester insists that it is a lie; he never had an alcohol problem.

McWane also was a massive violator of environmental laws. From 1995 to 2002 the company is known to have violated environmental laws at least 450 times. For example, rather than pay $750 to have 200 old tires safely disposed of, as was required by state law, the plant supervisor at Tyler Pipe ordered that the tires be burned. Supervisors admitted that they turned off equipment that would automatically shut down machinery if the pollution-controls malfunctioned. McWane plants routinely dumped contaminated water into rivers and streams in the dead of night rather than disposing of them safely.

DEATH AND TOBACCO

In the 1990s, the state of Connecticut joined about 40 other states in suing the major American tobacco companies to recover the $100 million per year it claimed to have paid for health care for smoking related illnesses. According to the suit, "More than 5,400 Connecticut residents die each year from tobacco-related causes." It further alleged that cigarette smoking shortened men's lives by an average of 11.6 years and women's by 12.8 years. ("Connecticut's Lawsuit Against the Tobacco Companies: Questions and Answers.")

The suit alleged that the tobacco companies knew as far back as 1953 that cigarette smoking was deadly but conspired to hide the truth from the public and to prevent research on the health hazards of cigarette smoking. In addition, although the tobacco industry had steadfastly denied that nicotine is addictive, it knew for decades that it is addictive and manipulated the nicotine content of its cigarettes in order to enhance its addictive properties in order to keep smokers hooked on them.

Finally, the suit alleged that the tobacco industry spent a lot of its $6 billion annual advertising budget to advertise to children, although the industry denied that it targeted children. The Connecticut suit pointed out that the average age when people begin to smoke is 13 and that 80 percent of adult smokers started smoking before they were 18.

The suit proceeded in part because Jeffrey Wigand, a scientist employed by the Brown & Williamson Tobacco Company, and Merrell Williams, a paralegal at the law firm of Wyatt Tarrant & Combs in Louisville, Kentucky, blew the whistle on the industry and provided insider information vital to the lawsuit. Wigand joined Brown & Williamson in 1988 in order to help create safer cigarettes. According to his account, he soon learned that the industry wasn't that interested. He said he learned that "cigarettes contain 600 additives and 4,000 to 8,000 chemical compounds, 'most of which you can't bury in a garbage dump, they're so toxic.' Some of the additives are designed 'to ameliorate the harshness of smoking and to facilitate and maintain addiction.'" ("Ex-'Insider' Jeffrey Wigand Says Tobacco Industry's Still Powerful.") He also learned that cigarettes cause fires that kill 1,000 to 1,500 people yearly. The project to create a safer cigarette was dropped when it became clear that it was probably impossible. Wigand was fired in 1993. Wigand signed an agreement with the company agreeing never to reveal information about the company and its activities.

According to Wigand, when he saw tobacco company executives lie under oath before a Congressional Committee headed by Representative Henry Waxman in 1994, he had had enough. The executives claimed that the management of the tobacco companies did not believe that cigarettes were a health hazard or that they were addictive, and claimed that they did not manipulate the nicotine content of cigarettes. Wigand knew that there were documents in Brown & Williamson's files that proved that the executives were lying. In 1995, Wigand agreed to testify before the Food and Drug Administration and at trials of cigarette companies, and he decided to make it public by going on the CBS program *60 Minutes*. According to some people, the producers of *60 Minutes* were afraid of being sued by Brown & Williamson because of its confidentiality agreement with Wigand and delayed the broadcast until the allegations were made public by the *Wall Street Journal*. Wigand also supplied documents he took from Brown & Williamson to the Food and Drug Administration to prove his allegations. Brown & Williamson sued Wigand for theft, fraud, and breach of contract.

Merrell Williams was a paralegal at a law firm that represented Brown & Williamson from 1989 to 1992. He was editing documents from Brown & Williamson in order to help the company hide the truth about cigarettes and what the company knew and did in order to help protect Brown & Williamson from lawsuits. When he read them, he says that his conscience bothered him, so he secretly photocopied about 4,000 documents and in 1993 gave them to people who made them public. The law firm sued Williams in 1993 for theft, fraud, breach of duties, and breach of contract ("Blowing the Whistle on Big Tobacco").

In June 1997, the tobacco companies reached an agreement both with the litigating states and the Federal government. The companies agreed to Federal control of cigarettes and their advertising, and to pay $368.5 billion over a 25-year period to compensate the states for the money they spent on medical care for smoking-related illnesses. Among other things, the agreement prohibits outdoor advertising of cigarettes and tobacco sponsorship of sports events. An important goal was reduction in teen smoking. Finally, the tobacco companies also had to agree to drop their suits against whistleblower Jeffrey Wigand.

In May 2000, the *Wall Street Journal* ran a story that claimed that the tobacco companies were still aggressively marketing cigarettes to children. M. Cass Wheeler, CEO of the American Heart Association, issued a statement commenting on the story. In it he said that the *Wall Street Journal's* allegations were corroborated by independent research by the Massachusetts Department of Public Health and the American Legacy Foundation, a group created by the settlement agreement with the tobacco companies to do research on tobacco-related issues. "Among the findings, the American Legacy Foundation . . . found that eight of the top 10 cigarette brands reached at least 70 percent of 12- to 17-year-old kids with five or more magazine advertisements in 1999" (http://www.americanheart.org/Support/Advocacy/youth_tobacco.html).

In August 2001, another series of allegations were published, this time by the *New York Times*. Reporter Alex Kuczynski claimed that although the tobacco companies said in their settlement with the states that they would not advertise in publications with more than 15 percent of or 2 million total readers under age 18, three of the four big tobacco companies were violating the agreement. The

Attorneys General of California, Oregon, New York, Ohio, and Washington sued the companies over the issue. For example, 23 percent of *Rolling Stone's* readers are under age 18, People magazine has 2.8 million readers under 18, *Sports Illustrated* has 4.9 million, and *TV Guide* has 5 million; nevertheless, tobacco companies still advertise in them. *Sports Illustrated* received $40 million in advertising from tobacco companies in 2000 according to Competitive Media reporting. Only the Philip Morris company abides by the agreement. R.J. Reynolds, Brown & Williamson, and Lorillard say they will not stop advertising in these magazines because "the limits they agreed to . . . were only guidelines, not laws."

The three tobacco companies said they were using different standards to determine whether a magazine was targeted at adults or youth. Brown & Williamson said it would not advertise in magazines with more than 15 percent of readers below age 18, but it would not follow the standard of not advertising in magazines where more than 2 million readers are under 18. The publisher of *People* magazine said he was "comfortable" accepting cigarette advertisements, and pointed out that there were no laws forbidding the magazine to accept cigarette ads and that the tobacco settlement applied to the tobacco companies, not to the magazine. The report also pointed out that at least 12 American newspapers, including the *New York Times*, decided not to run cigarette ads after May 1999 ("Tobacco Industry Still Advertises in Magazines Read by Youth").

In May 2001, the World Health Organization released a report that pointed to an increase in the number of women who smoke worldwide. According to the report, cigarette smoking causes 4 million premature deaths each year, but while smoking among men is decreasing, smoking among women is increasing. The report cited a number of causal factors, but one was an aggressive marketing campaign by tobacco companies specifically targeting women, some of which link smoking with "liberation" and "emancipation" ("Tobacco Companies Target Women").

In 1998, the American Heart Association claimed that "historically, tobacco companies have used their economic power to wield considerable influence on the political process." According to the AHA, the tobacco industry contributed "$4.75 million to the [political] parties in the first 18 months of the 1996 election cycle. . . ." Former Health and Human Services Secretary Louis Sullivan pointed out in 1992 that the tobacco companies were among the sponsors of the Republican National Convention that year, and Craig Fuller, a senior vice president of Philip Morris, was manager of the convention. The AHA also highlighted the fact that R.J. Reynolds canceled a $70 million per year Nabisco advertising account with Saatchi & Saatchi after the advertising company "produced an anti-smoking commercial for Northwest Airlines." The statement also said that some science and health writers "say that some of their articles dealing with smoking have been extensively edited when submitted to publications that carry cigarette advertising" ("Tobacco Industry's Economic and Political Clout").

In August 2001, the World Health Organization and the U.S. Centers for Disease Control and Prevention published a report detailing how the cigarette companies were marketing cigarettes to youth in poor countries. One way is to give teens free cigarettes to get them hooked. It is illegal in the United States for tobacco companies to give away free cigarettes to teens under age 18. According to the report, 11 percent of children 13 to 15 in Latin America and the Caribbean reported having been offered free cigarettes by tobacco company agents in 1999 and 2000. In South Africa it was 15.2 percent, in Moscow 16.7 percent, and in Jordan 24.8 percent. (It is illegal in Jordan to give cigarettes to teens under age 18.) In Moscow 33.8 percent of teens 13 to 15 are smokers, in South Africa and Costa Rica 26.6 percent , and in Jordan 17.7 percent. In Jordan, over 30 percent of boys 12 to 18 are smokers.

According to critics, the tobacco companies are desperate to find new customers because the number of smokers in the developed world is dropping because of anti-smoking campaigns and because their product kills their customers. Few people begin to smoke after the age of 18, so the tobacco companies must target those under 18, the younger the better.

According to the report, the tobacco companies employ many ways to attract teens. In the South Pacific, British American Tobacco puts sugar and honey in the cigarettes to sweeten them. The company denies that it is to make them especially appealing to teens, but documents from Brown & Williamson, its American subsidiary, show that as early as the 1970s the company was acutely aware that teens prefer sweet products and was considering sweeteners such as honey.

In Tirana, capital of Albania, young women, many under the age of 18, are paid by Philip Morris to don the costumes of Marlboro girls and give free cigarettes to people in the streets. One young girl who had the job said that as long as someone professed an interest in smoking and "doesn't look 14," it was OK to give him or her a free pack of cigarettes.

Although Philip Morris pledged to follow the same rules outside the United States that it follows inside it, the report claims that it has not adhered to its promise. "Health officials in many countries contend that the way Philip Morris products are promoted overseas often places cigarettes directly in the hands of children from Eastern Europe to Africa and the Middle East. Cigarettes are still handed out freely and sometimes by young people who are no more than children themselves" ("Enticing Third World Youth"). Philip Morris executives say that it is not company policy to give free cigarettes to teens but that some of its agents are overzealous and the company cannot monitor all agents in all countries to guarantee that they never put free cigarettes in the hands of people under 18. However, in 1990, Philip Morris commissioned a survey called the "youth generation study" that "examined Middle Eastern youth, from 13 to 15, tracking how much they smoked and how much extra spending money they had. Similar studies were done in Europe and Asia" ("Enticing Third World Youth").

"Connecticut's Lawsuit Against the Tobacco Companies: Questions and Answers," http://www.cslib.org/attygenl/tqanda.htm.

Mark Meltzer, "Ex-'Insider' Jeffrey Wigand Says Tobacco Industry's Still Powerful," *Atlanta Business Chronicle* (16 June 2000).

Hunt Helm, "Blowing the Whistle on Big Tobacco," *Louisville Courier-Journal* (25 May 1997), http://www.tobacco.org/ News/970525helms.html.

Alex Kuczynski, "Tobacco Industry Still Advertises in Magazines Read by Youth," *New York Times* (15 August 2001).

Gustavo Capdevila, "Tobacco Companies Target Women," DAWN Internet (www.dawn.com/2001/05/30/int14.htm).

"Tobacco Industry's Economic and Political Clout," American Heart Association, *1998*.

Greg Winter, "Enticing Third World Youth," *New York Times* (24 August 2001), p. C1.

ALLEGATIONS OF UNETHICAL PHARMACEUTICAL STUDIES IN NIGERIA

In August 2001, 30 Nigerian families brought suit in Federal court against Pfizer, Inc. The families claimed that Pfizer conducted unethical drug experiments on their children in Nigeria in 1996, when testing a drug named Trovan to determine whether it was safe and effective for treating children with meningitis. According to the suit, during a meningitis epidemic in Nigeria, Pfizer sent a research team to a hospital in Kano, Nigeria, to test the new medication. The team selected 100 children in the hospital to treat with Trovan and treated 100 other children at the hospital with chloramphenicol, a medication known to be safe and effective, as a control group. At the same hospital, the international organization Doctors Without Borders was already providing chloramphenicol free. The parents maintain that the Pfizer research team never told them that they were conducting an experiment with their children, never explained the potential dangers, and never informed them that they could refuse the experimental drug and still receive chloramphenicol free. Instead, the families said they thought that Pfizer was providing free treatment as an act of charity.

In addition, both the suit and newspaper reports claim that Pfizer never received the official approval required for conducting the experiment. But "when faced with an audit of its Trovan records by the Food and Drug Administration in 1997, the company produced a letter dated March 28, 1996, from the hospital saying the Trovan study had been approved by the hospital's ethics committee. But the suit contends that letter was written a year later and backdated—and that at the time the Pfizer trial took place, the hospital had neither an ethics committee nor the letterhead on which that letter was written." Pfizer was also accused of failing to provide proper follow-up treatment to the children in the experiment.

Finally, the suit claims that a Pfizer researcher, Dr. Juan Walterspiel, was fired after repeatedly warning management "that the company was violating international law, Federal regulations and medical ethics standards."

Tamar Lewin, "Families Sue Pfizer on Test of Antibiotics," *New York Times* (30 August 2001), p. C1.

TERRORISM, INTERROGATION, AND TORTURE

On February 7, 2002, after the terror attack of September 11, 2001, President George W. Bush, following the advice of White House Counsel Alberto Gonzales but against the advice of Secretary of State Colin Powell, decreed that the Geneva Conventions of 1949 on the treatment of prisoners of war, do not apply to suspected terrorists held in U.S. custody. The Geneva Conventions require that prisoners be treated "humanely," that they be protected "against acts of violence or intimidation and against insults and public curiosity," and that they "are entitled in all circumstances to respect for their persons and their honour."

The Convention specifies that the following qualify as prisoners of war:

1. Members of the armed forces of a Party to the conflict, as well as members of militias or volunteer corps forming part of such armed forces.

2. Members of other militias and members of other volunteer corps, including those of organized resistance movements, belonging to a Party to the conflict and operating in or outside their own territory, even if this territory is occupied, provided that such militias or volunteer corps, including such organized resistance movements, fulfill the following conditions:
    a.   that of being commanded by a person responsible for his subordinates;
    b.   that of having a fixed distinctive sign recognizable at a distance;
    c.   that of carrying arms openly;
    d.   that of conducting their operations in accordance with the laws and customs of war.

3. Members of regular armed forces who profess allegiance to a government or an authority not recognized by the Detaining Power.

4. Inhabitants of a non-occupied territory, who on the approach of the enemy spontaneously take up arms to resist the invading forces, without having had time to form themselves into regular armed units, provided they carry arms openly and respect the laws and customs of war.

According to the President, people accused of planning or committing terrorist acts do not fit any of the categories of prisoners that are explicitly mentioned in the Convention.

The United States also signed, although with explicitly stated reservations, the United Nations Convention Against Torture and Other Cruel, Inhuman, or Degrading Forms of Treatment or Punishment. According to its first Article,

> For the purposes of this Convention, torture means any act by which severe pain or suffering, whether physical or mental, is intentionally inflicted on a person for such purposes as obtaining from him or a third person information or a confession, punishing him for an act he or a third person has committed or is suspected of having committed, or intimidating or coercing him or a third person, ...

It requires states to prevent acts of torture from occurring on territory they control and states that, "No exceptional circumstances whatsoever, whether a state of war or a threat or war, internal political instability or any other public emergency, may be invoked as a justification of torture," and forbids a state to "extradite a person to another State where there are substantial grounds for believing that he would be in danger of being subjected to torture." It also states that the fact that one has been ordered by a superior to commit acts of torture is no justification or excuse.

The Bush administration did not want suspected terrorists to be covered by the Geneva Conventions because it thought that they would be particularly resistant to ordinary interrogation methods and would not divulge information about terrorist organizations and future terrorist attacks unless extreme measures were taken. In a memo to the President from White House Council Alberto Gonzales dated January 22, 2005, Gonzales wrote that the so-called war on terror, "is not the traditional clash between nations adhering to the rules of war that form the backdrop of" the Geneva Conventions. In the war on terror, Gonzales wrote, it is important to be able to extract information quickly.

Gonzales also wrote that some of the provisions of the Geneva Convention, such as that forbidding "outrages on personal dignity" and "inhuman treatment" are "undefined." In a Memorandum to the General Counsel of the Department of Defense written January 9, 2002, by John Yoo, Deputy Assistant Attorney General, Yoo seems to define torture as limited to activities that "cause great suffering or serious bodily injury." (Facsimiles of these memoranda were posted on the Internet.)

After the invasion of Iraq in 2003, the United States held thousands of people, mostly civilians, in its new military prison at Abu Ghraib, 20 miles from Baghdad. According to Seymour Hirsch, writing in the *New Yorker*, most were "civilians, many of whom had been picked up in random sweeps and at highway checkpoints." Some were considered "common criminals," but others were accused or suspected of being either active resistors of the U.S.-led occupation of Iraq or leaders of that resistance, whom the U.S. considered terrorists.[2]

Most of the officers and soldiers responsible for the prison were reservists with little or no experience or training in prison work. According to a Pentagon report written by Major General Antonio Taguba, from October to December, 2003, many prisoners suffered "sadistic, blatant, and wanton criminal abuse" at Abu Ghraib. Among the forms of abuse were:

> Breaking chemical lights and pouring the phosphoric liquid on detainees; pouring cold water on detainees; beating detainees with a broom handle and a chair; threatening male detainees with rape; allowing a military police guard to stitch the wound of a detainee who was injured after being slammed against the wall in his cell; sodomizing a detainee with a chemical light and perhaps a broom stick, and using military working dogs to frighten and intimidate detainees with threats of attack, and in one instance actually biting a detainee.[3]

Descriptions of the abuse and photographs of naked prisoners in humiliating positions taken by guards were publicized by Joseph Darby, an M.P. sickened by the mistreatment of prisoners. The revelations led to an explosion of international outrage.

According to Human Rights Watch, new information surfaced in 2005 when two sergeants and a captain in the U.S. Army described witnessing such treatment as the following:

> In one incident, a soldier is alleged to have broken a detainee's leg with a baseball bat. Detainees were also forced to hold five-gallon jugs of water with their arms outstretched and perform other acts until they passed out. Soldiers also . . . subjected detainees to forced stress positions, sleep deprivation, and extremes of hot and cold.[4]

Guards at Abu Ghraib maintained that true control of the prison and prisoners was in the hands of interrogators from military intelligence, the CIA, and private security firms under contract. The goal of much of the mistreatment of prisoners was to break their will so that they would be more cooperative and informative with interrogators.

There is reason to believe that in some cases, prisoners died under torture. In March 2005, the *New York Times* reported that military officials conceded that "at least 26 prisoners have died in American custody in Iraq and Afghanistan since 2002 in what Army and Navy investigators have concluded or suspect were acts of criminal homicide."[5] Only one of the deaths occurred at Abu Ghraib (most occurred at other locations), leading many observers to conclude that the prisoner abuse scandal was far more widespread than initially thought, going well beyond the single prison at Abu Ghraib. As of March 2005, the *New York Times* reported, "at least eight Army soldiers have now been convicted of crimes in the deaths of prisoners in American custody, including a lieutenant who pleaded guilty at Fort Hood, Texas, . . . to charges that included aggravated assault and battery, obstruction of justice and dereliction of duty."[6]

According to another report in the *New York Times*, "Two Afghan prisoners who died in American custody in Afghanistan in December 2002 were chained to the ceiling, kicked and beaten by American soldiers in sustained assaults that caused their deaths, according to Army criminal investigative reports that have not yet been made public." In the case of one prisoner identified only as Dilawar, "One soldier, Pfc. Willie V. Brand, acknowledged striking [him] 37 times, over a five-day period . . ., 'destroying his leg muscle tissue with repeated unlawful knee strikes.' The attacks on Mr. Dilawar were so severe that "even if he had survived, both legs would have had to be amputated."[7] According to a later published account, "Most of the interrogators had believed Mr. Dilawar was an innocent man who simply drove his taxi past the American base at the wrong time."[8]

According to the Army report, there is "credible information" that "four military interrogators assaulted Mr. Dilawar and another Afghan prisoner with 'kicks to the groin and leg, shoving or slamming him into walls/table, forcing the detainee to maintain painful, contorted body positions during interview and forcing water into his mouth until he could not breathe.'"[9] The last mentioned form of torture is called "water boarding."

According to a report aired by ABC News on November 29, 2005, "water boarding" was invented in the 1500s during the Italian Inquisition. "A prisoner, who is bound and gagged, has water poured over him to make him think he is about to drown." According to the report, "Current and former CIA officers tell ABC News that they were trained to handcuff the prisoner and cover his face with cellophane to enhance the distress." When CIA Director Porter Goss was asked on ABC's *Good Morning America* whether water boarding constituted torture, he replied, "I don't know," but assured interviewer Charles Gibson that the United States does not torture prisoners and that no pain is inflicted on prisoners. "What we do does not come close because torture, in terms of inflicting pain or something like that, physical pain or causing a disability, those kinds of things that probably would be a common definition for most Americans, sort of, you know it when you see it, we don't do that because it doesn't get what you want."[10]

The report said that "current and former CIA officers tell ABC News there is a presidential finding, signed in 2002, by President Bush, Condoleezza Rice and then-Attorney General John Ashcroft approving the techniques, including water boarding." However, "an Army major was sentenced to 10 years of hard labor for water boarding an insurgent in the Philippines," and water boarding was declared illegal by U.S. generals during the Vietnam War.[11]

Several low-level soldiers were tried and convicted of abusing prisoners, and the general in charge of Abu Ghraib, Janis Karpinski, was suspended from the military reserve. However, critics of the Bush administration allege that the executive branch and the Pentagon are more interested in covering up the abuse and protecting the large number of military officers responsible than in uncovering the truth and holding those responsible accountable. The executive branch and the Pentagon deny this. However, according to a report in *Newsweek*, Sgt. Samuel Provance tried to provide information about the abuse to General George Fay of military intelligence, who was given the task of investigating the role of military intelligence in the abuse, but was punished for it. The *Newsweek* reporter claimed that *Newsweek* had been shown a disciplinary order to Provance from Lt. Col. James Norwood notifying him "that he has lost his security clearance and is being 'flagged' for violating an order to keep quiet."[12] Even Congress has complained because of how much information is being kept from it by the Pentagon.

In November 2005, despite strong opposition from the Bush administration, with overwhelming majorities Congress passed legislation that would require that all agencies of the U.S. government, including the Pentagon and military intelligence, be bound by the Geneva Conventions that forbid torture or "cruel, inhuman, or degrading treatment." Vice President Dick Cheney then strongly urged that the CIA be exempted from that legislation, and President Bush threatened to veto the defense bill to which it was attached because it would hamper the President's ability to conduct the war on terrorism. Finally, the President felt compelled to sign the bill.[13] However, when President Bush signed the bill, he issued a "signing statement" specifying his interpretation of the bill. In effect, he said he would abide by its prohibition against torture and cruel, inhuman, and degrading treatment to the extent that it is compatible with his constitutional responsibilities as commander in chief. Critics were quick to claim that this provided a large loophole in the "absolute" prohibition that Congress intended. In effect, President Bush was claiming that as commander in chief, he has the authority to order torture and cruel, inhuman, and degrading prisoners if he thinks it is necessary for national security, despite the law passed by Congress absolutely forbidding it.[14]

Part of the context of this legislation is a November 2, 2005 story in the *Washington* Post alleging that "The CIA has been hiding and interrogating some of its most important al Qaeda captives at a Soviet-era compound in Eastern Europe..., part of a covert prison system set up by the CIA" as part of its "unconventional war on terrorism." The entire prison system was kept a secret from the public and almost all members of Congress. According to the report, "Virtually nothing is known about who is kept in the facilities, what interrogation methods are employed with them, or how decisions are made about whether they should be detained or for how long."[15] The CIA almost immediately began a criminal investigation into the leak of classified information about the secret prison system to the *Washington Post*.[16]

The CIA is also alleged to be practicing "rendition," whereby some suspected terrorists captured in Afghanistan or Iraq are handed over for interrogation to the security services of nations that are accused of routinely employing torture during interrogation. Critics claim that it is a way for the CIA to sidestep any U.S. laws forbidding torture.

On December 5, 2005, Secretary of State Condoleeza Rice answered critics by maintaining that the interrogation of detainees had provided information that enabled the United States and its allies to prevent several terrorist attacks in Europe. She said that the United States will use all and only legal measures during interrogation, and does not allow torture, but she still refused to confirm or deny allegations that the CIA has a system of secret detention centers in a number of foreign countries. However, she did say that the intelligence agencies of several allies had worked with the United States in interrogating detainees.[17]

INSURANCE FRAUD

In August, 2003, police in New York caught an insurance fraud ring that had staged thousands of fake accident and bilked auto insurance companies to the tune of $48 million. The ring had its own group of doctors, dentists, psychiatrists, and chiropractors, as well as medical clinics that participated in the fraud. Some clinics were owned by lawyers and accountants as lucrative investments.

Cars driven by experienced drivers would intentionally cut in front of other cars and slam on their brakes, causing the car behind them to crash into them. The drivers and passengers would then falsely claim to have a variety of injuries, attested to by the doctors and clinics in on the conspiracy. Doctors and clinics would order expensive medical tests they knew to be unnecessary, often not even bothering to actually have the fake patients tested, and then fill out forms for reimbursement from the insurance companies. If the insurance company hesitated to pay the claims, lawyers in the conspiracy would send letters threatening to sue the company if it did not pay.

New York was an easy target because the state has a no-fault insurance system that automatically authorizes up to $50,000 in medical expenses for anyone injured in an auto accident, regardless of who was at fault. According to state calculations, insurance fraud drives up the premium of everyone's auto insurance by about $177 annually.[18]

Although the drivers and phony "injured" passengers were not among society's more privileged members, we should take note of the fact that many of the participants in the fraud were well-to-do people from respected professions (doctors, psychiatrists, lawyers, and accountants) who could not excuse their behavior as motivated by desperation.

According to the U. S. Department of Agriculture, fraud committed by farmers in its farm insurance program totaled about $160 million in 2004. From 1997 to 2003, one farming couple, Robert and Viki Warren in Mississippi, submitted dozens of bogus totaling almost $10 million claims for lost tomato crops. The Warrens wove a complicated web of deception that included falsifying records about planting dates, acreage, yields, production, shipping manifests, and hailstorm damage. The Warrens created almost 200,000 false documents and records. In fact, they even faked a hailstorm by tossing ice on their tomato crop, breaking most of the plants by beating them with a stick, and photographing the damage to send to the insurance company. Though 16,000 tomatoes were planted, the Warrens claimed that 1.5 million were destroyed by the hailstorm. The insurance adjustor sent to investigate approved the claim despite the fact that its fraudulent nature was obvious on even the most casual inspection. His supervisor had instructed him to lie about the damage. The agent who sold the Warrens their crop insurance policy persuaded them to take out the policy in part by explaining to them how easy it is to commit fraud, and actually coached them on how to commit the fraud. To complete the circle, the Federal government helped the Warrens pay the premiums for their crop insurance and reimbursed the insurance companies for most of the losses from the policy. Experts say that the Warrens were one of the about 5 percent of insured farmers who commit fraud; the other 95 percent are honest.[19]

The office of Texas Governor Rick Perry listed on its website (December 2005) a variety of examples of insurance fraud encountered in Texas. They include a person collecting unemployment benefits because he claimed he was fired when in fact he quit his job, a person collecting unemployment benefits despite having an income that made her ineligible, a counseling agency that billed Medicaid for over $600,000 in counseling services it never provided, a physician who billed Medicaid and Medicare $1.3 million for allergy tests he did not perform, several individuals who faked water damage on homes they bought in order to collect a total of $5 million on the homeowners' insurance policies, and an insurance adjustor who added to legitimate claims many false repair bills totaling $150,000 from a fictitious company he created.

According to the FBI, citing a study by the Coalition Against Insurance Fraud, fraud in the property/casualty insurance field costs insurers, policy holders, and the government about $26 billion annually and is one of the main forces driving up the cost of insurance.

In a survey conducted in October 2002 by the Association of British Insurers, nearly half of the people contacted said that they would not rule out committing insurance fraud. Forty percent said they considered exaggerating an insurance claim as acceptable or borderline, and 36 percent thought that knowingly buying stolen goods is acceptable or borderline.[20]

POLICE BRUTALITY IN NEW YORK CITY

On August 9, 1997, Haitian immigrant Abner Louima was brutalized by two police officers in the 70th precinct station in Brooklyn, New York. Earlier that night, he had been picked up by police officer Justin Volpe in an apparent case of mistaken identity after a scuffle outside a nightclub. Someone in a crowd outside the nightclub hit Officer Volpe, knocking him to the ground. Volpe thought it was Louima. Volpe arrested Louima and brought him to the 70th precinct station. Louima was beaten in the patrol car on the way to the station. When they got to the station, Volpe took Louima to a men's room and while another officer held Louima down, Volpe shoved a broken broom handle up his rectum and into his mouth. Mr. Louima spent 64 days in the hospital and underwent three operations for a torn rectum and other internal injuries.

Investigators found a "blue wall of silence." Initially, no police officers in the precinct would come forward to testify against their fellow officers. A trustee of the P.B.A. (Patrolman's Benevolent Association) told officers not to talk about it. A P.B.A. lawyer publicly suggested that Mr. Louima was a homosexual and received his injuries during a consensual homosexual encounter with another man before he was arrested, although there was no shred of evidence for such a claim nor any reason to think that the story was true.

Finally, six days after the attack, Officer Eric Turetzky came forward to testify against Officer Volpe and the other officer who held Louima down during the attack. He was disgusted by the brutality of the attack on Louima. Officers of the Internal Affairs Bureau responsible for investigating allegations of police misconduct worried that Officer Turetzky would not be safe in the precinct station if other police officers knew he was cooperating in the investigation, and they sent a team to get him out of the station unharmed. A few days later, a second police officer, Thomas Wiese, came forward to testify against Volpe. He had accidentally barged into the men's room near the end of Volpe's attack on Louima. It was later determined that several officers knew that the attack was occurring and did nothing to stop it. They also tried to help Volpe cover it up, motivated by feelings of loyalty to a fellow police officer and the police department.

Volpe and another police officer went to jail. In July 2001, the city of New York agreed to pay Abner Louima $7.125 million and the Patrolman's Benevolent Association agreed to pay him $1.625 million. In a civil suit, Mr. Louima alleged that the city did not adequately oversee or discipline its police officers, creating a climate where officers thought they could behave brutally with impunity. In addition, the city gave responsibility for investigations and disciplinary actions regarding allegations of police brutality to the police department itself rather than to outside civilian review boards.

Michael Cooper, "Second Officer Gives Account of Sex Assault of Haitian," *New York Times* (18 August 1997).

"New York Settles in Brutality Case," *New York Times* (13 July 2001), p. A1.

Jim Dwyer, "Concern for Police Witness in Louima Case," *New York Times* (17 August 2001).

PROSECUTOR WITHHOLDS EVIDENCE
FROM THE DEFENSE

In August 2001, a state judge in Pennsylvania voided the conviction of a man, Dennis Counterman, sentenced to death in 1990 for setting a fire that killed his three sons because the police and prosecutors withheld vital evidence from the man's attorneys. For example, when police gave Counterman's attorneys a transcript of police interviews with his wife the day of the fire, they blotted out her statements—made to two different officers—that her husband was in bed asleep at the time of the fire and that her oldest son, Christopher, awakened her to tell her there was a fire. They also failed to inform Counterman's attorneys that in interviews neighbors told the police that Christopher had a history of setting fires.

Dennis Counterman is reported to have an IQ in the mid-70s and to have left school before completing the ninth grade. His wife is reported to be mentally retarded. Despite Ms. Counterman's statements in interviews the day of the fire, at her husband's trial months later she "testified that she had been awakened by the sound of a lighter and then saw her husband at the bottom of the stairs with a bucket." She also denied that her oldest son had a history of setting fires. The voided conviction meant that prosecutors had to decide whether to retry Counterman.

Raymond Bonner, "Sentence Thrown Out Over Withheld Evidence," *New York Times* (30 August 2001).

FLORIDA BAN ON GAY ADOPTIONS

In August, 2001, a Federal judge in Florida upheld a 1977 law forbidding gays to adopt children. The state of Florida argued that it is in a child's best interest to be brought up in a family consisting of a married mother and father. The judge, James Lawrence King, ruled that "Plaintiffs have not asserted that they can demonstrate that homosexual families are equivalently stable, are able to provide proper gender identification or are no more socially stigmatizing than married heterosexual families."

The lead plaintiff in Florida was Steven Lofton, "a gay pediatric nurse who raised from infancy three foster children who at birth tested positive for H.I.V., the virus that causes AIDS. Mr. Lofton quit his job to care for the children full-time...." Mr. Lofton once won the Children's Home Society's outstanding foster-parenting award. Mr. Lofton wanted to adopt one of the children, but was not permitted to because of his sexual identity.

The plaintiffs' attorney, Matthew Coles of the American Civil Liberties Union, argued that the choice often is not between having a married couple or having gays adopt children. Rather, it's between having gays adopt children or having no one adopt them. He pointed out that at the time, there were 3,400 children in foster care in Florida waiting to be adopted. Mr. Coles argued that the Florida ban "illegally discriminated against gays' fundamental family rights." However, the judge rejected this argument, ruling that there is no "fundamental right" to adoption. Mr. Coles pointed out that Florida law does not automatically disqualify drug abusers and those convicted of domestic violence from adopting children, but it does automatically disqualify gays.

Writer Dan Savage is a gay man who, along with his partner, has adopted a 3-year-old boy. He points out that, "It is an open secret among social workers that gay and lesbian couples are often willing to adopt children whom most heterosexual couples won't touch: H.I.V.-positive children, mixed-race children, disabled children and children who have been abused or neglected." He and his partner adopted the boy after a heterosexual couple decided not to adopt him because his teenaged mother drank and used drugs during her pregnancy.

Tamar Lewin, "Court Backs Florida Ban on Adoption by Gays," *New York Times* (31 August 2001), p. A14.

Dan Savage, "Is No Adoption Better Than Gay Adoption?" *New York Times* (8 September 2001), p. A23.

TAINTED EVIDENCE?

Jeffrey Pierce was convicted of raping a woman and spent 15 years in prison before being released in 2001 after prosecutors agreed that he had been wrongfully convicted. The jury convicted him in part because of the testimony of Oklahoma City police chemist Joyce Gilchrist, who testified that hairs of the rapist found at the scene were "microscopically consistent" with Pierce's hair. Pierce became a suspect 10 months after the attack after the victim picked his photo out of a police photo book as possibly her attacker, although she told police at the time that she didn't think he was her attacker. Two workers swore under oath at the trial that Pierce was at lunch with them when the rape occurred. Pierce was convicted and sentenced to 65 years in prison.

However, DNA retesting of the evidence in 2001 proved conclusively that the sperm and hairs of the rapists were not Pierce's, proving that he was innocent. (Sophisticated DNA testing of evidence only recently became available.) Was it an honest mistake on Gilchrist's part? Not according to critics. More of her cases were reexamined with new DNA tests, and new problems came to light. For example, Malcolm Rent Johnson, executed in 2000, was convicted partly on the basis of Gilchrist's 1982 testimony that six samples of sperm found at the scene were "consistent with his blood type." But a reexamination of the evidence in 2001 by chemist Laura Schille showed that there were no samples of sperm. The evidence never existed. Sperm takes decades to deteriorate. Similarly, "[t]wo appellate courts have ruled Gilchrist gave false testimony about semen evidence in the 1992 rape and murder trial of Alfred Brian Mitchell, whose sentence was overturned [in 2001] because of what one court called her 'untrue testimony'" ("Testimony Doubted in Oklahoma Execution"). The court ruled that she intentionally gave false testimony and that the prosecution deliberately withheld exculpatory evidence from Mitchell's attorneys.

Robert Lee Miller, Jr. was convicted of the 1986 rape and murder of Anne Laura Fowler partly on the basis of the same kind of forensic testimony by Joyce Gilchrist. After 10 years on death row, he was released when DNA retesting of the evidence proved that he was innocent. To compound the errors, the DNA testing proved that a man Gilchrist said the evidence showed wasn't involved turned out to be the rapist/murderer.

Gilchrist testified for the prosecution in over 3,000 cases. Some of the people convicted have already been executed. The FBI has begun reexamining more of those cases. It has already reexamined 8 and found that she made serious mistakes or misidentified evidence in 6 of them. In many she claimed a level of certainty for the forensic evidence that was far greater than good forensic science would permit. "She also appears to have withheld evidence from the defense and failed to perform tests that could have cleared defendants" ("When the Evidence Lies").

Critics charge that police forensic scientists are so closely identified with prosecutors that it is easy for them to lose their objectivity, a fundamental requirement of legitimate science. Gilchrist won praise, awards, and promotions from the police department for her ability to persuade juries to convict. But as early as 1987, her work was criticized. In 1987, a forensic scientist in the Kansas City police crime lab, John Wilson, filed a complaint about the quality of her work with the Southwestern Association of Forensic Scientists, but the Association took no action against her. Similarly, officers of the Oklahoma Criminal Defense Lawyers Association say that their organization had been "screaming" about her work for years. But, according to her critics, judges, police, and prosecutors protected her because she was so successful in helping them get convictions.

Joyce Gilchrist isn't the only police forensic scientist under a cloud. In August 2001, Fred S. Zain, a scientist with the state police crime lab in West Virginia, was on trial. In 1993, the West Virginia Supreme Court concluded that he had exaggerated the conclusions of lab tests and even faked lab tests in hundreds of cases. Since then, seven convictions have been overturned and scores are being reviewed. In 1993, the Court concluded that any testimony or documentary evidence offered by Zain at any time should be deemed "invalid, unreliable and inadmissible" ("Work by Expert Witness Is Now on Trial"). For example, in one trial Zain testified that an axe he tested that was suspected of being used in a murder showed that it had traces of blood from the victim. However, on reexamination, another expert found that the axe hadn't even been tested.

Like Gilchrist, Zain was popular with police and prosecutors because his expert testimony was often very persuasive in getting convictions. But Zain had been criticized by colleagues, and there had been complaints from defendants and their attorneys for many years before the Supreme Court's 1993 report. In 1998, a special grand jury recommended that the state police crime lab should be turned over to a private civilian agency to assure objectivity, competence, and impartiality, but the recommendation was sealed by court order until a special prosecutor in the Zain case asked that it be made public ("Revamp West Virginia's Crime Labs").

In addition to forensic scientists, police are sometimes accused of faking evidence. In September 2001, after a lengthy Federal investigation, 11 Miami police officers were charged with planting evidence (guns) in several police shootings and lying as part of a cover-up. They claimed that the men they shot were armed when in fact they were not armed. According to the indictment, some police officers kept guns they confiscated in arrests and raids instead of turning them over to the department. Later, they used some to plant at the scenes of police shootings to prove their (false) charge that the person they killed had a gun. In 2003 a judge issued a finding in civil court that "the preponderance of the evidence" confirmed the charges. In fact, "Miami has paid more than $20 million [between 1990 and 2003] to resolve more than 110 federal and state lawsuits alleging brutality, misconduct or unnecessary death caused by city officers."[21]

In terms of faking evidence, one of the notorious cases was that of 73-year-old Richard Brown. In 1996, police broke into his apartment searching for drugs and fired 123 bullets in his bedroom, hitting Mr. Brown with 9 of them while he cowered in a closet and his 14-year-old daughter hid in the bathroom. The police involved claimed Brown had fired at them first, but authorities now say that the gun found at the scene was planted by the police and that Brown did not have a gun. No drugs were found in the raid. According to the FBI, the evidence against the officers is overwhelming.

"Freed Convict Blames DA for Bad Verdict," Associated Press, *Amarillo Globe-News* (9 May 2001).

Belinda Luscombe, "When the Evidence Lies," *Time* (21 May 2001).

"Testimony Doubted in Oklahoma Execution," *New York Times* (29 August 2001).

Francis X. Clines, "Work by Expert Witness Is Now on Trial," *New York Times* (5 September 2001), p. A12.

"Revamp West Virginia's Crime Labs, *Herald-Dispatch* (Huntington, W. Virginia) (11 July 2001).

Dana Canedy, "11 Miami Officers Facing U. S. Charges in 3 Shooting Deaths," *New York Times* (8 September 2001).

THE TUSKEGEE SYPHILIS EXPERIMENT

In 1932, the U.S. Public Health Service began an experiment on 399 poor black male sharecroppers in Macon County, Alabama, one of the poorest counties in the state. The men, most of whom were illiterate, had syphilis, a bacterial disease contracted from sexual intercourse. (It also can be passed on in the womb from a mother to her newborn infant.) In its last or tertiary stage, untreated syphilis can lead to leaking heart valves, aneurysms, bone deterioration that can lead to facial mutilation as nose and palate bones are eaten away, paralysis, senility, blindness, and insanity ("'Bad Blood': A Case Study of the Tuskegee Syphilis Project").

The study was supposedly designed by the Public Health Service to determine whether syphilis affected blacks the same way as whites. Researchers offered free testing in Macon County, and 399 of those who tested positive for syphilis were selected. Local doctors, most of them black, and the hospital associated with the prestigious Tuskegee Institute, an all-black institution, cooperated. The men were told that they had "bad blood" and would be treated for it. They were not informed of the nature of their disease, nor were they informed that in fact they would not receive treatment designed to cure them. (In 1932, there were no antibiotics, but there were treatments for syphilis that were sometimes effective.) For the most part they received only aspirin, given in the form of pink pills to disguise it. In the late 1940s, penicillin was discovered, and it was a complete cure for syphilis. The men did not receive this treatment that could have cured them; steps were taken to make sure that they did not participate in free syphilis treatment offered in Macon County. The physicians who conducted the experiment even decided to violate a law passed in 1943, the Henderson Act, that required treatment for syphilis. Later, they also ignored the 1964 World Health Organization's Declaration of Helsinki requiring informed consent for human subjects of medical experiments ("The Tuskegee Syphilis Experiment").

In 1969, the Public Health Service gathered a "blue ribbon panel" to discuss the experiment. "The participants were all physicians, none of whom had training in medical ethics. In addition, none of them were of African descent." ("'Bad Blood:' A Case Study of the Tuskegee Syphilis Experiment.") The panel concluded that the study should continue.

Finally, Peter Buxton, a former employee of the Public Health Service familiar with the Tuskegee experiment, began to have doubts about the morality of the experiment. He contacted the Associated Press, and reporter Jean Heller researched the case and broke the story in the *Washington Star* on July 25, 1972. The study was immediately halted, although many of the people who conducted the study defended themselves by saying they were just following the orders of their superiors or that they were doing this to advance science and human knowledge for the greater good. "By the end of the experiment, 28 of the men had died directly of syphilis, 100 were dead of related complications, 40 of their wives had been infected, and 19 of their children had been born with congenital syphilis" ("The Tuskegee Syphilis Experiment"). Critics say that from its beginning the experiment was poorly designed and that it could not have provided any information that would have been useful in the treatment of syphilis. They say that nothing of medical value was learned from the study.

A. W. Fourtner, C. R. Fourtner, and C. F. Herreid, "'Bad Blood:' A Case Study of the Tuskegee Syphilis Project," SUNY at Buffalo (http://ublib.buffalo.edu/libraries /projects/cases/blood.htm).

Infoplease, "The Tuskegee Syphilis Experiment" (http://www.infoplease.com/ipa /A0762136.html).

EMBRYONIC STEM CELL RESEARCH

There is a type of cell in human embryos, called a stem cell, that has the ability to develop into any other kind of cell type in the body—blood cells, kidney cells, bone cells, and so on. There is great hope that stem cells can be used in the treatment of a variety of debilitating diseases. For example, some scientists think that some day they might be used to grow new hearts or livers for people, as well as provide treatment for such debilitating neurological illnesses as Parkinson's Disease.

Embryonic stem cells were first isolated in 1998 by the Geron Corporation, which financed research at the University of Wisconsin. As a result, the Geron Corporation was able to patent a variety of cell types that it generated from stem cells, such as liver cells and brain cells, as well as the technology for isolating them. As a result, "if someone were to figure out, say, how to turn stem cells into insulin-producing pancreatic cells to treat diabetes, Geron would demand royalties on sales of treatment" ("The Promise in Selling Stem Cells"). Scientists who want to do research using these stem cells must get approval from Geron. Some scientists claim that Geron "demands too many rights to discoveries or imposes too many restrictions" ("The Promise in Selling Stem Cells"). Geron thinks that most research done on stem cells will violate their patent rights unless the researchers reach a licensing agreement with the company.

Researchers decided to accept financing from Geron Corporation because there were limits on Federal funding of research on stem cells. Scientists "harvest" stem cells from human embryos; foes of abortion strongly oppose such research because it means the destruction of a human embryo, which they consider to be a human being with a right to life. In the summer of 2001, President George W. Bush had to decide whether to permit Federal funding of research that used embryonic stem cells. He decided that embryonic stem cells that come from fertility clinics that would have discarded and destroyed them in any case could be used in federally funded research. But he decided that there would be no Federal funding of research that used stem cells taken from embryos that were intentionally created for the sole purpose of harvesting their stem cells.

Critics of President Bush's decision say that there are not enough stem cell lines available and that many of those that exist are not safe for use in humans. For example, some stem cell lines were exposed to mouse cells while they were developing. They say that new embryos are needed and that there are not enough available from fertility clinics. "The vast majority of couples use their frozen embryos, or plan to use them, in attempts at pregnancy." Very few couples have agreed to permit their frozen embryos to be used in scientific research ("Researchers Say Embryos in Labs Are Not Available"). These critics say that the only way to provide researchers with the stem cells they need is to create new embryos in vitro explicitly for their stem cells.

The frozen embryos in fertility clinics "are one to five days old and consist of one to 120 cells. They are less than three-thousandths of an inch in diameter" ("Researchers Say Embryos in Labs Are Not Available"). Stem cells are normally harvested from embryos that are 5 to 6 days old. But embryos cannot be used for research purposes unless the donors of the egg and sperm agree to permit it. Most fertility clinics do not ask their clients if they want to donate the unused embryos to science for research. They also must agree to the particular research project in which the stem cells will be used. However, many embryos frozen in fertility clinics are not robust enough for research purposes. Commonly, the egg is from an older woman who has had difficulty conceiving, and frozen embryos are less robust than unfrozen ones. According to Dr. Barry Behr, director of the in vitro fertilization laboratory at Stanford University, "By far, by far, the vast majority of embryos that are frozen are not good. If we thawed 10,000 embryos, we would get 100 or so that are viable blastocysts" ("Researchers Say Embryos in Labs Are Not Available").

Embryos created for harvesting of their stem cells can be made from the egg and sperm of young and healthy donors and do not have to be frozen; therefore, they are likely to be of higher quality. Some researchers have already created human embryos in vitro (in petri dishes) and harvested their cells. Some opponents of abortion would like to see the practice outlawed, not just to deny Federal funding to research using stem cells from embryos created specifically for their stem cells.

Andrew Pollack, "The Promise in Selling Stem Cells," *New York Times* (26 August 2001), p. C1.

Gina Kolata, "Researchers Say Embryos in Labs Are Not Available," *New York Times* (26 August 2001), p. A1.

NANCY CRUZAN

In 1983, Nancy Cruzan was severely injured in an automobile accident. She received head injuries and her brain was deprived of oxygen for 12 to 14 minutes. Oxygen deprivation for 6 minutes causes permanent brain damage. The longer the brain is deprived of oxygen, the more severe the damage as brain cells die. She was in a coma, and after a few weeks, doctors diagnosed her as being in a persistent vegetative state, a condition in which one has permanently lost the capacity for consciousness and higher level mental functioning. With the permission of her husband at the time, doctors inserted a tube into her stomach for nutrition and hydration. She was in the Missouri State Hospital, and her care was being paid for by the state. After several years, her parents asked the hospital to discontinue nutrition and hydration so that their daughter could die. (Her husband had divorced her during that time.) If Nancy had been competent and had made the request herself, the hospital might have removed the nutrition and hydration tube, but because it was not the patient herself, the hospital refused and said it would comply with their request only if ordered to by a court.

Nancy Cruzan's parents went to court. Missouri law permitted withholding life-sustaining measures from an incompetent patient, but only if there were "clear and compelling" evidence that that is what the patient would have wanted if she were competent. Nancy had not left behind any written statements saying what she would want in the event of such catastrophic injuries, but a former roommate testified that Nancy had once told her she would not want to live if she couldn't live "halfway normally." Nancy Cruzan's parents believed that Nancy would not want to continue living in such a condition.

A state trial court sided with the parents on the grounds that people have a right under the Missouri and Federal Constitutions "to direct or refuse the withdrawal of death-prolonging procedures." (Note the use of the term *death-prolonging* instead of *life-prolonging*.) Apparently the court was satisfied that there was clear and compelling evidence that this is what Nancy would have wanted. It was convinced that her parents knew Nancy well enough to know what she would want in such circumstances, and it had the testimony of her former roommate.

On appeal, the State Supreme Court reversed the lower court's decision. It said that there is no unrestricted right even for competent patients to refuse treatment in either the state or Federal constitutions, that state policy clearly placed a high priority on preserving life, and that the evidence that her parents' were doing as Nancy would have wished was inadequate. It stated that no one has a right to decide to refuse treatment for an incompetent individual "in the absence of... clear and compelling evidence of the patient's wishes."

The case came before the United States Supreme Court in 1989, and in its majority 5–4 decision in 1990, it said that a competent person does have a Constitutional right to refuse "lifesaving hydration and nutrition" based on a person's right of self-determination. But of course, Nancy was not competent. In her case, it saw no Constitutional errors in Missouri's law that requires "clear and compelling evidence" of a person's wishes in cases where a surrogate given the right to make decisions for an incompetent patient makes a decision that will lead to the patient's death. The U.S. Supreme Court agreed with the Missouri Supreme Court that the Cruzans had failed to provide "clear and convincing proof" of what their daughter's wishes would have been. Therefore, the Supreme Court affirmed the decision of the State Supreme Court forbidding the discontinuation of hydration and nutrition to Nancy.

Cruzan v. Director, Missouri Department of Health, et al., United States Supreme Court (http://supct.law.cornell. edu/supct/html/88–1503.ZO.opinion. html).

THE PHILADELPHIA HEAD-INJURY STUDIES ON PRIMATES

Between 1970 and 1985, neurologist Thomas Gennarelli of the University of Pennsylvania Medical School studied head injuries in monkeys and baboons in order to improve treatment of head injuries in humans. In order to study them, he first had to cause them. In his laboratory, monkeys and baboons were given severe brain injuries by means of a pneumatic hammer smashing their skulls. Researchers in the program claim that the animals were sedated and felt no pain, but videotapes of experiments suggest otherwise. There are pictures of baboons struggling to free themselves from the restraints before the pneumatic hammer smashed their skulls. In some videotapes, researchers are heard making fun of the brain injured animals, and one researcher is seen deliberately lifting a baboon up by its injured arm after it had dislocated its shoulder. There is also evidence of "unsterile surgery, and horribly sloppy care of animals."

In 1984, members of the Animal Liberation Front broke into the laboratory and stole five years of audiovisual tapes of the experiments. They edited the tapes to show the worst abuses and gave the tape to television stations to broadcast. In 1985, People for the Ethical Treatment of Animals turned all the tapes over to the National Institutes of Health for review, hoping it would discontinue Federal funding of the experiments and forbid them to continue. The tapes were later reviewed by the Office for Protection from Research Risks, which appointed a neurosurgeon, a veterinary anesthesiologist, and a veterinary pathologist to investigate. The panel judged that the experiments were likely to yield information of value in the treatment of human head injuries, but it "criticized lack of anesthesia, inadequate supervision, poor training, inferior veterinary care, unnecessary multiple injuries to single animals, ... and 'statements in poor taste....'" The Secretary of Human Services rescinded the lab's Federal funding, effectively ending the lab's research.

Critics maintain that the research was not likely to yield insights valuable in the treatment of human head injuries. Many also say that even if it could yield such insights, it is morally wrong to use animals in this way for the benefit of human beings. The fact that monkeys and baboons are so closely related to human beings made it even worse, according to some people.

Prosecutors tried unsuccessfully to discover the identity of the members of the Animal Liberation Front in order to prosecute them for such crimes as breaking and entering, and theft.

Gregory Pence, *Classic Cases in Medical Ethics* (New York: McGraw Hill, 1990), pp. 171–172.

ENDNOTES

1. David Barstow and Lowell Bergman: "At a Texas Foundry, An Indifference to Life," *New York Times* (8 January 2003); "Family's Profits, Wrung From Blood and Sweat," *New York Times* (9 January 2003); "Deaths on the Job," *New York Times*" (10 January 2003).

2. Seymour Hirsch, "Torture at Abu Ghraib," *New Yorker* (online) (10 May 2004).

3. Ibid.

4. "New Accounts of Torture by U.S. Troops," Human Rights Watch (online) (24 September 2005).

5. Douglas Jehl, "U.S. Military Says 26 Inmate Deaths May Be Homicide," *New York Times* (online) (16 March 2005).

6. Ibid.

7. Douglas Jehl, "Army Details Scale of Abuse of Prisoners in an Afghan Jail," *New York Times* (online) (12 March 2005).

8. Tim Golden, "In U.S. Report, Brutal Details of 2 Afghan Inmates' Deaths," *New York Times* (online) (20 May 2005).

9. Ibid.

10. ABC News online (29 November 2005); William Branigan, "CIA Director Defends Detention Policy," *Washington Post* (online) (29 November 2005).

11. ABC News online (29 November 2005).

12. Michael Hirsh and John Barry, "The Abu Ghraib Scandal Cover-Up?" *Newsweek* (online) (7 June 2005).

13. Jeffrey H. Smith, "Exemption the CIA from the McCain Amendment Sends the Wrong Signal to Our Officers," *Washington Post* (online) (9 November 2005); "U.S. License to Abuse Would Put CIA Above the Law," Human Rights Watch (online) (26 October 2005).

14. Charles Savage, "Bush Could Bypass New Torture Ban," *Boston Globe* (online) (January 2006).

15. Dana Priest, "CIA Holds Terror Suspects in Secret Prisons," *Washington Post* (online) (2 November 2005).

16. CIA Begins Probe into Leak on Secret Prisons," *MSNBC* (online) (8 November 2005).

17. "Rice Defends U.S. Intelligence Tactics," *CBC News* (Canada) (5 December 2005); "Rice Defends Detainee Tactics" *Reuters* (5 December 2005).

18. Patrick Healy, "Investigators Say Fraud Ring Staged Thousands of Crashes," *New York Times* (online) (23 August 2003).

19. "Crop Insurance Fraud," *Morning Edition*, National Public Radio (online at NPR.org) (14 November 2005).

20. "Facts on Fraud No. 1," Association of British Insurers (February 2003).

21. Dan Christensen, "Judge in Miami Cops Case Opens Door to Civil Suits," *Miami Daily Business Review* (online) (April 11, 2003).

Index